MICROPROCESSORS
AND
MICROCOMPUTERS

HARDWARE AND SOFTWARE

MICROPROCESSORS
AND
MICROCOMPUTERS

HARDWARE AND SOFTWARE

SECOND EDITION

RONALD J. TOCCI

Monroe Community College

LESTER P. LASKOWSKI

Monroe Community College

PRENTICE-HALL, INC., Englewood Cliffs, New Jersey 07632

Library of Congress Cataloging in Publication Data

Tocci, Ronald J.
    Microprocessors and microcomputers.

    Includes index.
    1. Microprocessors.   2. Microcomputers.
I. Laskowski, Lester P.   II. Title.
QA76.5.T556 1982   001.64'04   81-11885
ISBN 0-13-581322-0   AACR2

Editorial/production supervision
  and interior design by *Mary Carnis*
Manufacturing buyer: *Gordon Osbourne*

Printed in the United States of America

10 9 8 7 6 5

ISBN 0-13-581322-0

Prentice-Hall International, Inc., *London*
Prentice-Hall of Australia Pty. Limited, *Sydney*
Prentice-Hall of Canada, Ltd., *Toronto*
Prentice-Hall of India Private Limited, *New Delhi*
Prentice-Hall of Japan, Inc., *Tokyo*
Prentice-Hall of Southeast Asia Pte. Ltd., *Singapore*
Whitehall Books Limited, *Wellington, New Zealand*

CONTENTS

Contents

PREFACE

This book was written to present a broad spectrum of readers with a practical introduction to the relatively new world of microprocessors and microcomputers. It should prove to be useful to the computer novice, technical student, and practicing engineer alike. A comprehensive review of digital principles and circuits is provided for readers with a minimum background.

As the title suggests, this book concentrates on the fundamentals of microprocessor-based systems and is *not* intended to be a survey of the numerous microprocessors and microprocessor applications. The authors have chosen to emphasize the ideas and principles common to all microprocessor systems. It should be relatively easy for an instructor to build on these fundamentals in the laboratory with a microprocessor and support devices of his or her own choosing, and with applications suited to available equipment.

It is difficult to predict what will happen in electronics over the next ten years or, for that matter, while this book is being prepared for publication, but basic ideas will probably remain the same while details on specific devices will change. For this reason, the book often stresses common concepts, although in some cases specific devices are used to illustrate techniques and applications, and to describe what is available *today*.

The programming material uses the 6502 microprocessor to teach programming techniques, and the reader should have no trouble extending this information to other microprocessors. Instructors who do not use the 6502 should still be able to use the rest of the text to develop understanding of microprocessor systems as was done by many first-edition users.

The text is divided into three parts: review material, hardware, and programming. Chapters 1 and 2 provide a thorough review of terminology, number systems, and digital circuits from basic gates to memory chips. Chapters 3 through 7 deal principally with computer structure and hardware, with some programming concepts introduced to show how the software and hardware work together. These chapters cover microcomputer structure, internal microprocessor organization, memory interfacing, and input/output modes and interfacing. Chapter 8 is a detailed treatment of microcomputer programming on a machine language level, with some elements of assembly language.

The text includes several valuable learning aids to facilitate the understanding of important concepts: (1) numerous thoroughly explained illustrative examples; (2) clear, uncomplicated diagrams and flowcharts; (3) extensive glossaries of new terms at the end of each chapter; and (4) over 200 end-of-chapter problems and questions of varied complexity which were not part of the first edition.

In addition to the end-of-chapter problems, this new edition contains many significant improvements: (1) the chapter on microprocessors has been updated to include discussion of 16-bit microprocessors, single-chip microcomputers, and bit-slice devices; (2) the chapter on I/O and interfacing has been divided into separate chapters on I/O modes and I/O interfacing; (3) the chapter on interfacing includes new material on I/O chips, parallel bus standards, serial standards, and modems; and (4) the treatment of conditional branching and relative addressing has been improved and expanded.

The authors are gratified by the large number of satisfied users of the first edition, and we hope that the updating and improvements in this new edition will be equally well received.

Ronald J. Tocci
Lester P. Laskowski

PART 1

INTRODUCTORY TOPICS

1

NUMBER SYSTEMS
AND CODES

Computers of all sizes have one thing in common—they handle *numbers*. In digital computers, these numbers are represented by binary digits. A *binary digit* is a digit that can only take on the values of 0 or 1, and no other value. The major reason why binary digits are used in computers is the simplicity with which electrical, magnetic, and mechanical devices can represent binary digits. Because the term "binary digit" is used so often in computer work, it is commonly abbreviated to *bit*. Henceforth, we shall use the latter form.

1.1 DIGITAL NUMBER SYSTEMS

Although actual computer operations use the binary number system, several other number systems are used to communicate with computers. The most common are the decimal, octal, and hexadecimal systems.

Decimal System

The *decimal system* is composed of the 10 symbols or digits: 0, 1, 2, 3, 4, 5, 6, 7, 8, and 9; using these symbols, we can express any quantity. The decimal system, also called the *base 10* system, because it has 10 digits, has evolved naturally as a result of the fact that human beings have 10 fingers. In fact, the word "digit" is the Latin word for "finger."

The decimal system is a *positional-value system*, in which the value of a digit depends on its position. For example, consider the decimal number 453. We know that the digit 4 actually represents 4 *hundreds*, the 5 represents 5 *tens*, and the 3 represents 3 *units*. In essence, the 4 carries the most weight of the three digits; it is referred to as the *most significant digit* (MSD). The 3 carries the least weight and is called the *least significant digit* (LSD).

The various positions relative to the decimal point carry weights that can be expressed as powers of 10. This is illustrated below, where the number 2745.214 is represented. The decimal point separates the positive powers of 10 from the negative powers. The number 2745.214 is thus equal to

$$(2 \times 10^{+3}) + (7 \times 10^{+2}) + (4 \times 10^{+1}) + (5 \times 10^{+0})$$
$$+ (2 \times 10^{-1}) + (1 \times 10^{-2}) + (4 \times 10^{-3})$$

In general, any number is simply the sum of the products of each digit value times its positional value:

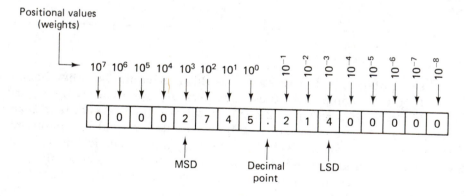

Decimal Counting

The number 9 is the largest digit value in the decimal system. Thus, as we are counting in decimal, a given digit will progress upward from 0 to 9. After 9, it goes back to 0 and the next higher digit position is incremented (goes up by 1). For example, note the digit changes in the following counting sequences: 25, 26, 27, 28, 29, 30; 196, 197, 198, 199, 200.

For a given number of digits, N, we can count decimal numbers from zero up to $10^N - 1$. In other words, with N digits we can have 10^N different numbers, including zero. To illustrate, with three decimal digits, we can count from 000 to 999, a total of 1000 different numbers.

Binary System

In the *binary system* there are only two symbols or possible digit values, 0 and 1. Even so, this *base 2 system* can be used to represent any quantity that can be represented in decimal or other number systems. In general, though, it will take a greater number of binary digits to express a given quantity.

All the statements made earlier concerning the decimal system are equally applicable to the binary system. The binary system is also a positional-value system, wherein each bit has its own value or weight expressed as powers of 2, as follows:

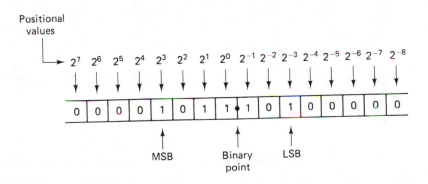

In the number expressed above, the positions to the left of the *binary point* (counterpart of the decimal point) are positive powers of 2 and the positions to the right of the binary point are negative powers of 2. The binary number 1011.101 is represented above, and its equivalent decimal value can be found by taking the sum of the products of each bit value (0 or 1) times its positional value.

$$1011.101_2 = (1 \times 2^3) + (0 \times 2^2) + (1 \times 2^1) + (1 \times 2^0)$$
$$+ (1 \times 2^{-1}) + (0 \times 2^{-2}) + (1 \times 2^{-3})$$

$$= 8 + 0 + 2 + 1 + .5 + 0 + .125$$

$$= 11.625_{10}$$

Notice in the preceding operation that subscripts (2 and 10) were used to indicate the base in which the particular number is expressed. This convention is used to avoid confusion whenever more than one number system is being employed.

Binary Counting The largest digit value in the binary system is 1. Thus, when counting in binary, a given digit will progress from 0 to 1. After it reaches 1, it recycles back to 0 and the next higher bit position is incremented:

	Binary				Decimal equivalent
Weights → $2^3 = 8$	$2^2 = 4$	$2^1 = 2$	$2^0 = 1$		
			0		0
			1		1
		1	0		2
		1	1		3
	1	0	0		4
	1	0	1		5
	1	1	0		6
	1	1	1		7
1	0	0	0		8
1	0	0	1		9
1	0	1	0		10
1	0	1	1		11
1	1	0	0		12
1	1	0	1		13
1	1	1	0		14
1	1	1	1		15

LSB

Note in this example that the least-significant-bit (LSB) position changes value at each step in the counting sequence. The next higher bit (2^1) changes value every two counts, the 2^2 bit changes value every four counts, and so on.

In the binary system, using N bits, we can count through 2^N different numbers, including zero. For example, with 2 bits, we can count 00, 01, 10, 11 for four different numbers. Similarly, with 4 bits, we can count from 0000 up to 1111, a total of $2^4 = 16$ different numbers. The largest number that can be represented by N bits is always equal to $2^N - 1$ in decimal. Thus, with 4 bits, the largest binary number is 1111_2, which is equivalent to $2^4 - 1 = 15_{10}$.

Binary-to-Decimal Conversion As explained earlier, the binary number system is a positional system where each bit carries a certain weight based on its position relative to the binary point. Any binary number can be converted to its decimal equivalent simply by summing together the weights of the various positions in the binary number which contain a 1. To illustrate:

$$1 \quad 1 \quad 0 \quad 1 \quad 1 \quad \text{(binary)}$$
$$2^4 + 2^3 + 0 + 2^1 + 2^0 = 16 + 8 + 2 + 1$$
$$= 27_{10} \text{ (decimal)}$$

The same method is used for binary numbers which contain a fractional part.

$$1 \quad 0 \quad 1 \; . \; 1 \quad 0 \quad 1 = 2^2 + 2^0 + 2^{-1} + 2^{-3}$$
$$= 4 + 1 + .5 + .125$$
$$= 5.625_{10}$$

The following conversions should be performed and verified by the reader:

1. $1 \quad 0 \quad 0 \quad 1 \quad 1 \quad 0_2 = 38_{10}$.
2. $0 \; . \; 1 \quad 1 \quad 0 \quad 0 \quad 0 \quad 1_2 = .765625_{10}$.
3. $1 \quad 1 \quad 1 \quad 1 \quad 0 \quad 0 \quad 1 \quad 1 \; . \; 0 \quad 1 \quad 0 \quad 1_2 = 243.3125_{10}$.

There are several ways to convert a decimal number to its equivalent binary system representation. A method that is convenient for small numbers is just the reverse of the process described in the preceding section. The decimal number is simply expressed as a sum of powers of 2 and then 1s and 0s are written in the appropriate bit positions. To illustrate:

$$13_{10} = 8 + 4 + 1 = 2^3 + 2^2 + 0 + 2^0$$
$$= 1 \quad 1 \quad 0 \quad 1_2$$

Another example:

$$25.375_{10} = 16 + 8 + 1 + .25 + .125$$
$$= 2^4 + 2^3 + 0 + 0 + 2^0 + 0 + 2^{-2} + 2^{-3}$$
$$= 1 \quad 1 \quad 0 \quad 0 \quad 1 \; .0 \quad 1 \quad 1_2$$

For larger decimal numbers, the foregoing method is laborious. A more convenient method entails separate conversion of the integer and fractional parts. For example, take the decimal number 25.375, which was converted above. The first step is to convert the integer portion, 25. This conversion is accomplished by repeatedly *dividing* 25 by 2 and writing down the remainders after each division until a quotient of zero is obtained.

$$\frac{25}{2} = 12 + \text{remainder of } 1$$

$$\frac{12}{2} = 6 + \text{remainder of } 0$$

$$\frac{6}{2} = 3 + \text{remainder of } 0$$

$$\frac{3}{2} = 1 + \text{remainder of } 1$$

$$\frac{1}{2} = 0 + \text{remainder of } 1$$

MSB ↓   LSB

$$25_{10} = \boxed{1 \quad 1 \quad 0 \quad 0 \quad 1}_2$$

The desired binary conversion is obtained by writing down the remainders, as shown above. Note that the *first* remainder is the LSB and the *last* remainder is the MSB.

The fractional part of the number (.375) is converted to binary by repeatedly *multiplying* it by 2 and recording any carries into the integer position.

$$.375 \times 2 = .75 = .75 \text{ with carry of } 0$$
$$.75 \times 2 = 1.50 = .50 \text{ with carry of } 1$$
$$.50 \times 2 = 1.00 = .00 \text{ with carry of } 1$$

$$.375_{10} = \boxed{.0 \quad 1 \quad 1}_2$$

Note that the repeated multiplications continue until a product of 1.00 is reached,* since any further multiplications result in all zeros. Notice here that the *first* carry is written in the first position to the right of the binary point.

Finally, the complete conversion for 25.375 can be written as the combination of the integer and fraction conversions.

$$25.375_{10} = 1 \quad 1 \quad 0 \quad 0 \quad 1 \; . \; 0 \quad 1 \quad 1_2$$

---

*Most of the time, 1.00 will not occur and the process is terminated after a suitable number of places in the binary fractional number is reached.

The reader should apply this method to verify the following conversion:

$$632.85_{10} = 1\ \ 0\ \ 0\ \ 1\ \ 1\ \ 1\ \ 1\ \ 0\ \ 0\ \ 0\ .\ 1\ \ 1\ \ 0\ \ 1\ \ 1_2$$

Octal Number System

The *octal number system* has a *base of eight*, meaning that it has eight possible digits: 0, 1, 2, 3, 4, 5, 6, and 7. Thus, each digit of an octal number can have any value from 0 to 7. The digit positions in an octal number have weights that are powers of 8:

$$\longleftarrow - - - \boxed{8^4 \quad 8^3 \quad 8^2 \quad 8^1 \quad 8^0 \quad 8^{-1} \quad 8^{-2} \quad 8^{-3} \quad 8^{-4} \quad 8^{-5}} - - - \longrightarrow$$

$$\text{octal point} \longrightarrow \uparrow$$

An octal number, then, can be easily converted to its decimal equivalent by multiplying each octal digit by its positional weight. For example,

$$372_8 = 3 \times (8^2) + 7 \times (8^1) + 2 \times (8^0)$$
$$= 3 \times 64 + 7 \times 8 + 2 \times 1$$
$$= 250_{10}$$

Another example:

$$24.6_8 = 2 \times (8^1) + 4 \times (8^0) + 6 \times (8^{-1})$$
$$= 20.75_{10}$$

Counting in Octal The largest octal digit is 7, so when counting in octal, a digit is incremented upward from 0 to 7. Once it reaches 7, it recycles to 0 on the next count and causes the next higher digit to be incremented. This is illustrated in the following sequences of octal counting: 64, 65, 66, 67, 70; 275, 276, 277, 300.

With N octal digits, we can count from zero up to $8^N - 1$, for a total of 8^N different counts. For example, with three octal digits we can count from 000_8 to 777_8, which is a total of $8^3 = 512_{10}$ different octal numbers.

Conversion between Octal and Binary The primary advantage of the octal number system is the ease with which conversions can be made between binary and octal numbers. The conversion from octal to binary is performed by converting *each* octal digit to its 3-bit binary equivalent. The eight possible digits are converted as follows:

Octal Digit	0	1	2	3	4	5	6	7
Binary Equivalent	000	001	010	011	100	101	110	111

Using these conversions, any octal number is converted to binary by individually converting each digit. For example, we can convert 472_8 to binary as follows:

$$\begin{matrix} 4 & 7 & 2 \\ \downarrow & \downarrow & \downarrow \\ 100 & 111 & 010 \end{matrix}$$

Hence, octal 472 is equivalent to binary 100111010. As another example, consider converting 54.31_8 to binary.

$$\begin{matrix} 5 & 4 & . & 3 & 1 \\ \downarrow & \downarrow & & \downarrow & \downarrow \\ 101 & 100 & . & 011 & 001 \end{matrix}$$

Thus, $54.31_8 = 101100.011001_2$.

Converting from binary to octal is simply the reverse of the foregoing process. The binary digits are grouped into groups of 3 on each side of the binary point, with zeros added on either side if needed to complete a group of 3 bits. Then, each group of 3 is converted to its octal equivalent. To illustrate, consider the conversion of 11010.1011_2 to octal:

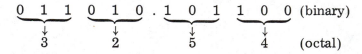

Note that 0s were added on each end to complete the groups of 3 bits. Here are two more examples: $11110_2 = 36_8$, $10011.01_2 = 23.2_8$.

Usefulness of Octal System The ease with which conversions can be made between octal and binary make the octal system attractive as a shorthand means of expressing large binary numbers. In computer work, binary numbers with up to 36 bits are not uncommon. These binary numbers, as we shall see, do not always represent a numerical quantity but often are some type of code that conveys nonnumerical information. In computers, binary numbers might represent (1) actual numerical data, (2) numbers corresponding to a location (address) in memory, (3) an instruction code, (4) a code representing alphabetic and other nonnumerical characters, or (5) a group of bits representing the status of devices internal or external to the computer.

When dealing with a large quantity of binary numbers of many bits, it is convenient and more efficient for us to write the numbers in octal rather than binary. Keep in mind, however, that the digital system works strictly in binary and we are using octal only as a convenience for the operators of the system.

Hexadecimal Number System

The *hexadecimal system* uses *base 16*. Thus, it has 16 possible digit symbols. It uses the digits 0 through 9 plus the letters A, B, C, D, E, and F as the 16 digit symbols. Table 1.1 shows the relationships among hexadecimal, decimal, and binary. Note that each hexadecimal digit represents a group of 4 bits. Many computers utilize the hexadecimal system, rather than octal, to represent large binary numbers. The conversions between hexadecimal and binary are done in exactly the same manner as octal and binary, except that groups of 4 bits are used. The following examples illustrate:

$$1\ 1\ 1\ 0\ 1\ 0\ 0\ 1\ 1\ 0_2 = \underbrace{0\ 0\ 1\ 1}_{3}\ \underbrace{1\ 0\ 1\ 0}_{A}\ \underbrace{0\ 1\ 1\ 0}_{6}$$

$$= 3\ A\ 6_{16}$$

$$9\ F\ 2_{16} = \quad 9 \qquad\qquad F \qquad\qquad 2$$

$$1\ 0\ 0\ 1 \quad 1\ 1\ 1\ 1 \quad 0\ 0\ 1\ 0$$

$$= 100111110010_2$$

TABLE 1.1

Hexadecimal	Decimal	Binary
0	0	0000
1	1	0001
2	2	0010
3	3	0011
4	4	0100
5	5	0101
6	6	0110
7	7	0111
8	8	1000
9	9	1001
A	10	1010
B	11	1011
C	12	1100
D	13	1101
E	14	1110
F	15	1111

Counting in Hexadecimal When counting in *hex* (abbreviation for hexadecimal), each digit can be incremented from 0 up to F. Once it reaches F, the next count causes it to recycle to 0 and the next higher digit is incremented. This is illustrated in the following hex counting sequences: 38, 39, 3A, 3B, 3C, 3D, 3E, 3F, 40; 6B8, 6B9, 6BA, 6BB, 6BC, 6BD, 6BE, 6BF, 6C0.

Hexadecimal-to-Decimal Conversion Occasionally, it is necessary to convert from a hexadecimal number to its equivalent decimal number. This is easily done if it is remembered that the various digit positions in a hex number have weights that are powers of 16. The conversion process is as follows:

$$356_{16} = 3 \times 16^2 + 5 \times 16^1 + 6 \times 16^0$$
$$= 768 + 80 + 6$$
$$= 854_{10}$$
$$2AF_{16} = 2 \times 16^2 + 10 \times 16^1 + 15 \times 16^0$$
$$= 512 + 160 + 15$$
$$= 687_{10}$$

Note in the second example that the value 10 was substituted for A and the value 15 for F in the conversion to decimal.

1.2 CODES

When numbers, letters, words, or other information is represented by a special group of symbols, the process is called *encoding* and the group of symbols is called a *code*.

We have seen that any decimal number can be represented by an equivalent binary number. The group of 0s and 1s in the binary number can be thought of as a code representing the decimal number. When a decimal number is represented by its equivalent binary number, we call it *straight binary coding*. If the decimal number is represented by its octal equivalent, we call it *octal coding*, and similarly for *hex coding*. Each of these types of coding is really just a different number system. In digital systems, many codes are used that do not fall into this classification.

BCD Code

Digital systems all use some form of binary numbers for their internal operation, but the external world is decimal in nature. This means that conversions between the decimal and binary systems are being performed often.

These conversions between decimal and binary can become long and complicated for large numbers. For this reason, another means of encoding decimal numbers which combines some features of both the decimal and binary system is sometimes used.

If *each* digit of a decimal number is represented by its binary equivalent, this produces a code called *binary-coded decimal* (hereafter abbreviated BCD). Since a decimal digit can be as large as 9, 4 bits are required to code each digit (binary code for 9 is 1001).

To illustrate the BCD code, take a decimal number such as 874. Each digit is changed to its binary equivalent as follows:

$$
\begin{array}{ccc}
8 & 7 & 4 \\
\downarrow & \downarrow & \downarrow \\
1000 & 0111 & 0100
\end{array}
$$

As another example, let us change 94.3 to its BCD-code representation.

$$
\begin{array}{cccc}
9 & 4 & . & 3 \\
\downarrow & \downarrow & & \downarrow \\
1001 & 0100 & & .0011
\end{array}
$$

Once again, each decimal digit is changed to its straight binary equivalent.

The BCD code, then, represents each digit of the decimal number by a 4-bit binary number. Clearly, only the 4-bit binary numbers from 0000 through 1001 are used. The BCD code does not use the numbers 1010, 1011, 1100, 1101, 1110, and 1111. In other words, only 10 of the 16 possible 4-bit binary code groups are used. If any of these "forbidden" 4-bit numbers ever occurs in a machine using the BCD code, it is usually an indication that an error has occurred.

EXAMPLE 1.1 Convert the BCD number 0110100000111001 to its decimal equivalent.

Solution:

$$
\begin{array}{cccc}
0110 & 1000 & 0011 & 1001 \\
6 & 8 & 3 & 9
\end{array}
$$

EXAMPLE 1.2 Convert the BCD number 011111000001 to its decimal equivalent.

Solution:

$$
\begin{array}{ccc}
0111 & \underline{1100} & 0001 \\
7 & & 1
\end{array}
$$

└→forbidden code group indicates error in BCD number

Comparison of BCD with Straight Binary It is important to realize that a BCD number is *not* the same as a straight binary number. A straight binary code takes the *complete* decimal number and represents it in binary; the BCD code converts *each* decimal *digit* to binary individually. To illustrate, take the number 137 and compare its straight binary and BCD codes:

$$1\quad 3\quad 7_{10} = 1\ 0\ 0\ 0\ 1\ 0\ 0\ 1_2 \quad \text{(binary)}$$
$$1\quad 3\quad 7_{10} = 0001\quad 0011\quad 0111 \qquad \text{(BCD)}$$

The BCD code requires 12 bits to represent 137, whereas the straight binary code requires only 8 bits. It is always true that the BCD code for a given decimal number requires more code bits than the straight code. This is because BCD does not use all possible 4-bit groups, as pointed out earlier.

The main advantage of the BCD code is the relative ease of converting to and from decimal. Only the 4-bit code groups for the decimal digits 0 through 9 need be remembered. This ease of conversion is especially important from a hardware standpoint because in a digital system, it is the logic circuits that perform the conversions.

BCD is used in digital machines whenever decimal information is either applied as inputs or displayed as outputs. Digital voltmeters, frequency counters, and digital clocks all use BCD because they display output information in decimal. Electronic calculators use BCD because the input numbers are entered in decimal via the keyboard and the output numbers are displayed in decimal.

Alphanumeric Codes

If it is to be very useful, a computer must be capable of handling nonnumeric information. In other words, a computer must be able to recognize codes that represent numbers, letters, and special characters. These codes are classified as *alphanumeric codes*. A complete and adequate set of necessary characters includes (1) 26 lowercase letters, (2) 26 uppercase letters, (3) 10 numeric digits, and (4) about 25 special characters, including +, /, #, and %.

This totals up to 87 characters. To represent 87 characters with some type of binary code would require at least 7 bits. With 7 bits, there are $2^7 = 128$ possible binary numbers; 87 of these arrangements of 0 and 1 bits serve as the code groups representing the 87 different characters. For example, the code group 1010101 might represent the letter U.

The most common alphanumeric code is known as the American Standard Code for Information Interchange (ASCII) and is used by most minicomputer and microcomputer manufacturers. Table 1.2 shows a partial listing of the 7-bit ASCII code. For each character, the octal and hex equivalents

TABLE 1.2 Partial Listing of ASCII Code

Character	7-Bit ASCII	Octal	Hex
A	100 0001	101	41
B	100 0010	102	42
C	100 0011	103	43
D	100 0100	104	44
E	100 0101	105	45
F	100 0110	106	46
G	100 0111	107	47
H	100 1000	110	48
I	100 1001	111	49
J	100 1010	112	4A
K	100 1011	113	4B
L	100 1100	114	4C
M	100 1101	115	4D
N	100 1110	116	4E
O	100 1111	117	4F
P	101 0000	120	50
Q	101 0001	121	51
R	101 0010	122	52
S	101 0011	123	53
T	101 0100	124	54
U	101 0101	125	55
V	101 0110	126	56
W	101 0111	127	57
X	101 1000	130	58
Y	101 1001	131	59
Z	101 1010	132	5A
0	011 0000	060	30
1	011 0001	061	31
2	011 0010	062	32
3	011 0011	063	33
4	011 0100	064	34
5	011 0101	065	35
6	011 0110	066	36
7	011 0111	067	37
8	011 1000	070	38
9	011 1001	071	39
Blank	010 0000	040	20
.	010 1110	056	2E
(	010 1000	050	28
+	010 1011	053	2B
$	010 0100	044	24
*	010 1010	052	2A
)	010 1001	051	29
—	010 1101	055	2D
/	010 1111	057	2F
,	010 1100	054	2C
=	011 1101	075	3D

are also shown. The ASCII code is used in the transmission of alphanumeric information between a computer and external input/output devices like a teletypewriter (TTY) or cathode-ray tube (CRT).

Parity

The process of transferring binary-coded information is subject to error, although modern equipment has been designed to reduce the probability of errors occurring. However, even relatively infrequent errors can cause useless results, so it is desirable to detect them whenever possible. One of the most widely used schemes for error detection is the *parity method*.

A *parity bit* is an extra bit that is attached to a code group which is being transferred from one location to another. The parity bit is made either 0 or 1, depending on the number of 1s that are contained in the code group. There are two different methods that are used.

In the *even-parity method*, the value of the parity bit is chosen so that the total number of 1s in the code group (including the parity bit) is an *even* number. For example, suppose that the code group is 1000011. This is the ASCII character C. The code group has *three* 1s. Therefore, we will add a parity bit of 1 to make the total number of 1s an even number. The *new* code group, including the parity bit, thus becomes

$$\boxed{1} \quad 1 \quad 0 \quad 0 \quad 0 \quad 0 \quad 1 \quad 1$$

added parity bit

If the code group contains an even number of 1s to begin with, then the parity bit is given a value of 0. For example, if the code group is 1000001 (the character A), the assigned parity bit would be 0, so the new code, including the parity bit, would be 01000001.

The *odd-parity method* is used in exactly the same way except that the parity bit is chosen so that the total number of 1s (including the parity bit) is an *odd* number. For example, for the code group 1000001, the assigned parity bit would be a 1. For the code group 1000011, the bit would be a 0.

Regardless of whether even parity or odd parity is used, the parity bit becomes an actual part of the code word. For example, adding a parity bit to the 7-bit ASCII code produces an 8-bit code.

The parity bit is used to ensure that during the transmission of a character code from one place to another (e.g., TTY to computer), any *single* errors can be detected. For example, if odd parity is being used and the recipient of the transmitted character detects an *even* number of 1 bits, clearly the character code must be in error.

Obviously, the parity method has limitations insofar that it can only detect single errors and it cannot detect which bit is in error. There are more elaborate schemes used not only to check for multiple errors, but also to detect where the errors are and to correct them. The error-correction schemes are not important to our study of microcomputers, so they are not discussed in this book.

1.3 BINARY ARITHMETIC

Arithmetic operations can be performed on binary numbers in exactly the same way as on decimal numbers. In some cases, however, certain binary operations are done differently than their decimal counterparts because of hardware considerations.

Binary Addition

The addition of two binary numbers is performed in exactly the same manner as the addition of decimal numbers. In fact, binary addition is simpler since there are fewer cases to learn. Let us first review a decimal addition.

```
   3   7   6    LSD
 + 4   6   1
 ─────────────
   8   3   7
```

The least-significant-digit (LSD) position is operated on first, producing a sum of 7. The digits in the second position are then added to produce a sum of 13, which produces a *carry* of 1 into the third position. This produces a sum of 8 in the third position.

The same general steps are followed in binary addition. However, there are only four cases which can occur in adding the binary digits (bits) in any position. They are:

$$0 + 0 = 0$$

$$1 + 0 = 1$$

$$1 + 1 = 0 \quad \text{plus a carry of 1 into the next position}$$

$$1 + 1 + 1 = 1 \quad \text{plus a carry of 1 into the next position}$$

This last case occurs when the two bits in a certain position are 1 and there is a carry from the previous position. Here are several examples of the addition of two binary numbers:

```
    0 1 1 (3)          1 0 0 1 ( 9)          1 1.0 1 1 (3.375)
  + 1 1 0 (6)        + 1 1 1 1 (15)        + 1 0.1 1 0 (2.750)
  ───────────        ─────────────        ───────────────────
    1 0 0 1 (9)        1 1 0 0 0 (24)        1 1 0.0 0 1 (6.125)
```

Addition is the most important arithmetic operation in digital systems because the operations of subtraction, multiplication, and division as they are performed in most modern digital computers and calculators actually use only addition as their basic operation.

Binary Subtraction

In many large computers and in most microcomputers, the operation of subtraction is performed using the operation of addition. This process requires the use of the *2's-complement form.*

The 2's-complement of a binary number is obtained by replacing each 0 with a 1, and each 1 with a 0, then adding 1 to the resulting number. The first step of changing each bit is called *1's-complementing.* For example, the 1's-complement of 10110110 is 01001001.

The 2's-complement of a binary number is formed by adding 1 to the 1's-complement of the number. For example, the 2's-complement of 10110110 is obtained as follows:

number	10110110
1's-complement	01001001
add 1	+_____1
2's-complement	01001010

The operation of subtraction can be performed by converting the *subtrahend* (the number to be subtracted) to its 2's-complement and then *adding* it to the *minuend* (the number being subtracted from). To illustrate, consider subtracting the number 1001 from 1100 (decimal 9 from decimal 12).

Normal Subtraction		2's-Complement Subtraction	
Minuend	1100	Minuend	1100
Subtrahend	−1001	2's-Complement of subtrahend	+0111
Difference	0011	Sum	10011
		disregard final carry	

Thus, the final result is 0011 (decimal 3).

We will say more about 2's-complement subtraction after we introduce signed numbers.

Signed Numbers

In binary machines, the binary numbers are represented by a set of binary storage devices (e.g., flip-flops). Each device represents one bit. For example, a 6-bit flip-flop register could store binary numbers ranging from 000000 to

111111 (zero to 63 in decimal). This represents the *magnitude* of the number. Since digital computers and calculators must handle negative as well as positive numbers, some means is required for representing the *sign* of the number (+ or -). This is usually done by adding another bit to the number, called the *sign bit*. In general, the common convention which has been adopted is that a 0 in the sign bit represents a positive number and a 1 in the sign bit represents a negative number. This is illustrated below. This number is divided into two parts: the leftmost bit is the sign bit, which is 0, indicating +; the other 7 bits are the value or magnitude of the number. Thus, the number is $+52_{10}$.

$$\boxed{0}\ 0\ 1\ 1\ 0\ 1\ 0\ 0_2\ =\ +52_{10}$$

sign bit ⟶

In the same manner, the following number is -52_{10}.

$$\boxed{1}\ 0\ 1\ 1\ 0\ 1\ 0\ 0_2\ =\ -52_{10}$$

sign bit ⟶

This method for representing signed numbers is called the *true-magnitude form* because the true value of the binary number is used for both + and - numbers and only a sign bit is added.

Computers that use the 2's-complement system use a different technique for representing *negative* numbers. Instead of using the true magnitude of the number, the 2's-complement of the number is used. This is illustrated below for the number -52.

$$\boxed{1}\ \underbrace{1\ 0\ 0\ 1\ 1\ 0\ 0}\ =\ -52_{10}$$

sign bit ⟶   2's-complement of 0110100_2

1.4 ADDITION USING SIGNED NUMBERS

Next, we will investigate how the operations of addition and subtraction are performed in digital computers which use the 2's-complement representation for negative numbers. In the various cases to be considered, it is important to remember that the sign-bit portion of each number is operated on the same as the magnitude portion.

Case I: Two Positive Numbers

The addition of two positive numbers is straightforward. Consider the addition of +9 and +4.

```
    +9 ⟶   ┌─────┐
           │ 0 │ 1   0   0   1  (augend)
  +(+4) ⟶  │ 0 │ 0   1   0   0  (addend)
           ├─────┤
           │ 0 │ 1   1   0   1  (sum = +13)
           └─────┘
             └── sign bits
```

Note that the sign bits of the *augend* and *addend* are both 0 and the sign bit of the sum is 0, indicating that the sum is positive.

Case II: Positive Number and Smaller Negative Number

Consider the addition of +9 and –4. Remember that the –4 will be in its 2's-complement form.

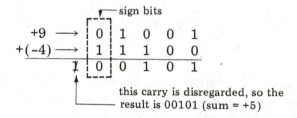

```
                         ┌─ sign bits
     +9 ⟶    ┌───┐
             │ 0 │ 1   0   0   1
   +(–4) ⟶   │ 1 │ 1   1   0   0
          ┌──┼───┤
          1 │ 0 │ 0   1   0   1
          └──┴───┘
             ↑
             │   this carry is disregarded, so the
             └── result is 00101 (sum = +5)
```

In this case, the sign bit of the addend is 1. Note that the sign bits also participate in the addition process. In fact, a carry is generated in the last position of addition. *This carry is disregarded*, so the final sum is 00101, which is equivalent to +5.

Case III: Positive Number and Larger Negative Number

Consider the addition of –9 and +4.

```
     -9 ⟶    1   0   1   1   1
   +(+4) ⟶   0   0   1   0   0
            ─────────────────────
             1   1   0   1   1   (sum = –5)
```

The sum here has a sign bit of 1, indicating a negative number. Since the sum is negative, it is in 2's-complement form, so the last four bits (1011) represent the 2's-complement of 0101 (equivalent to decimal 5). Thus, 11011 is equivalent to –5, the correct expected result.

Case IV: Two Negative Numbers

$$
\begin{array}{r}
-9 \longrightarrow 1 \quad 0 \quad 1 \quad 1 \quad 1 \\
+(-4) \longrightarrow 1 \quad 1 \quad 1 \quad 0 \quad 0 \\
\hline
1 \quad 1 \quad 0 \quad 0 \quad 1 \quad 1
\end{array}
$$

└── this carry is disregarded, so the
result is 10011 (sum = –13)

The final result is again negative and in 2's-complement form with a sign bit of 1.

Case V: Equal and Opposite Numbers

$$
\begin{array}{r}
-9 \longrightarrow 1 \quad 0 \quad 1 \quad 1 \quad 1 \\
+(+9) \longrightarrow 0 \quad 1 \quad 0 \quad 0 \quad 1 \\
\hline
1 \quad 0 \quad 0 \quad 0 \quad 0 \quad 0
\end{array}
$$

└── disregard so the result is 00000
(sum = +0)

The final result is obviously "plus zero," as expected.

1.5 SUBTRACTION IN THE 2'S-COMPLEMENT SYSTEM

The subtraction operation using the 2's-complement system actually involves the operation of addition and is really no different from the cases considered in the preceding section. When subtracting one binary number (the *subtrahend*) from another binary number (the *minuend*), the procedure is as follows:

1. Take the 2's-complement of the subtrahend, *including* the sign bit. If the subtrahend is a positive number, this will change it to a negative number in 2's-complement form. If the subtrahend is a negative number, this will change it to a positive number in true binary form. In other words, we are changing the sign of the subtrahend.
2. After taking the 2's-complement of the subtrahend, it is *added* to the minuend. The minuend is kept in its original form. The result of this addition represents the required *difference*. The sign bit of this difference determines whether it is + or – and whether it is in true binary form or 2's-complement form.

Let us consider the case where +4 is to be subtracted from +9.

$$\text{minuend} \quad (+9) \longrightarrow 0 \quad 1 \quad 0 \quad 0 \quad 1$$

$$\text{subtrahend} \ (+4) \longrightarrow 0 \quad 0 \quad 1 \quad 0 \quad 0$$

Change subtrahend to its 2's-complement form (11100). Now add this to the minuend.

```
      0  1  0  0  1
    +1  1  1  0  0
  1   0  0  1  0  1
  ↑
  └── disregard so the result is 00101 = +5
```

When the subtrahend is changed to its 2's-complement, it actually becomes −4, so we are adding +9 and −4, which is the same as subtracting +4 from +9. This is the same as case II of the preceding section. Any subtraction operation, then, actually becomes one of addition when the 2's-complement system is used. This feature of the 2's-complement system has made it the most widely used method since it allows addition and subtraction to be performed by the same circuitry.

The reader should verify the results of using the foregoing procedure for the following subtractions.

1. +9 − (−4)
2. −9 − (+4)
3. −9 − (−4)
4. +4 − (−4)

Remember: When the result has a sign bit of 1, it is negative and in 2's-complement form.

1.6 MULTIPLICATION OF BINARY NUMBERS

The multiplication of binary numbers is done in the same manner as multiplication of decimal numbers. The process is actually simpler since the multiplier digits are either 0 or 1, so that at any time we are multiplying by 0 or 1 and no other digits. The following example illustrates:

```
            1  0  0  1 ←── multiplicand = 9₁₀
            1  0  1  1 ←── multiplier = 11₁₀
            1  0  0  1 ⎫
         1  0  0  1    ⎪
      0  0  0  0       ⎬ partial products
   1  0  0  1          ⎭
   1  1  0  0  0  1  1 ←── final product = 99₁₀
```

In this example the multiplicand and multiplier are in true binary form and no sign bits are used. The steps followed in the process are exactly the same as in decimal multiplication. First, the LSB of the multiplier is examined; in our example it is a 1. This 1 multiplies the multiplicand to product 1001, which is written down as the first partial product. Next, the second bit of the multiplier is examined. It is a 1, so 1001 is written for the second partial product. Note that this second partial product is *shifted* one place to the left relative to the first one. The third bit of the multiplier is 0, so 0000 is written as the third partial product; again, it is shifted one place to the left relative to the previous partial product. The fourth multiplier bit is 1, so the last partial product is 1001, shifted again one position to the left. The four partial products are then summed up to produce the final product.

Most digital machines can only add two binary numbers at a time. For this reason, the partial products formed during multiplication cannot all be added together at the same time. Instead, they are added together two at a time; that is, the first is added to the second and their sum is added to the third, and so on. This process is illustrated for the preceding example.

```
      add {        1   0   0   1  ←— first partial product
              1   0   0   1          ←— second partial product shifted left
      add {    1   1   0   1   1  ←— sum of first two partial products
            0   0   0   0              ←— third partial product shifted left
    add {    0   1   1   0   1   1  ←— sum of first three partial products
          1   0   0   1                  ←— fourth partial product shifted left
          1   1   0   0   0   1   1  ←— sum of four partial products, which
                                          equals final total product.
```

1.7 BINARY DIVISION

The process for dividing one binary number (the *dividend*) by another (the *divisor*) is the same as that which is followed for decimal numbers, what we usually refer to as "long division." The actual process is simpler in binary because when we are checking to see how many times the divisor "goes into" the dividend, there are only two possibilities, 0 or 1. To illustrate, consider the following examples of division:

```
            0   0   1   1
    1   1 ⟌ 1   0   0   1        (9 ÷ 3 = 3)
            0   1   1
            0   0   1   1
```

```
              0   0   1 0 . 1
    1   0   0 ⟌ 1   0   1 0 . 0    (10 ÷ 4 = 2.5)
              1   0   0
                  1   0   0
                  1   0   0
                          0
```

In most modern digital machines, the subtractions that are part of the division operation are usually carried out using 2's-complement subtraction, that is, complementing the subtrahend and adding.

1.8 BCD ARITHMETIC OPERATIONS

Many computers (and all calculators) have the capability of performing arithmetic operations on numbers that are encoded in BCD. These operations are somewhat more complex than binary arithmetic operations because BCD is not a number system but a code. Despite this fact, BCD arithmetic is frequently used because, as mentioned earlier, BCD offers a more convenient way for the computer to communicate with a decimal world.

BCD Addition

The addition of decimal numbers that are in BCD form can be best understood by considering the two cases that can occur when two decimal digits are added.

Sum Equals Nine or Less Consider adding 5 and 4 using BCD to represent each digit.

$$
\begin{array}{rl}
5 & \quad 0101 \longleftarrow \text{BCD for 5} \\
+4 & \quad +0100 \longleftarrow \text{BCD for 4} \\
\hline
9 & \quad 1001 \longleftarrow \text{BCD for 9}
\end{array}
$$

The addition is carried out as in normal binary addition and the sum is 1001, which is the BCD code for 9. As another example, take 45 added to 33.

$$
\begin{array}{rl}
45 & \quad 0100\ 0101 \longleftarrow \text{BCD for 45} \\
+33 & \quad +0011\ 0011 \longleftarrow \text{BCD for 33} \\
\hline
78 & \quad 0111\ 1000 \longleftarrow \text{BCD for 78}
\end{array}
$$

In this example, the 4-bit codes for 5 and 3 are added in binary to produce 1000, which is BCD for 8. Similarly, the second decimal digit positions produce 0111, which is BCD for 7. The total is 0111 1000, which is the BCD code for 78.

In the two preceding examples, none of the sums of the pairs of decimal digits exceeded 9; therefore, *no decimal carries were produced.* For these cases, the BCD addition process is straightforward and is actually the same as binary addition.

Sum Greater than Nine Consider the addition of 6 and 7 in BCD.

```
     6         0110 ◄── BCD for 6
   + 7        +0111 ◄── BCD for 7
   ───        ─────
    13         1101 ◄── invalid code group for BCD
```

The sum 1101 does not exist in the BCD code; it is one of the six forbidden or invalid 4-bit code groups. This has occurred because the sum of the two digits exceeds 9. Whenever this occurs, the sum has to be corrected by the addition of six (0110) to skip over the six invalid code groups.

```
      6         0110 ◄── BCD for 6
    + 7        +0111 ◄── BCD for 7
    ───        ─────
     13         1101 ◄── invalid sum
               +0110 ◄── add 6 for correction
              ─────────
     0001       0011 ◄── BCD for 13
      ‿          ‿
      1          3
```

As shown, 0110 is added to the invalid sum and produces the correct BCD result. Note that a carry is produced into the second decimal position. This addition of 0110 has to be performed whenever the sum of the two decimal digits is greater than 9.

As another example, take 47 plus 35 in BCD.

```
   47        0100 0111 ◄── BCD for 47
  +35       +0011 0101 ◄── BCD for 35
  ───       ──────────
   82        0111 1100 ◄── invalid sum in first digit
        +         0110 ◄── add 6
            ──────────
             1000 0010 ◄── correct BCD sum
               8    2
```

The addition of the 4-bit codes for the seven and five digits results in an invalid sum and is corrected by adding 0110. Note that this generates a carry of 1, which is carried over to be added to the BCD sum of the second-position digits.

To summarize the BCD addition procedure:

1. Add the BCD code groups for each digit position using ordinary binary addition.
2. For those positions where the sum is nine or less, no correction is needed. The sum is in proper BCD form.
3. When the sum of two digits is greater than nine, a correction of 0110 should be added to that sum to get the proper BCD result. This will always produce a carry into the next decimal position.

The procedure for BCD addition is clearly more complicated than straight binary addition. This is also true of the other BCD arithmetic operations, which we will not elaborate on further at this time.

1.9 HEXADECIMAL ARITHMETIC

Later in our work we shall have need to add and subtract hexadecimal numbers. The procedures for these operations will now be illustrated.

Addition

$$
\begin{array}{rrr}
4 & 7 & A \\
+2 & 9 & 2 \\
\hline
7 & 0 & C
\end{array}
$$

Note that $A + 2 = C$, since $A = 10$ (decimal) and $C = 12$ (decimal). Also note that $7 + 9 = 0$ with a carry into the next position.

Subtraction

Hexadecimal subtraction can be done in several ways. One method is to convert the subtrahend to binary, take its 2's-complement, convert back to hexadecimal, and then add it to the minuend. This is illustrated for subtracting 292 from 47A:

$$
\begin{array}{l}
\text{subtrahend} = 292_{16} = 001010010010 \\
\qquad\qquad\qquad\quad\ 110101101110 \longleftarrow \text{2's-complement} \\
\qquad\qquad\qquad\quad\ \ D\quad\ 6\quad\ E \qquad\qquad \text{convert to hex} \\
\qquad\qquad\qquad\ +4\quad\ 7\quad\ A \qquad\qquad \text{add minuend} \\
\qquad\qquad\qquad\ \boxed{1}\ 1\quad E\quad\ 8
\end{array}
$$

disregard carry ⟶

Thus, the final result is 1E8.

GLOSSARY

Alphanumeric Codes   Codes that represent numbers, letters, and operation characteristics (e.g., ASCII code).

BCD Code   Binary-coded-decimal system, in which each digit of a decimal number is encoded in its 4-bit binary equivalent.

Binary Number System   Number system that uses only the digits 0 and 1.

Bit   Abbreviation for "binary digit."

Hexadecimal Number System   Number system that uses the digits 0 through 9 and the alphabet letters A through F.

Octal Number System   Number system that uses the digits 0 through 7.

1's-Complement   Result obtained by taking a binary number and changing each bit to its opposite value.

Parity Bit   Extra bit that is attached to a code group to make the number of 1s conform to a predetermined form (odd or even).

2's-Complement   Result obtained by adding 1 to the 1's-complement of a binary number.

QUESTIONS AND PROBLEMS

1.1   Perform each of the following conversions.

(a) 236_{10} = _____ $_2$

(b) 896_{10} = _____ BCD

(c) 11011011_2 = _____ $_{10}$

(d) 1110111011_2 = _____ $_8$

(e) 110101011110_2 = ____ $_{16}$

(f) 100100111000_{BCD} = _____ $_{10}$

(g) 967_{10} = _____ BCD

(h) 1537_8 = _____ $_2$

(i) $FEA3_{16}$ _____ $_2$

1.2   Add an even-parity bit to the following data words.

(a) ___ 100110000111   (b) ___ 000101111011

1.3   Perform the following operations using the 2's-complement system.

(a)   +10   (b)   +11   (c)   +15   (d)   -10   (e)   -7

   +(+ 5)   +(- 6)   -(+ 5)   +(+ 5)   -(-8)

1.4   Perform the following using BCD to represent the decimal values.

(a) 301_{10} (b) 455_{10}

   +214_{10} +126_{10}

1.5   Perform the following hexadecimal operations.

(a) 597_{16} (b)   849

   +612_{16} -$5F4_{16}$

1.6   Octal and hexadecimal counting sequences are shown in the table. Write the next *four* numbers in each sequence.

Octal	Hexidecimal
372	3FB
373	3FC
374	3FD
375	3FE
—	—
—	—
—	—
—	—

1.7 The code words below are written in the 7-bit ASCII code with an *odd*-parity bit added as the most significant bit (MSB). What is the coded message?

11001000/01000101/01001100/01001100/01001111

1.8 Take the equation $I = E/R$ and write it using the ASCII code. Attach an *even*-parity bit to each code word.

1.9 Take the binary codes generated in Problem 1.8 and convert them to hexadecimal.

2

DIGITAL CIRCUITS

The circuitry of digital systems and digital computers is designed to operate on voltage signals that are digital in nature; that is, these signals can have only two possible values at any time. Figure 2.1 shows a typical digital waveform which goes between the levels of 0 volts (V) and +5 V. These voltage levels are assigned the binary values 0 and 1, respectively. These 0 and 1 representations are called *logic levels*. Although the logic levels in Fig. 2.1 are shown as exactly 0 V and +5 V, in practical systems each logic level will represent a range of voltages. For example, logic 0 (also referred to as a Low) might be any voltage between 0 V and +0.8 V, and logic 1 (also called a HIGH) might range from +2 V to +5 V. Incidentally, these are the logic-level ranges for the transistor-transistor logic (TTL) family of integrated circuits.

In digital computers, the digital voltage signals can represent different things. A single digital voltage signal can represent one bit of a binary number, one bit of some binary code (e.g., BCD, ASCII), a logic or control level that signals the status of some situation, or several other possibilities. Regardless of what these digital or logic signals represent, the circuits that operate

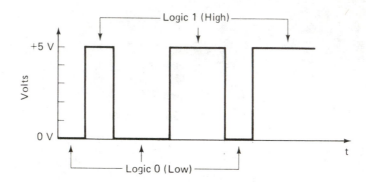

FIGURE 2.1   Typical digital signal.

on these signals are called *digital logic circuits*. This chapter reviews all the logic circuits needed to understand and use computers.

2.1 PARALLEL AND SERIAL TRANSMISSION

It is generally necessary to transmit signals representing complete binary numbers consisting of several bits from one part of a system to another. There are basically two ways of doing this: parallel transmission and serial transmission.

In *parallel representation* or *transmission* of binary numbers, or codes, each bit is derived from a separate circuit output and transmitted over a separate line. Figure 2.2A illustrates the arrangement for a 5-bit number. Each circuit output represents one binary digit (bit) and can be either 0 V (binary 0) or 5 V (binary 1). The five circuit outputs are present simultaneously, so at any time the complete binary number is available at the outputs. In Fig. 2.2A, the binary number 10110 is represented.

In *serial transmission*, which is illustrated in Fig. 2.2B, only *one* signal output line is used to transmit the binary number. This output line transmits the various bits one at a time in sequence, generally starting with the least significant bit. It should be apparent that some sort of timing is needed to be able to distinguish among the various bits. In the figure, a *clock signal* is used to provide the sequencing. A clock signal is an important part of most digital systems and is used to provide accurate timing of operations. In serial transmission, each time a clock pulse occurs, the output signal changes to the next bit of the binary number. In Fig. 2.2B, the output sequences through the bits 01011 (note that time increases from left to right). The actual binary number being transmitted is 11010, since the LSB is transmitted first.

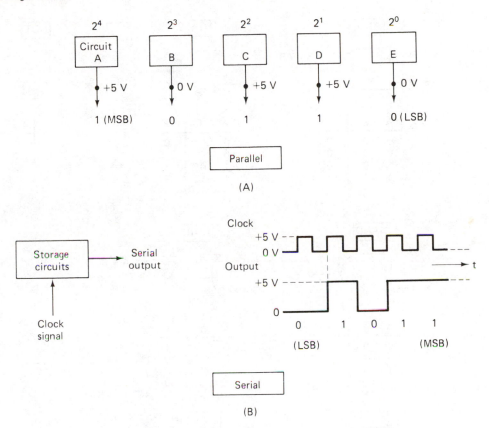

FIGURE 2.2 Parallel and serial transmission of numbers.

2.2 LOGIC GATES

Logic gates are digital circuits that have two or more logic inputs and produce a single output with a logic level determined by the logic levels present at the inputs. Figure 2.3 shows each of the basic logic gates, the mathematical expressions for their operation, and a table showing the output level for each combination of input levels.

AND Gate The AND gate operates such that the output will be at the 1 level *only when all* inputs are 1. The mathematical expression for the two-input AND gate is written as $X = AB$, the same as ordinary multiplication. For a three-input gate, it would be $X = ABC$; and so on for more inputs.

OR Gate The OR gate produces a one-output when *any* input is at the 1

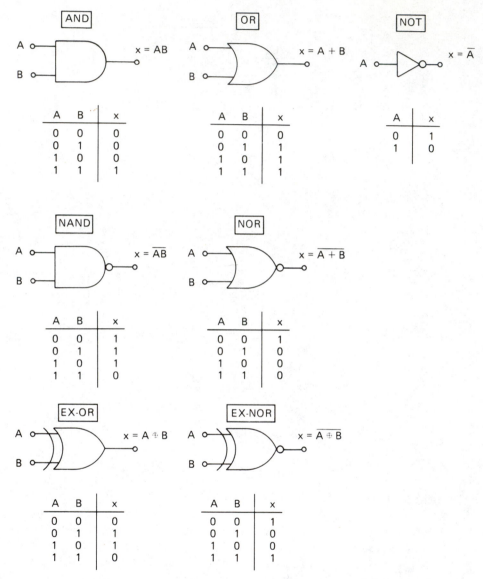

FIGURE 2.3 Basic logic gates.

level. Its mathematical expression is $X = A + B$, where the + stands for the OR operation and not normal addition. For a three-input OR gate, it would be $X = A + B + C$; and so on.

NOT Gate This is actually not a gate since it can only have one input. It is commonly called an *inverter* and it produces an output whose logic level is always *opposite* of the input logic level. The mathematical statement of its operation is $X = \overline{A}$. The overbar always indicates the inversion (NOT) operation.

NAND Gate The NAND gate combines the AND and NOT operations, such that the output will be 0 *only when all* inputs are 1. Its logic expression is $X = \overline{AB}$, which indicates that inputs A and B are first ANDed and then the result inverted. Thus, a NAND gate always produces an output that is the inverse (opposite) of an AND gate.

NOR Gate The NOR gate combines the OR and NOT operations such that the output will be 0 when *any* input is 1. Its logic expression is $X = \overline{A + B}$, which indicates that A and B are first ORed and then the result inverted. A NOR gate always gives an output logic level that is the inverse of an OR gate.

EXCLUSIVE-OR Gate The EX-OR gate produces a 1 output only when the two inputs are at *different* logic levels. An EX-OR gate always has two inputs, and its output expression is $X = A \oplus B$.

EXCLUSIVE-NOR Gate This gate is the inverse of the EX-OR gate. It produces a 1 output only when the inputs are at the *same* logic level. The EX-NOR output expression is $X = \overline{A \oplus B}$.

2.3 LOGIC EQUIVALENCES

The same logic operations can be implemented in more than one way. The most obvious examples of this are shown in Fig. 2.4A, where the AND operation is implemented with two NAND gates and the OR operation is implemented with two NOR gates. In each case, the second gate is used as a NOT gate.

Two less obvious equivalences are shown in Fig. 2.4B and C. In B, we see that a NAND gate is equivalent to an OR gate which has inverters on each input. The small circles on the OR gate inputs represent the inversion operation and act just like NOT gates. These two representations, although equivalent, can be interpreted differently, as shown in the diagram. The decision as to which representation should be used in a logic-circuit schematic depends on which of the output conditions is the *normal* condition and which is the *activated* condition. For example, if the output is normally HIGH during the circuit operation and goes LOW (is activated) only at certain special times, the representation on the left is used. On the other hand, if the output is normally LOW and goes HIGH (is activated) only at certain times, the representation on the right is used.

In other words, when the LOW output state is the active state which causes other things in the circuit to happen, the representation in (a) is used. The small circle on the output indicates that the LOW state is the active output state. When the HIGH output state is the active state which causes other

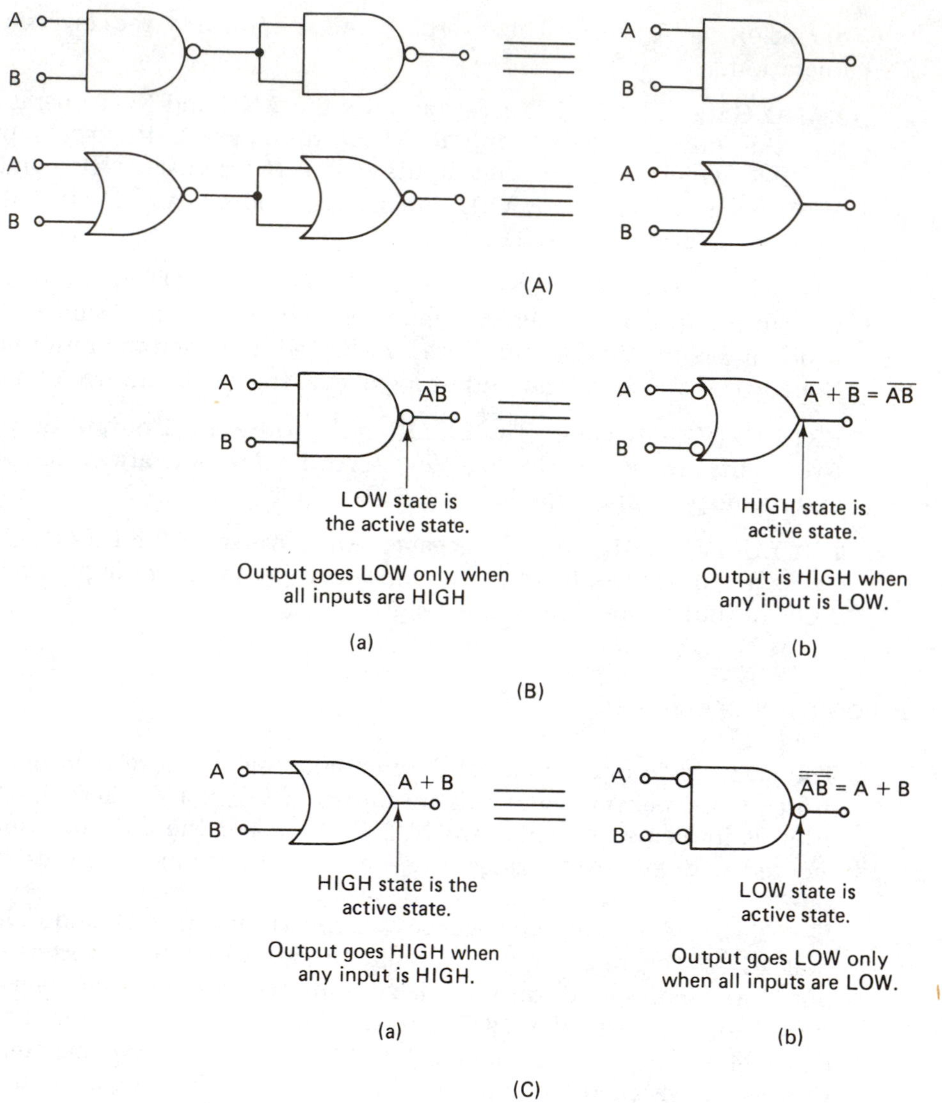

(A)

LOW state is
the active state.

Output goes LOW only when
all inputs are HIGH

(a)

HIGH state is
active state.

Output is HIGH when
any input is LOW.

(b)

(B)

HIGH state is the
active state.

Output goes HIGH when
any input is HIGH.

(a)

LOW state is
active state.

Output goes LOW only
when all inputs are LOW.

(b)

(C)

FIGURE 2.4 Some logic-gate equivalences.

things to happen, (b) is used. The absence of a circle on the output indicates
that the HIGH output state is the active state.

The same idea is used for other logic operations, such as the OR operation shown in Fig. 2.4C. Again, both representations are equivalent to the
OR operation. The representation in (a) is used when the HIGH state is the
active output state, and (b) is used when the LOW state is the active output
state.

2.4 INTEGRATED-CIRCUIT LOGIC FAMILIES

It is not our intention here to go into detail on all the integrated-circuit (IC) logic families and subfamilies, but we should briefly mention the principal characteristics that distinguish the various families. The three most important characteristics are *operating speed*, *power consumption*, and *packing density* (number of elements per chip area).

Operating Speed The bipolar logic families excel here with emitter-coupled logic (ECL) being the fastest, followed by Schottky TTL, integrated injection logic (I^2L), and conventional TTL. The MOS families are all slower, with CMOS being the fastest MOS family, followed by NMOS and then PMOS.

Power Consumption CMOS is the best here, followed by I^2L, low-power TTL, PMOS, and NMOS. The ECL and Schottky TTL families dissipate the most power.

Packing Density PMOS and NMOS are the leaders in this area, but I^2L is catching up. CMOS comes next, followed by TTL and ECL.

2.5 TRISTATE LOGIC

Until a few years ago, all digital logic circuits were characterized by outputs that were at either of two voltage levels. The recent development of *bus-organized* computers (discussed later) led to the development of a type of logic circuitry that has *three* distinct output states. These devices, called *tristate logic* (TSL) devices, have a third output condition in addition to the normal HIGH and LOW logic voltage levels. This third condition is called the *high-impedance*, or *high-Z* state.

Figure 2.5 shows the symbol and operation for a TSL inverter. The DISABLE input controls the output operation so that the output either acts as a normal inverter output (DISABLE = 0) or as a high-impedance output (DISABLE = 1). In the *enabled* condition, the circuit behaves exactly as any logic inverter, producing an output voltage level opposite to the input logic level. In the *disabled* high-Z state, the output terminal acts as if it were disconnected from the inverter; in other words, think of it as a virtual open circuit.

Many types of logic circuits are currently available with tristate outputs. Another common one is the *tristate buffer*, which operates exactly like the inverter in Fig. 2.5, except that it does not produce the inversion operation in the enabled state. Its symbol is the same as shown in Fig. 2.5, except there is no circle on the output.

Other tristate circuits include flip-flops, registers, memories, and almost all microprocessor and microprocessor interface chips.

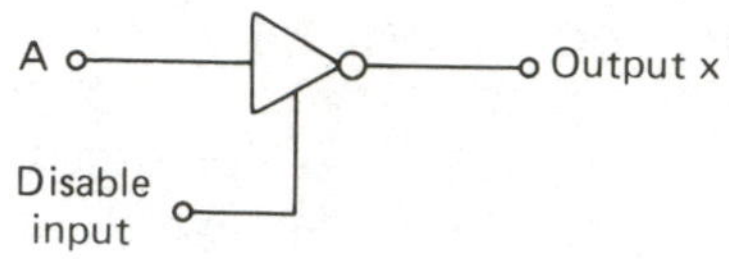

	Operation
DISABLE = 0 (the enabled condition)	Operates as normal inverter with $x = \overline{A}$
DISABLE = 1 (the disabled condition)	Output is in high-impedance state; acts as if output terminal is disconnected from the inverter

FIGURE 2.5 Tristate logic inverter.

The usefulness of TSL should become very clear when we discuss data transfer and data bussing. It will not become fully appreciated, however, until we study the complete microcomputer system.

Enable Inputs Some IC manufacturers prefer to call the control input on a tristate device an ENABLE input rather than a DISABLE input. This, of course, means that the ENABLE input would be active on the opposite logic level as the DISABLE input. For example, if the control input of Fig. 2.5 were an ENABLE input, it would be active-LOW, since a 0 *enables* the device. This would be indicated by a small circle on the device symbol.

2.6 FLIP-FLOPS

Logic gates produce outputs that depend on the *current* logic states of the inputs. Digital systems of almost any degree of complexity also require logic circuits which can produce outputs that depend on the *previous* states of the inputs, in other words, circuits with memory. The most widely used memory circuit is the *flip-flop* (FF).

Flip-flops are logic circuits that have two outputs, which are the inverse of each other. Figure 2.6 indicates these outputs as Q and $\overline{Q}$ (actually any letter could be used, but Q is the most common). The Q output is called the normal FF output and $\overline{Q}$ is the inverted FF output. When a FF is said to be in the high (1) state or the low (0) state, this is the condition at the Q output. Of course, the $\overline{Q}$ output is always the inverse of Q.

There are two possible operating states for the FF: (1) $Q = 0$, $\overline{Q} = 1$; and (2) $Q = 1$, $\overline{Q} = 0$. The FF has one or more inputs, which are used to cause

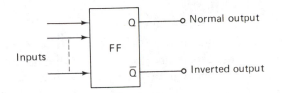

FIGURE 2.6 General flip-flop symbol.

the FF to switch back and forth between these two states. Once an input signal causes a FF to go to a given state, the FF will remain in that state even after that input signal is terminated. This is its memory characteristic.

The flip-flop is known by several other names, including bistable multivibrator, latch, and binary, but we will generally use flip-flop because it is the most common designation in the digital field.

Basic FF Circuit

Figure 2.7 shows how two cross-coupled NAND gates are arranged to form the basic SET/CLEAR FF (SC FF). The circuit has two inputs, SET and CLEAR. These inputs are normally both 1. If the SET input is brought to 0, the Q output goes to the 1 state (and $\overline{Q} = 0$). Even if SET returns to 1, Q will remain at 1, owing to the internal feedback. This is called *setting* the FF. Similarly, when the CLEAR input is brought to 0, Q will go to the 0 state and stay there. This is called *clearing* the FF. The table in Fig. 2.7 summarizes this FF's operation. Note that SET and CLEAR should not go LOW simultaneously or an ambiguous output state will result.

It should be mentioned here that the CLEAR input is often called the RESET input, and resetting the FF is the same as clearing the FF.

The FF of Fig. 2.7 has limited usefulness in itself, but it is the basic building block of many types of IC FFs. These IC FFs all utilize a *clock* input to synchronize the changing from one state to another. We will describe clocked FFs after a brief look at clock signals.

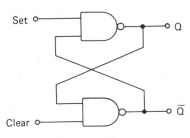

SET	CLEAR	Q
1	1	No change*
0	1	1
1	0	0
0	0	Ambiguous

*Q remains at previous value

FIGURE 2.7 Basic SC flip-flop made from NAND gates.

2.7 CLOCK SIGNALS

Most digital systems operate as *synchronous sequential systems*. What this means is that the sequence of operations that takes place is synchronized by a *master clock signal*, which generates periodic pulses that are distributed to all parts of the system. This clock signal is usually one of the forms shown in Fig. 2.8; most often it is a square wave (50 percent duty cycle), such as the one shown in Fig. 2.8B.

The clock signal is the signal that causes things to happen at regularly spaced intervals. In particular, operations in the system are made to take place at times when the clock signal is making a transition from 0 to 1 or from 1 to 0. These transition times are pointed out in Fig. 2.8. The 0-to-1 transition is called the *rising edge* or *positive-going edge* of the clock signal; the 1-to-0 transition is called the *falling edge* or *negative-going edge* of the clock signal.

The synchronizing action of the clock signal is the result of using *clocked flip-flops*, which are designed to change states on either (but not both) the rising edge or the falling edge of the clock signal. In other words, the clocked FFs will change states at the appropriate clock transition and will rest between successive clock pulses. The frequency of the clock pulses is generally determined by how long it takes the FFs and gates in the circuit to respond to the level changes initiated by the clock pulse, that is, the propagation delays of the various logic circuits.

Some computers, including many microcomputers, have their timing controlled by two or more related clock signals. One common combination shown in Fig. 2.9 utilizes two clock signals identified by the symbols ϕ_1 and ϕ_2 (phase 1 and phase 2). This more complex clocking arrangement provides four different edges and three different states per period, compared to only two edges and two states per period for a single clock signal. We will utilize ϕ_1 and ϕ_2 in our discussion of microcomputers.

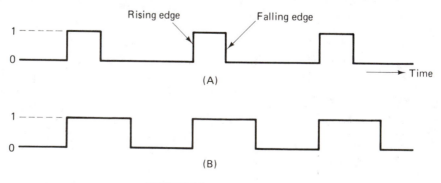

FIGURE 2.8 Clock signals.

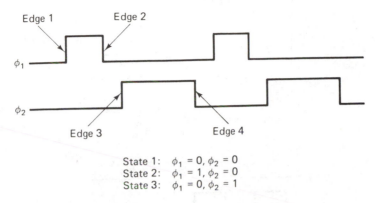

State 1: $\phi_1 = 0, \phi_2 = 0$
State 2: $\phi_1 = 1, \phi_2 = 0$
State 3: $\phi_1 = 0, \phi_2 = 1$

FIGURE 2.9 Two-phase clock signals.

2.8 CLOCKED FLIP-FLOPS

Clocked FFs all have at least two types of inputs: a clock input (abbreviated CLK) and one or more control inputs. The control inputs are used to determine what state the FF output will go to when a signal is applied to the CLK input. The signal at the CLK input is the actual triggering signal which causes the FF to respond according to the control inputs.

Edge-triggered D Flip-flop

Figure 2.10A shows the symbol and truth table for an edge-triggered D FF. It is so called because it has a single control input, D. This FF operates such that the logic level present at the D input is transferred to the Q output *only* on the positive-going edge of the CLK input signal. The D input has no effect on Q at any other time, as illustrated by the example waveforms shown in Fig. 2.10B.

Note that the negative-going edge of the CLK signal has no effect on the FF output. There are edge-triggered D FFs that trigger *only* on the negative-going edge of the CLK input. These otherwise operate exactly the same and have the same symbol except for a small circle on the CLK input to indicate negative-edge triggering.

Edge-triggered JK Flip-flop

The edge-triggered JK flip-flop is the most versatile type of FF available. As shown in Fig. 2.11, it uses two control inputs, J and K. These determine what will happen to the Q output when the positive edge of the CLK signal occurs, according to the accompanying truth table.

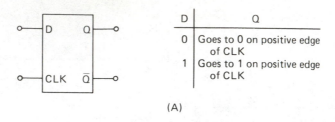

D	Q
0	Goes to 0 on positive edge of CLK
1	Goes to 1 on positive edge of CLK

(A)

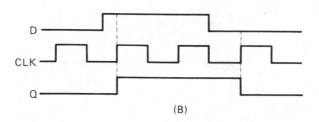

(B)

FIGURE 2.10   Positive-edge-triggered D FF.

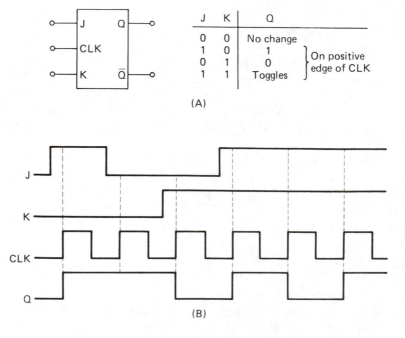

J	K	Q	
0	0	No change	
1	0	1	On positive edge of CLK
0	1	0	
1	1	Toggles	

(A)

(B)

FIGURE 2.11   Edge-triggered JK FF.

40

J = K = 0: If this condition is present when the positive edge of the CLK signal occurs, there will be no change in the state of the FF (see waveforms in Fig. 2.11B).

J = 1, K = 0: This condition always produces Q = 1 on the occurrence of the positive edge of the CLK signal.

J = 0, K = 1: This always produces Q = 0 on the occurrence of the positive edge of the CLK signal.

J = 1, K = 1: If this condition is present when the positive edge of the CLK signal occurs, the Q output will switch to its opposite state (toggle).

Again, note that nothing happens to Q except on the positive edge of the CLK signal. There are negative-edge triggered JK FFs whose operation is otherwise exactly the same. A small circle on the CLK input symbolizes negative-edge triggering.

D-type Latch

The edge-triggered FFs can change states only when the appropriate edge of the CLK signal occurs. The D-type latch is similar to the edge-triggered D FF except that it can change states during the HIGH portion of the CLK signal. Figure 2.12 shows the D-type latch symbol and operation. As long as the

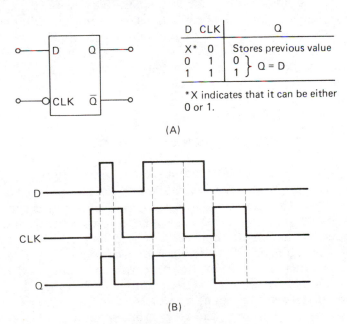

D	CLK	Q
X*	0	Stores previous value
0	1	0 ⎫
1	1	1 ⎭ Q = D

*X indicates that it can be either 0 or 1.

(A)

(B)

FIGURE 2.12 D-Type latch.

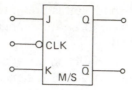

FIGURE 2.13 JK master/slave FF.

CLK is HIGH, output Q will follow the D input even if it changes. When the CLK goes LOW, Q will store (or latch) the last value it had and the D input has no further effect. A circle is shown on the CLK input of the latch to indicate that it stores or latches the D value when CLK goes LOW.

JK Master/Slave FF

In certain applications, the control inputs to a clocked FF will be making a transition at approximately the same time as the triggering edge of the CLK input occurs. This can often lead to unpredictable triggering. To overcome this problem, the JK master/slave FF was developed. This FF actually contains two internal FFs (master and slave) and *always* triggers on the negative edge of the CLK input. The *master* is used to store the conditions present on the J and K inputs just prior to the negative edge of the CLK so that if J and K do change at the same time as the CLK, the *slave* will respond to the old J, K values, thus producing a predictable Q output. Figure 2.13 shows the symbol for this FF. The notation M/S is not always used in circuit diagrams, but manufacturers' data sheets will tell you whether the FF is edge-triggered or master/slave.

2.9 SYNCHRONOUS AND ASYNCHRONOUS FF INPUTS

For the clocked flip-flops that we have been studying, the J, K, and D inputs have been referred to as *control inputs*. These inputs are also called *synchronous inputs*, because their effect on the FF output is synchronized with the CLK input. As we have seen, the synchronous control inputs must be used in conjunction with a clock signal to trigger the FF.

Most clocked FFs also have one or more *asynchronous inputs* which operate independently of the synchronous inputs and clock input. These asynchronous inputs can be used to set the FF to the 1 state or clear the FF to the 0 state at any time, regardless of the conditions at the other inputs. Stated in another way, the asynchronous inputs are *override* inputs, which

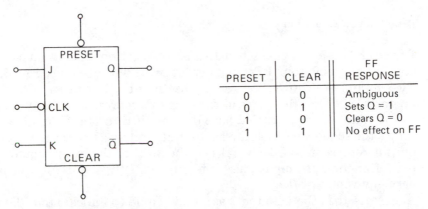

PRESET	CLEAR	FF RESPONSE
0	0	Ambiguous
0	1	Sets Q = 1
1	0	Clears Q = 0
1	1	No effect on FF

FIGURE 2.14 Clocked JK FF with asynchronous inputs.

can be used to override all the other inputs in order to place the FF in one state or the other.

Figure 2.14 shows a clocked J-K FF with PRESET and CLEAR inputs. These asynchronous inputs are activated by a 0 level, as indicated by the small circles on the FF symbol. The accompanying truth table indicates how these inputs operate. A LOW on the PRESET input *immediately* sets Q to the 1 state. A LOW on the CLEAR *immediately* clears Q to the 0 state. Simultaneous low levels on PRESET and CLEAR are forbidden since it leads to an ambiguous condition. When neither of these inputs is LOW, the FF is free to respond to the J, K, and CLK inputs, as previously described.

It is important to realize that these asynchronous inputs respond to dc levels. This means that if a constant 0 is held on the PRESET input, the FF will remain in the Q = 1 state regardless of what is occurring at the other inputs. Similarly, a constant LOW on the CLEAR input holds the FF in the Q = 0 state. Thus, the asynchronous inputs can be used to hold the FF in a particular state for any desired interval. Most often, however, the asynchronous inputs are used to set or clear the FF to the desired state by application of a momentary pulse.

2.10 BINARY COUNTERS

Flip-flops can be connected in various arrangements to function as binary counters that count input clock pulses. A wide variety of counters are available as standard integrated-circuit packages and it is seldom necessary to construct a counter from individual FFs. For this reason, we will not go into the internal operation of a counter. Instead, we will review the external operating characteristics of currently available IC counters.

Basic Counter Operation

Figure 2.15 shows the schematic representation of a 4-bit counter. This counter contains four FFs, one per bit, with outputs labeled A, B, C, and D. Two inputs are shown, the clock pulse input, CP, and RESET. The counter operates such that the states of the four FFs represent a binary number equal to the number of pulses that have been applied to the CP input. The diagram shows the sequence which the FF outputs follow as pulses are applied. The A output represents the LSB and D is the MSB of the binary count. For example, after the *fifth* input pulse, the outputs DCBA = 0101, which is the binary equivalent of *five*.

Note that the CP input has a small circle to indicate that the FFs in the counter change states on the negative-going edge of the clock pulses. Counters that trigger on positive-going edges are also available and they do not have the circle on the CP input.

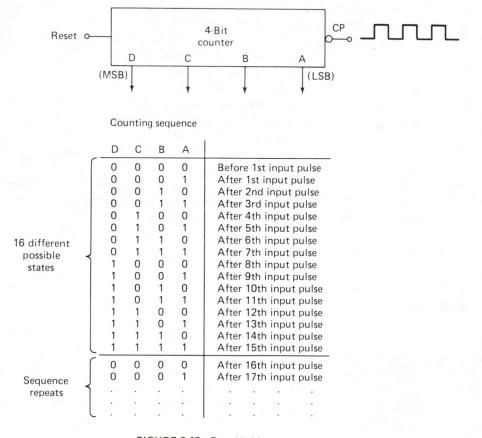

Counting sequence

D	C	B	A	
0	0	0	0	Before 1st input pulse
0	0	0	1	After 1st input pulse
0	0	1	0	After 2nd input pulse
0	0	1	1	After 3rd input pulse
0	1	0	0	After 4th input pulse
0	1	0	1	After 5th input pulse
0	1	1	0	After 6th input pulse
0	1	1	1	After 7th input pulse
1	0	0	0	After 8th input pulse
1	0	0	1	After 9th input pulse
1	0	1	0	After 10th input pulse
1	0	1	1	After 11th input pulse
1	1	0	0	After 12th input pulse
1	1	0	1	After 13th input pulse
1	1	1	0	After 14th input pulse
1	1	1	1	After 15th input pulse
0	0	0	0	After 16th input pulse
0	0	0	1	After 17th input pulse

16 different possible states

Sequence repeats

FIGURE 2.15 Four-bit binary counter.

Counting Sequence

This 4-bit counter can count from 0000_2 (zero) to 1111_2 (fifteen), for a total of 16 different states. After it reaches the maximum counter of 1111, the next input pulse will cause the FF outputs to recycle to the 0000 count. The counting sequence is then repeated for subsequent pulses. In general, a counter with N FFs can count from 0 up to $2^N - 1$, for a total of 2^N different states. The total number of different states is called the counter's *MOD number*. The counter in Fig. 2.15 is a MOD-16 counter. A counter with N FFs would be a MOD-2^N counter.

The counting sequence can be cut short at any time by applying the proper logic level to the RESET input. In Fig. 2.15, a HIGH on the RESET input will immediately reset all the FFs to the 0 state and will hold them there until RESET returns LOW. A small circle on the RESET input would indicate that a LOW is needed to reset the counter to 0000.

Many IC counters are internally designed so that they do not count through the complete sequence up to $2^N - 1$ but up to some lesser count before recycling to zero. For example, a common IC counter is the *decade counter*, which counts from 0000 to 1001 (0 to 9) and then recycles to 0000. It has 10 distinct states and is, therefore, a MOD-10 counter. It is also called a *BCD counter* because the FF outputs count through the 10 BCD-code groups.

Some IC counters are designed so that the user can vary the counting sequence through appropriate external connections. These are usually referred to as *variable-MOD* counters.

Frequency Division

In addition to counting pulses, all counters can perform frequency division. This is illustrated in Fig. 2.16 for the 4-bit, MOD-16 counter. The output A is seen to be a frequency exactly $\frac{1}{2}$ of the CP input frequency. The B output frequency is $\frac{1}{4}$ of the input frequency, C is $\frac{1}{8}$ of the input frequency, and D is $\frac{1}{16}$ of the input frequency.

In general, the waveform out of the MSB FF of a counter will divide the input frequency by the MOD number. For example, the D FF of a decade counter will have a frequency that is $\frac{1}{10}$ of the clock input.

Up/Down Counters

The counters we have talked about so far can count *up* from zero to some maximum count and then reset to zero. There are several IC counters that can count in either direction and are called *up/down counters*. Figure 2.17 shows the two basic up/down counter arrangements.

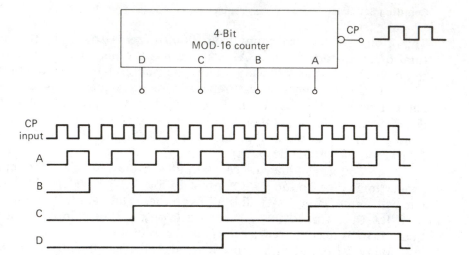

FIGURE 2.16   Counter waveforms showing frequency division.

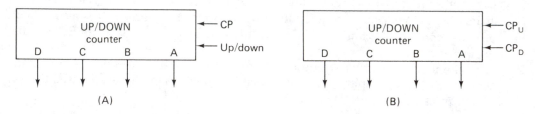

FIGURE 2.17   Representation of two types of up/down counters.

The counter in 2.17A has a single CP input that is used for both count-up and count-down operations. The UP/DOWN input is used to control the counting direction. One logic level applied to this input causes the counter to count *up* from 0000 to 1111 as pulses are applied to CP. The other logic level applied to UP/DOWN causes the counter to count *down* from 1111 to 0000 as pulses are applied to CP.

The counter in 2.17B does not use an UP/DOWN control input. Instead, it uses separate clock inputs CP_U and CP_D for counting up and down, respectively. Pulses applied to CP_U cause the counter to count up, and pulses applied to CP_D cause the counter to count down. Only one CP input can be pulsed at one time, or erratic operations will occur.

2.11   FF REGISTERS

A simple *register* is a group of memory devices used to store binary information. More complex registers can modify the stored information in some manner. The most common register device is the FF, and a counter is an example of a FF register. Two other types of FF registers are buffer (storage) registers and shift registers.

As we will see, registers play a significant role in digital computer systems. In fact, in its simplest form, a computer is a system of registers in which binary information is transferred from one register to another register, operated on in some way and then transferred to another register. For the time being, we will concentrate on the operation of transferring information from one register to another.

Parallel Transfer

Figure 2.18 shows two 3-bit registers. The X register consists of FFs X_1, X_2, and X_3; the Y register consists of FFs Y_1, Y_2, and Y_3. Each FF is an edge-triggered D FF. The TRANSFER pulse applied to the CLK inputs of the Y register causes the value of X_1 to be transferred to Y_1, X_2 to Y_2, and X_3 to Y_3. This transfer of the contents of the X register into the Y register is a *parallel* transfer, since the 3 bits are transferred simultaneously. Since we will be dealing with register-to-register transfers quite a bit, we will use the following shorthand notation to indicate such a transfer:

$$[X] \longrightarrow [Y]$$

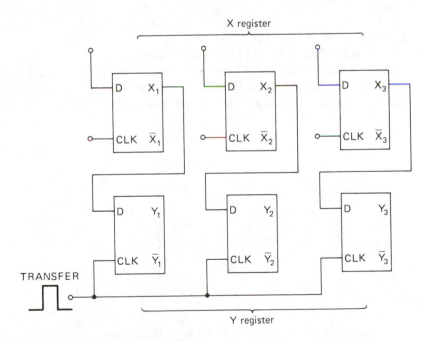

FIGURE 2.18 Parallel transfer from X register to Y register.

The symbol [X] will mean the contents of the X register and similarly for [Y]. The arrow indicates the direction of the transfer.

Serial Transfer

Serial transfer from one register to another occurs 1 bit at a time. Before examining serial transfer, we will look at the operation of a shift register. Figure 2.19 shows a 3-bit shift register using master/slave JK FFs. The FFs are connected such that the current content of each FF is transferred to the FF on its right when the negative edge of a SHIFT pulse occurs. In addition, the level present on the serial input S is transferred into FF X_2.

To illustrate, assume that the X-register contents are $X_2 = 1$, $X_1 = 0$, $X_0 = 1$. Using the shorthand notation, we can write this as [X] = 101. Also, assume that S = 0. Each of these logic levels is setting up the succeeding FF to take on its value when the shift pulse occurs. Thus, after the occurrence of the negative edge of the shift pulse, the register contents are [X] = 010; that is, the level on S has shifted to X_2, the *previous* level of X_2 has shifted to X_1, and the *previous* level of X_1 has shifted to X_0. The *previous* value of X_0 is lost.

If S is now changed to 1 and a second shift pulse occurs, the result is [X] = 101. With S = 1, a third shift pulse produces [X] = 110; and so on.

Shift registers can also be constructed using D FFs. In either arrangement, the FFs have to be master/slave type for proper transfer. This is because the levels on the FF control inputs (J, K, or D) can be changing as the negative edge of the shift pulse occurs.

Figure 2.20 shows two 3-bit shift registers connected so that the contents of the X register will transfer serially into the Y register. The complete transfer requires *three* shift pulses, one per bit. The complete transfer sequence is shown in the diagram, assuming that S = 0, [X] = 101, and [Y] = 011.

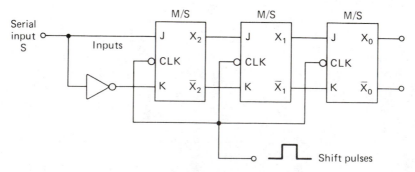

FIGURE 2.19 Shift register.

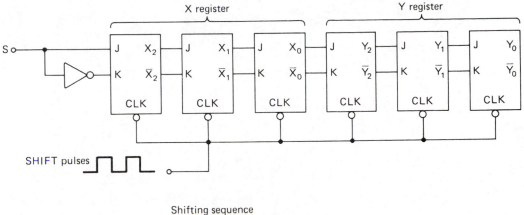

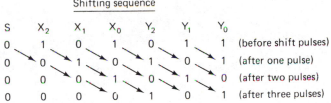

FIGURE 2.20 [X] → [Y] using serial transfer.

Serial transfer requires more time than parallel transfer because of the need to shift 1 bit at a time. On the other hand, serial requires fewer interconnections between the two registers.

2.12 IC REGISTERS

It is rarely necessary to construct registers from individual FFs because of the availability of a wide variety of integrated-circuit registers. We will not attempt to show all the numerous variations but will concentrate on the basic types used in microcomputer applications.

Data-latching Registers

The data-latching type of register uses the D-type latches discussed earlier. Figure 2.21 shows the representation for a 4-bit latching register. The CLK input is common to each latch and causes the data outputs Q_3, Q_2, Q_1, and Q_0 to respond to the data inputs D_3, D_2, D_1, and D_0 as follows:

1. While CLK is HIGH, each Q output follows the logic levels present on its corresponding D input (e.g., Q_3 follows D_3).

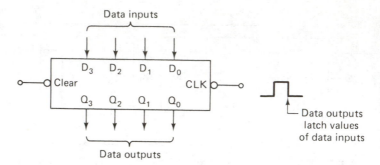

FIGURE 2.21 Four-bit latching register.

2. When CLK goes LOW, each Q output latches (holds) the last D value and cannot change even if the D input changes.

The CLEAR input is used to clear each output to 0 simultaneously on a low level.

Edge-triggered Register

The edge-triggered type of register (Fig. 2.22) uses edge-triggered D FFs and operates exactly like the register in Fig. 2.21 except that the data inputs only affect the data outputs at the instant when CLK makes a *low-to-high* transition. At that time, the levels present on the D inputs transfer to the Q outputs. Variations in the D input levels will cause no change in the Q outputs, but for proper data transfer to occur, it is necessary that the D inputs be stable when the CLK transition occurs.

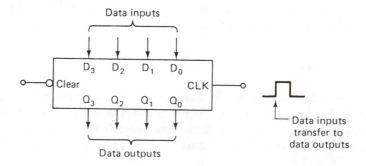

FIGURE 2.22 Four-bit edge-triggered register.

Shift Registers

There are several integrated variations of the basic shift register circuit. They differ as to how the data can enter the register (serial, parallel, or both) and as to whether the output data are available in parallel as well as in serial form. Some also have control inputs to determine the direction of the shift operation (left to right, or vice versa). To illustrate, Fig. 2.23 shows the block representation of two common IC shift registers.

The IC in Fig. 2.23A is called a *parallel-in, serial-out* shift register. It consists of eight FFs arranged to shift data left to right on the low-to-high

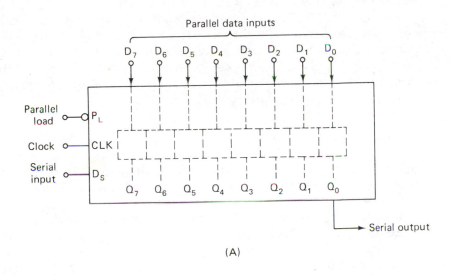

(A)

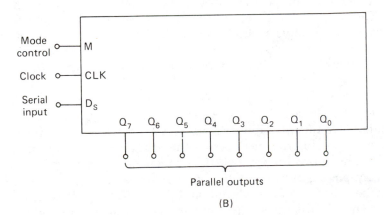

(B)

FIGURE 2.23 IC shift registers.

transition of the clock pulses. Data can be entered into the register in two different ways. *Serial* data can be entered through the serial input D_S. These data are shifted into FF Q_7 on the clock pulses. *Parallel* data can be entered via the data inputs D_0 through D_7 under the control of the parallel-load input, P_L. Whenever P_L goes low, the levels on D_0 through D_7 are immediately loaded (transferred) into the register FFs. With P_L at a high level, the parallel data inputs are disabled (have no effect).

This IC has only one FF output, Q_0, which is the rightmost bit. It represents the serial output which would occur as data are shifted left to right. The reason that the Q_1 through Q_7 outputs are not available is because of the limited number of IC pins (usually 14 or 16).

Figure 2.23B shows a *serial-in, parallel-out* shift register. Data can only enter this register serially through D_S on the low-to-high edge of the clock pulses. All eight FF outputs are available for external use as data are shifted on the clock pulses. The mode control, M, is used to control the shifting direction. For one logic level on M, the shifting will be left to right. For the other logic level on M, shifting will be right to left.

Tristate Registers

In most modern computers, the transfer of data from register to register takes place over a group of connecting lines called a *bus*. These *bus-organized* computers utilize tristate devices, for reasons that will soon become clear. The tristate register is one of these devices. A typical 4-bit tristate register is represented in Fig. 2.24. It contains four edge-triggered D FFs with a common clock input. The outputs O_0 through O_3 are tristate outputs that operate as normal outputs as long as the *output disable input*, OUTD, is kept low. A high on OUTD places the outputs in the high-impedance (high-Z) state.

The outputs are all cleared to 0 by a low level on the CLR input. This condition will always clear the register independent of all other inputs. However, if OUTD = 1 when CLR goes LOW, the outputs will not register as 0s, since they are in the high-Z state. When OUTD returns to 0, the cleared outputs will be 0.

The *input disable input*, IND, is used to inhibit the effect of the CLK and D inputs. With IND = 0, the data inputs will be transferred to the data outputs on the high-to-low edge of CLK. With IND = 1, the D and CLK inputs are essentially disabled so that the data outputs are not affected.

Although this is a typical tristate register, some of the input designations will vary among the many IC manufacturers. For example, the IND input might be called the LOAD input, and the OUTD input might be the ENABLE input. The manufacturers' IC data sheets will always provide information as to the functions of the various inputs.

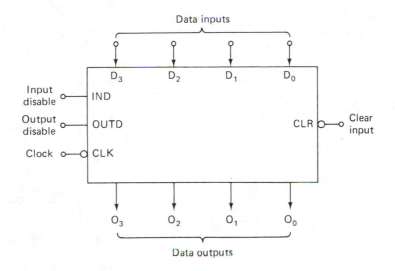

IND	OUTD	CLR	Data outputs
X	0	0	All 0
0	0	1	= D inputs on negative edge of clock
1	0	1	Store previous values—clock has no effect
X	1	X	High-impedance state

"X" always
means it can
be either 0
or 1

FIGURE 2.24 Tristate register.

2.13 DATA BUS

We mentioned the term *bus* as being very important in computer systems. Its total significance cannot be appreciated until our study of microcomputers. For now, the bus concept can be illustrated for register-to-register transfers.

A *data bus* is a group of wires used as a common path connecting all the inputs and outputs of several registers, such that data can be easily transferred from any one register to any other, using appropriate control signals. Figure 2.25 shows a bus-organized system of three registers. Each register is a 4-bit tristate register like the one in Fig. 2.24.

In this arrangement, there are four lines that make up the data bus since the registers are each 4 bits wide. Corresponding outputs of each register are connected to the same one line of the bus (e.g., each O_0 is connected to the DB_0 line). This appears to be an ambiguous situation for determining the logic level on each bus line. The ambiguity, however, is removed by ensuring

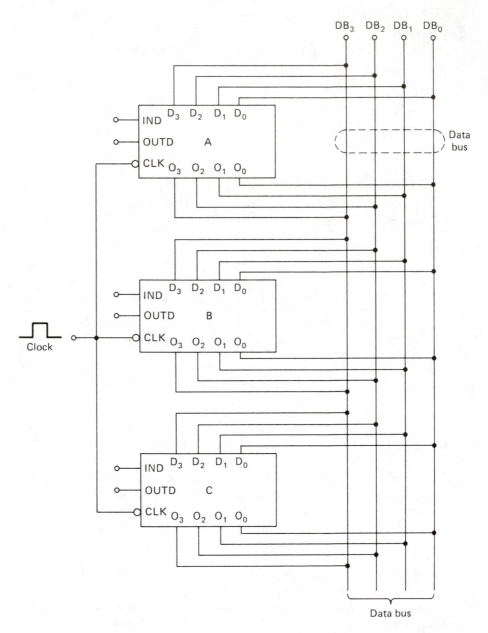

FIGURE 2.25 Registers connected to a common bus.

that only *one* of the three registers has its outputs enabled while the other two register outputs are in the high-Z state. For example, assume that registers A and B have their OUTD = 1 while register C has OUTD = 0. This essentially disconnects the register A and B outputs from the data bus so that only the register C outputs have their logic levels present on the data bus lines.

The data inputs to each register are also connected to the corresponding bus lines. Thus, the levels on the bus are always ready to be transferred to any one of the registers. Normally, though, only the register that is to receive the data will have IND = 0.

Data-Transfer Operation

Consider transferring the contents of register A to register C. To perform this transfer, the data outputs of register A must be placed on the data bus by setting $OUTD_A = 0$. Also, register C must have $IND_C = 0$ so that it can receive the data. All other disable inputs must be kept at the 1 level. Summarizing,

$$\left.\begin{array}{l} IND_A = 1, OUTD_A = 0 \\ IND_B = 1, OUTD_B = 1 \\ IND_C = 0, OUTD_C = 1 \end{array}\right\} \begin{array}{c} \text{conditions needed for} \\ [A] \longrightarrow [C] \end{array}$$

With these levels on the disable inputs, a pulse applied to the common CLK inputs will cause the levels on the data bus (A outputs) to be transferred to register C.

It should be easy to see how we can add more registers to the data bus by repeating the same connections for each register. Of course, each register adds two more disable inputs that have to be controlled for each data transfer. For the time being, we will not be concerned about what provides the signals to these disable inputs.

Simplified Representation of Bus

In all but the simplest computer systems, there will be many devices, as well as registers, connected to the same bus. On a circuit schematic, this can produce a very confusing array of lines and connections, especially for larger numbers of lines per bus. For this reason, we will often use a simplified representation for bus organization where a group of wires is replaced by one wide line. This is illustrated in Fig. 2.26 for a three-register, 8-bit bus arrangement. The bracketed numbers inside the register always indicate the number of bits the register contains. Similarly, the bracketed numbers inside the wide lines indicate the number of actual wires which they represent.

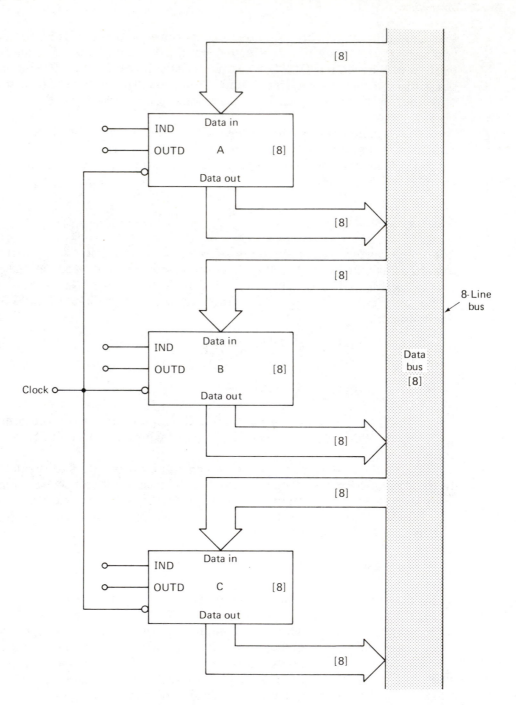

FIGURE 2.26 Simplified drawing of bus arrangement.

Bidirectional Bussing

Refer again to Fig. 2.25. Since each register has both its inputs and its outputs tied to the data bus, it is obvious that corresponding inputs and outputs are shorted together. For example, output O_3 and input D_3 for each register are connected to bus line DB_3, and therefore they are connected to each other. As we have seen, there is nothing wrong with this because in normal operation a register will never have both its data inputs and outputs enabled at the same time.

Since inputs and outputs are going to be tied together anyway, many IC manufacturers *internally* connect them. This reduces the number of pins that have to be used for the IC. Instead of four separate pins for data input and four for output, there are just four input/output (I/O) pins (see Fig. 2.27A). Depending on the status of the DISABLE inputs, the I/O lines function as in-

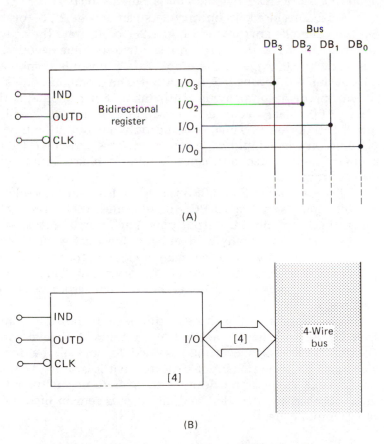

(A)

(B)

FIGURE 2.27 (A) Bidirectional register; (B) simplified diagram.

puts or outputs and are, therefore, called *bidirectional data lines*. The simplified representation for these bidirectional registers is shown in Fig. 2.27B,
where the double-pointed arrow indicates that it is *bidirectional*.

2.14 DECODERS

In digital computers, binary codes are used to represent many different types
of information, such as instructions, numerical data, memory addresses, and
control commands. A code group that contains N bits can have 2^N different
combinations, each of which represents a different piece of information. A
logic circuit is required which can take the N-bit code as logic inputs and
then generate an appropriate output signal to identify which of the 2^N combinations is present. Such a circuit is called a *decoder*.

Most integrated-circuit decoders can decode 2-, 3-, or 4-bit input codes.
Several examples are shown in Fig. 2.28 to illustrate the characteristics of decoder circuits. The top diagram is a 3-line-to-8-line decoder. It has a 3-bit input code (C, B, A) and, therefore, $2^3 = 8$ possible combinations. The eight
output lines 0 through 7 indicate which combination is present. This is
shown in the accompanying truth table. For example, if the input code is
$CBA = 100$ (binary equivalent of 4_{10}), then output 4 will be a 1 while all
other outputs are 0. Thus, one and only one output will be active (high) depending on which input code is present. This particular decoder is also called
a *binary-to-octal* decoder, since it takes a binary input code and produces
eight outputs.

The decoder in Fig. 2.28B is a 4-line-to-10-line decoder. Although it has
a 4-bit input, only the 10 BCD input codes (0000 through 1001) are used.
Thus, there are only 10 output pins. Each output pin is active-LOW, which
means that it is normally high and goes low only when the corresponding input code is present. Note the small circles and the inverter* signs on the outputs (e.g., $\overline{O_3}$) indicating active-LOW operation. This decoder is commonly
called a *BCD-to-decimal* decoder, since it converts a BCD-coded input into a
decimal output.

The decoder in Fig. 2.28C utilizes all 16 possible combinations of the
four inputs, so it has 16 active-LOW outputs. A special control input called
$\overline{\text{ENABLE}}$ (also called $\overline{\text{STROBE}}$) is used to control the decoder's operation.
The small circle on this input indicates that it is active-LOW meaning that a 0
on $\overline{\text{ENABLE}}$ *enables* the decoder to operate normally; a 1 on the $\overline{\text{ENABLE}}$
input *disables* the decoder, and all outputs remain high independent of the
binary input code.

---

*Inversion bars are often used to indicate active-LOW inputs or outputs.

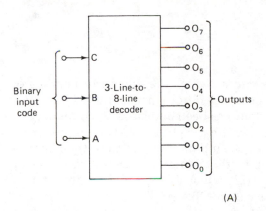

C	B	A	Outputs
0	0	0	$O_0 = 1$; all others 0
0	0	1	$O_1 = 1$; all others 0
0	1	0	$O_2 = 1$; all others 0
0	1	1	$O_3 = 1$; all others 0
1	0	0	$O_4 = 1$; all others 0
1	0	1	$O_5 = 1$; all others 0
1	1	0	$O_6 = 1$; all others 0
1	1	1	$O_7 = 1$; all others 0

(A)

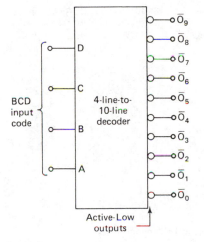

D	C	B	A	Outputs
0	0	0	0	$O_0 = 0$; all others 1
0	0	0	1	$O_1 = 0$; all others 1
0	0	1	0	$O_2 = 0$; all others 1
0	0	1	1	$O_3 = 0$; all others 1
0	1	0	0	$O_4 = 0$; all others 1
0	1	0	1	$O_5 = 0$; all others 1
0	1	1	0	$O_6 = 0$; all others 1
0	1	1	1	$O_7 = 0$; all others 1
1	0	0	0	$O_8 = 0$; all others 1
1	0	0	1	$O_9 = 0$; all others 1
1	0	1	0	All outputs = 1
1	0	1	1	All outputs = 1
1	1	0	0	All outputs = 1
1	1	0	1	All outputs = 1
1	1	1	0	All outputs = 1
1	1	1	1	All outputs = 1

(B)

OPERATION

(1) ENABLE = 0. Operates as a normal decoder with active-LOW outputs.

(2) ENABLE = 1. All outputs are kept HIGH.

(C)

FIGURE 2.28 Various IC decoders.

59

2.15 ENCODERS

A decoder takes an input code and activates the one corresponding output. An *encoder* performs the opposite operation; it generates a binary output code corresponding to which input has been activated. A commonly used IC encoder is represented in Fig. 2.29. It has eight active-LOW inputs, which are kept normally high. When one of the inputs is driven to 0, the binary output code is generated corresponding to that input. For example, when input $\bar{I}_3$ = 0, the outputs will be CBA = 011, which is the binary equivalent of decimal 3. When $\bar{I}_6$ = 0, the outputs will be CBA = 110.

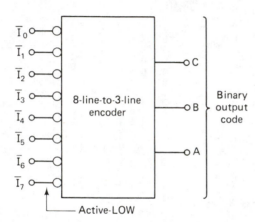

Output code CBA corresponds to input, which is activated (LOW).

FIGURE 2.29 Typical IC encoder.

Priority Encoders

What happens if more than one of the encoder inputs is made low? For some encoders, the outputs would be garbage. For a *priority encoder*, the outputs would be the binary code for the *highest* numbered input that is activated. For example, assume that the encoder of Fig. 2.29 is a priority encoder and that inputs $\bar{I}_4$ and $\bar{I}_7$ are simultaneously made low. The output code will be CBA = 111, corresponding to input $\bar{I}_7$. No matter how many inputs are activated, the code for the highest one will appear at the output.

2.16 MULTIPLEXERS (DATA SELECTORS)

A *multiplexer* or *data selector* is a logic circuit that accepts several data inputs and allows only *one* of them at a time to get through to the output. The routing of the desired data input to the output is controlled by SELECT in-

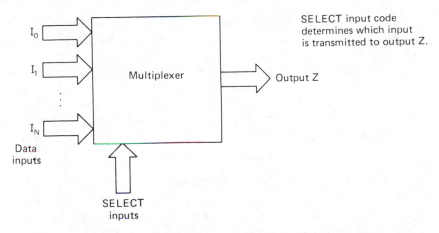

FIGURE 2.30 General diagram of digital multiplexer.

puts (sometimes referred to as ADDRESS inputs). Figure 2.30 shows a general multiplexer. In this diagram, the inputs and outputs are drawn as large arrows to indicate that they may be one or more lines.

There are many IC multiplexers with various numbers of data inputs and select inputs. Since the basic operation is similar for all of these, we will only look at one representative example (Fig. 2.31). This is called a *four-input, 2-bit multiplexer*. Each set of inputs consists of 2 bits, and there are four sets of inputs called *input ports*. For instance, A_1 and A_0 are one input port, and B_1 and B_0 are another. There is only one set of outputs (output

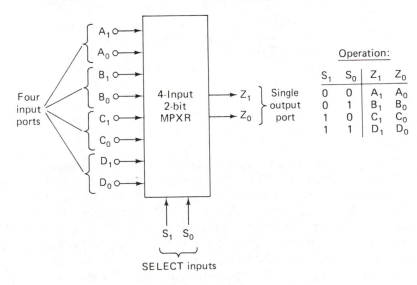

FIGURE 2.31 Four-input, 2-bit multiplexer.

port), Z_1 and Z_0, whose logic levels at any time will be identical to the logic levels present at *one* of the input ports as selected by the SELECT inputs S_0 and S_1.

To illustrate, with $S_1 = S_0 = 0$, the A input port is selected so that $Z_1 = A_1$ and $Z_0 = A_0$. Similarly, with $S_1 = 1$ and $S_0 = 0$, the C input port is selected so that $Z_1 = C_1$ and $Z_0 = C_0$. Only the selected inputs will affect the output. Clearly, this multiplexer behaves like a multipole, multiposition switch whose position is controlled by the logic levels at S_1 and S_0.

2.17 DEMULTIPLEXERS (DATA DISTRIBUTORS)

A *demultiplexer* has a single input port and many output ports (Fig. 2.32) and it transmits data from the input port to one of the output ports as determined by the SELECT inputs.

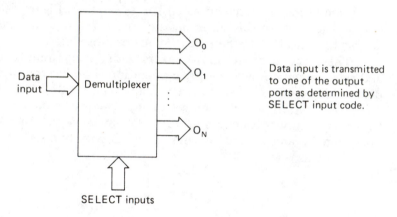

FIGURE 2.32 General demultiplexer.

2.18 ARITHMETIC CIRCUITS

A computer is capable of performing arithmetic, logical, and data manipulation operations on binary numbers. The circuitry that performs these operations is internal to the computer and is not normally accessible to the user. For this reason, we choose not to spend any time showing how logic circuits can be arranged to act as adders, subtractors, and so on. Instead, we will consider the collection of these arithmetic circuits as a single unit called the *arithmetic/logic unit* (ALU).

A typical ALU is diagrammed in Fig. 2.33 together with its associated registers. The ALU portion consists of logic circuitry that will perform oper-

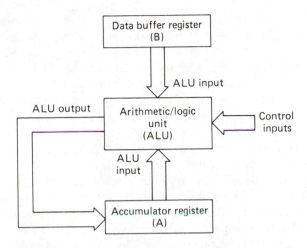

FIGURE 2.33 Typical computer arithmetic/logic unit.

ations such as addition, subtraction, multiplication, division, square roots, exponentials, data manipulations (e.g., shifting), and logical operations (AND, OR, etc.) on the *two* binary numbers contained in the two input registers. Some or all of these operations are available in any computer, depending on its sophistication and complexity. Larger, more expensive computers have an ALU that can do all of these functions and even more. Small, cheap microcomputers have an ALU that can only do a few simple operations. However, through proper programming even these simple computers can be made to perform the more complex operations but at a sacrifice in speed compared to the more complex computers.

The two registers feed the two binary numbers which the ALU will operate on. These numbers are referred to as *operands* and the ALU operates on them in accordance with the control inputs. For example, one operand is stored in the *Data Buffer register* (B) and the other operand is stored in the *Accumulator register* (A). The control inputs determine what the ALU will do with these operands. The results of the operation appear at the ALU output and are then immediately transferred to the accumulator. In other words, the results of any ALU operation end up stored in the accumulator.

Much more will be said about the ALU and its operations in later chapters.

2.19 MEMORY DEVICES

One of the major advantages that digital systems have over analog systems is the ability to easily store large quantities of digital information and data for short or long periods of time. This memory capability is what makes digital systems so versatile and adaptable to many situations. For example, in a digital computer the internal main memory stores instructions that tell the computer what to do under *all* possible circumstances so that the computer will do its job with a minimum amount of human intervention.

We have already become very familiar with the flip-flop, which is an electronic memory device. We have also seen how groups of FFs called registers can be used to store information and how this information can be transferred to other locations. FF registers are high-speed memory elements which are used extensively in the internal operations of a digital computer where digital information is continually being moved from one location to another. Recent advances in large-scale-integrated (LSI) technology have made it possible to obtain large numbers of FFs on a single chip arranged in various memory-array formats. These bipolar and metal-oxide-semiconductor (MOS) memories are the fastest memory devices available and their cost has been continuously decreasing as LSI technology improves.

Because of their high speed, semiconductor memories can be used as the *internal* memory of a computer, where fast operation is important. The internal memory of a computer is in constant communication with the rest of the computer as it executes a program of instructions. In fact, the instructions and data are usually stored in this internal memory.

A reasonably good compromise between speed and cost is provided by magnetic-core memories. This type of memory has been widely used as the internal working memory of digital computers since the later 1950s. Its popularity is due mainly to its high speed at relatively low cost. Recently, MOS memories have begun to replace magnetic cores in many computers. The MOS memories are smaller, faster, and require less power than magnetic cores, and their cost is approaching that of magnetic cores. The IBM 370, a very large computer, uses MOS memory for internal storage. Many minicomputers and almost all microcomputers use MOS (or bipolar) memories for internal storage.

Although semiconductor and magnetic core memories are well suited for high-speed internal memory, their cost per bit of storage prohibits their use as *bulk* memory devices. Bulk memory refers to memory *external* to the main computer, which is capable of storing large quantities of information (millions of bits). External bulk memory, which is normally much slower than internal memory, is used to transfer data and information to a computer's internal memory; likewise, data from internal memory is often transferred to bulk memory for long-term storage. Magnetic tape, magnetic disk, and magnetic drum are popular bulk memory devices that are much less expensive in cost per bit than internal memory devices. Two newer entries into the bulk memory field are *charge-coupled devices* (CCD) and *magnetic bubble memory* (MBM). These are semiconductor devices which have not been around long enough to predict their impact in the area of bulk storage.

2.20 SEMICONDUCTOR MEMORIES — ORGANIZATION

IC memory chips store binary information in groups called *words*. A word is the basic unit of information or data used in a computer. The number of bits that constitute a word will vary from computer to computer, ranging typically from 4 bits to 36 bits. A single memory chip will store a given number of words of so many bits per word. For example, a popular memory chip has a storage capacity of 1024 words of 4 bits each (i.e., a 1024×4 chip).

It is helpful to think of a memory chip as consisting of a group of registers, each register storing one word (see Fig. 2.34). The width of each register is the number of bits per word. The number of registers is the number of words stored in the memory. This general diagram represents a memory that stores N words of M bits each (i.e., an $N \times M$ memory). Common values for the number of words per chip are 64, 256, 512, 1024, 2048, and 4096. These are all powers of 2. Common values for the word size are 1, 4, and 8. As we shall see, it is possible to obtain other word sizes by combining several memory chips.

The contents of each register are subject to two possible operations, *reading* and *writing*. Reading is the process of getting the word which is stored in the register and sending it to some other place, where it can be used. The contents of the register are not changed by the read operation. Writing is the process of putting a new word into a particular register. Of course, this writing operation destroys the word that was previously stored in the register. As we will see, not all memory chips are capable of having their contents written into.

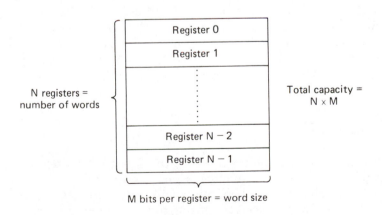

FIGURE 2.34 Memory arranged as group of registers.

Addressing

Each register or word is assigned a number beginning with 0 and continuing as high as needed. This number uniquely specifies the location of the register and the word it is storing, and is referred to as its *address*. For instance, address 2 refers to register 2 or word 2. Anytime that we want to refer to a particular word in the memory, we will use its address. The address of each word is an important number because it is the means by which a device external to the memory chip can select which memory word it desires access to for a read or a write operation.

To understand how addressing is used, we must take a more detailed look at the internal organization of a typical memory chip (Fig. 2.35). This particular chip stores 64 words of 4 bits each (i.e., a 64 × 4 memory). These words have addresses ranging from 0 to 63_{10}. In order to select one of the 64 address locations for reading or writing, a binary address code is applied to a decoder circuit. Since $2^6 = 64$, the decoder requires a 6-bit input code. Each address code activates one particular decoder output, which, in turn, enables its corresponding register. For example, assume an applied address code of

$$A_5 A_4 A_3 A_2 A_1 A_0 = 011010$$

Since $011010_2 = 26_{10}$, decoder output 26 will go HIGH, enabling register 26.

Read Operation

The address code picks out one register in the memory chip for reading or writing. In order to *read* the contents of the selected register, the READ/WRITE (R/W) input must be a 1. In addition, the CHIP SELECT (CS) input must be activated (a 1 in this case). The combination of R/W = 1 and CS = 1 enables the output buffers so that the contents of the selected register will appear at the four data outputs. R/W = 1 also *disables* the input buffers so that the data inputs do not affect the memory during a read operation.

Write Operation

To write a new 4-bit word into the selected register requires that R/W = 0 and CS = 1. This combination enables the input buffers so that the 4-bit word applied to the data inputs will be loaded into the selected register. The R/W = 0 also *disables* the output buffers, which are tristate, so that the data outputs are in their open-circuited state.

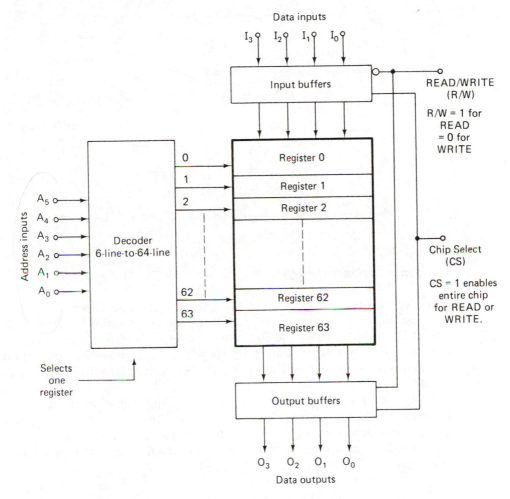

FIGURE 2.35   Internal organization of a 64 × 4 memory chip.

Chip Select

Most memory chips have one or more CHIP SELECT (CS) inputs which are used to enable the entire chip or disable it completely. In the disabled mode all data inputs and data outputs are disabled, so neither a read or write operation can take place. In this mode, the contents of the memory are unaffected. The reason for having CS inputs will become clear when we combine memory chips to obtain larger memories. It should be noted that many manufacturers call these inputs CHIP ENABLE (CE) rather than CS.

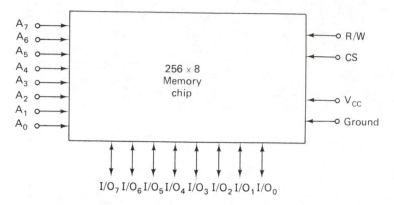

FIGURE 2.36 Pin-function diagram for a 256 × 8 memory IC.

Common Input/Output Pins

In order to conserve pins on an IC package, manufacturers often combine the data input and data output functions using common input/output pins. The R/W input controls the function of these I/O pins. During a read operation, the I/O pins act as data outputs which reproduce the contents of the selected address location. During a write operation, the I/O pins act as data inputs.

We can see why this is done by considering the chip in Fig. 2.35. With separate input and output pins, a total of 18 pins is required (including ground and power supply). With four common I/O pins, only 14 pins are required. The pin saving becomes even more significant for chips with larger word size.

EXAMPLE 2.1 How many pins would be required for a memory chip that stores 256 8-bit words and has common I/O lines?

Solution: There are 256 address locations and $2^8 = 256$. Therefore, eight address inputs are needed to select any address from 00000000 to 11111111 (255_{10}). There are eight I/O lines since the word size is 8 bits. Adding one R/W line, one CS line, power, and ground gives a total of 20 pins (see Fig. 2.36).

2.21 SEMICONDUCTOR MEMORIES — OPERATING SPEED

There are several ways of measuring the speed of IC memories. Unfortunately, there has not been a great degree of standardization among the memory manufacturers. Thus, it sometimes happens that different manufacturers specify the speed of supposedly equivalent memory chips as being different. The three most often used specifications of memory speed are *read-cycle time*, t_{RC}; *write-cycle time*, t_{WC}; and *access time*, t_A. Since each of these is a time measurement, the smaller the number, the faster is the memory.

Read-Cycle Time

Read-cycle time (t_{RC}) is the total time required for reading data from a given memory address. It is measured from the instant when the correct address and CS inputs are applied to when the memory is ready for the next read operation. In other words, it is the total time required between successive read operations. The value of t_{RC} can range from as short as 15 nanoseconds (ns) for ECL memories to 2000 ns for slow MOS memories.

Access Time

Access time (t_A) is probably the one most often cited when comparing memories. It is the time from the start of the read cycle to the time when the memory data outputs are valid. This might appear to be the same as read-cycle time. In some cases, it is, but in many cases, t_A is less than t_{RC}. This is because the data outputs might be ready before the memory is actually ready for the next read operation. For instance, a memory might have a read cycle time of 500 ns and an access time of 400 ns.

Write-Cycle Time

Write-cycle time (t_{WC}) is the total time required for writing a data word into an addressed location. t_{WC} is often the same value as t_{RC}, but it is sometimes a little shorter.

IC Comparisons

The bipolar IC memories are the fastest available. These include ECL (the fastest), Schottky TTL (second fastest), TTL, and current injection logic ($I^2 L$). These faster memory devices also consume more power per bit of storage.

MOSFET memories tend to be slower than bipolar memories. PMOS, the oldest MOS process, is the slowest. NMOS is somewhat faster and is probably the one most commonly used today. CMOS is the fastest of the MOS memories but is still somewhat slower than the bipolar types.

The big advantages of MOS memories are power dissipation and density. MOS memories use much less power per bit than bipolars. In addition, because the MOS fabrication process is simpler, more bits can be stored in a given chip area. Thus, almost all large-memory ICs will be MOS. CMOS memories consume almost zero power under static (dc) conditions, but the power dissipation goes up as operating frequency increases.

2.22 SEMICONDUCTOR MEMORIES – TYPES

Memory ICs come in several types which differ in their internal structure and how they are applied. Actually, there are two broad classifications which include all of them. These two classifications are based on the relative frequency of read operations versus write operations which are to be performed on the memory.

Read-Write Memories

Memories that can be read from and written into with equal ease are called *read-write memories* (RWM). The memory examples discussed in Section 2.20 were of this type and we saw that the read or write operation was selected by the R/W input. The term "RWM," however, is seldom used, although it is more accurate than the term that is used —*random-access memory* (RAM).

RAM *actually* describes any memory capable of having any one of its address locations accessed without having to sequence through other locations. Magnetic tape, for instance, would not be classified as a RAM. Present convention has established RAM to mean RWM, and so we will always use RAM to signify a memory device that can be easily read from or written into.

RAMs are used in computers for the *temporary* storage of programs and data. The contents of many of the RAM locations will continually change as the computer executes a program. This demands fast read- and write-cycle times for the RAM so as not to slow down the computer.

A major disadvantage of semiconductor RAMs is that they are *volatile*, which means that when electrical power is removed from the chip, the RAM loses all its stored information. Some RAMs, however, use such small amounts of power in the standby mode (no read or write operations taking place) that they can be powered from batteries in the event that power fails or is turned off.

Read-Only Memories

Read-only memories (ROM) encompass those types that are designed primarily for having data read from them. In fact, during normal operation, no new data can be written into a ROM. Some types of ROMs can be written into only once. Others can be written into as many times as desired, but the process is not a simple one. Before we look at the variations of ROMs, we will examine the basic ROM symbol shown in Fig. 2.37.

The example in Fig. 2.37 is a ROM that is storing 1024 8-bit words. This would be called a 1024 × 8 ROM or, more simply, a 1K × 8 ROM, where 1K represents 1024. Similarly, a 4096 × 8 can be written as a 4K × 8, and so on. Since this ROM stores 1024 different words, it requires 10 address inputs ($2^{10} = 1024$). The word size is 8 bits, so there are eight output lines. The CHIP SELECT input is used to enable or disable the memory outputs. With $\overline{CS} = 0$, the outputs are enabled and will produce the data word stored in the location selected by the address code inputs. With $\overline{CS} = 1$, the outputs are disabled (open-circuited).

Note that there are no data inputs or R/W control because the write operation is not part of the ROM's normal operation. Some ROMs do have special input pins used for initially writing the data into the ROM, but these are not shown on the ROM symbol because they are generally not used once the ROM is placed in a circuit.

Obviously, ROMs are used to store data that do not change. A principal use for ROMs is to store programs and data in dedicated microcomputer systems, such as the type used in many of the newer sophisticated electronic cash registers. Such systems usually also contain a small amount of RAM to handle the variable data involved in a transaction. The information in the ROM would be written in during manufacture or installation of the machine, and this information would not be erased by turning off the power. In other words, *all ROMs are nonvolatile memories.*

ROMs can be subdivided into several types, which differ as to how information is written or *programmed* into the memory storage locations.

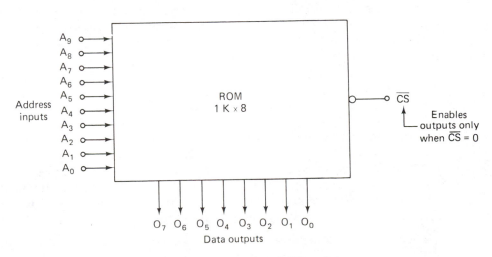

FIGURE 2.37 Typical ROM symbol.

Mask-programmed ROM   This type of ROM has its storage locations written into (programmed) by the manufacturer as the IC is being made. A photographic negative called a *mask* is used to control the electrical interconnections on the chip. A special mask is required for each different set of information to be stored in the ROM. Since these masks are expensive, this type of ROM is economical only if you need a large quantity of the same ROM. Some ROMs of this type are available as off-the-shelf devices preprogrammed with commonly used information or data, such as certain mathematical tables and character-generator codes for CRT displays.

Programmable ROM (PROM)   A PROM is a ROM that can be programmed by the user after he has purchased it. The most common PROM contains tiny Nichrome wires that act as fuses. The user can selectively "burn out" some of the fuses with currents applied at the appropriate IC pins and thereby program the PROM according to his truth table.* Once this programming process is complete, however, the program cannot be changed, so it has to be done right the first time. The IC manufacturer or distributor can program it for you according to your truth table. This will cost extra, but it will eliminate the worry over making a mistake.

Erasable Programmable ROM (EPROM)   An EPROM can be programmed by the user and it can also be *erased* and reprogrammed by the user as often as he desires. Once programmed, the EPROM is a nonvolatile memory that will hold its stored data indefinitely. EPROMs are written into electronically by applying pulses at the appropriate IC pins. The entire programming process, if done manually, can take a good deal of time. Several types of EPROM programmers are commercially available, which can cut programming time down to less than 1 minute.

There are two erasure processes used in currently available EPROMs. One process involves the application of strong ultraviolet light through a quartz window on the chip. The other process utilizes voltages applied to appropriate pins on the chip. Both the ultraviolet and electrical erasing processes erase the entire memory so that complete reprogramming is required. The electrically erased EPROMs are often referred to as *electrically alterable* PROMs (EAPROMs).

2.23   RAMs—STATIC AND DYNAMIC MODES

RAM memories are available in two possible operating modes, *static* and *dynamic*. The static RAM consists essentially of FF registers, one FF per bit, and the necessary circuitry for decoding the address inputs and selecting the right register. This circuitry can get quite complex, requiring up to 10 tran-

---

*"Truth table" here means the list of all the addresses and the word to be stored at each address location.

sistors per bit of storage. This tends to limit static RAMs to a storage capacity of around 16K bits per chip. The advantage of static RAMs is that the stored information will remain valid as long as electrical power is applied.

To overcome the density limitations of static memories, the *dynamic* RAMs do not store binary data in FFs. Instead, the 0s and 1s are stored as the charge on tiny capacitors. The capacitors require no special fabrication because they are provided by the gate capacitance of MOS transistors. With this technique only a few transistors are required per bit of storage, typically three. This allows many more bits of storage per chip than static memories. 64K dynamic memory chips are not uncommon.

The reason why this type of memory is called dynamic is because the capacitors will tend to discharge and must therefore be periodically recharged if they are to retain their data. This periodic recharging is called *refreshing* the memory. Refreshing is done by cycling through each address location at a rate of at least once every 2 milliseconds (ms). In most cases, external circuitry is required for this refreshing process and can sometimes complicate the design of a complete memory system.

In addition to the increased number of bits per chip, dynamic RAMs also offer a reduced power consumption, including power needed for refreshing. This power reduction is due to the fact that the data are stored as voltages on the capacitors. Of course, dynamic RAMs, like static RAMs, are volatile and will lose all stored data if power is removed from the chip.

2.24 COMBINING MEMORY CHIPS

In most IC memory applications the required memory capacity or word size cannot be satisfied by one memory chip. Instead, several memory chips have to be combined to provide the desired capacity and word size. We will see how this is done through several examples that illustrate all the important concepts that will be needed when we interface memory chips to a microprocessor.

Expanding Word Size

Suppose that we need a memory which can store 16 8-bit words and all we have are chips that are arranged as 16 × 4 memories. We can combine two of these 16 × 4 chips to produce the desired memory. The configuration for doing so is shown in Fig. 2.38. Examine this diagram carefully and see what you can find out from it before reading on.

Since each chip can store 16 4-bit words and we want to store 16 8-bit words, we are using each chip to store *half* of each word. In other words, RAM-0 stores the four *higher*-order bits of each of the 16 words, and

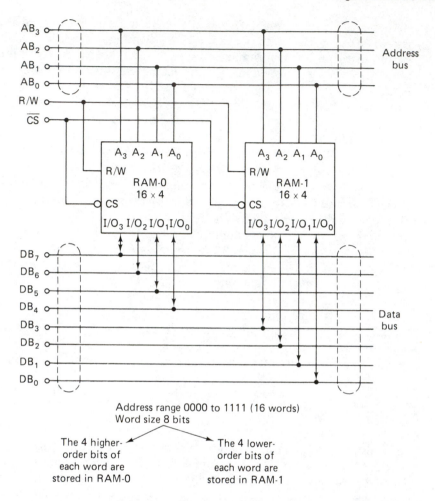

FIGURE 2.38 Combining two 16 × 4 RAMs for a 16 × 8 memory.

RAM-1 stores the four *lower*-order bits of each of the 16 words. A full 8-bit word is available at the RAM outputs connected to the data bus.

Any one of the 16 words is selected by applying the appropriate address code to the four-line *address bus* (AB_3, AB_2, AB_1, AB_0). For now, we will not be concerned with where these address inputs come from. Note that each address bus line is connected to the corresponding address input of each chip. This means that once an address code is placed on the address bus, this same address code is applied to both chips so that the same location in each chip is accessed at the same time.

Once the address is selected, we can read or write at this address under control of the common R/W line. To read, R/W must be high and $\overline{CS}$ must be low. This causes the RAM I/O lines to act as *outputs*. RAM-0 places its selected 4-bit word on the upper four data bus lines and RAM-1 places its selected 4-bit word on the lower four data bus lines. The data bus then contains the full selected 8-bit word, which can now be transmitted to some other device (i.e., a register).

To write, $R/W = 0$ and $\overline{CS} = 0$ causes the RAM I/O lines to act as *inputs*. The 8-bit word to be written is placed on the data bus from some external device. The upper 4 bits will be written into the selected location of RAM-0 and the lower 4 bits will be written into RAM-1.

The same basic idea for expanding word size will work for many different situations. Read the following example and draw a rough diagram showing what the system will look like.

EXAMPLE 2.2   How many 1024×1 RAM chips are needed to construct a 1024×8 memory system?

Solution: Eight chips. Figure 2.39 shows the arrangement.

Expanding Capacity

Suppose that we need a memory which can store 32 4-bit words and all we have are the 16×4 chips. By combining two 16×4 chips as shown in Fig. 2.40, we can produce the desired memory. Once again, examine this diagram and see what you can determine from it before reading on.

To obtain a total of 32 4-bit words, we are using each RAM to store 16 words. The two RAMs share the 4-bit data bus since only one of them will be enabled at one time. The one that is enabled will place its data on the data bus during a read operation or will receive data from the data bus during a write operation.

How can we select 1 of 32 different words if each chip has only four address lines? We simply use the CS input as a fifth address input. There are five address bus lines which are required to access the 32 different addresses. The lower four lines, AB_3, AB_2, AB_1, and AB_0, are connected to the address inputs of each chip. These four lines select 1 of the 16 locations in both RAMs. The AB_4 line is used to select *which* RAM is actually going to be read from or written into at that selected location.

To illustrate, when $AB_4 = 0$, the CS of RAM-0 enables this chip for read or write. Then, any address location in RAM-0 can be accessed by AB_3 through AB_0. These four lines can range from 0000 to 1111 to select the desired location. Thus, the range of addresses representing locations in RAM-0 are

$$AB_4\, AB_3\, AB_2\, AB_1\, AB_0 = 00000 \text{ to } 01111$$

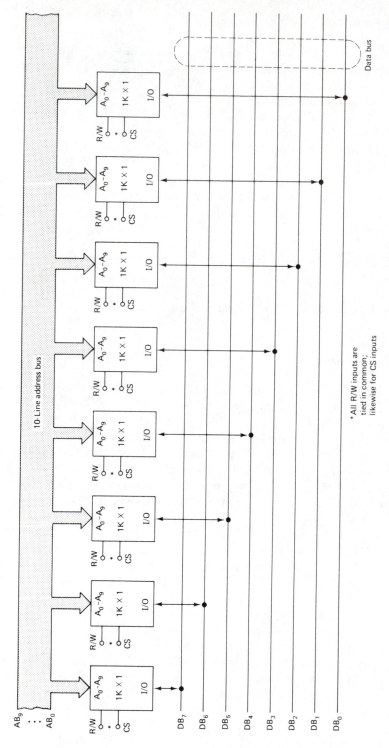

FIGURE 2.39 Eight 1K × 1 chips arranged as a 1K × 8 memory.

*All R/W inputs are tied in common; likewise for CS inputs

10-Line address bus

AB_9 . . . AB_0

Data bus

DB_7
DB_6
DB_5
DB_4
DB_3
DB_2
DB_1
DB_0

$A_0 - A_9$ 1K × 1 I/O R/W CS

76

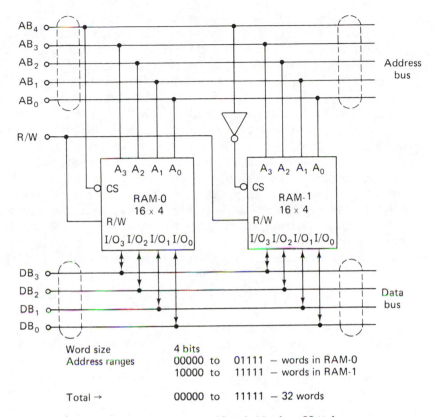

FIGURE 2.40 Combining two 16 × 4 chips for a 32 × 4 memory.

Note that when $AB_4 = 0$, the CS of RAM-1 is HIGH, so its I/O lines are disabled and cannot communicate (give or take data) with the data bus.

It should be clear that when $AB_4 = 1$, the roles of RAM-0 and RAM-1 are reversed. RAM-1 is now enabled and the AB_3 through AB_0 lines select one of its locations. Thus, the range of addresses located in RAM-1 are

$$AB_4\, AB_3\, AB_2\, AB_1\, AB_0 = 10000 \text{ to } 11111$$

EXAMPLE 2.3 It is desired to combine several 256 × 8 PROMs to produce a total capacity of 1024 × 8. How many PROM chips are needed? How many address bus lines are required?

Solution: Four PROM chips are required with each one storing 256 of the 1024 words. Since $1024 = 2^{10}$, the address bus must have 10 lines.

The configuration for the memory of Example 2.3 is similar to the 32×4 memory of Fig. 2.40. However, it is slightly more complex because it requires a decoder circuit for generating the CS input signals. The complete diagram for this 1024×8 memory is shown in Fig. 2.41.

Since the total capacity is 1024 words, 10 address bus lines are required. The two highest-order lines, AB_9 and AB_8, are used to select *one* of the PROM chips; the other eight address bus lines go to each PROM to select the desired location within the selected PROM. The PROM selection is accomplished by feeding AB_9 and AB_8 into the decoder circuit. The four possible combinations of AB_9, AB_8 are decoded to generate active-LOW signals which are applied to the CS inputs. For example, when $AB_9 = AB_8 = 0$, the 0 output of the decoder goes LOW (all others are HIGH) and enables PROM-0. This causes the PROM-0 outputs to generate the data word stored at the address determined by AB_7 through AB_0. All other PROMs are disabled.

Thus, all addresses in the following range are stored in PROM-0:

$$AB_9\,AB_8\,AB_7\,\ldots\,AB_0 = 0000000000 \text{ to } 0011111111$$

These are the first 256 addresses in the memory. For convenience, these addresses can be more easily written in hexadecimal code to give a range of 000_{16} to $0FF_{16}$.

Similarly, $AB_9 = 0$, $AB_8 = 1$ selects PROM-1 to give it an address range of

$$0100000000 \text{ to } 0111111111 \quad \text{(binary)}$$

or

$$100 \text{ to } 1FF \text{ (hex)}$$

The reader should verify the PROM-2 and PROM-3 address ranges given in Fig. 2.41.

EXAMPLE 2.4   A decoder of what size would be needed to expand the memory of Fig. 2.41 to $4K \times 8$? How many address bus lines are needed?

Solution: A 4K capacity is $4 \times 1024 = 4096$ words, which requires $4096/256 = 16$ PROM chips. To select 1 of 16 chips will require a 4-line-to-16-line decoder. With a capacity of 4096 words, a total of 12 address bus lines are needed; 4 go to the decoder to select the PROM and the other 8 go to each PROM to select the address in the PROM.

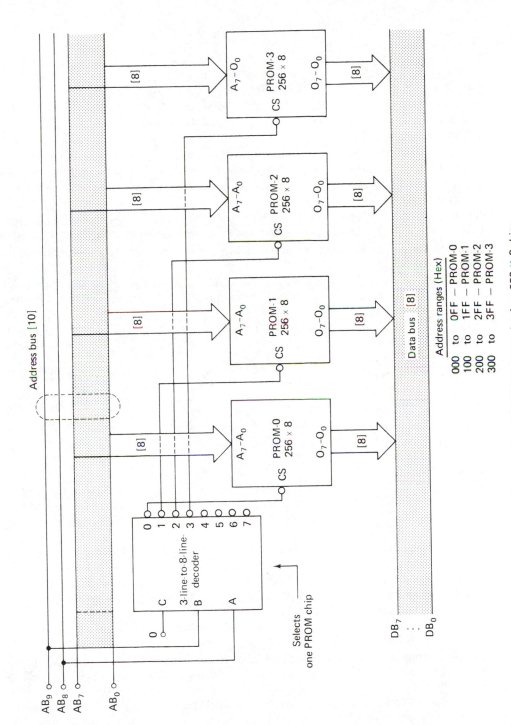

FIGURE 2.41 1K × 8 PROM memory using four 256 × 8 chips.

Address ranges (Hex)

000	to	0FF	— PROM-0
100	to	1FF	— PROM-1
200	to	2FF	— PROM-2
300	to	3FF	— PROM-3

GLOSSARY

Access Time (t_A) Speed specification of a memory device. It is the time from the initiation of a read cycle to when memory data outputs are valid.

Accumulator Register Location where the results of any ALU operation are stored.

Address Number that uniquely specifies a location in memory where instructions or data are stored.

Arithmetic/Logic Unit (ALU) Collection of arithmetic and logic circuits used to perform arithmetic, logical, and data manipulations on binary numbers in a computer.

Asynchronous FF Inputs Inputs that override all other inputs to place the FF in the Set or Cleared state.

Bidirectional Bus Sharing of common bus lines by input and output. Depending upon the state of the disable inputs, information can flow as an output or an input.

Binary Counter Various arrangements of FF interconnections used to count clock pulses and divide frequencies.

Bus Group of wires used as a common path connecting all the inputs and outputs of several registers so that data can be easily transferred from any one register to any other using various control signals.

Chip Select One or more inputs on an IC used to enable the entire chip or disable it completely. In the disabled state, it behaves as though it were not connected to the circuit.

Clocked FF FF that will respond to the control inputs only on the occurrence of the appropriate clock signal.

Clock Signal Signal used to synchronize the operations of digital systems.

Decoder Logic circuit that can take an N-bit code representing instructions, data, or control commands as its logic inputs and generate an appropriate output signal to identify which of the 2^N combinations is present.

Demultiplexer Logic circuit that takes a single input and routes it to one of several outputs, dependent upon the state of the SELECT inputs.

Dynamic RAM Memory devices that store binary data by charging the gate capacitances of MOS transistors and therefore need to be refreshed periodically so as not to lose the charge when present.

Encoder Logic circuit that generates a binary output code corresponding to which input was activated.

Erasable Programmable ROM (EPROM) Semiconductor ROM memory device with which the user can completely erase and reprogram the contents of memory as many times as desired.

FF Logic circuits with memory; in other words, their outputs depend on the previous states of the inputs.

Mask-programmed ROM Semiconductor ROM memory device which requires the manufacturer to load the information into the ROM using a photographic negative (mask) technique.

Master/Slave FF FF that contains two internal FFs (master and slave) which allow for reliable operation even when the control inputs are making a transition at the same time the CLK input occurs.

Multiplexer Logic circuit that selects one of several inputs to become its output. The input selected is dependent upon the state of the SELECT inputs.

Nonvolatile Memory devices that retain stored information for an indefinite length of time and do not need electrical power to do so.

Parallel Transmission Transfer of binary information during which all bits of a word are transferred at the same time and over individual lines.

Priority Encoder Encoder that responds by giving the binary output code for the highest numbered input which is activated if more than one input is activated simultaneously.

Programmable ROM (PROM) Semiconductor ROM memory device which can be programmed once by the user after purchase.

Random-Access Memory (RAM) Any memory device that can go directly to an address without having to sequence through other locations. RAM is also generally used to describe a memory device that can be easily read from or written into.

Read-Cycle Time (t_{RC}) Total time required between two successive READ operations.

Read-Only Memories (ROM) Semiconductor memory devices designed primarily for having data read from them.

Read Operation Process of getting a word from memory and sending it to some other place where it can be used.

Register Group of memory devices (FFs) used to store binary information.

Serial Transmission Transfer of binary information where the bits of a word are transmitted sequentially over a single output line.

Static RAM Semiconductor RAM memory device which consists essentially of FF registers and the necessary circuitry for decoding. Information will remain valid as long as power is on.

Tristate Logic (TSL) TTL logic circuits that operate as normal TTL devices when enabled and high-Z (disconnected) when disabled.

Volatile Memory devices that lose all stored information when power is removed.

Word Basic unit of information or data used in a computer.

Write-Cycle Time (t_{WC}) Total amount of time required for writing a data word into a memory location.

Write Operation Process of getting a word placed into a specific memory location or external device.

QUESTIONS AND PROBLEMS

Sections 2.1–2.5

2.1 (a) How many different logic outputs are required to represent an 8-bit binary number using *parallel* representation? (b) How many are required using *serial* representation?

2.2 Look at the logic-gate symbols in Fig. 2.42. Which one would you use in a logic schematic to represent a gate whose output is normally HIGH and goes LOW when any input goes LOW?

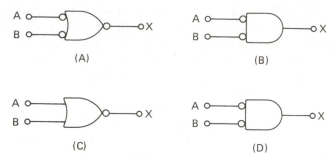

FIGURE 2.42

2.3 Repeat Question 2.2 for a gate whose output is normally Low and goes High only when both inputs are Low.

2.4 The device in Fig. 2.43 is a tristate buffer. Fill in the truth table.

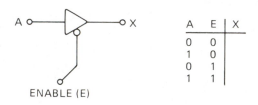

A	E	X
0	0	
1	0	
0	1	
1	1	

FIGURE 2.43

Sections 2.6–2.13

2.5 Explain the difference between an edge-triggered D flip-flop and a D-type latch.

2.6 What type of input is common to all edge-triggered flip-flops?

2.7 Explain the difference between flip-flop synchronous and asynchronous inputs.

2.8 What two functions are performed by all IC counters?

2.9 Compare the relative advantages of parallel and serial transfer of data between two registers.

2.10 An 8-bit shift register holds the data word 10110010. What will the register contents be after *three left* shifts? (Assume that serial input = 0.)

2.11 Which of the registers of Fig. 2.23 could be used to convert a parallel data word to a serial data word?

2.12 What logic conditions are needed to cause the transfer of data from register C to register B in Fig. 2.25?

2.13 Using the simplified bus representation, draw the diagram of a bus system arrangement that includes two 8-bit registers with separate input and output lines, and two 8-bit bidirectional registers.

Sections 2.14–2.18

2.14 Match the device in column I with its function from column II.

I	*II*
(A) decoder	(1) switches one logic input channel to one of several output channels
(B) encoder	
(C) multiplexer	(2) produces binary-coded output corresponding to the activated input
(D) demultiplexer	
	(3) activates one output corresponding to the binary input code
	(4) switches one of several input channels to a single output channel

2.15 What are the functions of the Accumulator register in a computer arithmetic/logic unit?

Sections 2.19–2.23

2.16 A certain IC memory chip has a capacity of 512×8.
   (a) How many words does it store?
   (b) What is the word size?
   (c) How many total bits does it store?
   (d) How many address lines does it have?

2.17 How many pins are required for a memory chip that stores 1024 1-bit words and has separate I/O lines?

2.18 To which type(s) of memory chip does each of the following descriptions apply (i.e., RAM, RWM, ROM, PROM, EPROM)?
   (a) Any memory where each address location is directly accessible.
   (b) Is nonvolatile.
   (c) Is programmed by the manufacturer.
   (d) Can be programmed only once by the user.
   (e) Can be programmed and erased by the user as often as desired.
   (f) Can be read from or written into with equal ease.
   (g) Is used to store variable data.
   (h) Does not require a R/W line.

2.19 List the comparative advantages and disadvantages of dynamic and static RAMs.

Section 2.24

2.20 Show how to combine four RAM chips like those in Fig. 2.40 to produce a memory with a capacity of 64×4. (*Hint:* Decoding logic is required for the CS inputs.)

2.21 Combine four of these RAM chips to produce a memory with a 32×8 capacity.

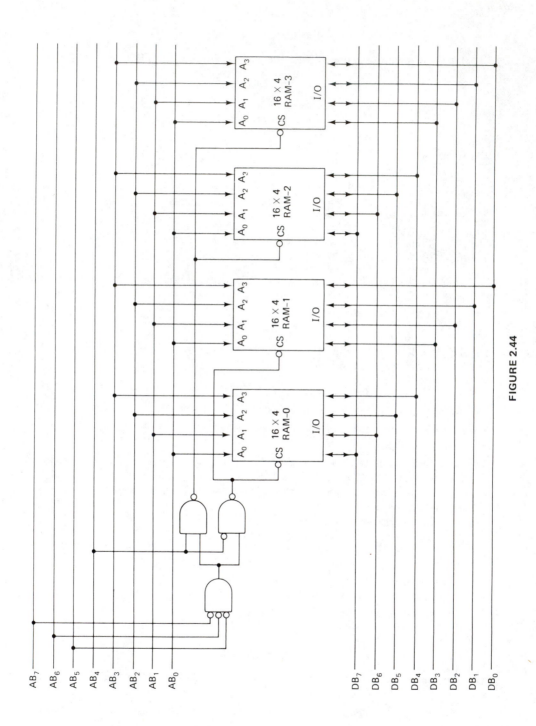

FIGURE 2.44

2.22 Expand the capacity of the memory arrangement in Fig. 2.41 to 2K $\times$ 8. (*Hint:* Add another address line to the address bus and consider the decoder's C input.)

2.23 Consider the memory arrangement of Fig. 2.44.
   (a) What is the total capacity?
   (b) Determine the range of addresses (in binary and hex) stored in the RAM-0/ RAM-1 module.
   (c) Repeat (b) for the RAM-2/RAM-3 module.

3

INTRODUCTION TO COMPUTERS

From the first electronic digital computers of the 1940s to today's versatile full-size computers and revolutionary microcomputers, very little has changed as far as basic computer operation is concerned. In the last 20 years, vast improvements in the size, speed, and capabilities of computers have taken place; but today's digital computers still process 0s and 1s using the same basic logic operations as their predecessors. This means that there are many basic concepts that can be applied to all types of computers, including the microcomputer. Certainly, there are exceptions to, and variations of, these basic concepts, but once these concepts are understood, the mystery about how any computer works will begin to disappear.

3.1 WHAT CAN COMPUTERS DO?

For the most part, human beings can do whatever computers can do, but computers can do it with much greater speed and accuracy. This is in spite of the fact that computers perform all their calculations and operations one

86

step at a time. For example, a human being can take a list of 10 numbers and find their sum all in one operation by listing the numbers one over the other and adding them column by column. A computer, on the other hand, can add numbers only two at a time, so adding this same list of numbers will take nine actual addition steps. Of course, the fact that the computer requires only a microsecond or less per step makes up for this apparent inefficiency.

A computer is faster and more accurate than people, but unlike most people it has to be given a complete set of instructions that tell it *exactly* what to do at each step of its operation. This set of instructions, called a *program*, is prepared by one or more persons for each job the computer is to do. These programs are placed in the computer's memory unit in binary-coded form, with each instruction having a unique code. The computer takes these instruction codes from memory *one at a time* and performs the operation called for by the code. Much more will be said on this later.

It would be impossible to list all the applications which use computers today and which will use computers in the future. Instead, we will look at three examples from the areas of business, industrial control, and scientific-engineering problem solving. These examples will not give a complete picture of how the computer performs in a given application, nor will they encompass all the areas in which computers are used today. Rather, they are intended to show why computers are so extremely useful.

Business

A typical business task is the processing of paychecks for employees who work at an hourly rate. In a noncomputerized payroll system servicing a large company (i.e., 1000 employees) a substantial amount of paperwork and energy is expended in meeting the pay schedule. Calculations must be made concerning items like regular and overtime hours worked, wage rate, gross earnings, federal and state taxes, Social Security, union dues, insurance deductions, and net earnings. Summaries must also be made on items such as earnings to date, taxes to date, Social Security accumulation, vacation, and sick leave. Each of the calculations would have to be performed manually (calculator) for each employee, consuming a large amount of time and energy.

By contrast, a computer payroll system requires much less time and man-power, is less prone to error, and provides a better record-keeping system. In such a system a master file is generated for each employee, containing all the necessary data (e.g., wage rate, tax exemptions, etc.). The master files of all the employees, representing a massive amount of data, are stored on magnetic tape and updated each payroll cycle. The computer is programmed to read the data from the master file tape, combine it with data for the pay period in question, and make all the necessary calculations. Some of the advantages of the computerized system are:

1. Payroll calculation time is shortened.
2. Accumulated earnings can be generated automatically.
3. Accurate payroll documents are prepared automatically.
4. Clerical effort is greatly reduced.
5. One master employee file is used to prepare all reports.
6. Data are readily available for budgeting control and cost analysis.

Science and Engineering

Scientists and engineers use mathematics as a language that defines the operation of physical systems. In many cases, the mathematical relationships are extremely complex and must be evaluated for many different values of the system variables. A computer can evaluate these complex mathematical expressions at high speeds. In addition, it can perform repeated calculations using different sets of data, tabulate the results, and determine which sets of values produced the best results. In many cases, the computer can save an engineer hours, even days, of tedious calculations, thereby providing more time for creative work.

Process Control

Time is not a critical factor when a computer is used to process business data or do engineering calculations in the sense that the results are not required immediately (i.e., within a few milliseconds or seconds). Computers are often used in applications where the results of their calculations are required immediately to be used in controlling a process. These are called *real-time* applications.

An example of a real-time application can be found in industrial process control, which is used in industries such as paper mills, oil refineries, chemical plants, and many others. A non-computer-controlled system might involve one or more technicians located in a central control room. Instruments are used to monitor the various process parameters and send signals back to the control console, which displays pertinent readings on analog or digital meters. The technician records these readings, interprets them, and decides on what corrective actions, if any, are necessary. Corrections are made using various controls on the control console.

If the same system were under computer control, the measuring instruments would send their signals to the computer, which processes them and responds with appropriate control signals to be sent back to the process. Some advantages of the computer-controlled system are:

1. It reacts much faster and with greater precision to variations in the measured process parameters. Thus, serious conditions in the process can be detected and corrected much more quickly than can be done with human intervention.
2. Certain economic savings can be realized because the computer can be programmed to keep the process operating at maximum efficiency in the use of materials and energy.
3. Continuous records can be kept of the process parameter variations, thereby enabling certain trends to be detected prior to the occurrence of an actual problem. These records can be kept in much less space, since magnetic tape would replace a bulky paper-filing system.

These examples of what computers can do are really not indicative of the recent trends in computer usage that have been brought about by microprocessors and microcomputers. These developments have brought computers into commercial products such as automobiles, cash registers, traffic controllers, and copy machines, as well as into the home.

3.2 HOW MANY TYPES OF COMPUTERS ARE THERE?

The answer depends on what criteria are used to classify them. Computers are often classified according to physical size, which usually, but not always, is also indicative of their relative capabilities. The *microcomputer* is the smallest and newest member of the computer family. It generally consists of several IC chips, including a *microprocessor* chip, memory chips, and *input/output interface* chips. These chips are a result of tremendous advances in large-scale integration, which have also served to bring prices down so that it is possible to buy a fully assembled microcomputer now for less than $100.

Minicomputers are larger than microcomputers and have prices that go into the tens of thousands of dollars (including input/output peripheral equipment). Minis are widely used in industrial control systems, scientific applications for schools and research laboratories, and in business applications for small businesses. Although more expensive than microcomputers, minicomputers continue to be widely used because they are generally faster and possess more capabilities. These differences in speed and capability, however, are gradually shrinking.

The largest computers, called *mainframes*, are those found in large corporations, banks, universities, and scientific laboratories. These "maxicomputers" can cost as much as several million dollars and include complete systems of peripheral equipment, such as magnetic-tape units, magnetic-disk units, punched-card punchers and readers, keyboards, printers, and many more. Applications of mainframes range from computationally oriented science and engineering problem solving to the data-oriented business applications, where emphasis is on maintaining and updating large quantities of data and information.

Most of the computer principles and concepts which are about to be introduced are common to all categories of computers, although there can be tremendous variations from computer to computer. Of course, since our major objective is to learn about microcomputers, the discussions will always be more oriented toward microcomputers.

3.3 HOW DO COMPUTERS THINK?

Computers do not think! The computer *programmer* provides a *program* of instructions and data which specifies every detail of what to do, what to do it to, and when to do it. The computer is simply a high-speed machine which can manipulate data, solve problems, and make decisions, all under the control of the program. If the programmer makes a mistake in the program or puts in the wrong data, the computer will produce wrong results. A popular saying in the computer field is "garbage in gives you garbage out."

Perhaps a better question to ask at this point is: How does a computer go about executing a program of instructions? Typically, this question is answered by showing a diagram of a computer's architecture (arrangement of its various elements) and then going through the step-by-step process that the computer follows in executing the program. We will do this — but not yet. First, we will look at a somewhat farfetched analogy that contains many of the concepts involved in a computer operation.

Secret Agent 89

Secret Agent 89 is trying to find out how many days before a certain world leader is to be assassinated. His contact tells him that this information is located in a series of post office boxes. In order to ensure that no one else gets the information, it is spread through 10 boxes. His contact gives him the 10 keys along with the following instructions:

1. The information in each box is written in code.
2. Open box 1 first and execute the instruction located there.
3. Continue through the rest of the boxes in sequence unless instructed to do otherwise.
4. One of the boxes is wired to explode upon opening.

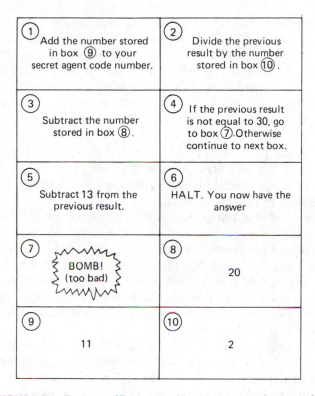

FIGURE 3.1 Ten post office boxes with coded message for Agent 89.

Agent 89 takes the 10 keys and proceeds to the post office, code book in hand.

Figure 3.1 shows the contents of the 10 post office boxes after having been decoded. Assume that you are Agent 89; begin at box 1 and go through the sequence of operations to find the number of days before the assassination attempt. Of course, it should not be as much work for you as it was for Agent 89, because you do not have to decode the messages. The answer is given in the next paragraph.

If you have proceeded correctly, you should have ended up at box 6, with an answer of 17. If you made a mistake, you might have opened box 7, in which case you are no longer with us. As you went through the sequence of operations, you essentially duplicated the types of operations and encountered many of the concepts that are part of a computer. We will now discuss these operations and concepts in the context of the secret agent analogy and see how they are related to actual computers.

In case you have not already guessed, the post office boxes are like the *memory* in a computer, where *instructions* and *data* are stored. Post office boxes 1 through 6 contain instructions to be executed by the secret agent, and boxes 8 through 10 contain the data called for by the instructions. (The contents of box 7, to our knowledge, has no counterpart in computers.) The numbers on each box are like the *addresses* of the locations in memory.

Three different classes of instructions are present in boxes 1 through 6. Boxes 1, 2, 3, and 5 are instructions that call for *arithmetic operations*. Box 4 contains a *decision-making* instruction, called a *conditional jump* or *conditional branch*. This instruction calls for the agent (or computer) to decide whether to jump to address 7 or to continue to address 5, depending on the result of the previous arithmetic operation. Box 6 contains a simple control instruction that requires no data or refers to no other address (box number). This *halt* instruction tells the agent that the problem is finished (program is completed) and to go no further.

Each of the arithmetic and conditional jump instructions consists of two parts — an *operation* and an *address*. For example, the first part of the first instruction specifies the operation of addition. The second part gives the address (box 9) of the data to be used in the addition. These data are usually called the *operand* and their address is called the *operand address*. The instruction in box 5 is a special case in which there is no operand address specified. Instead, the operand (data) to be used in the subtraction operation is included as part of the instruction.

A computer, like the secret agent, decodes and then executes the instructions stored in memory *sequentially*, beginning with the first location. The instructions are executed in order unless some type of *branch* instruction (such as box 4) causes the operation to branch or jump to a new address location to obtain the next instruction. Once the branching occurs, instructions are executed sequentially beginning at the new address.

This is about as much information as we can extract from the secret agent analogy. Each of the concepts we encountered will be encountered again in subsequent material. Hopefully, the analogy has furnished insights that should prove useful as we begin a thorough study of computers.

3.4 BASIC COMPUTER SYSTEM ORGANIZATION

Every computer contains five essential elements or units; the *arithmetic/logic unit* (ALU), the *memory unit*, the *control unit*, the *input unit*, and the *output unit*. The basic interconnection of these units is shown in Fig. 3.2. The arrows in this diagram indicate the direction in which data, information, or control signals are flowing. Two different-size arrows are used; the larger arrows represent data or information that actually consists of a relatively large number of parallel lines, and the smaller arrows represent control signals that are normally only one or a few lines. The various arrows are also numbered to allow easy reference to them in the following descriptions.

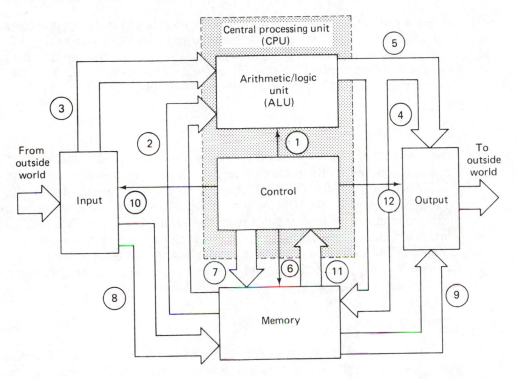

FIGURE 3.2 Basic computer organization.

Arithmetic/Logic Unit

The *arithmetic/logic unit* (ALU) is the area of the computer in which arithmetic and logic operations are performed on data. The type of operation to be performed is determined by signals from the control unit (arrow 1). The data that are to be operated on by the ALU can come from either the memory unit (arrow 2) or the input unit (arrow 3). Results of operations performed in the ALU can be transferred to either the memory unit for storage (arrow 4) or to the output unit (arrow 5).

Memory Unit

The *memory unit* stores groups of binary digits (words) that can represent instructions (program) which the computer is to perform and the data that are to be operated on by the program. The memory also serves as storage for intermediate and final results of arithmetic operations (arrow 4). Operation of the memory is controlled by the control unit (arrow 6), which signals for either a read or a write operation. A given location in memory is accessed by the control unit, providing the appropriate address code (arrow 7). Information can be written into the memory from the ALU or the input unit (arrow 8), again under control of the control unit. Information can be read from memory into the ALU (arrow 2) or into the output unit (arrow 9).

Input Unit

The *input unit* consists of all the devices used to take information and data that are external to the computer and put it into the memory unit (arrow 8) or the ALU (arrow 3). The control unit determines where the input information is sent (arrow 10). The input unit is used to enter the program and data into the memory unit prior to starting the computer. This unit is also used to enter data into the ALU from an external device during the execution of a program. Some of the common input devices are keyboards, toggle switches, teletypewriters, punched-card and punched-paper-tape readers, magnetic-tape readers, and analog-to-digital converters (ADC).

Output Unit

The *output unit* consists of the devices used to transfer data and information from the computer to the "outside world." The output devices are directed by the control unit (arrow 12) and can receive data from memory (arrow 9) or the ALU (arrow 5), which are then put into appropriate form for external use. Examples of common output devices are light-emitting-diode (LED) readouts, indicator lights, teletypewriters, printers, cathode-ray-tube (CRT) displays, and digital-to-analog converters (DAC).

Control Unit

The function of the *control unit* should now be obvious. It directs the operation of all the other units by providing timing and control signals. In a sense, the control unit is like the conductor of an orchestra, who is responsible for keeping each of the orchestra members in proper synchronization. This unit contains logic and timing circuits that generate the signals necessary to execute each instruction in a program.

The control unit *fetches* an instruction from memory by sending an address (arrow 7) and a read command (arrow 6) to the memory unit. The instruction word stored at the memory location is then transferred to the control unit (arrow 11). This instruction word, which is in some form of binary code, is then decoded by logic circuitry in the control unit to determine which instruction is being called for. The control unit uses this information to generate the necessary signals for *executing* the instruction.

Central Processing Unit

In Fig. 3.2, the ALU and control units are shown combined into one unit called the *central processing unit* (CPU). This is commonly done to separate the actual "brains" of the computer from the other units. We will use the CPU designation in all our work on microcomputers because, as we shall see, in microcomputers the CPU is often on a single LSI chip, called the *microprocessor chip.*

3.5 COMPUTER WORDS

The preceding description of how the various units in a computer interact has been, by necessity, somewhat oversimplified. To proceed in more detail, we must define the various forms of information that are continually being transferred and manipulated within the computer.

In a computer, the most elementary unit of information is the binary digit (bit). A single bit, however, can impart very little information. For this reason, the primary unit of information in a computer is a group of bits referred to as the *computer word*. Word size is so important that it is often used in describing a computer. For example, a 16-bit computer is a computer in which data and instructions are processed in 16-bit units. Of course, the word size also indicates the word size of the memory unit. Thus, a 16-bit computer has a memory unit that stores a certain number of 16-bit words.

A large variety of word sizes have been used by computer manufacturers. The larger (maxi) computers have word sizes that range from 16 to 64 bits, with 32 bits being the most common. Minicomputer word sizes run from 8 to 32, with 16 bits representing the overwhelming majority. Most microcomputers use an 8-bit word size. There are several 4-bit microcomputers, which are designed for replacing digital logic circuits, and a few 16-bit microcomputers, which are aimed at competing with minicomputers.

The Byte

A group of 8 bits is called a *byte* and represents a universally used unit in the computer industry. For example, a microcomputer with an 8-bit word size is said to have a word size of one byte. A 16-bit computer can be said to have a word size of two bytes. When we deal with microcomputers that have an 8-bit word size, we will use the terms "word" and "byte" interchangeably.

The 4-bit microcomputers have a word size of one-half byte, commonly referred to as a *nibble*. Thus, each word in a 4-bit microcomputer is a nibble, and two nibbles constitute a byte.

Types of Computer Words

A word stored in a computer's memory unit can contain several different types of information, depending on what the programmer intended for that particular word. We can classify computer words into three categories: (1) pure binary numerical data, (2) coded data, and (3) instructions. These will now be examined in detail.

3.6 BINARY DATA WORDS

These are words which simply represent a numerical quantity in the binary number system. For example, a certain location in the memory of an 8-bit (single-byte) microcomputer might contain the world 01110011, representing the desired process temperature in Fahrenheit degrees. This binary number 01110011 is equivalent to 115_{10}.

Here is an example of a 16-bit data word:

$$1010000101001001$$

which is equivalent to $41,289_{10}$.

Obviously, a wider range of numerical data can be represented with a larger word size. With an 8-bit word size, the largest data word (11111111_2) is equivalent to $2^8 - 1 = 255_{10}$. With a 16-bit word size, the largest data word is equivalent to $2^{16} - 1 = 65,535_{10}$. With 32 bits (four bytes) we can represent numbers greater than 4 billion.

Signed Data Words

A computer would not be too useful if it could only handle positive numbers. For this reason, most computers use the signed 2's-complement system discussed in Chapter 1. Recall that the most significant bit (MSB) is used as the *sign* bit (0 is positive and 1 is negative). Here is how the values +9 and –9 would be represented in an 8-bit computer:

$$+9 \longrightarrow \underline{0}0001001$$

+ └── binary for 9_{10}

$$-9 \longrightarrow \underline{1}1110111$$

– └── 2's-complement of 0001001

Here, of course, only 7 bits are reserved for the magnitude of the number. Thus, in the signed 2's-complement system, we can only represent numbers from -127_{10} to $+127_{10}$. Similarly, with 16-bit words, we can have a range from $-32,767_{10}$ to $+32,767_{10}$.

Multiword Data Units

Very often a computer needs to process data that extend beyond the range possible with a single word. For such cases, two or more memory words can be used to store the data in parts. For example, the 16-bit data word 1010101100101001_2 can be stored in two consecutive 8-bit memory locations:

Memory Address	Contents		
0030	10101011	←	8 high-order bits of 16-bit number
0031	00101001	←	8 low-order bits of 16-bit number

Here, address location 0030_{16} stores the 8 higher-order bits of the 16-bit data word. This is also called the *high-order byte*. Similarly, address 0031_{16} stores the *low-order byte*. The two bytes combined make up the full data word.

There is no actual limit to the number of memory words that can be combined to store large numbers.

Octal and Hexadecimal Data Representation

For purposes of convenience in writing and displaying data words, they can be represented in either octal or hexadecimal codes. For example, the number $+116_{10}$ can be represented in a single byte as 01110100_2. Its hex and octal representations are

$$01110100_2 = 74_{16}$$

$$01110100_2 = 164_8$$

It is important to realize that the use of hex or octal representations is solely for convenience of the computer user; the computer memory still stores the binary numbers (0s and 1s), and these are what the computer processes.

3.7 CODED DATA WORDS

Data processed by a computer do not have to be pure binary numbers. One of the other common data forms uses the BCD code (Chapter 1), where each group of 4 bits can represent a single decimal digit. Thus, an 8-bit word can represent two decimal digits, a 16-bit word can represent four decimal digits, and so on. Many computers can perform arithmetic operations on BCD-coded numbers as part of their normal instruction repertoire; others, especially some microcomputers, require special effort on the part of the programmer in order to do BCD arithmetic.

Data words are not restricted to representing only numbers. They are often used to represent alphabetic characters and other special characters or symbols using codes such as the 7-bit ASCII code (Chapter 1). The ASCII code is used by all minicomputer and microcomputer manufacturers. Although the basic ASCII code uses 7 bits, an extra parity bit (Chapter 1) is added to each code word, producing a one-byte ASCII code. The example below shows how a message might be stored in a sequence of memory locations using ASCII code with an *even* parity bit. The contents of each location are also given in hex code. Use Table 1.2 to determine the message. Note that the leftmost bit is the parity bit and the first character is stored in location $012A_{16}$.

Address Location	Binary	Hex
012A	11001001	C9
012B	10111101	BD
012C	01010110	56
012D	10101111	AF
012E	11010010	D2
	ASCII	

The decoded message is the familiar electrical Ohm's law, $I = V/R$.

The one-byte ASCII code is particularly suited to computers with an 8-bit word size. However, computers with other word sizes still use one-byte ASCII. For example, a 16-bit computer can pack two bytes into one memory word so that each word represents two characters. This is illustrated below, where the characters I and = are stored in one 16-bit word.

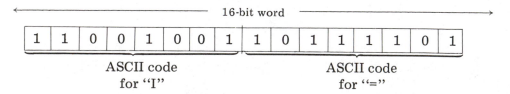

On the other hand, a 4-bit microcomputer would have to use two consecutive memory locations to represent one byte of ASCII.

Interpretation of Data Words

Suppose you are told that a particular data word in a microcomputer's memory is 01010110. This word can be interpreted in several ways. It could be the binary representation of 86_{10}, it could be the BCD representation of 56_{10}, or it could be the ASCII code for the character V. How should this data word be interpreted? It is up to the programmer since he or she is the one who places the data in memory together with instructions that make up the program. The programmer knows what type of data word is being used and must make sure that the program of instructions executed by the computer interprets the data properly.

3.8 INSTRUCTION WORDS

The format used for data words varies only slightly among different computers, especially those with the same word size. This is not true, however, of the format for *instruction* words. These words contain the information necessary for a computer to execute its various operations, and the format and codes for these can vary widely from computer to computer. Depending on the computer, the information contained in an instruction word can be different. But, for most computers, the instruction words carry two basic units of information: the *operation* to be performed and the *address* of the *operand* (data) that is to be operated upon.

Figure 3.3 shows an example of a *single-address instruction word* for a hypothetical 20-bit computer. The 20 bits of the instruction word are divided into two parts. The first part of the word (bits 16 through 19) contains the *operation code* (*op code*, for short). The 4-bit op code represents the operation that the computer is being instructed to perform, such as addition or subtraction. The second part (bits 0 through 15) is the *operand address*, which represents the location in memory where the operand is stored.

With 4 bits used for the op code, there are $2^4 = 16$ different possible op codes, with each one indicating a different instruction. This means that a computer using this instruction-word format is limited to 16 different possible instructions which it can perform. A more versatile computer would

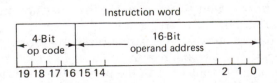

FIGURE 3.3 Typical single-address instruction word.

have a greater number of instructions and would therefore require more bits in its op code. In any case, each instruction which a computer can perform has a specific op code that the computer (control unit) must interpret (decode).

The instruction word of Fig. 3.3 has 16 bits reserved for the operand address code. With 16 bits, there are 2^{16} = 65,536 different possible addresses. Thus, this instruction word can specify 16 different instructions and 65,536 operand addresses. As an example, a 20-bit instruction word might be

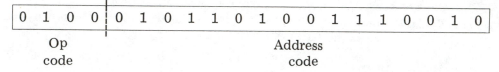

The op code 0100 represents one of 16 possible operations; let us assume that it is the code for *addition* (ADD). The address code is 0101101001110010 or, more conveniently, 5A72 in hexadecimal. In fact, this complete instruction word can be expressed in hexadecimal as

$$\underset{\substack{\text{Op}\\\text{code}}}{4} \quad \underset{\text{Address}}{\underbrace{5 \quad A \quad 7 \quad 2}}$$

This complete instruction word, then, tells the computer to do the following:

> Fetch the data word stored in address location 5A72, send it to the ALU, and *add* it to the number in the Accumulator register. The sum will then be stored in the Accumulator (the previous contents of the Accumulator is lost).

We will examine this and other instructions more thoroughly later.

Multiple-Address Instructions

The single-address instruction is the basic type used in microcomputers and was once the principal type used in larger computers. The larger computers, however, have begun to use several other instruction formats, which provide more information per instruction word.

Figure 3.4 shows two instruction-word formats that contain more than one address. The two-address instruction has the op code plus the addresses of *both* operands that are to take part in the specified operation. The three-address instruction has the addresses of both operands plus the address in memory where the result is to be stored.

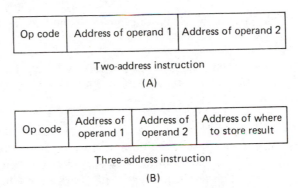

Two-address instruction

(A)

Three-address instruction

(B)

FIGURE 3.4 Multiple-address instruction formats.

These multiple-address instruction words have the obvious advantage that they contain more information than the single-address instruction. This means that a computer using multiple-address instructions will require fewer instructions to execute a particular program. Of course, the longer instruction words require a memory unit with a larger word size. We will not concern ourselves further with multiple-address instructions, since they are not used in microcomputers.

3.9 SIMPLE PROGRAM EXAMPLE

Now that we have looked at some of the types of data and instruction words, the next step is to combine data and instructions in a program. For our programming example, we will use a fictitious computer called the S-16. The "S" stands for *small* while the "16" represents the number of instructions this computer can perform and also the number of words in its memory. Although the S-16 is smaller than most practical computers, its operation is exactly the same as any larger computer. Its small size is simply a convenience for purposes of illustration.

The S-16 is an 8-bit computer. Its instruction-word format is

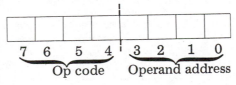

With a 4-bit op code, any of $2^4 = 16$ different instructions can be specified. The 4-bit operand address code means that there are $2^4 = 16$ different address locations in memory.

EXAMPLE 3.1 What is the complete capacity of the S-16 memory? How many FFs are in its Accumulator register?

Solution: We know it stores 16 words and each word is 8 bits long. Thus, the memory capacity is 16 8-bit words (i.e., a 16 × 8 memory chip). Since a data word is 8 bits, the Accumulator register has 8 FFs.

Table 3.1 describes some of the S-16 instructions. Each instruction is accompanied by its 4-bit op code and also by a *symbolic* code made up of three or four letters. The symbolic codes are easier to remember than the op codes and they play an important role in the advanced programming concepts we will encounter later. Read the description of each instruction carefully because each is typical of the instructions available in most computers. Remember that the *operand* referred to in these descriptions is the data word stored at the operand-address location.

Using the partial set of S-16 instructions from Table 3.1, we will write a simple program that will do the following:

1. SUBTRACT one number (X) from another number (Y).
2. STORE the result, Q, in location $1001 = 9_{16}$.
3. If the result is *zero*, HALT the computer at location 0101 (5_{16}). Otherwise, HALT the computer at location 0100 (4_{16}).

TABLE 3.1

Symbolic Code	Binary Op Code	Description of Operation
LDA	1100	LOAD Accumulator: the data stored at the operand address are loaded into the Accumulator register.
ADD	0100	ADD: the operand is added to the number stored in the Accumulator and the resultant sum is stored in the Accumulator.
SUB	0101	SUBTRACT: the operand is subtracted from the contents of the Accumulator and the result is stored in the Accumulator.
STA	0111	STORE Accumulator: the contents of the Accumulator is stored in memory at the location specified by the operand address.
JMP	1000	JUMP (unconditionally): the next instruction is taken from the location specified by the operand address instead of in sequence.
JPZ	1001	JUMP ON ZERO: the next instruction is taken from operand address *if* the Accumulator contents is *zero*. Otherwise, the next instruction is taken in sequence.
HLT	0001	HALT: The computer operation is halted. No further instructions are executed.

TABLE 3.2

Memory Address (Hex)	Memory Word (Binary)	Symbolic Code	Description
0	11001000	LDA 8	LOAD Y into Accumulator
1	01010111	SUB 7	SUBTRACT X from Accumulator
2	01111001	STA 9	STORE result Q in location 9
3	10010101	JPZ 5	If Q = 0, JUMP to 5
4	00010000	HLT	If Q ≠ 0, HALT here
5	00010000	HLT	If Q = 0, HALT here
6	-Not used-		
7	$X_7 X_6 X_5 X_4 X_3 X_2 X_1 X_0$	X	Data word X
8	$Y_7 Y_6 Y_5 Y_4 Y_3 Y_2 Y_1 Y_0$	Y	Data word Y
9	????????	Q	Location where Q will be stored
A	Not used		
B			
C			
D			
E			
F			

The complete program as it appears in the S-16 memory is shown in Table 3.2. The 16 memory locations are indicated by their hexadecimal addresses 0 through F. The words stored in locations 0 through 5 are the sequence of instruction words used in the program. Locations 7, 8, and 9 are used for data words. The numbers X and Y are data required by the program and are initially stored in 7 and 8, respectively. Location 9 is reserved for storing the result, Q. The locations 6 and A through F are not used in this sample program.

Program Execution

Once the program is in the computer's memory, it is ready to be executed by the computer (do not be concerned, for now, about how the program got into memory). We will now proceed through the program and explain what the computer does at each step.

1. Operation is initiated by the computer user, usually by activating a START or RUN switch on the computer console. This causes the Control unit to begin fetching instructions from memory, starting at address 0.* This first instruction is LDA 8 and tells the Control unit

*In many computers the user can set the starting address to something other than address 0.

to *read* the data word stored in address 8 and load it into the Accumulator. The data word at address 8 is the value of Y.

2. After executing the instruction at address 0, the Control unit automatically sequences to address 1 for its next instruction. This sequencing is provided by a Program Counter (PC), which starts at 0 and is automatically incremented as each instruction is executed so that it always contains the address of the next instruction.

   The instruction at address 1 is SUB 7 and causes the Control unit to go to address 7 to obtain the data word (X). These data are then sent to the ALU to be subtracted from the contents of the Accumulator. The result of this operation (Q) is stored in the Accumulator.

3. The PC is incremented to address 2, so the Control unit takes its next instruction from that location. This instruction, STA 9, causes the Control unit to store (write) the contents of the Accumulator into address 9. The value of Q = Y - X is now in memory location 9 as well as still being in the Accumulator.

4. The PC is incremented to 3 and the Control unit fetches the next instruction from that location. This instruction, JPZ 5, causes the Control unit to examine the contents of the Accumulator. If the value is *not* exactly equal to zero, the Control unit increments PC to 4. If the Accumulator value *is* exactly zero, the Control unit sets PC to 5. Thus, the next instruction may be taken from either address 4 or address 5, depending on the value of Q.

5. If PC is now 4, the Control unit fetches the instruction at address 4. This instruction causes the computer to HALT and no further instructions will be executed. But, if PC is now 5, the Control unit obtains its next instruction from address 5 (rather than 4). This instruction causes the computer to HALT so that no more instructions will be executed.

6. This completes the execution of our small program. The computer will do nothing more until the user either presses the START button to reexecute the same program or puts a new program into memory for execution.

This simple example program did not even begin to illustrate the real assets of a computer but was intended to show the sequencing action that occurs in all computers. The operation takes place one step at a time as explained. Of course, each step is executed in a very short time interval, which depends on the speed of the computer. For example, this short program would take even the slowest microcomputer around 10 microseconds (μs) to execute.

3.10 COMPUTER OPERATING CYCLES

We now have the basic idea of how a computer sequences through a program. In essence, the computer is always doing one of two things: (1) fetching an instruction word from memory and interpreting that instruction, or (2) executing the operations called for by the instruction word. The computer operation, then, is comprised of two types of cycles: an *instruction* cycle and an *execution* cycle. We will examine these two cycles and describe the flow of information between the various computer units for each.

Instruction Cycle

Refer to Fig. 3.5, which is a diagram of those computer elements that are involved in the instruction cycle. The arrows on the diagram are simply used to indicate the direction of information flow. The circled numbers correspond to the steps in the following description:

1. The instruction cycle begins when the address of the next instruction is transferred from the Program Counter (PC) to the Memory Address Register (MAR). The PC keeps track of which instruction is being fetched from memory. It is incremented at the end of each instruction cycle. The MAR is used to hold any memory address that is being accessed for a read or write operation.
2. The Control unit generates a READ pulse, which causes the Memory unit to read the instruction word from the memory location specified by the MAR. This instruction word is clocked into the Memory Data Register (MDR). The MDR functions as a buffer register for all data read from or written into memory.
3. The op-code portion of the instruction word, which is now in the MDR, is transferred to the Instruction Register (IR) in the Control unit. Simultaneously, the operand-address portion of the instruction word is transferred to the MAR (replacing its previous contents).
4. The op code in the IR is fed to the Instruction Decoder (ID), which determines which op code is present. This information is sent to the control-signal-generating portion of the Control unit to determine which control signals will be needed to execute the instruction during the execution cycle.
5. The PC is incremented to prepare for the next instruction cycle. (Note that the PC contents is not now in the MAR.)

To summarize, during the instruction cycle, the instruction word is

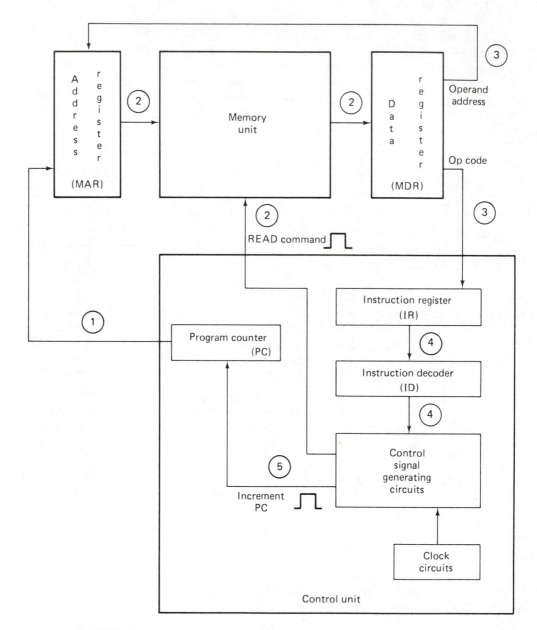

FIGURE 3.5 Flow of information during a computer's instruction cycle.

fetched from memory, the op-code portion is decoded, the address portion is placed in the MAR, and the PC is incremented.

Execution Cycle

An instruction cycle is followed by an execution cycle, during which the instruction is actually carried out. The exact sequence of operations during the execution cycle will, of course, depend on the instruction. Refer to Fig. 3.6, showing the flow of information during a typical execution cycle.

1. The IR still holds the op code and the ID indicates which instruction

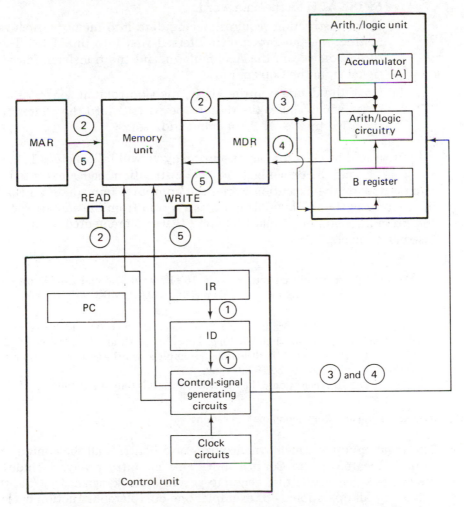

FIGURE 3.6 Flow of information during a computer's execution cycle.

is being executed; this determines which signals will be generated by the control-signal-generating circuitry during the following steps.

2. If the instruction requires fetching a data word from memory, the Control unit generates a READ pulse, which takes the data word from the address specified by the MAR and places it in the MDR. Recall that the MAR is holding the operand address from the instruction cycle.

3. Once in the MDR, the data word can be transferred to the ALU, where it might be placed in the Accumulator or in the B register. The Control unit generates the control signals to produce this transfer and also to determine what operation, if any, is to be performed by the ALU on the data word.

4. If the instruction requires placing data into memory, such as a STA instruction, the data are transferred first into the MDR. These data often come from the Accumulator and the transfer is initiated by a signal from the Control unit.

5. Once the data are in the MDR, the Control unit generates a WRITE pulse which causes the data to be written into the address location specified by the MAR (operand address).

It should be clear that an execution cycle will follow steps 1, 2, and 3 or steps 1, 4, and 5, depending on the instruction being executed. At the completion of the execution cycle, the computer immediately goes into an instruction cycle and takes its next instruction from the address specified by the Program Counter. Recall that the PC was incremented at the end of the instruction cycle.

EXAMPLE 3.2   A certain computer has a 16-bit word size and a 6-bit op code. How many bits does it have in each of its registers (MAR, MDR, PC, IR, A)?

Solution: With a 16-bit word size and a 6-bit op code, the operand-address portion of an instruction word will be 10 bits long. Thus, the MAR and PC must be 10 bits each.
      The MDR and A both handle a complete word as it comes from memory, so these registers have to be 16 bits long.
      The IR receives only the op-code bits and is only 6 bits long.

Synchronizing and Controlling the Operations

The logic circuitry which synchronizes and controls all the computer operations is located in the Control unit. This circuitry always includes one or more clock generators that generate periodic clock signals to act as the time frame for all operations. For example, one complete instruction cycle or one complete execution cycle might require four clock pulses. Figure 3.7 illustrates the timing for such a situation.

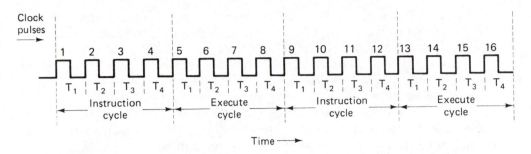

FIGURE 3.7   Typical timing sequence for computer cycles.

As shown in the diagram, each series of four clock pulses constitutes one operating cycle. Pulses 1 through 4 comprise the first instruction cycle, followed by pulses 5 through 8, which comprise the first execution cycle. Pulses 9 through 12 constitute the second instruction cycle, followed by pulses 13 through 16 for the second execution cycle. This sequence continues for as many cycles as are necessary to process all the instructions in a given program.

Each operating cycle is divided into four time intervals, and certain operations occur at each of these times. For example, during the first interval (T_1) of each instruction cycle, the contents of the Program Counter is transferred to the MAR. Actually, this transfer takes place on the leading edge of the T_1 pulse in the instruction cycle. As another example, during the execution of an ADD instruction, the addition of the numbers in the Accumulator and the B register occurs during the T_4 interval of the execution cycle.

The Control unit sends control signals to the other computer units during each of the clock time intervals. The sequence of control signals will be the same for each instruction cycle, but the sequence will vary during the execution cycle depending on the instruction being executed (the op code). Clearly, the ultimate speed of the computer operation depends to a great extent on the clock signal. In general, a higher-frequency clock signal indicates a faster computer. We will go into more detail on timing sequences in our study of microprocessors and microcomputers.

3.11   TYPICAL MICROCOMPUTER INSTRUCTION WORD FORMATS

We have looked at instruction-word formats that contain op-code and operand-address information in a *single* word. In other words, a complete instruction such as those in Fig. 3.3 or 3.4 is stored in a *single* memory location. This is typical of computers with relatively large word sizes. For most microcomputers and many minicomputers, the smaller word size makes it impossible to provide op code and operand addresses in a single word.

Since the vast majority of microcomputers use an 8-bit (one byte) word length, we will describe the instruction formats used in 8-bit computers. With a one-byte word size there are *three* basic instruction formats: single-byte, two-byte, and three-byte. These are illustrated in Fig. 3.8.

The single-byte instruction contains only an 8-bit op code with no address portion. Clearly, this type of instruction does not specify any data from memory to be operated on. As such, single-byte instructions are used for operations that do not require memory data. An example would be the instruction *Clear the Accumulator Register to Zero* (CLA), which instructs the computer to clear all the FFs in the ALU's Accumulator.

The first byte of the two-byte instruction is an op code and the second byte can be an 8-bit address code specifying the location of the operand, or an 8-bit data word. In the three-byte instruction, the second and third bytes form a 16-bit operand address. For these multibyte instructions, the two or three bytes making up the complete instruction have to be stored in successive memory locations. This is illustrated below for a three-byte instruction. The left-hand column lists the address locations in memory where each byte (word) is stored. These addresses are given in hexadecimal code. The second

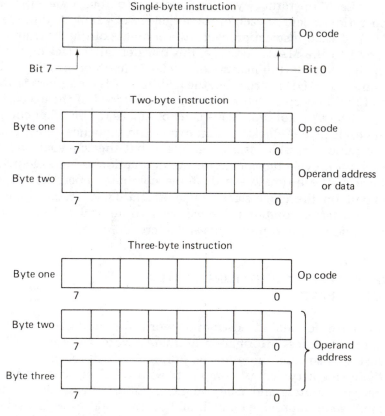

FIGURE 3.8 Instruction formats used in 8-bit microcomputers.

column gives the binary word as it is actually stored in memory; the third column is the hex equivalent of this word. Examine this complete example before reading further and try to figure out what it represents.

| Memory | Memory Word | | Description |
Address (Hex)	Binary	Hex	
0020	01001010	4A	Op code for ADD
0021	11110110	F6	Low-order address bits (LO)
0022	00110101	35	High-order address bits (HI)
.	.	.	
.	.	.	
35F6	01111100	7C	Operand

The three bytes stored in locations 0020, 0021, and 0022 constitute the complete instruction for adding the data word stored in address location 35F6 to the Accumulator. The second and third bytes hold the 8 low-order bits (LO), and 8 high-order bits (HI), respectively, of the operand address. Some microcomputers use the reverse order, with HI stored in the second byte and LO in the third byte of the instruction sequence. Memory location 35F6 is also shown; its contents is the data word which the control unit of the computer will fetch and send to the ALU for addition.

A Typical Microcomputer Program Example

Below is a short program which is stored in memory locations 0020_{16} to 0029_{16} of an 8-bit microcomputer. Note that since each word is one byte (8 bits) in length, it takes two successive bytes to represent a 16-bit operand address code. This program takes two pieces of data and performs an addition, stores the result in memory, and then halts.

Memory Address (Hex)	Memory Word (Hex)	Symbolic Code	Description
0020	49	LDA	LOAD Accumulator (ACC) with X
0021	50		⎡Address of⎤
0022	01		⎣operand X⎦
0023	7E	ADD	ADD Y to contents of ACC
0024	51		⎡Address of⎤
0025	01		⎣operand Y⎦
0026	B2	STA	STORE ACC contents
0027	52		⎡Address where ACC⎤
0028	01		⎣will be stored⎦
0029	EF	HLT	HALT operation

The CPU* begins the program with an instruction cycle by READING the contents of memory location 0020. The word stored there (49) is taken into the CPU and is interpreted as an instruction op code. (In other words, the CPU *always* interprets the first word of a program as an instruction and the programmer must *always* adhere to this format.) The CPU decodes this op code to determine the operation to be performed and to determine if an operand address follows the op code. In this case, an operand address is required and is stored in the next two successive bytes in the program. Thus, the CPU continues the instruction cycle and must READ locations 0021 and 0022 to obtain the address of data X. Once this address (0150) has been read into the CPU, the CPU has completed the instruction cycle. It then proceeds to the execution cycle, which involves executing the LDA instruction by READING memory location 0150 and putting its contents into the accumulator. Thus, the complete execution of this first instruction requires *three* separate READ operations for the instruction cycle, and *one* READ operation for the execution cycle.

Three READ operations are needed for the instruction cycle and one READ operation for the execution cycle of the second instruction, which begins at 0023. This instruction also uses a two-byte operand address and requires reading the contents of this address for transfer to the CPU's arithmetic unit.

The third instruction begins at 0026 and uses a two-byte operand address. The CPU uses *three* READ operations during the instruction cycle to obtain these. However, the instruction STA calls for a WRITE operation during the execution cycle, whereby the CPU transfers the contents of the accumulator to memory location 0152.

The final instruction at 0029 is simply an op code with no operand address. The CPU READS this op code (EF) during the instruction cycle, decodes it, and then halts any further operations during the execution cycle.

In summary, a microcomputer uses a multibyte instruction format where one, two, or three bytes specify a complete instruction (i.e., op code and operand address). Computers with larger word sizes can have the complete instruction specified in a single word. Regardless of the instruction format, however, all computers perform the same basic operations during the instruction and execution cycles. Because of its multibyte instruction format, the microcomputer's instruction cycle will necessarily be longer than that of a larger-word-size computer. We will have much more to say regarding the microcomputer instruction format in the work that follows.

3.12 HARDWARE AND SOFTWARE

A computer system consists of hardware and software. The *hardware* refers to the electronic, mechanical, and magnetic elements from which the computer is fabricated. This hardware, especially in large-scale computer systems,

*CPU (Central Processing Unit) is the combination of the ALU and Control Unit.

can be somewhat awe-inspiring. But, regardless of the complexity of the computer hardware, the computer is a useless maze of wire unless it has a function to perform and a program to tell it how to do it.

Software refers to the totality of programs and programming systems used by a computer. These programs are all initially written on paper (software) before being transferred to some storage media (hardware), and completely control the computer's operation from startup to shutdown. Many types of programs are supplied by computer manufacturers, but the user will often have program needs that are unique and so must write his or her own programs. This is especially true for microcomputers, which are relatively new and are applied for such a wide variety of purposes.

Some Programming Language Concepts

One of the hardest things to explain to someone is that a computer cannot do a thing without a program to tell it what to do and when to do it. This is true for all computers, from the multimillion-dollar IBM 370/168 down to the cheapest microcomputer. In other words, all the computer *hardware* is useless without *software*. Software, remember, refers to the binary patterns stored somewhere in the computer system memory which represent instructions that control the operation of the computer. A *program* is any sequence of instructions that causes the computer to perform some useful function. A *programmer* is one who develops this sequence of instructions in some form that can be easily deposited in the computer memory.

Machine Language

Programming involves writing a program in some code or language which the computer can interpret and execute. There are many different programming languages in use today; they range from the use of 0s and 1s all the way up to the use of English-language statements. Each type of language has its advantages and shortcomings relative to the other types, as we shall see. Regardless of what type of language the programmer uses to write his program, however, the program must eventually be translated to the *only* language any computer understands—the language of 0s and 1s, which is referred to as *machine language*. The computer performs specific operations in response to specific binary patterns (op codes) which form its instruction set. These binary patterns represent the actual language the machine (computer) understands and works with.

Manufacturers define the *machine language* their computers understand and the set of instructions represented. In general, any two different computers will have different machine languages. For example, Motorola's 6800 microprocessor uses the code 10111001_2 for its addition instruction, while MOS Technology's 6502 uses the code 01101101_2. This means that a machine language program written for one microcomputer will not work on any other microcomputer. There are a few exceptions to this, when one microcomputer manufacturer purposely duplicates the instruction set of another manufacturer. A prime example is Zilog's Z-80, whose instruction set contains Intel's 8080A instruction set as well as many additional instructions.

The *object* of any programming task is to place the machine language codes for a particular sequence of instructions into the computer's memory. For this reason, the machine language program stored in memory is also referred to as the *object program*. When a programmer actually writes a program on paper in machine language, it will consist of sequences of 0s and 1s. For example, below is a short object program for adding two numbers using the 6502 machine language:

```
10101001
00010000
00011000
01101001
00100000
10001101
00000000
00000010
```

Clearly, the function of this program is far from obvious to anyone except the person who wrote it or perhaps someone who has all the 6502 codes memorized. Even the person who wrote it would have a hard time recognizing it after not having seen it for a while.

Writing programs directly in binary machine language has several disadvantages. First, it is very difficult to write all but the simplest programs without making an error, because after a while the strings of 0s and 1s all begin to look alike. Likewise, errors are difficult to detect; a misplaced 0 or 1 can easily get lost among hundreds or thousands of bits. Furthermore, the process of entering a machine language program into the computer's memory can be extremely tedious and prone to error. Each byte is entered via eight binary switches on the computer's front panel. This means, for example, that a program of 100 bytes, not very long by most standards, will require 800 different switch settings.

Machine language programming can be improved through the use of octal or hexadecimal codes. The programmer writes the program using the octal or hexadecimal equivalents of each instruction. The same addition program using hexadecimal is as follows:

A9
10
18
69
20
8D
00
02

Writing a program in hexadecimal is certainly simpler and less prone to error since each entry requires only two digits rather than eight. Furthermore, an error in any of the digits would be much easier to detect, and entering the program from a hex keyboard would be less tiresome and prone to error than binary switches. Of course, this requires a keyboard monitor program (ROM) for monitoring the keyboard and converting each hex key actuation into machine language (binary).

Assembly Language

The next higher step up from machine language is *assembly language*, also called *symbolic language*. This language uses alphabetic abbreviations for each type of instruction rather than binary or hex op codes. For example, abbreviations such as LDA or ADC are used instead of numbers. These abbreviations are often called *mnemonics* because they are more easily remembered than the binary or hex machine language codes. Likewise, in assembly language, addresses are often referred to by names or *labels*, such as VALU1 or RESULT, instead of by actual numerical values. Written in assembly language, the program for adding two numbers might appear as follows:

```
START    LDA   VALU1
         CLC
         ADC   VALU2

         STA   RESULT
```

Clearly, writing this program would be much easier than its machine language counterpart because the programmer would not have to keep looking up number codes for each operation; the mnemonics are very quickly committed to memory because they are closely related to the instruction they represent. The mnemonic for the instruction "Load Accumulator from Memory" is LDA and the mnemonic for Clear the Carry flag is CLC. This greatly reduces the chance for programming errors caused by entering the wrong codes.

Another aspect of assembly language which is convenient is that the programmer does not have to use numerical addresses. As shown in the example above, the labels VALU1, VALU2, and RESULT represent memory locations for data being used by the program. This relieves the programmer of the task of keeping track of numerical addresses, which, as we shall see, can be a sizable task in many programs.

A natural question now arises: How does this assembly language program finally become the machine language object program stored in the computer memory? One way is to do it manually. The programmer writes the program in the more convenient assembly language, goes over it, and modifies and corrects it as required. When he is satisfied that the program will do the required job, he then translates each instruction into machine language by consulting a table of machine language codes. This process of converting an assembly program into machine language is called *assembly*. Manual assembly is fine for short programs but becomes somewhat tedious for long programs.

The assembly process can also be carried out by the computer itself. To do so, the computer must have a special program called an *assembler* stored in its memory. The assembler is a big program that takes up a considerable amount of memory space depending on the complexity of the computer's instruction set (i.e., number of different instructions) and the number of special features included. An assembler program can be purchased from the computer manufacturer or from other software sources, and stored on a bulk memory medium such as magnetic tape or disk until it is needed. The assembly process typically follows these steps:

1. The assembler is loaded into the computer memory. If the assembler is stored on a cassette tape, it will be read into the computer memory using a tape I/O program which is probably stored in ROM.
2. The computer is commanded to execute the assembler program (e.g., punch in the address of the assembler program and hit the RUN key).
3. The assembler program is now being executed and it is waiting for input from the keyboard.
4. The programmer can now type in his program in assembly language. Clearly, an ASCII keyboard is necessary if alphanumeric characters are to be used. As each instruction mnemonic is typed in, the assembler program converts it to its machine language equivalent and stores it in memory. For example, if the programmer types in L—D—A, the ASCII codes for these characters are transmitted to the computer. The assembler program interprets these codes and responds by putting the binary machine language code 10101001 (hex A9) into memory. The assembler performs other functions, such as converting the address labels of the assembly program into actual numerical addresses and many other functions (which we will not discuss here).

5. After the programmer has entered the complete assembly language program, the corresponding machine language program (object program) has been stored in memory and is ready to be executed.

High-Level Languages

Although assembly language is much more convenient than machine language for all but the simplest programs, it still requires that the programmer be very familiar with the computer's internal structure and its complete set of instruction mnemonics. In addition, the programmer has to write an instruction for each step the computer has to perform. For example, to add two numbers, he has to tell the computer to fetch the first number, place it in the Accumulator, fetch the second number, add it to the Accumulator, and store the result in a memory location. This step-by-step process can become quite laborious for complex programs. In fact, to become an accomplished machine or assembly language programmer, it takes a great deal of practice and a great deal of time.

To overcome these difficulties, a number of high-level languages have been developed. These *high-level* languages make it possible to communicate with a computer using English-language words and mathematical symbols without the need for detailed knowledge of the computer's internal architecture or instruction set. Furthermore, with high-level languages, one statement can contain many steps, corresponding to many machine language instructions. To illustrate, the following is a statement written in a language called BASIC:

$$\text{LET RESULT} = A + B$$

It should be obvious, even to a nonprogrammer, that this single instruction statement represents a program for adding two numbers. It should also be obvious that this program is much easier to write and understand than its machine language and assembly language counterparts.

A large number of high-level languages are in use, each of which is designed specifically for certain types of tasks. The three most widely used are FORTRAN, COBOL, and BASIC. FORTRAN (*for*mula *tran*slation) is a language designed for scientific and engineering applications, although its use now pervades other fields. COBOL (*c*ommon *b*usiness-*o*riented *l*anguage) is used in business data-processing applications. BASIC (*b*eginner's *a*ll-purpose *s*ymbolic *i*nstruction *c*ode) is a simple language developed for solving numerical problems. It is used in educational, business, and entertainment applications and is the most widely used high-level language in microcomputer systems. The latest entry into the field of high-level language programming is PASCAL. Programming in this language is said to be easier and more quickly mastered than in BASIC, COBOL, or FORTRAN. Some people say that

PASCAL will replace BASIC as the high-level language programming standard for microcomputers.

The main purpose of any high-level language is to relieve the computer user from having to worry about the details of machine or assembly language programming. Instead, the programmer can concentrate on solving the problem at hand using the straightforward uncoded commands and rules of the high-level languages. Another advantage of high-level languages is that the same program can be run on two completely different computers, assuming that both computers *understand* the particular language being used. For example, a program written in BASIC for a 6502-based microcomputer would also work on a 8080A-based microcomputer, provided that both computers have some means for *translating* the BASIC language into their particular machine languages.

How does a computer translate a high-level language such as BASIC? Just as the use of assembly language required a special *assembler program*, the use of a high-level language requires a special program. This special program can be classified as either an *interpreter program* or as a *compiler program*. Both are much larger programs than assemblers and require much more memory space.

Interpreters and compilers differ in the process used for translating high-level language. An interpreter takes each high-level instruction or command statement (e.g., LET RESULT = A + B) and causes the computer to go through the steps required to execute the operation. It does *not* convert each statement into machine language codes to be placed in memory; that is, it does not create an object program. A compiler, on the other hand, translates each statement into the sequence of machine language codes required to execute the operation. It creates an object program in memory, which must then be run to perform the programmed task. Stated another way, a compiler translates the *complete* high-level program into an object program that is placed in memory for later execution, while an interpreter translates small chunks of the program and executes them as it goes along without creating an object program.

High-level languages do have some drawbacks that make them unsuitable for some applications. They usually produce programs that run slower and use more memory than machine or assembly language programs. One reason is that these high-level languages perform according to prescribed rules which cannot take advantage of all the idiosyncrasies and subtleties of a particular computer. A programmer using machine or assembly language can often take advantage of his intimate knowledge of the computer to produce a more efficient program. Another reason is that the interpreter or compiler translation process takes a certain amount of time. Interpreters are particularly slow with typical program execution times that are 10 to 50 times longer than a machine language version.

Of course, the use of any high-level language requires the compiler or interpreter program to be in memory. These fairly expansive programs can be purchased from the computer manufacturer and are usually stored on paper tape or magnetic tape until needed. As you can see, then, using a high-level language requires a good deal of input/output equipment; a bulk storage media for the interpreter or compiler, and a teletype or video terminal for entering the programs are a minimum requirement.

Many microprocessor applications are involved in some type of control problem which involves the computer acquiring input data from a process and generating control signals to output to the process. This type of situation does not lend itself to an efficient use of high-level language programming. Therefore, machine language with some elements of assembly language programming will be covered in much more detail in a later chapter.

3.13 INPUT/OUTPUT

We have said very little about the computer's input and output units so far, and we do not intend to say much until later. This does not mean that these units are of secondary importance. In fact, it is often the input and output devices that are used to distinguish one computer system from another.

These units represent the means through which the computer communicates with the external world. For example, the instructions and data that constitute a program must be placed in the computer's internal memory before being executed. In large computer systems, this might be done by a punched-card reader which translates holes punched on "IBM" cards into the instruction and data codes required by the computer. In a microcomputer, the instructions and data might be entered from a keyboard or from sets of toggle switches. Of course, there are many other types of input devices in common usage, such as paper-tape readers, magnetic-tape readers, and analog-to-digital (A/D) converters.

Once the computer executes its program, it usually has results or control signals which it must present to the external world. For example, a large computer system might have a line printer as an output device. Here, the computer sends out signals to print out the results on paper. A microcomputer might display its results on indicator lights or on LED displays. Again, there are many other types of output devices, such as CRT displays, paper-tape punches, and digital-to-analog (D/A) converters.

Interfacing

The most important aspect of the I/O units involves *interfacing*, which can be defined as the joining of dissimilar devices in such a way that they are able to function in a compatible and coordinated manner. *Computer interfacing* is more specifically defined as the synchronization of digital information transmission between the computer and external input/output devices.

Many input/output devices are not directly compatible with the computer because of differences in characteristics, such as operating speed, data format (e.g., hex, ASCII, binary), data transmission mode (e.g., serial, parallel), and logic signal level. Such I/O devices require special interface circuits which allow them to communicate with the Control, Memory, and ALU portions of the computer system. A common example is the popular teletypewriter (abbreviated TTY), which can operate both as an input and an output device. The TTY transmits and receives data serially (1 bit at a time) while most computers handle data in parallel form. Thus, a TTY requires interface circuitry in order to send data to or receive data from a computer. We will discuss this and other interface circuits when we deal with microcomputer I/O techniques.

GLOSSARY

Byte   Set of adjoining binary bits, usually 8, which are operated on as a unit.

Central Processor Unit (CPU)   That unit of a computing system which fetches, decodes, and executes programmed instructions and maintains the status of results as the program is executed. The subunits of a CPU typically include Accumulator and Operand registers, instruction logic, arithmetic/logic unit, and I/O control logic.

Conditional Branch (Conditional Jump)   Instruction causing a program transfer to an instruction other than the next sequential instruction only if a specific condition tested by the instruction is satisfied. If the condition is not satisfied, the next sequential instruction in the program is executed.

Data Word   Information stored in the computer memory which is operated on during the execution of an instruction.

Execution Cycle   Time during which a specific computer instruction is performed.

Hardware   Electronic, mechanical, and magnetic elements from which the computer is fabricated.

Instruction Cycle   Time during which the instruction word is fetched from memory, the op-code portion decoded, the address portion placed in MAR, and the PC incremented.

Instruction Word   Information in the computer memory which is necessary for the computer to execute its various operations. Generally, instruction words consists of two units of information: the op-code portion, and the address of operand portion.

Interfacing   Synchronization of digital information transmission between the computer and external input/output devices.

Jump   Instruction that causes the computer to fetch the next instruction to be executed from a location other than the next sequential location.

Mainframe   A very large computer system.

Memory   Any storage medium for binary data.

Memory Address Register (MAR)   Internal register used to hold the address of data which the CPU is reading or writing into memory.

Microcomputer Class of computer containing a microprocessor chip, memory chips, and input/output interface on a single printed circuit board.

Microprocessor Single LSI circuit which performs the functions of a CPU.

Multibyte Instruction Op code and operand address making up the complete instruction are stored in successive memory locations.

Operand Any of the quantities taking part in the execution of a computer instruction. An operand can be a constant, a result of a computation, a parameter, and so on.

Operation Code (Op Code) That part of a computer binary instruction word representing the operation that the Computer is being instructed to perform, such as addition (ADD) or subtraction (SUB).

Program Complete sequence of computer instructions necessary to solve a specific problem or perform a specific task.

Program Counter (PC) Internal register that always contains the address in memory of the next instruction the CPU is to fetch.

Software Programs and programming systems that control the operation of the computer hardware.

Symbolic Code Three- or four-letter code used as an aid in remembering the op codes.

QUESTIONS AND PROBLEMS

Sections 3.1–3.4

3.1 List each of the five basic units of every computer, and state the principal function of each.

3.2 Which two units of a computer are combined and referred to as the *central processing unit* (CPU)?

Sections 3.5–3.8

3.3 A certain computer has a word size that can accommodate four bytes. How many bits is this word size?

3.4 The contents of two consecutive memory locations in a certain computer is shown in the table. All values are in hexadecimal.

Memory Address	Contents
0350	24
0351	B8

(a) If the two data words represent the two halves of a large binary number, what is the *decimal* value of that number?

(b) If the two data words are in ASCII code with an *even*-parity bit (MSB), what do the words represent?

3.5 A certain computer has the following instruction word format.

Op Code	Operand Address
8 bits	16 bits

(a) How many different instructions can this instruction word specify?
(b) How many different memory addresses can it specify?
(c) What internal memory capacity would this computer require to operate at full capacity?

3.6 What advantages do multiple-address instructions have over single-address instructions?

Section 3.9

3.7 The table lists the memory contents of the S-16 computer. The Program Counter (PC) is set to 0 and the computer begins executing the program.
(a) Describe the sequence of operations that occur as this program is executed (see Section 3.9).
(b) What value is stored in location F after the computer halts?

Memory Address (Hex)	Memory Word (Hex)
0	C9
1	5A
2	5B
3	9D
4	48
5	8D
6	00
7	00
8	02
9	09
A	05
B	03
C	00
D	7F
E	10
F	00

3.8 Change the contents of memory location B to 04 and repeat Problem 3.7.

Section 3.10

3.9 Which of the following operations is *not* part of a computer's *instruction* cycle?
(a) The address of the instruction word is transferred from PC to MAR.

(b) The control unit generates signals needed to perform the operation called for by the instruction.

(c) The op-code portion of the instruction word is sent to the Instruction Decoder.

(d) The control unit fetches the instruction word from memory.

3.10 Which of the following is *not* normally used during a computer execution cycle?

(a) MAR   (b) Accumulator   (c) Instruction Decoder   (d) PC

Section 3.11

3.11 List the different events that occur in a typical computer instruction cycle.

3.12 Repeat Problem 3.11 for an execution cycle of an ADD instruction.

3.13 Repeat Problem 3.11 for an execution cycle of a STA instruction.

3.14 Consider the following typical microcomputer three-byte instruction:

8D
00
02

(a) What portion of the instruction is contained in the first byte?

(b) What do the other two bytes represent?

(c) What is the word size of this microcomputer?

(d) How many READ operations must the control unit perform in order to fetch this complete instruction?

(e) If "8D" is the op code for a STA operation, how many READ operations must be performed during the execution cycle?

3.15 How many different types of instructions can be specified using a multibyte format? How many different operand addresses?

Section 3.12

3.16 What is the only language that a computer's circuitry understands?

3.17 What are the disadvantages of programming in binary machine language?

3.18 What type of programming language uses alphabetic abbreviations for each type of instruction?

3.19 What are the advantages of programming in assembly language as compared to machine language?

3.20 What function does an assembler program perform?

3.21 Which of the following types of programming languages require a familiarity with the computer's internal architecture?
(a) machine language   (b) assembly language   (c) high-level languages (BASIC, FORTRAN, etc.)

3.22 What are the advantages of high-level languages compared to machine and assembly language?

3.23 What are the disadvantages of high-level languages?

3.24 Explain the difference between an *interpreter* and a *compiler*.

PART 2

MICROCOMPUTER HARDWARE

4

MICROCOMPUTER STRUCTURE AND OPERATION

Developments in the semiconductor industry over the past 20 years can indeed be termed revolutionary. Advances in large-scale integration (LSI) and very large-scale integration (VLSI) are taking place at a staggering rate, with IC chips containing over 1 million components now readily available.

The principal impact of this LSI technology has been economic. It is now possible to integrate the control and arithmetic portions of a computer on a *single* chip. In other words, a central processing unit (CPU) is available as a single circuit component referred to as a *microprocessor* (μP) at a cost of $30 or less. In addition, LSI has made it possible to construct large-capacity memories from low-cost LSI memory chips, and has produced a wide variety of LSI input/output interface chips.

What this means is that a relatively small number of LSI chips can be configured to operate as a complete computer — a *microcomputer* (μC). Right now the cost of a microcomputer typically ranges from $50 to $1000. Their relative low cost coupled with their small size has made it possible to use computers in areas where cost and size were formerly prohibitive. This includes application areas such as appliances, automobiles, electronic instrumentation, all kinds of consumer products, and personal computers for the home.

4.1 BASIC μC ELEMENTS

It is important that we understand the distinction between the microcomputer and the microprocessor. A μC contains many elements, one of which is the μP. The μP is the central processing unit (CPU) portion of the μC. This is illustrated in Fig. 4.1, where the basic elements of a μC are shown. The μP is typically a single LSI chip that contains all the control and arithmetic circuits of the μC. The μP may consist of more than one chip. This is true, for example, of bipolar μPs (TTL, Schottky TTL, ECL) which do not have the high packing densities of the MOS devices, so require two or more chips to produce a μP with appropriate word size.

The memory unit shows both RAM and ROM devices, typical of most μCs, although one or the other might not be present in certain applications. The RAM section consists of one or more LSI chips arranged to provide the designed memory capacity. This section of memory is used to store programs

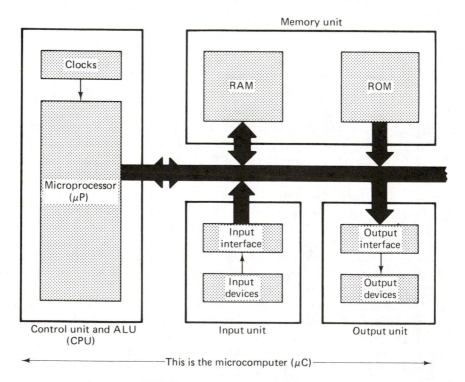

FIGURE 4.1 Basic elements of a μC.

and data that will change often during the course of operation. It is also used as storage for intermediate and final results of operations performed during execution of a program.

The ROM section consists of one or more LSI chips to store instructions and data that does not change. For example, it might store a program that causes the μC to continually monitor a keyboard, or it might store a table of ASCII codes needed for outputting information to a teletype unit.

The input and output sections contain the interface circuits needed to allow the I/O devices to properly communicate with the rest of the computer. In some cases, these interface circuits are LSI chips designed by μP manufacturers to interface their μPs to a variety of I/O devices. In other cases, the interface circuits may be as simple as a buffer register.

The microprocessor, then, is generally a single LSI chip that incorporates the functions of a control unit (fetching, interpreting, and executing instructions) and an arithmetic/logic unit, but lacks the memory and I/O interface circuitry needed to make a complete computer. The microcomputer is thus a microprocessor chip supported by appropriate memory devices and I/O chips.

These definitions are not as clear-cut as they may seem. LSI technology is constantly developing new devices that tend to incorporate more and more functions on one chip. There are already available from several manufacturers devices called *single-chip microcomputers*, which contain a CPU, a nominal amount of RAM and ROM, and some I/O circuitry all on a single chip. These single-chip μCs contain all the elements needed to function as a complete μC, although they sometimes require additional memory and I/O support chips to expand their capabilities.

4.2 WHY μPs AND μCs?

When the first single-chip μPs were introduced a few years ago, it was difficult to foresee the tremendous impact these devices would have on the creation of new products. But designers have rapidly become aware of the capabilities and versatility of these devices. Microprocessors are being utilized in new products in place of *random logic*; random logic refers to conventional logic designs using flip-flops, gates, counters, registers, and other medium-scale integration (MSI) functions. For instance, a traffic-light controller that previously required 200 TTL chips can now be built with 12 chips using a μP system costing less than $250.

There are several fundamental reasons for the superiority of μP-based designs over random logic designs:

1. Fewer IC packages, printed-circuit boards, and connectors, thereby reducing assembly costs.

2. Greater reliability, owing to the decreased number of IC interconnections.

3. Lower power requirements, making power supply design easier.

4. Simpler system testing, evaluation, and redesign. Since μP-based equipment operates under the control of a program in memory (usually ROM), its operation is easily modified by simply changing the program (replacing or reprogramming the ROM). It is easier to change the *software* in such a system than to change the wiring in a random logic system.

5. Since product features can be added to μP-based equipment by adding to the software, manufacturers are increasing the capabililies and value of their products. For example, makers of μP-controlled cash registers are adding automatic tax computation by putting extra steps into the program stored in ROM if the tax rate changes, the ROM can be replaced or reprogrammed to take care of the change.

Despite these advantages, μPs and μCs cannot compete with random logic in areas where high speed is required. Even those μPs which utilize high-speed bipolar technology are at a speed disadvantage because of the sequential nature of programmed computer control. μCs perform operations one at a time in anywhere from 0.1 to 20 microseconds (μs) per operation; in random logic systems many operations can be performed in parallel (simultaneously). Of course, μPs can be utilized in those portions of high-speed systems where speed is not critical.

Typical Applications

In a typical application a μC receives *input* information or data, executes a sequence of instructions which somehow operates on or *processes* this input information, and then provides *output* information or data. The input and output operations, of course, involve interfacing with the outside world, while the processing function is done inside the μC under the control of a program stored in memory (RAM or ROM).

For example, in a μC-controlled engine status display system for an automobile (Fig. 4.2A), the *input* information consists of engine parameters such as temperature, oil pressure, and fuel consumption rate. Each of these physical quantities is converted to an electrical quantity by some type of transducer. The electrical quantities are then converted into a digital form to be inputted to the μC. The μC then *processes* the input data (puts them into the correct format to be displayed) and then *outputs* the formatted data to the display panel.

Another example is a μC-controlled electric oven (Fig. 4.2B). Here

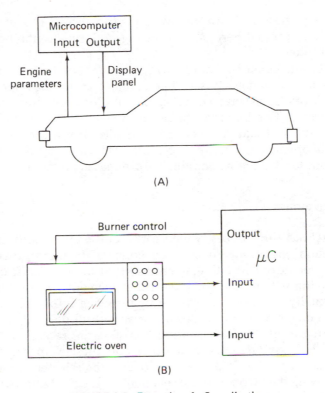

FIGURE 4.2 Examples of μC applications.

input information is entered by the user via a keyboard to tell the μC the desired cooking temperature and cooking time. The μC responds to this input information by executing a program which generates an *output* signal to control the oven burners for the desired temperature and time duration. During this control process, the oven temperature is transduced to electrical and then digital form and serves as another μC *input*. The temperature input allows the μC to compare the actual oven temperature with the desired temperature in order to properly control the burners.

4.3 TYPICAL μC STRUCTURE

We are now prepared to take a more detailed look at μC organization. The many possible μC structures are essentially the same in principle, although they vary as to the size of the data and address buses, and the types of control signals they use.

To provide the clearest means for learning the principles of μC operation, it is necessary to choose a single type of μC structure and study it in detail. Once a solid understanding of this typical μC is obtained, it will be relatively easy to learn about any other type. The μC structure we have chosen to present here, shown in Fig. 4.3, represents the most common one in use today.

The diagram shows the basic elements of an 8-bit microcomputer system and the various buses that connect them together. Although this diagram looks somewhat complex, it still does not show all the details of the μC system. For the time being, however, it will be sufficient for our purposes. We will add the pertinent details after a thorough discussion of the overall operation. Examine this diagram carefully and try to get as much information from it as possible before reading further.

The Bus System

The μC has three buses, which carry all the information and signals involved in system operation. These buses connect the microprocessor (CPU) to each of the memory and I/O elements so that data and information can flow between the μP and any of these other elements. In other words, the CPU is continually involved in sending or receiving information to or from a location in memory, an input device, or an output device.*

In the μC, all information transfers are referenced to the CPU. When the CPU is sending data to another computer element, it is called a WRITE operation and the CPU is WRITING into the selected element. When the CPU is receiving data from another element, it is called a READ operation and the CPU is READING from the selected element. It is very important to realize that the terms READ and WRITE always refer to operations performed by the CPU.

The buses involved in all the data transfers have functions described as follows:

1. *Address bus.* This is a *unidirectional* bus, because information flows over it in only one direction, from the CPU to the memory or I/O elements. The CPU alone can place logic levels on the 16 lines of the address bus, thereby generating $2^{16} = 65,536$ different possible addresses. Each of these addresses corresponds to one memory location or one I/O element. For example, address $20A0_{16}$ might be a location in RAM or ROM where an 8-bit word is stored, or it might be an 8-bit buffer register that is part of the interface circuitry for a keyboard input device.

   When the CPU wants to communicate with (READ or WRITE), a certain memory location or I/O device, it places the appropriate

---

*In some μC systems, it is possible for I/O devices to send data directly to or receive data directly from memory without the CPU being involved. This type of operation is called *direct memory access* (DMA) and will be discussed later.

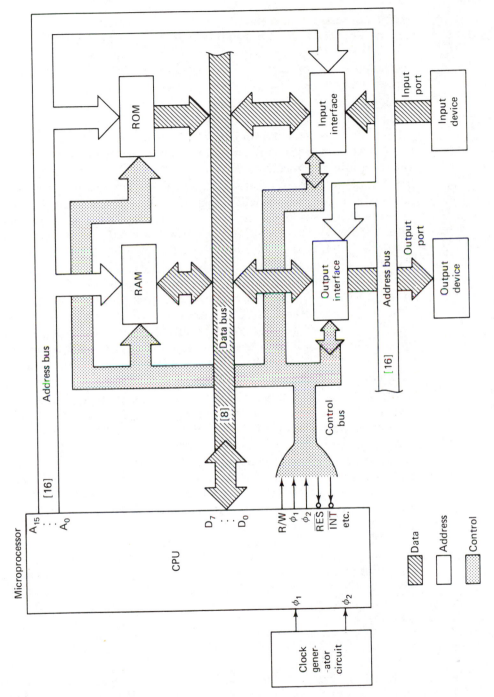

FIGURE 4.3 Typical 8-bit μC structure.

133

16-bit address code on its 16 address pin outputs, A_0 through A_{15}, and on to the address bus. These address bits are then *decoded* to select the desired memory location or I/O device. This decoding process usually requires decoder circuitry not shown on this diagram but which will be introduced later.

2. *Data bus.* This is a bidirectional bus, because data can flow to or from the CPU. The CPU's eight data pins, D_0 through D_7, can be either inputs or outputs, depending on whether the CPU is performing a READ or a WRITE operation. During a READ operation they act as inputs and receive data that has been placed on the data bus by the memory or I/O element selected by the address code on the address bus. During a WRITE operation the CPU's data pins act as outputs and place data on the data bus which is then sent to the selected memory or I/O element. In all cases, the transmitted data words are 8 bits long because the CPU handles 8-bit data words, making this an 8-bit μC.

In some microprocessors, the data pins are used to transmit other information in addition to data (e.g., address bits or CPU status information). That is, the data pins are time-shared or *multiplexed*, which means that special control signals must be generated by the CPU to tell the other elements exactly what is on the data bus at a particular time. We will not concern ourselves with this type of operation for the time being.

3. *Control bus.* This is the set of signals that is used to synchronize the activities of the separate μC elements. Some of these control signals, such as R/W, are signals the CPU sends to the other elements to tell them what type of operation is currently in progress. The I/O elements can send control signals to the CPU. An example is the RESET input of the CPU, which, when driven LOW, causes the CPU to reset to a particular starting state. Another example is the CPU's interrupt input (INT), used by I/O devices to get the attention of the CPU when it is performing other tasks.

The control bus signals will vary widely from one μC to another. There are certain control signals that all μCs use, but there are also many control signals that are peculiar to the μP upon which the μC is based. We will include only the essential control signals in our initial discussion and then add the more specialized ones as they are needed.

Timing Signals

The most important signals on the control bus are the system clock signals that generate the time intervals during which all system operations take place. Different μCs use different kinds of clock signals, depending on the type of μP being used. Some μPs, such as MOS Technology's 6502 and Zilog's Z-80, do not require an external clock generating circuit. A crystal or *RC* network connected to the appropriate μP pins sets the operating frequency for the clock signals, which are generated on the μP chip. Other μPs, such as Intel's 8080A and Motorola's 6800, require an external circuit to generate the clock signals needed by the CPU and the other μC elements. These manufacturers often provide a special clock-generator chip designed to be used with their μP.

Many of the currently popular μPs (8080, 6800, 6502) use a two-phase clock system with nonoverlapping pulses such as those shown in Fig. 4.4. Other widely used μPs (Z-80, RCA 1802) operate from a single clock signal. In our subsequent discussions, we will use the two-phase clock system. The two clock phases, ϕ_1 and ϕ_2, are always part of the control bus. Other timing signals, derived from ϕ_1 and ϕ_2, are sometimes generated by the CPU and become part of the control bus.

I/O Ports

During the execution of a program, the CPU is constantly READING or WRITING into memory. The program may also call on the CPU to READ from one of the input devices or WRITE into one of the output devices. Although the diagram of the 8-bit μC (repeated in Fig. 4.5) only shows one input and one output device, there can be any number of each tied to the μC bus system. Each I/O device is normally connected to the μC bus system through some type of interface circuit. The function of the interface is to make the μC and the device compatible so that data can be easily passed between them. The interface is needed whenever the I/O device uses different signal levels, signal timing, or signal format than the μC.

For example, a typical input device is the standard teletypewriter unit (abbreviated TTY), which sends ASCII-coded information to the computer in *serial* fashion (1 bit at a time over a single line). The μC, however, accepts data from the data bus at 8 *parallel* bits. Thus, an interface circuit is used to convert the TTY's serial signal to an 8-bit parallel data word.

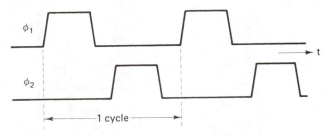

FIGURE 4.4 Two-phase clock system.

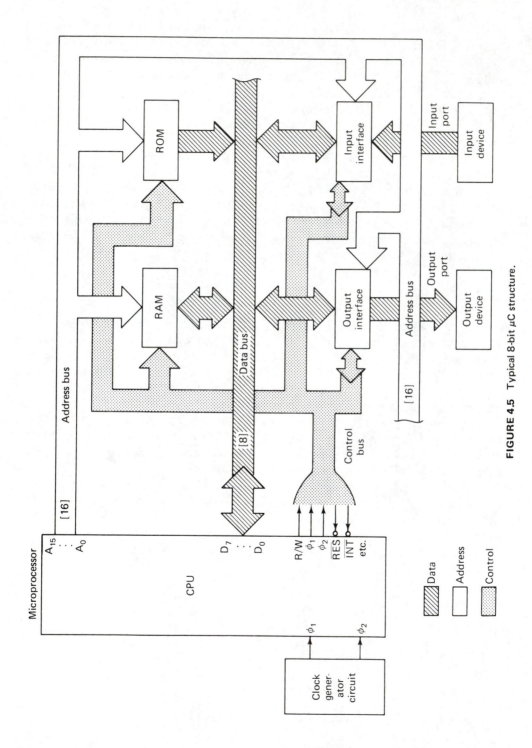

FIGURE 4.5 Typical 8-bit μC structure.

It was mentioned during the discussion of the address bus that the CPU places a 16-bit address on this bus to select a certain memory location or a certain I/O device. This means that each I/O device has a specific address just like any location in memory. In many μCs, the CPU does not distinguish between memory and I/O, and it communicates with both in the same way, using the same control signals. This method is called *memory-mapped I/O*. Other μCs use separate control signals and separate address decoders for I/O. This is called *isolated I/O*. We will concentrate mainly on the memory-mapped I/O technique, since it is the most common and has several advantages over the isolated I/O technique.

Although I/O devices are treated like memory locations, they are significantly different than memory in some respects. One big difference is that I/O devices can have the capability to *interrupt* the μC while it is executing a program. What this means is that an I/O device can send a signal to the μP chip's INTERRUPT ($\overline{\text{INT}}$) input to tell the CPU that it wishes to communicate with it. The CPU will then suspend execution of the program it is currently working on and will perform the appropriate operation with the interrupting I/O device. RAM and ROM do not normally have interrupting capability. Much more will be said about interrupts in subsequent material.

4.4 READ AND WRITE OPERATIONS

We are now ready to take a more detailed look at how the μP communicates with the other μC elements. Remember, the μP is the CPU and contains all the control and arithmetic/logic circuitry needed to execute a program of instructions stored in RAM or ROM. The CPU is continually performing READ and WRITE operations as it executes a program. It fetches each instruction from memory with a READ operation. After interpreting the instruction, it may have to perform a READ operation to obtain the operand from memory, or it may have to WRITE data into memory. In some cases, the instruction may call for the CPU to READ data from an input device (such as a keyboard or TTY) or to WRITE data into an output device (such as an LED display or a magnetic-tape cassette).

The Read Operation

The following steps take place during a READ operation:

1. The CPU generates the proper logic level on its R/W line for initiating a READ operation. Normally, R/W = 1 for READ. The R/W line is part of the control bus and goes to all the memory and I/O elements.

2. Simultaneously, the CPU places the 16-bit address code onto the address bus to select the particular memory location or I/O device which the CPU wants to receive data from.

3. The selected memory or I/O element places an 8-bit word on the data bus. All nonselected memory and I/O elements will not affect the data bus, because their *tristate* outputs will be in the disabled (high-Z) condition.

4. The CPU receives the 8-bit word from the data bus on its data pins, D_0 through D_7. These data pins act as inputs whenever R/W = 1. This 8-bit word is then latched into one of the CPU's internal registers, such as the Accumulator.

This sequence can be better understood with the help of a timing diagram showing the interrelationship between the signals on the various buses (see Fig. 4.6). Everything is referenced to the ϕ_1 and ϕ_2 clock signals. The complete READ operation occurs in one clock cycle. This is typically 1 μs for MOS microprocessors. The leading edge of ϕ_1 initiates the CPU's generation of the proper R/W and address signals. After a short delay, typically 100 ns for a MOS μP, the R/W line goes HIGH and the address bus holds the new address code (point 1 on timing diagram). Note that the address bus waveform shows both possible transitions (LOW to HIGH and HIGH to LOW) because some of the 16 address lines will be changing in one direction while others will be changing in the opposite direction.

During the ϕ_2 pulse, the selected memory or I/O device is enabled (point 2) and it proceeds to put its data word on the data bus. Prior to this, the data bus is in its high-Z state, since no device connected to it has been enabled. At some point during the ϕ_2 pulse, the data on the data bus become stable (point 3). Again, both possible data line transitions are shown on the diagram. The delay between the start of the ϕ_2 pulse and the data bus stabilizing depends on the speed of the memory and I/O elements. For memory this delay would be its *access time* (Chapter 2). On the falling edge of ϕ_2, the data on the data bus are latched into the CPU (point 4). Clearly, then, the memory and I/O devices must be capable of putting data on the bus prior to the falling edge of ϕ_2 or proper transfer to the CPU will not occur. Thus, it is necessary to ensure that these devices have a speed compatible with the μC clock frequency.

EXAMPLE 4.1   A certain type of PROM has an access time specified as 750 ns (typical) and 1 μs (maximum). Can it be used with a μC that has a clock frequency of 1 MHz?

Solution: No, with a clock frequency of 1 MHz, the ϕ_2 pulse duration will be less than 500 ns. Thus, the PROM would have to have an access time of less than 500 ns for proper data transfer to the CPU.

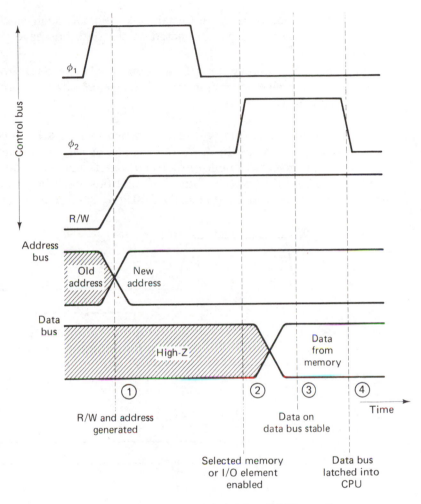

FIGURE 4.6 Typical μC timing for a READ operation.

The Write Operation

The following steps occur during a WRITE operation:

1. The CPU generates the proper logic level on the R/W line for initiating a WRITE operation. Normally, R/W = 0 for WRITE.
2. Simultaneously, the CPU issues the 16-bit address code onto the address bus.
3. The CPU then places an 8-bit word on the data bus via its data pins D_0 through D_7, which are now acting as outputs. This 8-bit word

typically comes from an internal CPU register, such as the Accumulator. All other devices connected to the data bus have their outputs disabled.

4. The selected memory or I/O element takes the data from the data bus. All nonselected memory and I/O elements will not have their inputs enabled.

This sequence has the timing diagram shown in Fig. 4.7. Once again, the leading edge of ϕ_1 initiates the R/W and address bus signals (point 1). During the ϕ_2 pulse, the selected memory or I/O device is enabled (point 2) and the CPU places its data on the data bus. The data-bus levels become stabilized a short time into the ϕ_2 pulse (typically 100 ns). These data are then written

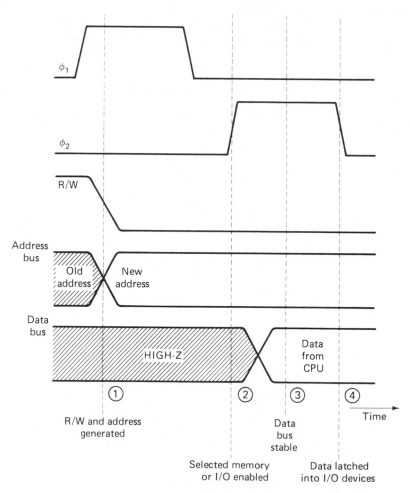

FIGURE 4.7 Typical μC timing for a WRITE operation.

into the selected memory location while ϕ_2 is high. If an I/O device has been selected, it usually latches the data from the data bus on the falling edge of ϕ_2 (point 4).

The READ and WRITE operations encompass most of the μC activity that takes place outside the CPU. The following example illustrates.

EXAMPLE 4.2 Below is a short program which is stored in memory locations 0020_{16} to 0029_{16} of an 8-bit μC. Note that since each word is one byte (8 bits), it takes two successive bytes to represent a 16-bit operand address code. Determine the total number of READ and WRITE operations which the μC will perform as it executes this program.

Memory Address (Hex)	Memory Word (Hex)	Symbolic Code	Description
0020	49	LDA	LOAD Accumulator (ACC) with X
0021	50		⌈Address of⌉
0022	01		⌊operand X⌋
0023	7E	ADD	ADD Y to contents of ACC
0024	51		⌈Address of⌉
0025	01		⌊operand Y⌋
0026	B2	STA	STORE ACC contents
0027	52		⌈Address where ACC⌉
0028	01		⌊will be stored⌋
0029	EF	HLT	HALT operation

Solution: The CPU begins executing the program by READING the contents of memory location 0020. The word stored there (49) is taken into the CPU and is interpreted as an instruction op code. (In other words, the CPU *always* interprets the first word of a program as an instruction and the programmer must *always* adhere to this format.) The CPU decodes this op code to determine the operation to be performed and to determine if an operand address follows the op code. In this case, an operand address is required and is stored in the next two successive bytes in the program. Thus, the CPU must READ locations 0021 and 0022 to obtain the address of data X. Once this address (0150) has been read into the CPU, the CPU proceeds to execute the LDA instruction by READING memory location 0150 and putting its contents into the Accumulator. Thus, the complete execution of this first instruction requires *four* separate READ operations: one for the op code, two for the address, and one for the LDA operation.

Four READ operations are needed for the second instruction, which begins at 0023. This instruction also uses a two-byte operand address and requires reading the contents of this address for transfer to the CPU's arithmetic unit.

The third instruction begins at 0026 and uses a two-byte operand address. The CPU uses *three* READ operations to obtain these. However, the instruction STA calls for a WRITE operation whereby the CPU transfers the contents of the Accumulator to memory location 0152.

The final instruction at 0029 is simply an op code with no operand address. The CPU READS this op code (EF), decodes it, and then halts any further operations.

The total number of READ operations, then, is *twelve* and the total number of WRITE operations is *one*.

4.5 ADDRESS-ALLOCATION TECHNIQUES

We mentioned earlier that some type of decoding circuitry is needed to help the CPU select the memory location or I/O device which it is trying to READ from or WRITE into. When the CPU places a 16-bit address on the address bus, we want it to activate one and only one memory location or I/O device. The actual decoding circuitry depends on what type of memory chips are used for RAM and ROM. As we saw in Section 2.24, the decoders are used to drive the chip select inputs of the various memory chips so that only the chip or group of chips that are storing the desired word will be activated. Before expanding further on the decoding circuits, we will say a few words about memory organization.

The ROM portion of an 8-bit μC memory is usually implemented in single chips which store a certain number of 8-bit words per chip. For example, a μC might have 1024 words (1K) of ROM. This could be implemented on a single 1024×8 ROM chip or it might be on four 256×8 ROM chips. On the other hand, RAMs require more logic on each chip since they can be written into as well as read from. Thus, typically, several RAM chips have to combine to handle 8-bit words. Figure 4.8 shows two common methods for implementing 1K of RAM.

In Fig. 4.8A, eight 1024×1 RAM chips are used with each chip storing 1 bit of each word. For example, RAM 7 contains the MSBs and RAM 0 contains the LSBs of each of the 1024 words. This complete arrangement is called a memory *module*. In this case, it is a 1024-word module. In a module, all the chips are selected simultaneously, as evidenced by the common line going to the Chip Select (CS) inputs.

In Fig. 4.8B, we are using 256×4 RAM chips. Two of these chips are combined to form a 256×8 module so that a total of four 256×8 modules are implemented with the eight chips shown. Each module has a separate *Module Select* input and only one module is selected at one time for READ or WRITE.

Memory Space

The total number of addresses that a CPU can select using a 16-bit address code is 65,536. In hexadecimal, these addresses range from 0000 to FFFF and constitute the μC's total *memory space*. Rarely is this total memory

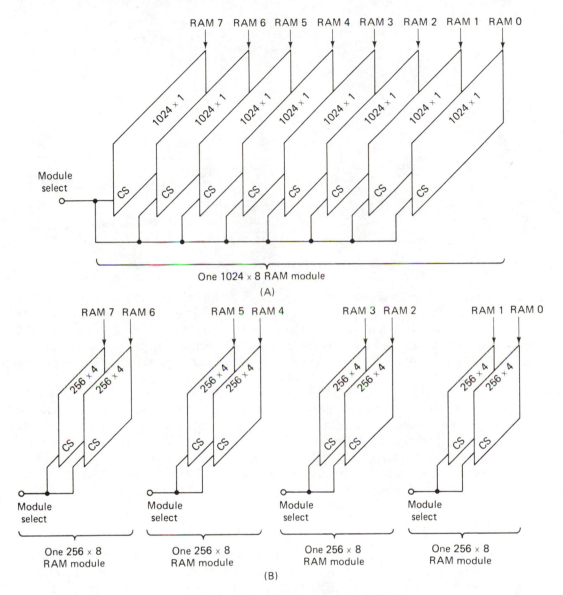

FIGURE 4.8 Two typical ways of implementing 1024 8-bit words of RAM.

space used in a typical microcomputer. A typical situation is illustrated in Fig. 4.9, where we see how the total memory space might be allocated among RAM, ROM, and I/O devices.

As shown, hex addresses 0000 through 03FF have been allocated for RAM. This is a total of 1024_{10} address locations. Addresses F000 through F7FF have been allocated for I/O devices, for a total of 2048_{10} (2K) ad-

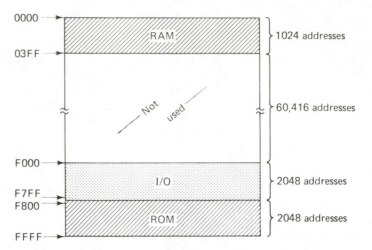

FIGURE 4.9 Typical memory-space allocation in a small μC.

dresses. This does not mean that 2048 different I/O devices are used with this μC, because, as we shall see, it is convenient to use a range of addresses, rather than one address, to select a particular I/O device. Addresses F800 through FFFF are used for ROM to store permanent programs and data, a total of 2048_{10} address locations. This leaves addresses 0400 through EFFF which are not being used in this example.

The actual address allocations for RAM, ROM, and I/O are chosen by the μC designer but also depend to some extent on the μP being used. For example, when the 8080A μP is reset by a low level on its $\overline{\text{RES}}$ input, its internal Program Counter (PC) goes to 0000_{16} and that is where the μP takes its first instruction from. This, of course, means that the lower-numbered addresses, beginning with 0000, have to be ROM or RAM program storage rather than data storage.

Memory Pages

Many μCs divide their 65,536 available addresses into 256 blocks of 256 addresses. Each of these blocks is called a *page*. Figure 4.10 shows how a μC's memory space can be organized as pages.* Note that each page covers a range of 256 addresses. For example, page 00 includes address locations 0000 through 00FF, and page 69 includes address locations 6900 through 69FF. Also, note that the page number is the same as the first two hex digits of the addresses on that page. For example, all addresses starting with 69 are on page 69.

Using this page organization, we can think of each address as consisting

*Some μCs use a different number of addresses per page.

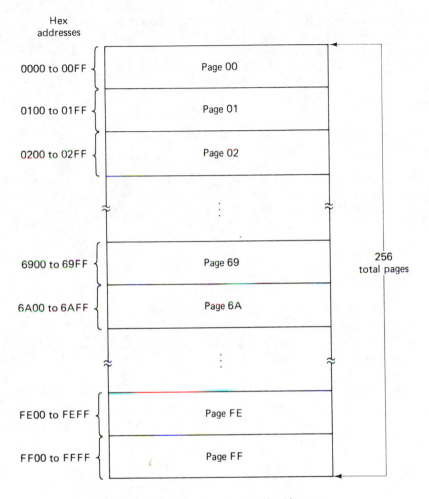

FIGURE 4.10 Memory space organized into pages.

of a page number and a word number. To illustrate, consider address 1E66:

$$\underbrace{1 \qquad E}_{\substack{\text{Page} \\ \text{number}}} \quad \underbrace{6 \qquad 6}_{\substack{\text{Word on} \\ \text{that page}}}$$

The first two digits specify page 1E and the last two digits specify word 66 on that page.

EXAMPLE 4.3 Refer to the typical memory-space allocations given in Fig. 4.9. How many pages have been allocated for RAM? Repeat for I/O and ROM.

Solution: The RAM occupies addresses 0000 through 03FF; this includes pages 00, 01, 02, and 03 for a total of *four* pages.

The I/O uses pages F0, F1, F2, F3, F4, F5, F6, and F7 for a total of *eight* pages.

The ROM occupies pages F8, F9, FA, FB, FC, FD, FE, and FF for a total of *eight* pages.

EXAMPLE 4.4   Refer to Fig. 4.8 and determine how many pages of memory can be stored in each module.

Solution: The 1024 × 8 module in Fig. 4.8A can store *four* pages of memory because one page is 256 words. The 256 × 8 modules in Fig. 4.8B can each store *one* page of memory.

4.6   ADDRESS-DECODING TECHNIQUES

We are now ready to develop the address-decoding circuitry that is needed to select the single memory location or I/O device which the CPU is addressing. There are several approaches to the decoding problem, which are all basically the same. Rather than showing several variations of decoding logic, we have chosen to develop one method whose concepts and ideas are applicable to all decoding schemes. The approach we will use is straightforward and utilizes page-organized addressing. We will develop the complete decoding logic for an 8-bit μC which uses 16-bit addresses and whose memory-space allocation is given in Fig. 4.11.

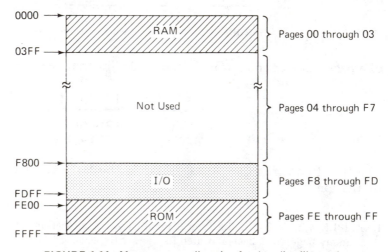

FIGURE 4.11   Memory-space allocation for decoding illustration.

Decoding for RAM

Before we can develop the decoding logic for the RAM addresses, we have to choose the type of chip we want to use to implement the RAM. Since we are going to use a page-organized method, we will use the RAM modules of Fig. 4.8B, each of which can store one page. With a RAM address allocation of 0000 to 03FF, ranging over four pages, we will need eight 256×4 RAM chips such as Intel's 2112. This chip has eight address inputs, a R/W input, a Chip Select input, and four data I/O lines.

The complete decoding circuitry for the four pages of RAM is shown in Fig. 4.12. Note the following points:

1. Two RAM chips constitute a one-page module storing 256 8-bit words, with each RAM contributing 4 bits of each word.

2. The CPU R/W control output is connected to each RAM chip's R/W input. Of course, only one RAM module will actually READ or WRITE, depending on which one has its CS input activated.

3. The CPU's eight higher-order address lines, A_{15} through A_8, are fed to the decoding logic, which includes a 3-line-to-8-line decoder such as the 74138. This decoder takes the 3-bit binary input code, CBA, and activates the corresponding output to select the memory page module that is being addressed.

4. The CPU's eight lower-order address lines, A_7 through A_0, are connected to the address inputs of *each* RAM chip. These address lines select the memory word from the selected page module.

EXAMPLE 4.5 Assume that the CPU is performing a WRITE operation into memory location $02A5_{16}$. It places a low level on R/W and generates the address code at its address outputs. This address code in binary is

$$02A5_{16} = 0000 \mid 0010 \mid 1010 \mid 0101$$
$$\quad\quad\quad\ \ A_{15} \quad\ \ A_8\ \ A_7 \quad\quad A_0$$

The six MSBs of this address code produce a Low level at the NAND-gate output which is applied to the decoder's C input. Address lines A_9 and A_8 place a 1 and 0 at the decoder's B and A inputs, respectively. Thus, the decoder input binary code is CBA = 010, which produces a Low at decoder output 2. The Low drives the PAGE 2 SELECT line to enable RAMs 5 and 6.

The eight lower-order address lines select address 10100101 from page 2 as the location the CPU will write into. The CPU places its data on the data bus and writes them into this location during ϕ_2. Notice that the decoder is not enabled until ϕ_2, since ϕ_2 drives its CHIP ENABLE (CE) input. This is done to ensure that the levels on the address lines have stabilized before the memory is activated. Otherwise, it is possible that one or more RAM locations might accidently get activated as the address lines are changing from the old address code to the new address code.

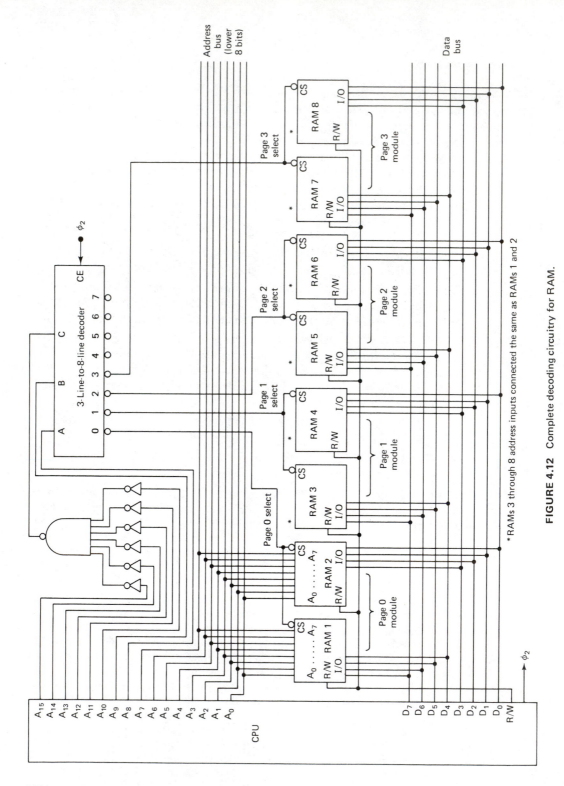

FIGURE 4.12 Complete decoding circuitry for RAM.

*RAMs 3 through 8 address inputs connected the same as RAMs 1 and 2

148

This example should clearly show how the decoding circuitry selects the exact address specified by the CPU. The trick here is to notice that we are only using address locations 0000 through 03FF for RAM. For this address range, address lines A_{15} through A_{10} will all be LOW, so the inverters and NAND gate will produce a LOW at decoder input C. Address lines A_9 and A_8, then, actually select the page module being addressed. It should be obvious that any combination on lines A_{15} through A_{10} other than all LOWS will produce a HIGH at decoder input C. This prevents outputs 0 through 3 of the decoder from being activated. Decoder outputs 4 through 7 are not used.

Decoding for ROM and I/O

Referring to Fig. 4.11, we see that addresses F800 through FDFF (pages F8 through FD) are reserved for I/O and addresses FE00 through FFFF (pages FE and FF) are ROM. Since the I/O and ROM allocations are adjacent, we can develop the decoding circuitry for both simultaneously. First, we must specify the type of ROM chip we want to use. A good choice would be a 256 × 8 ROM such as Intel's 1702A PROM. Two of these are needed to store two pages.

As far as I/O is concerned, let as assume that the μC is connected to *six* different peripheral devices — three *input* devices and *three* output devices. Each device will have an interface circuit which connects it to the μC. Since six pages have been allocated in memory space for I/O, we can assign one page per interface circuit. In other words, we can assign all addresses in page FD to interface 1, all addresses in page FC to interface 2, and so on. The reason for doing this is that it only requires decoding the eight higher-order address lines and thereby minimizes I/O address decoding circuitry. The following table summarizes the I/O organization we will be using.

Interface	Type	Addresses
1	Output	FD00 through FDFF (page FD)
2	Output	FC00 through FCFF (page FC)
3	Output	FB00 through FBFF (page FB)
4	Input	FA00 through FAFF (page FA)
5	Input	F900 through F9FF (page F9)
6	Input	F800 through F8FF (page F8)

The complete decoding circuitry for I/O and ROM is shown in Fig. 4.13. Note the following points:

1. Two 256 × 8 ROM chips are used, one per page.

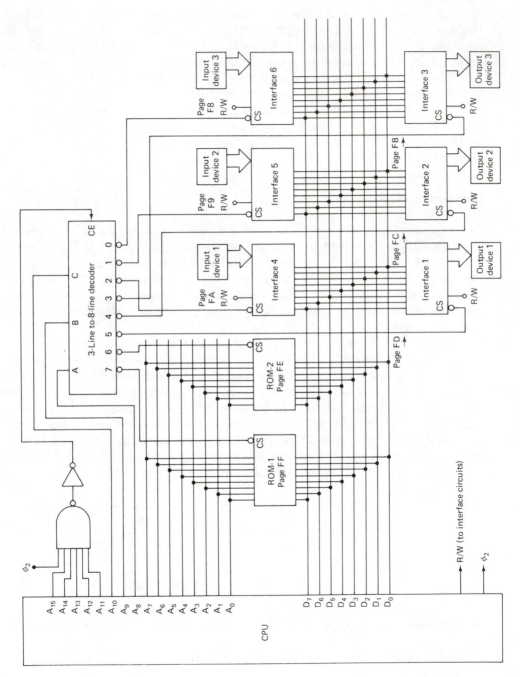

FIGURE 4.13 ROM and I/O selection circuitry.

2. Interface circuits 1, 2, and 3 are used for output devices, while inter- face circuits 4, 5, and 6 are used for input devices. Typically, the six interface circuits would all be different. They could be as simple as buffer circuits or FF registers, or as complex as an LSI interface chip such as a UART (e.g., used for teletypewriter or tape cassette). For now, however, we will use the general symbol shown and will not be concerned with the details of the interface circuits until a little later.

3. The CPU's eight higher-order address lines go to the decoding logic, which includes a 3-to-8 decoder. This decoder generates eight PAGE SELECT outputs, only one of which will be activated, depending on the address code.

4. The CPU's eight lower-order address lines are connected to the ad- dress inputs of each ROM to select one word from the selected page.

5. The CPU's R/W line is not connected to the ROM chips. A ROM does not have a R/W input because it cannot be written into. The R/W line is, however, connected to the interface circuits. There are two reasons for this. First, some interface circuits are capable of be- ing written into or read from. For example, it may be an output interface through which the CPU can both send data to an output device (WRITE) and receive status information from the output de- vice (READ).

The second reason is to avoid accidental conflicts on the data bus. To illustrate, interface circuit 4 is selected by any address on page FA whenever the CPU wants to read data from input device 1. Suppose that through some programming error the CPU is perform- ing a WRITE operation on address FA00. This address will select interface circuit 4 and will cause data from input device 1 to be placed on the data bus. However, since the CPU is performing a WRITE operation, a data word from one of its internal registers will also be placed on the data bus. These two different sets of logic levels on the data bus can cause damage to the CPU chip or the in- terface chip. This problem is avoided by using the R/W line from the CPU to disable interface circuit 4 during a CPU WRITE operation (R/W = 0).

EXAMPLE 4.6 Describe the process by which the decoding circuitry selects ROM ad- dress FE77.

Solution: The CPU places FE77 on the address bus. In binary, this address code is

$$FE77_{16} = 1111 \mid 1110 \mid 0111 \mid 0111$$
$$\phantom{FE77_{16} = }A_{15} A_8 \; A_7 A_0$$

The five MSBs, A_{15} through A_{11}, produce a Low level at the NAND-gate output (when $\phi_2 = 1$), which is inverted and applied to the decoder's chip enable to activate the decoder. Address lines A_{10}, A_9, and A_8 produce a code of 110 at the decoder inputs to activate decoder output 6. The Low at output 6 drives the Page FE Select line to enable ROM-2.

The lower-order address lines (A_7 through A_0) select location 01110111 in ROM-2 as the actual location whose word is placed on the data bus via ROM-2's data output pins. This word does not appear on the data bus until ϕ_2 because ϕ_2 has to be High for the decoder to be activated. During ϕ_2, the CPU takes the word from the data bus and places it in one of its internal registers.

EXAMPLE 4.7 Describe the process by which the CPU writes a word into output device 2.

Solution: The Chip Select input of interface circuit 2 is driven by decoder output 4, which is the Page FC Select line. This means that any address whose first two hex digits are FC will select interface circuit 2 and hence output device 2. Thus, to write data into output device 2, the CPU must set R/W = 0 and generate an address of the form FCXX, where XX can be any hex digits. Then, it must place the word to be written on the data bus, from there it is transmitted by interface circuit 2 to output device 2.

These examples showed how the decoding circuitry selects the ROM location or I/O device specified by the CPU. The main point used in designing this circuitry is that for all addresses in the range F800 through FFFF, address lines A_{15} through A_{11} will be High. This condition produces a High at the CE input of the decoder. Address lines A_{10}, A_9, and A_8, then, select the appropriate decoder output. Notice that any combination on lines A_{15} through A_{11} other than all Highs will produce a Low at CE, thereby disabling all decoder outputs (all High) so that no ROM or I/O is selected.

Complete Decoding Circuitry

The complete decoding circuitry for our example microcomputer is obtained by combining the circuits of Fig. 4.12 and 4.13. The resultant circuit includes two NAND gates, seven inverters, two 3-line-to-8-line decoders, eight 256×4 RAMs, two 256×8 ROMs, and six different interface circuits. Of course, if the amount of RAM or ROM memory is to be expanded at a later time, the necessary decoder circuitry must be added. Many μC manufacturers include enough decoder circuitry on their memory boards so that future memory expansion only requires adding the necessary RAM or ROM chips.

Buffering the Address and Data Lines

Looking at Figs. 4.12 and 4.13, you will notice that all of the CPU's address lines are driving two or more loads. This will usually require some buffer circuits, especially if the CPU is a MOS device and the loads are TTL. For example, CPU address line A_{15} is driving an inverter (Fig. 4.12) and a NAND gate (Fig. 4.13). Typically, logic gates and decoders are TTL devices because of their speed and availability. If the CPU is MOS, its outputs will normally be capable of driving only one TTL load. Thus, A_{15} cannot drive both TTL loads directly. The same is true for A_{14} through A_8. These eight address lines must, therefore, be coupled to their loads through some type of buffer circuit (such as a 74126 or 8T97) which can easily drive several TTL loads. This is illustrated in Fig. 4.14A for line A_{15}.

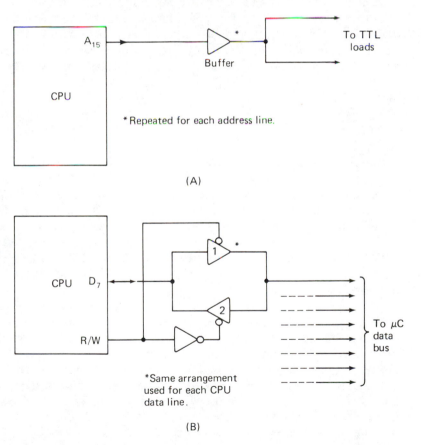

(A)

(B)

FIGURE 4.14 (A) Buffered address line; (B) bidirectional buffers for CPU data lines.

Address lines A_0 through A_7 are each driving eight RAM chips and two ROM chips. These memory chips are normally MOS devices, and so their inputs draw negligible current from the signal sources driving them. However, there is still a loading problem due to the capacitance present at each input [typically 2 to 5 picofarads (pF)]. The accumulated effect of these capacitances can drastically slow down the signals on the address bus lines and cause improper operation. For this reason, buffers should be used on all the address lines. The buffer circuits will have a very low output resistance so that they can drive capacitive loads without significant signal deterioration.

The same considerations apply for the CPU's data lines, D_0 through D_7. There is an important difference, however, because these lines are bidirectional. Figure 4.14B shows a common way to buffer these data lines using two tristate buffers. The R/W signal from the CPU is used to control which buffer is activated. For a WRITE operation R/W is LOW and buffer 1 is activated to allow data from the CPU data line on to the data bus. For a READ operation R/W is HIGH and buffer 2 is activated to allow data from the data bus into the CPU. Note that only one buffer is activated at any given time. This same arrangement is used for each CPU data line.

4.7 ISOLATED I/O

As mentioned earlier, the two basic methods by which the CPU can communicate with I/O devices are *memory-mapped I/O* and *isolated I/O*. The discussions thus far have concentrated on memory-mapped I/O, where the I/O devices are treated just like memory locations; that is, they have addresses just like memory, and the CPU uses the R/W control signal to control the direction of data transfer. The same instructions are used by the CPU to communicate with I/O devices as with RAM and ROM. In other words, for memory-mapped I/O the CPU makes no distinction between memory and I/O devices.

Some microprocessors, such as the 8080/8085 and Z-80, are designed to use isolated I/O techniques where the CPU treats memory and I/O devices separately, using different control signals for each. Figure 4.15 shows how the 8085 microprocessor performs isolated I/O. The 8085 uses *three* control signals to specify which operation is being performed. The signal $\overline{RD}$ is driven LOW by the μP for any read operation from memory or I/O. The $\overline{WR}$ line is driven LOW by the μP for any write operation from memory or I/O. The μP uses the IO/$\overline{M}$ line to specify whether memory or I/O is being communicated with; a HIGH specifies I/O, a LOW specifies memory.

The table in Fig. 4.15 shows the logic levels that the μP places on these

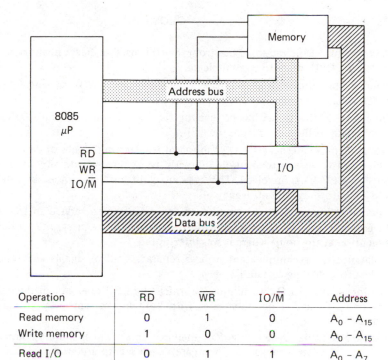

Operation	$\overline{RD}$	$\overline{WR}$	$IO/\overline{M}$	Address
Read memory	0	1	0	$A_0 - A_{15}$
Write memory	1	0	0	$A_0 - A_{15}$
Read I/O	0	1	1	$A_0 - A_7$
Write I/O	1	0	1	$A_0 - A_7$

FIGURE 4.15 Isolated I/O as implemented using the 8085 μP.

lines for each of the four possible operations. Note that only address lines A_0 through A_7 are used for I/O. This means that the μP can communicate with $2^8 = 256$ I/O devices. For example, when the μP wants to read from an input device, it generates $\overline{RD} = 0$, $\overline{WR} = 1$, $IO/\overline{M} = 1$, and places an 8-bit *device* address on the address bus. The I/O decoding circuitry decodes the device address to select the correct input device. The memory devices will not respond to the address bus since $IO/\overline{M} = 1$.

Since the $IO/\overline{M}$ line distinguishes between memory and I/O, the memory can use all the 65,536 addresses that are possible with 16 address lines. This is an advantage of isolated I/O over memory-mapped I/O. A disadvantage of isolated I/O is that special program instructions are required to perform I/O operations. The two most common are IN and OUT instructions. Memory-mapped I/O uses the same instructions for I/O and memory and does not require special instructions. In addition, memory-mapped I/O has the advantage of being able to use the same wide variety of instructions for I/O that are available for memory, thereby providing more programming flexibility.

GLOSSARY

Address Bus Unidirectional bus from the CPU used to select memory or I/O devices with which the CPU wants to communicate.

Control Bus Bidirectional bus carrying signals such as R/W, ϕ_1, and ϕ_2, which are used to synchronize the activities of separate μC elements.

Data Bus Bidirectional bus connecting the CPU to memory and I/O elements. This bus allows data to flow to or from the CPU.

Direct Memory Access (DMA) Method of transferring blocks of data which makes it possible for I/O devices to send data directly to or receive data directly from memory without the CPU being involved. This system significantly increases the rate of data transfer and, therefore, system efficiency.

Interrupt Suspension of normal program execution to service an I/O device that wants to communicate with the CPU. After servicing the request, the CPU resumes program execution at the point where it was interrupted.

Isolated I/O Technique that utilizes separate control signals and separate address decoders for selecting certain I/O devices.

Memory-Mapped I/O Technique by which the CPU does not distinguish between memory and I/O, and it communicates with both in the same way, using the same control signals.

Memory Module Arrangement of memory chips which share a common CHIP SELECT (CS) input. This arrangement is organized to set up a given word size for the μP being used.

Memory Page Block of memory spaces, typically 256 addresses. With 16 address bits, 256 such memory blocks are possible.

Microprocessor Typically, a single LSI chip that contains all the control and arithmetic circuits of the μC. It is the CPU portion of the μC.

Random Logic Circuits Conventional logic designs utilizing flip-flops, gates, counters, registers, and other medium-scale-integration (MSI) functions.

QUESTIONS AND PROBLEMS

Sections 4.1–4.3

4.1 Which of the following is an advantage which microcomputers have over minicomputers and large general-purpose computers?
   (a) easier to program
   (b) more computational capability
   (c) smaller, cheaper
   (d) faster speed

4.2 Which of the following is *not* an advantage that a microprocessor system has over hard-wired logic in performing a complex logic control function?
   (a) generally easier to design
   (b) operates at higher speed
   (c) is more flexible — can be modified more easily
   (d) uses fewer chips

4.3 The address bus is an example of a *bidirectional* bus which allows the μP to communicate with memory or I/O devices. True or false?

4.4 When I/O devices are treated like memory locations by the μP, it is referred to as:
   (a) isolated I/O
   (b) direct memory access
   (c) memory-mapped I/O
   (d) user-initiated I/O

4.5 Explain the difference between a *microprocessor* and a *microcomputer*.

4.6 What are the advantages of microprocessor-based designs over random logic designs? What is their main disadvantage?

4.7 Describe the functions of the three buses in a typical μC.

Sections 4.4 and 4.5

4.8 Which one of the following steps does *not* occur during the μP's READ operation?
   (a) The μP makes the R/W line = 1.
   (b) The μP places the 16-bit address code onto the address bus to select a particular memory location.
   (c) The μP places an 8-bit data word onto the data bus.
   (d) The selected memory or I/O element outputs become activated while all other memory or I/O elements will not be affected, since their tristate outputs will be in the disabled state.

4.9 Which one of the following steps does *not* occur during the μP's WRITE operation?
   (a) The μP makes the R/W line = 1.
   (b) The μP places a 16-bit address on the address bus.
   (c) The μP places an 8-bit data word onto the data bus.
   (d) The selected I/O or memory element takes the data from the data bus.

4.10 A μP places 1011 0101 0011 1110 onto the address bus. What *page* in memory is being accessed?
   (a) B53E   (b) 254   (c) 3E   (d) B5

4.11 Signals such as R/W, RESET, ϕ_2, and INT are part of the μC's:
   (a) peripheral bus   (c) control bus
   (b) address bus   (d) data bus

4.12 When a μC is performing a READ operation, the data are latched into the μP:
   (a) as soon as ϕ_1 goes high
   (b) as soon as the memory places the data on the data bus
   (c) on the falling edge of ϕ_2
   (d) as soon as R/W goes high

4.13 A certain μC has the following memory-space allocations:

   0000 to 07FF   ROM
   2000 to 3FFF   RAM
   CB00 to CFFF   I/O

   (a) How many ROM locations are these? (b) RAM locations?
   (c) How many different I/O devices can be addressed?

Sections 4.6 and 4.7

4.14 Why is ϕ_2 connected to the decoder in Fig. 4.12?

4.15 Modify the circuitry in Fig. 4.12 to include four more pages of RAM (pages 4 through 7). (*Hint:* The logic feeding decoder input C must be modified.)

4.16 Design the complete address decoding circuitry for a microcomputer that has the following address allocations:

RAM	0000 to 07FF using 1K $\times$ 4 RAM chips
ROM	2000 to 23FF using 256 $\times$ 8 ROM chips
I/O	C000 to C3FF for *four* different I/O devices

4.17 In some microcomputers it is not feasible to allocate one complete page of addresses to a single input/output device because the addresses might be required for future memory expansion. Change the I/O address requirements for Problem 4.16 to the following and design the necessary decoding logic:

I/O device 1	C000 to C03F
I/O device 2	C040 to C07F
I/O device 3	C080 to C0BF
I/O device 4	C0C0 to C0FF

4.18 Consider a complete microcomputer made up of the combined circuitry of Figs. 4.12 and 4.13. Assume that all the circuitry was on one printed-circuit (PC) board. While checking out the microcomputer operation, a technician finds that he can write into any RAM location and can read from any RAM location with no problem. However, he finds that whenever he tries to read from ROM-1 or ROM-2, he gets erroneous results, even after he replaces the ROM chips. He later determines that he can read correctly from ROM-1 (page FF) only if he removes RAMs 7 and 8 from the PC board, and he can read from ROM-2 (page FE) only if he removes RAMs 5 and 6.

Which of the following would be possible reasons for the malfunction observed by the technician?
(a) RAM chips 5 to 8 are damaged.
(b) Input C of the RAM decoder is shorted to ground.
(c) There is a break in the connection between address line A_{10} and the decoder in Fig. 4.13.
(d) The hex-inverter chip used in Fig. 4.12 has lost its connection to $+V_{cc}$.

4.19 Why is it necessary to buffer a microprocessor's data and address lines?

4.20 Describe the major differences between isolated I/O and memory-mapped I/O, giving their relative advantages and disadvantages. Which one is used in Figs. 4.12 and 4.13?

5

THE MICROPROCESSOR –
HEART OF THE MICROCOMPUTER

All microcomputers, though they vary in their architecture, have one element in common — the microprocessor chip. As we know, the μP functions as the central processing unit of the μC. In essence, the μP is the heart of the μC because its capabilities determine the capabilities of the μC. Its speed determines the maximum speed of the μC, its address and data pins determine the μC's memory capacity and word size, and its control pins determine the type of I/O interfacing that must be used.

The μP performs a large number of functions, including:

1. Providing timing and control signals for all elements of the μC.
2. Fetching instructions and data from memory.
3. Transferring data to and from I/O devices.
4. Decoding instructions.
5. Performing arithmetic and logic operations called for by instructions.
6. Responding to I/O-generated control signals such as RESET and INTERRUPT.

159

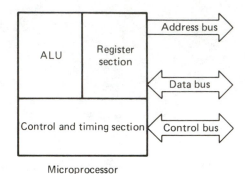

Microprocessor

FIGURE 5.1 Major functional areas of a μP chip.

The μP contains all the logic circuitry for performing these functions, but it should be kept in mind that a great deal of the μP's internal logic is not externally accessible. For example, we cannot apply an external signal to the μP chip to increment the Program Counter (PC). Instead, the μP elements are *software*-accessible. This means that we can affect the internal μP circuitry only by the *program* we put in memory for the μP to execute. This is what makes the μP so versatile and flexible — when we want to change the μP's operation, we simply change the program (e.g., by changing the ROMs that store the program). This is generally easier than rewiring hardware.

Since we must construct programs that tell the internal μP logic what to do, we need to become familiar with the internal μP structure, its characteristics, and its capabilities. The μP logic is extremely complex, but we can divide it into three areas: the register section, the control and timing section, and the ALU (see Fig. 5.1). Although there is some overlap among these three areas, for clarity we will consider them separately.

5.1 TIMING AND CONTROL SECTION

We will not discuss this part of the μP in too much detail for two reasons. First, it is the one area on the μP chip over which we have very little control. Second, we do not have to know the detailed structure of the timing and control section to develop useful programs for the μP.

The major function of this μP section is to fetch and decode instructions from program memory and then to generate the necessary control signals required by the ALU and register section for executing these instructions. The fetching and decoding functions correspond to the *instruction cycle*, and control-signal generation takes place during the *execution cycle*. Both these cycles were discussed in Chapter 3, and we need not elaborate on them further.

Control Bus Signals

The control section also generates *external* control signals that are sent to other μC elements as part of the system's control bus. We used some of these control bus signals in our description of the μC in Chapter 4, namely R/W and ϕ_2. In addition to generating output signals for the control bus, the μP control section also responds to control bus signals that are sent from other μC elements to the μP chip. The RESET and INT (INTERRUPT) mentioned in Chapter 4 are examples.

     Each μP has its own unique set of input and output control signals that are described in detail in the manufacturers' operation manuals. We will not attempt to define all of these here. Instead, we will describe some of the control bus signals that are common to several different microprocessors.

Reset   All μPs have this input. When this input is activated, most of the μP's internal registers are reset to 0. In many μPs, the program counter (PC) is reset to 0 so that the instruction stored at memory location 0000_{16} is the first to be executed. In some μPs, activating the RESET input does not clear the PC. Instead, the PC is loaded from two specific memory locations (such as FFFE and FFFF). In other words, upon RESET the address of the first instruction is taken from these memory locations (each one stores one byte of the 16-bit address). Usually, this starting address is stored in ROM and is often referred to as an *address vector*.

R/W   This μP output line informs the rest of the μC as to whether the μP is in a READ or WRITE operation. Some μPs use separate control lines, RD to indicate a READ operation and WR to indicate a WRITE operation.

MREQ (Memory Request)   This μP output indicates that a memory access is in progress.

IORQ (I/O Request)   A μP output which indicates that an I/O device is being accessed. Some μPs use this signal along with MREQ to distinguish between memory and I/O operations. This allows memory and I/O to use the same address space, because the IORQ and MREQ signals determine which one (I/O or memory) is enabled. This technique of treating I/O separately from memory is called *isolated I/O*.

Ready   This μP input is used by slow memory or I/O devices which cannot respond to a μP access request within one μP clock cycle. When the slow device is selected by the address decoding circuitry, it immediately sends a READY signal to the μP. In response, the μP suspends all its internal operations and enters what is called a WAIT state. It remains there until the device is ready to send or receive data, which the device so indicates by removing the READY signal.

Hold This μP input is used for direct memory access (DMA) operations which we will discuss later. When an external device activates this input, the μP finishes executing the instruction it is currently working on and then *floats* its address and data buses. This means that it disables its tristate data and address pins so that they are effectively disconnected from the μC buses. This allows other external devices to use the address and data buses as long as HOLD is active.

HLDA (Hold Acknowledge) This is an output signal which the μP generates to indicate to external logic that the μP is in a HOLD state and the data and address buses are available. A similar μP output is BA (buses available).

INT or IRQ (Interrupt Request) This is a μP input which is used by I/O devices to interrupt the execution of the current program and cause the μP to jump to a special program, called the *interrupt service routine*. The μP executes this special program, which normally involves servicing the interrupting device. When this execution is complete, the μP resumes execution of the program it had been working on when it was interrupted.

INTE (Interrupt Enable) This is a μP output that indicates to external devices whether or not the internal μP interrupt logic is enabled or disabled. If enabled (INTE = 1), the μP can be interrupted as described above. If disabled (INTE = 0), the μP will not respond to the INT or IRQ inputs. The state of INTE can be software-controlled. For example, a program can contain an instruction that makes INTE = 0 so that the interrupt operation is disabled.

NMI (Nonmaskable Interrupt) This is another μP interrupt input, but it differs from INT or IRQ in that its effect cannot be disabled. In other words, the proper signal on NMI will always interrupt the μP regardless of the interrupt enable status.

5.2 REGISTER SECTION

The most common operation that takes place *inside* the μP chip is the transfer of binary information from one register to another. The number and types of registers that a μP contains is a key part of its architecture and has a major effect on the programming effort required in a given application. The register structure of different μPs varies considerably from manufacturer to manufacturer. However, the basic functions performed by the various registers is essentially the same in all μPs. They are used to store data, addresses, instruction codes, and information on the status of various μP operations. Some are used as counters which can be controlled by software (program instructions) to keep track of things such as the number of times a particular sequence of instructions has been executed or sequential memory locations where data are to be taken from.

We will describe the most common types of registers, their functions, and how they can be affected by software. It should be stated that this latter item is an extremely important one from the programmer's viewpoint; this will become increasingly apparent as we get further into programming and applications.

Instruction Register

The function of the *Instruction register* (IR) has already been discussed. When the CPU* fetches an instruction word from memory, it sends it to the IR. It is stored here while the instruction decoding circuitry determines which instruction is to be executed. The IR is automatically used by the CPU during each instruction cycle, and the programmer never has a need to access this register. The size of the IR will be the same as the word size. For an 8-bit μP, the IR is 8 bits long.

Program Counter

The *Program Counter* (PC) has also been discussed previously. The PC always contains the address in memory of the next instruction (or portion of an instruction) which the CPU is to fetch. When the μP RESET input is activated, the PC is set to the address of the first instruction to be executed. The μP places the contents of PC on the address bus and fetches the first byte of the instruction from that memory location. (Recall that in 8-bit μCs, one byte is used for the op code and the following one or two bytes for the operand address.) The μC automatically increments the PC after each use and in this way executes the stored program sequentially unless the program contains an instruction that alters the sequence (e.g., a JUMP instruction).

The size of the PC depends on the number of address bits the μP can handle. Most of the more common μPs use 16-bit addresses, but some use 12 bits. In either case, the PC will have the same number of bits as the address bus. In many μPs, the PC is divided into two smaller registers, PCH and PCL, each of which holds one-half of an address. This is illustrated in Fig. 5.2. PCH holds the 8 high-order bits of the 16-bit address, and PCL holds the 8 low-order bits. The reason for using PCH and PCL is that, as we will see later, it is often necessary to store the contents of PC in memory. Since the memory stores 8-bit words, the 16-bit PC must be broken into two halves and stored in two successive memory locations.

The programmer has no direct access to the PC. That is, there are no direct instructions to load the PC from memory or to store the PC contents in memory. However, there are many instructions which cause the PC to take on a value other than its normal sequential value. JMP (JUMP) and JPZ

*Since the μP is the CPU of a μC, we will use the terms μP and CPU interchangeably.

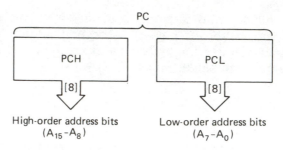

FIGURE 5.2 Sixteen-bit PC broken into 8-bit units.

(JUMP-ON-ZERO) are examples of instructions that change the PC so that the CPU executes instructions out of their normal sequential order.

Memory Address Register

The *Memory Address register* (MAR) is sometimes called a *storage address register* or an *address latching register*. It is used to hold the address of data which the CPU is reading from or writing into memory. For example, when executing an ADD instruction, the CPU places the operand address portion of the ADD instruction into the MAR. The contents of the MAR are then placed on the address bus so that the CPU can fetch the data during the next clock cycle.

It should now be apparent that there are two sources of addresses for the μP's address bus, the PC and the MAR. The PC is used for *instruction* addresses and the MAR is used for *data* addresses. A multiplexer is used to switch either the PC or MAR onto the address bus, depending on whether

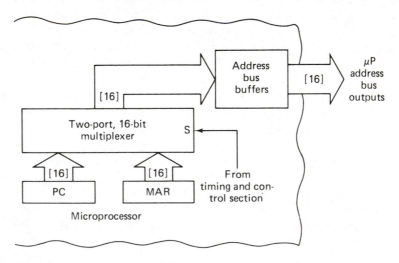

FIGURE 5.3 Portion of the μP showing how address source is selected for the address bus.

the CPU is in an instruction cycle or an execution cycle. This is illustrated in Fig. 5.3. Here the PC and MAR outputs are fed to a two-port multiplexer. The multiplexer's single output port is connected to the μP's address bus via the address bus buffers. The multiplexer's select input S is controlled by a signal from the μP's control section. One value of S selects the PC to be placed onto the address bus and the other value of S selects the MAR.

Accumulator

The *Accumulator* is a register that takes part in most of the operations performed by the ALU. It is also the register in which the results are placed after most ALU operations. In many ALU instructions, the Accumulator is the source of one of the operands and the destination of the result.

In addition to its use in ALU instructions, the Accumulator has other uses; for instance, it can be used as a storage register for data that are being sent to an output device or as a receiving register for data that are being read from an input device. Some μPs have more than one Accumulator. In these μPs, the instruction op codes specify which Accumulator is to be used.

The Accumulator generally has the same number of bits as the μP's word size. Thus, an 8-bit μP will have an 8-bit Accumulator. Some μPs also have an *Extension register*, which is used in conjunction with the Accumulator for handling binary numbers with more than 8 bits. For example, the μP has an arithmetic mode called *double-precision arithmetic*, wherein each number is 16 bits long and is stored in two words of memory. When these 16-bit data words are sent to the CPU, the Extension register stores the 8 least significant bits and the Accumulator stores the 8 most significant bits. These two registers can be considered to be one 16-bit register.

In many μPs the ALU cannot perform an operation on a word in memory directly. The word must first be read from memory and placed in the Accumulator. The operation is performed on the Accumulator contents and then written back into memory. This sequence requires three separate program instructions and is illustrated below for the operation of *1's-complementing* a memory data word.

	Hex Code	Description
	A9	LOAD Accumulator (LDA)
Instruction 1	20	
	05	Address of data (0520_{16})[a]
Instruction 2	67	Complement Accumulator (CMA)
	85	Store Accumulator (STA)
Instruction 3	20	
	05	Address of result (0520_{16})

[a]Here we are assuming a μP which specifies the LO-order address byte before the HI-order address byte.

The first instruction requires three bytes and instructs the CPU to load the Accumulator (LDA) with the contents of memory location 0520_{16}. The second instruction is only a single byte and instructs the CPU to perform a 1's-complement on the Accumulator contents (CMA). The third instruction requires three bytes and causes the CPU to store the new contents of the Accumulator (STA) in memory location 0520_{16}. Some μPs do allow some operations to be performed on memory words without using the Accumulator as an intermediate storage location. This greatly reduces the number of instructions required for the operation, but requires more complex μP circuitry. To illustrate, the 1's-complement operation for such a μP would only require the following single instruction:

	Hex Code	Description
Single instruction	69	Complement memory (CMM)
	20	Address of data to be
	05	complemented

General-Purpose Register

General-Purpose registers are used for many of the temporary storage functions required inside the CPU. They can be used to store data that is used frequently during a program, thereby speeding up the program execution since the CPU does not have to perform a memory READ operation each time the data are needed. They can also be used to store partial results of arithmetic operations while the Accumulator is being used for a different arithmetic operation. In some μPs, the General-Purpose registers can also be used as index registers (described below) or as Accumulators. The number of General-Purpose registers will vary from μP to μP. Some μPs have none, while others may have 12 or more.

There are normally several instructions which the programmer can use to access a General-Purpose (GP) register. The most common are:

1. Load GP from memory — $[M] \longrightarrow [GP]$.
2. Store GP in memory — $[GP] \longrightarrow [M]$.
3. Transfer contents of GP to Accumulator — $[GP] \longrightarrow [A]$.
4. Transfer contents of Accumulator to GP — $[A] \longrightarrow [GP]$.
5. Transfer contents of one GP register to another GP register — $[GP_1] \longrightarrow [GP_2]$.
6. Increment GP by 1 — $[GP + 1] \longrightarrow [GP]$.
7. Decrement GP by 1 — $[GP - 1] \longrightarrow [GP]$.

The final two instructions are extremely useful to a programmer. They allow him or her to use GP as an up or down counter to keep track of the number of times a particular operation or sequence of operations is executed. This is illustrated in Fig. 5.4, which shows a *flowchart* of a portion of a program. A flowchart is essentially a block diagram showing the sequence of major steps in a program. It is used to document the logical operation of a program such that any programmer can look at it and determine what the program is doing. The programmer usually lays out the flowchart prior to actually writing the program; this is especially helpful to him or her in complex programs containing many branches.

The flowchart in Fig. 5.4 represents a small portion of a larger program flowchart. It shows how GP is used as a down counter to keep track of the number of times the instruction sequence in block 2 is executed. At the start of the program GP is loaded from memory with the value COUNT (block 1). COUNT represents the number of times the programmer wants the sequence

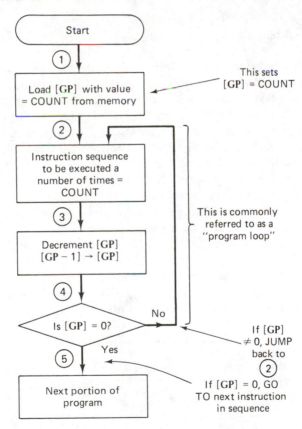

FIGURE 5.4 Flowchart that illustrates the use of a General-Purpose register as a counter.

in block 2 to be executed. After executing block 2, the contents of GP is decremented (block 3). The program then moves to block 4, which is called a *decision block*. A decision block is always drawn in the shape of a diamond. In this block, the new contents of GP is examined to see if it is exactly zero. If [GP] ≠ 0, the program will jump back to block 2 to reexecute the sequence there; if [GP] = 0, the program will go on to block 5. This can be accomplished with a JUMP instruction such as JUMP-ON-NOT-ZERO (JNZ).

It should be clear that the program will execute blocks 2, 3, and 4 for a number of times equal to COUNT, at which time GP will have been decremented to 0, causing the program to go on to block 5. As pointed out in the diagram, the portion of the program that gets executed several times is called a *program loop*. Program loops are very common in all but the simplest programs. In fact, many programs use more than one CPU register as counters to produce a loop within a loop. More will be said on this in our work on µC programming.

Index Register

An *index register*, like a General-Purpose register, can be used for general CPU storage functions and as a counter. In addition, it has a special function which is of great use in a program where tables or arrays of data must be handled. In this function, the Index register takes part in determining the addresses of data the CPU is accessing. This operation is called *indexed addressing* and is a special form of addressing available to the programmer. There are several different forms of indexed addressing. We will describe one of the most common forms here and show how it can be valuable in certain types of programming operations.

The basic idea of indexed addressing is that the actual or *effective* operand address called for by an instruction is the sum of the operand address portion of the instruction *plus* the contents of the Index register. To illustrate, let us assume that Index register X is 8-bits long and holds the number 04_{16}. Let us also assume that the CPU is executing a load-Accumulator instruction using indexed addressing (the symbolic code for this instruction would be LDA,X). This instruction might be stored in memory as follows:

Address of Memory Word	Memory Word	
0200	6F ←——————	code for LDA,X
0201	50	
0202	04	the "base" address 0450

To execute this instruction, the CPU fetches the op code 6F from location 0200. It determines that a LDA,X operation is to be performed in which a data word is to be loaded into the Accumulator. The effective address of this data word is determined by taking the operand address portion of this instruction from memory locations 0201 and 0202, called the *base* address, and adding to it the contents of the Index register X. Thus,

$$\text{effective address} = \text{base address} + [\text{X}]$$
$$= 0450 \qquad + 04$$
$$= 0454$$

This effective address 0454, then, is the address from which the CPU reads the data word to be placed into the Accumulator.

As this example has shown, the actual address from which data are to be taken depends on the current contents of Index register X. If the contents of X are changed and this instruction is repeated, a new data address would be used. This characteristic makes indexed addressing extremely useful in handling tables of data stored in memory. We will show this in the following simple program example.

EXAMPLE 5.1   A table of seven data words is stored in memory locations 2061 through 2067. Draw the flowchart for a program that will add these seven data words and store the sum in memory address 2068. Use indexed addressing.

Solution: The required flowchart is shown in Fig. 5.5. Examine it closely and note the following important points: (1) the Accumulator is cleared to zero before any ADD operation occurs; (2) the Index register X is initially loaded with the number 07; (3) the instructions in blocks, 3, 4, and 5 are executed a total of *seven* times before the program goes on to block 6; and (4) the ADD instruction (block 3) is executed using data from a different address each time, starting with 2067 and ending with 2061. In this way, the complete table of data has been added to the Accumulator.

This example only begins to illustrate the value of indexed addressing and index registers. Some of the other indexed addressing techniques will be described when we discuss programming concepts in detail.

Status Register

Also referred to as a *Process Status register* or *Condition register*, the *Status register* consists of individual bits with different meanings assigned by the μP manufacturer. These bits are called *flags*, and each flag is used to indicate the status of a particular μP condition. The value of some of the flags can be examined under program control to determine what sequence of instructions to follow. Two of the most common flags are the Zero flag, Z, and the Carry flag, C. The value of Z will always indicate whether or not the previous data

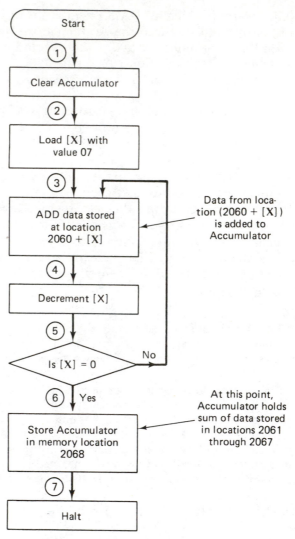

FIGURE 5.5 Flowchart of a short program that uses indexed addressing to add seven numbers stored in sequential memory locations.

manipulation instruction* produced a result of zero. Normally, a μP control signal sets Z to the HIGH state when the result of an instruction is zero and clears Z to a LOW when the result of an instruction is not zero. The value of C always indicates whether the previous instruction produced a result that exceeded the μP word size. For example, whenever the addition of two 8-bit data words produces a sum that exceeds 8 bits (i.e., a carry out of the eighth position), the C flag will be set to 1. If the addition produces no carry, C will be 0. The C flag can be thought of as the ninth bit of any arithmetic result.

*This is an instruction that performs any operation on data.

Some µPs have one or more of their status register bits connected to pins on the µP chip for direct interfacing with external devices. This is illustrated in Fig. 5.6, where bits 6 and 7 of the status register are directly accessible at the µP pins. Bit 6 is a *Flag Output* (FO) which the µP can use to control an external device under program control. That is, the logic level of FO can be set or cleared by instructions within a program. For example, at some point in a program the level of FO can be set to the HIGH state by the execution of an SFO instruction. SFO is the symbolic code for *Set Flag Output*. This HIGH at FO might be used to turn on an external device (e.g., a tape recorder, a motor, a light bulb, etc.) or it might be a signal to an external device that the CPU has reached a particular point in its program execution. A *Clear Flag Output* instruction (CFO) is used to bring FO back to the LOW state.

Bit 7 is a *Sense Input* (SI), which is set or cleared only by an external signal applied to the corresponding µP pin. This allows an external device to communicate directly with the CPU via SI. The CPU can examine the level of SI under program control and can branch to different sequences of instructions depending on the value of SI.

This latter operation is an example of the most common use of flags. Most µP instruction sets contain several *conditional branch* instructions, which determine the sequence of instructions to be executed depending on the flag values. The JUMP-ON-ZERO (JPZ) instruction is a prime example. When the CPU executes the JPZ instruction, it examines the value of the Zero flag. If the Zero flag is LOW, indicating that the previous instruction produced a nonzero result, the next instruction to be executed will be taken in normal sequence. If the Zero flag is HIGH, indicating a zero result, the program will jump to the operand address for its next instruction and will continue in sequence from there. Other examples are JUMP-ON-CARRY-SET (JCS) and JUMP-ON-CARRY-CLEARED (JCC), both of which examine the Carry flag. We will introduce some of the other common flags during our work on programming.

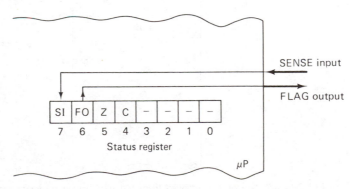

FIGURE 5.6 Some µP Status registers have one or more bits connected directly to µP pins.

Stack Pointer Register

Before defining the function of the Stack Pointer register, we must define the *stack*. The stack is a portion of RAM reserved for the temporary storage and retrieval of information, typically the contents of the μP's internal registers. This area of memory is called a stack because it operates as follows:

1. Each time a word is to be stored in this area of RAM, it is placed in an address location which is one less than the address of the previous word stored on the stack. To help illustrate this, refer to Fig. 5.7. Let us assume that we have four words that we want to store on the stack. Word A, the first word, will be stored at address 0165. Word B, the second word, will be stored at address 0164. Similarly, word C goes into address 0163 and word D into 0162.

2. Words stored on the stack are read from the stack in the opposite order from that in which they were placed on the stack. Referring to Fig. 5.7, this means that word D must be read first, then word C, word B, and finally word A.

3. Once a word is read from the stack, its location on the stack is available for storage.

The operation of the stack can be likened to the manner in which we stack plates in a cupboard. Each time we add a plate to the stack, we place it

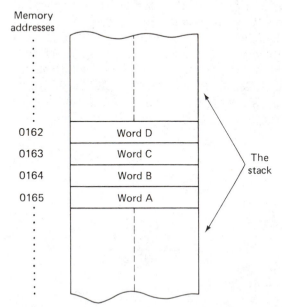

FIGURE 5.7 Words are removed from the stack in the opposite order from that in which they were placed on the stack.

on top of the stack; each time we remove a plate from the stack, we take it from the top of the stack. The last plate placed on the stack is the first plate removed from the stack. In fact, this type of stack is often referred to as a *last-in, first-out* (LIFO) stack.

The amount of RAM that is reserved for the stack will vary from one μP to another. For example, the 6502 uses page 01 of RAM for its stack, whereas in the 8080A, the location and size of the stack are indeterminate, being left to the programmer's discretion. Some μPs, such as National Semiconductor's PACE, do not use external RAM for the stack; instead they have a small stack right in the μP chip. For example, PACE has a 10-word stack.

This brings us to the *Stack Pointer register* (SP). This register acts as a special memory address register used only for the stack portion of RAM. Whenever a word is to be stored on the stack, it is stored at the address contained in the SP. Likewise, whenever a word is to be read from the stack, it is read from the address specified by the SP. The contents of the SP are initialized by the programmer at the beginning of the program. Thereafter, the SP is automatically decremented *after* a word is stored on the stack and incremented *before* a word is read from the stack. (The incrementing and decrementing is done automatically by the μP control section.)

The operation of the SP is illustrated in Fig. 5.8. Let us assume that the most recent stack operation stored a word in location 0164. After that operation, the SP was decremented to 0163 to indicate that location 0163 is the

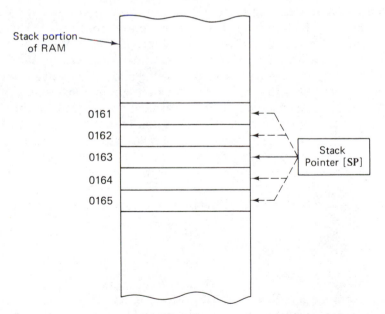

FIGURE 5.8 The Stack Pointer register points to the next available location on stack.

next location available on the stack.* This is symbolized in Fig. 5.8 by the SP pointing to location 0163. If the next stack operation is a store, a word will be stored in 0163, and the SP will be decremented to 0162. Another store operation will place a word in 0162 and decrement the SP to 0161. Now, let us assume that a stack READ operation is to be performed. The stack pointer is pointing to 0161 and is automatically incremented to 0162 and the word stored there is read by the CPU. Similarly, subsequent READ operations would increment the SP to 0163, 0164, 1065, and so on.

There are several instances in which the stack portion of memory is used. As we shall see later, the μP automatically saves return addresses and other critical information on the stack during subroutine calls and interrupts. The programmer can also store data and information on the stack at any time by using special instructions. For example, the contents of the Accumulator can be stored on the stack using an instruction of the type

PHA   *push* Accumulator on the stack

This instruction stores [A] at the stack location indicated by the SP, and then decrements the SP.

The opposite operation can be performed using an instruction such as

PLA   *pull* Accumulator off the stack

This instruction causes the SP to be incremented, and then loads the Accumulator from the stack location indicated by the SP. These *push* and *pull* instructions are useful because the programmer does not have to specify a memory address. The address is, of course, specified by the SP.

The μP takes care of incrementing and decrementing the SP, so the programmer really does not have to worry about that aspect of the operation. The programmer, however, must take care of initializing the SP and he or she must also ensure that the SP never points to locations outside the RAM area reserved for the stack; otherwise, a stack storage operation might write over a word in the program or data area of RAM. In addition, the programmer must be sure to take words off the stack in the reverse order that they were placed on the stack. We will expand on this in our discussion of programming concepts, where we will show how the stack is used by the programmer.

5.3 ARITHMETIC/LOGIC UNIT

Most modern μPs have arithmetic/logic units (ALUs) which are capable of performing a wide variety of arithmetic and logical operations. These operations can involve two operands, such as the Accumulator and a data word

*The SP always points to the next available storage location on the stack.

from memory, or the Accumulator and another μP internal register. Some of the operations involve only a single operand, such as the Accumulator, a register, or a word from memory.

A simplified diagram of a typical ALU is shown in Fig. 5.9. The ALU block represents all the logic circuitry used to perform arithmetic, logic, and manipulation operations on the operand inputs. Two 8-bit operands are shown as inputs to the ALU, although frequently only one operand is used. Also shown as an input to the ALU is the Carry flag, C, from the μP Status register. The reason for this will be explained later. The functions the ALU will perform are determined by the control signal inputs from the μP control section. The number of these control inputs varies from μP to μP.

The ALU produces two sets of outputs. One set is an 8-bit output representing the results of the operation performed on the operands. The other is a set of status signals which are sent to the μP Status register to set or clear various flag bits. For example, if the result of an ALU operation is exactly zero, a signal is sent to the Z flag in the Status register to set it to the HIGH state. If the result of the ALU operation produces a carry into the ninth bit position, a signal is sent to set the C flag in the status register. Other signals from the ALU will set or clear other flags in the status register.

The operand inputs A and B can come from several sources. When two operands are to be operated on by the ALU, one of the operands comes from the Accumulator and the other operand comes from a data word fetched from memory which is stored in a data buffer register within the μP. In some μPs, the second operand can also be the contents of one of the General-Purpose registers. The result of the ALU operation performed on the two operands is normally sent to the Accumulator.

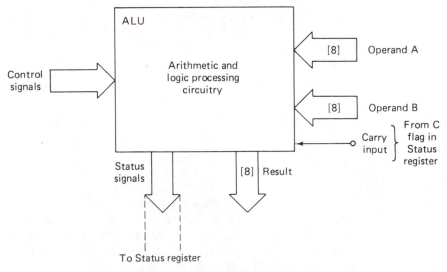

FIGURE 5.9 Simplified diagram of a typical μP ALU.

When only one operand is to be operated on by the ALU, the operand can be the contents of the Accumulator, a General-Purpose register, an Index register, or a memory data word. The result of the ALU operation is then sent back to the source of the operand. When the single operand is a memory word, the result is sent to a data buffer register, from where the CPU writes it back into the memory location of the operand.

Single-Operand Operations

We will now describe some of the common ALU operations performed on a single operand.

1. CLEAR. All bits of the operand are cleared to 0. If the operand comes from the Accumulator, for example, we can symbolically represent this operation as $0 \longrightarrow [A]$.

2. COMPLEMENT (or INVERT). All bits are changed to their opposite logic level. If the operand comes from register X, for example, this operation is represented as $[\overline{X}] \longrightarrow [X]$.

3. INCREMENT. The operand is increased by 1. For example, if the operand is 11010011, it will have 00000001 added to it in the ALU to produce a result of 11010100. This instruction is very useful when the program is using one of the μP registers as a counter. Symbolically, this is represented as $[X + 1] \longrightarrow [X]$.

4. DECREMENT. The operand is decreased by 1. In other words, the number 00000001 is subtracted from the operand. This instruction is useful in programs where a register is used to count down from an initial value, as was done in our earlier examples of General-Purpose and Index registers (Figs. 5.4 and 5.5). Symbolically, this operation is represented as $[X - 1] \longrightarrow [X]$.

5. SHIFT. The bits of the operand are shifted to the left or to the right one place and the empty bit is made a 0. This process is illustrated below for a SHIFT-LEFT operation.

| 1 | 0 | 0 | 1 | 1 | 1 | 0 | 1 | Operand before shift

| 0 | 0 | 1 | 1 | 1 | 0 | 1 | 0 | After shift

Note that a 0 is shifted into the rightmost bit. Also, note that the original leftmost bit is shifted out and is lost. In most μPs the bit that is shifted out of the operand is not lost; instead, it is shifted into the Carry flag bit, C, of the status register. This is illustrated below for a SHIFT-RIGHT operation.

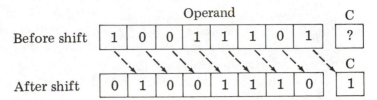

Note that a 0 is shifted into the leftmost bit and also note that the original rightmost bit is shifted into C (the original value of C is lost). For the corresponding SHIFT-LEFT operation, the leftmost bit would be shifted into C. This type of operation is used by the programmer to test the value of a specific bit in an operand. He does this by shifting the operand the required number of times until the bit value is in the C flag. A CONDITIONAL JUMP instruction is then used to test the C flag to determine what instruction to execute next.

6. ROTATE. This is a modified SHIFT operation in which the C flag becomes part of a circulating shift register along with the operand; that is, the value shifted out of the operand is shifted into C and the value of C is shifted into the empty bit of the operand. This is illustrated below for a ROTATE-RIGHT operation.

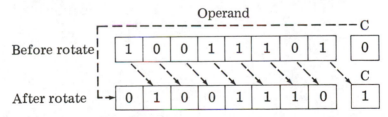

Note that the original C bit is shifted into the leftmost bit of the operand and that the rightmost bit of the operand is shifted into C. A ROTATE-LEFT operates in the same manner except in the opposite direction.

Two-Operand ALU Operations

We will now describe some of the ALU operations performed on two operands.

1. ADD. The ALU produces the binary sum of the two operands. Generally, one of the operands comes from the Accumulator, the other from memory, and the result is sent to the Accumulator. Symbolically, this operation is $[A] + [M] \longrightarrow [A]$. If the addition of the

two operands produces a carry out of the MSB position, the Carry flag, C, in the status register is set to 1. Otherwise, C is cleared to 0. In other words, C serves as the ninth bit of the result.

2. SUBTRACT. The ALU subtracts one operand (obtained from mem-memory) from the second operand (the Accumulator) and places the result in the Accumulator. Symbolically, this is [A] - [M] ⟶ [A]. Most μPs use the 2's-complement method of subtraction (Chapter 1) whereby the operand from memory is 2's-complemented and then added to the operand from the Accumulator. Once again, the Carry bit generated by this operation is stored in the C flag.

3. COMPARE. This operation is the same as subtraction except that the result is not placed in the Accumulator. Symbolically, this is [A] - [M]. The subtraction is performed solely as a means for determining which operand is larger without affecting the contents of the Accumulator. Depending on whether the result is positive, negative, or zero, various condition flags will be affected. The programmer can then use CONDITIONAL JUMP instructions to test these flags.

4. LOGICAL AND. The corresponding bits of the two operands are ANDed and the result is placed in the Accumulator. Symbolically, this is written as [A] · [M] ⟶ [A]. One of the operands is always the Accumulator and the other comes from memory. As an example, let us assume that [A] = 10110101 and [M] = 01100001. The AND operation is performed as follows:

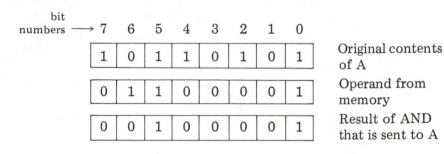

Note that each bit of the result is obtained by ANDing the corresponding bits of the operands. For example, bit 7 of the Accumulator is a 1 and bit 7 of the memory word is a 0. Thus, bit 7 of the result is 1 · 0 = 0. Similarly, bit 5 of each operand is a 1, so bit 5 of the result is 1 · 1 = 1.

5. LOGICAL OR. The corresponding bits of the two operands are ORed and the result placed in the Accumulator. Symbolically, this is shown as [A] OR [M] ⟶ [A]. A plus sign (+) can be used in place

of OR, but it might cause confusion with the binary addition operation. Using the same two operands used in the illustration of the AND operation above, the result of the OR operation will be 11110101.

6. EXCLUSIVE-OR. The corresponding bits of the two operands are EX-ORed and the result is placed in the Accumulator. Symbolically, this is [A] ⊕ [M] ⟶ [A]. Using the same two operands used in the prior illustrations, the result of the EX-OR operation will be 11010100. The logic AND, OR, and EX-OR operations are very useful to a programmer. We will examine some of their uses under programming concepts.

7. Decimal (BCD) arithmetic. Many μPs have some provision for performing addition and subtraction in the BCD system whereby an 8-bit data word is treated as two BCD-digits. As we pointed out in Chapter 1, arithmetic operations on BCD numbers require extra steps to obtain the correct results. While in some μPs these extra steps are performed automatically whenever BCD arithmetic instructions are executed, other μPs require the programmer to insert special instructions to correct the results.

This list of arithmetic/logic operations does not include the more complex operations of multiplication, division, square roots, and so on. These operations are not explicitly performed by most currently available μP because of the extra circuitry they would require. To perform such operations, the programmer can instruct the μP to execute an appropriate series of simple arithmetic operations. For example, the multiplication operation can be obtained through a series of shifting and adding operations, and the division operation by a series of shifting and subtracting operations.

The sequences of instructions which the programmer develops for performing such complex arithmetic operations are called *subroutines*. A multiplication subroutine for obtaining the product of two 8-bit numbers might consist of as many as 20 or 30 instruction steps, requiring 200 μs to execute. If this long execution time is undesirable, it is possible to use an external LSI chip containing a high-speed multiplier. Such LSI multipliers are available with execution times of only ns and can be connected to the μP as I/O devices. In addition to multiplier chips, there are *arithmetic processing chips*, which can be interfaced to a μP to perform most of the operations available on a scientific calculator. These chips are fairly expensive ($150 to $200) and are used only when a great many high-speed computations are required. Another alternative to slow subroutines is to use a ROM as a storage table which can store such data as multiplication tables, trigonometric tables, and logarithmic tables.

Signed Numbers

The circuitry in the ALU performs the ADD and SUBTRACT operations in the binary number system and always treats the two operands as 8-bit binary numbers. This is true even when the program calls for BCD arithmetic, the only difference being the extra steps needed to correct the BCD result. With an 8-bit data word, decimal numbers from 0 to 255 can be represented in binary code, assuming that all 8 bits are used for the numerical value. However, if the programmer wishes to use both positive and negative numbers, the MSB of each data word is used as the *sign bit* with 0 for + and 1 for −. The other 7 bits of each data word represent the magnitude; for positive numbers the magnitude is in true binary form, while for negative numbers the magnitude is in 2's-complement form.

The beauty of this method for representing signed numbers is that it requires no special operations by the ALU. The circuitry in the ALU will perform addition and subtraction on the two operands in the same manner regardless of whether the operands are unsigned 8-bit data words or 7-bit data words plus a sign bit. As was shown in Chapter 1, the sign bit participates in the add and subtract operations just like the rest of the bits. What this means is that the μP really does not know or care whether the data it is processing are signed or unsigned. Only the programmer is concerned about the distinction, and he or she must at all times know the format of the data being used in the program.

As an aid to the programmer, almost all μPs transfer the value of bit 7 of the ALU result to a flag bit in the status register. This flag bit, sometimes called the Sign flag, S, or the Negative flag, N, will be set to 1 if the ALU result has a 1 in bit 7 and will be cleared to 0 if bit 7 is a 0. The program can then test to see if the result was positive or negative by performing a CONDITIONAL JUMP instruction based on the Sign flag. For example, a JUMP-ON-NEGATIVE instruction (JPN) will cause the CPU to examine the Sign flag in the status register to determine what sequence of instructions to follow next.

5.4 TYPICAL 8-BIT MICROCOMPUTERS

In the preceding sections we described some of the basic characteristics of microprocessors and tried to be general in our discussion. Now we are going to describe briefly four of the most popular μPs on the market today. These descriptions will focus mostly on the structure of the μP chip and will not go into the instruction sets of each μP. The latter area is discussed in Chapter 7. In making comparisons among various μPs, it must be kept in mind that it is very difficult to say that one μP is better than another μP. It really depends on the application or types of applications for which the μP is being considered. Each μP generally has something it can do to be better than other μPs and some areas in which it is lacking; this is because μP manufacturers decide for what types of applications they are designing their products.

A particular area where comparisons must be made carefully is the area of *execution speed*, that is, the speed at which a μP executes instructions. One cannot generalize and say that a μP which has a higher clock frequency will have a greater execution speed. This is because the number of clock cycles required to execute an instruction will vary from one μP to another. Furthermore, one μP may complete a certain program faster than another, but a different program might be just the reverse. For these reasons, a potential user should test the speed of a μP by having it execute a program similar to what it will be executing in the intended application. For our purposes here, we will try to give some degree of speed comparison among the various μPs by indicating the amount of time required for each μP to execute an ADD instruction.

8080/8085

Manufactured primarily by Intel Corporation using *N*-channel MOS technology, the 8080 was the first powerful μP to hit the market. It is the most widely known μP and, at present, it is also the most widely used μP, although this position is being challenged by the other μPs we will discuss. It has an 8-bit word size, can address up to 65,536 words of memory, and has 78 types of instructions.

Figure 5.10 shows the primary elements of the 8080 chip and its external connections. Note that the chip requires *three* power-supply voltages, +5 V, +12 V, and –5 V, and two clock inputs, ϕ_1 and ϕ_2. These clock signals have to be externally generated with the proper phase relationship, pulse duration, and so on. A special clock-generator chip, the 8224, is manufactured by Intel for direct connection to the 8080 and other microcomputer elements. The maximum clock frequency of the 8080 varies from 1 to 4 megahertz (MHz), depending upon the version being used. The diagram also shows the 16-bit address bus, the 8-bit bidirectional data bus, and a 10-line control bus. The control bus signals include $\overline{\text{WR}}$ (memory or I/O write), RE-SET, READY, HOLD, and INT (INTERRUPT).

There are 10 principal registers in the 8080 of concern to the user. The 16-bit Program Counter is used to place instruction addresses on the address bus. The 8-bit Accumulator participates in arithmetic/logic operations and stores results. There are six 8-bit General-Purpose registers, B, C, D, E, H, and L. These are often used in pairs (B–C, D–E, H–L) to act as 16-bit General-Purpose registers. The 16-bit Stack Pointer is used to address the stack portion of RAM. Since the programmer can load any 16-bit number into this SP, the stack can be located in any area of RAM. The Status register holds five

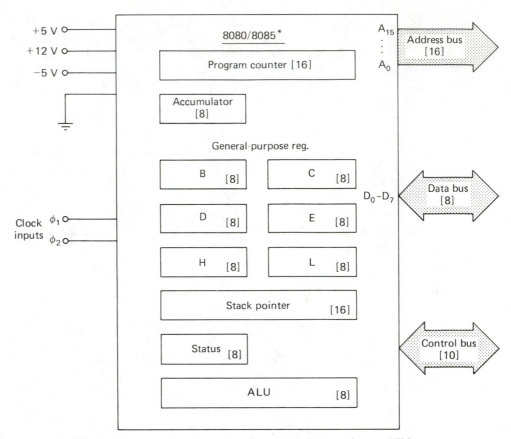

*The 8085 has on-chip system controller and clock-generating capabilities, uses a single +5-V supply and has more bus control functions and interrupt capabilities.

FIGURE 5.10   8080/8085 microprocessor.

condition flags, including the Carry (C), Sign (S), and Zero (Z) flags. The 8080's ALU can perform a wide variety of operations, including addition, subtraction, compare, shift, rotate, AND, OR, and EX-OR. It can also do BCD arithmetic, although it requires the use of a special *decimal-adjust* instruction after *each* BCD operation to correct the BCD result.

The 8080A can operate at a 2-MHz clock frequency, which means that its clock cycle time is 500 ns. To give you some indication of its execution speed, the 8080A requires *seven* clock cycles to perform an ADD operation. That is, it requires 3.5 μs to add two 8-bit operands. This assumes that one operand is already in the accumulator. Intel manufactures a faster version of the 8080A, called the 8080A-1, which can run at a clock frequency of 3.125 MHz, which is 60 percent faster than the 8080A. Of course, the higher speed of the 8080A-1 can be of value only if faster memory devices are used in the system. Intel also has introduced a new μP, the 8085, which offers many improvements over the 8080. The 8085 chip has an on-chip clock generator, uses a single +5-V supply, and has more bus control functions and interrupt inputs than the 8080.

Z-80

The Z-80 is an *N*-channel MOS microprocessor manufactured by Zilog, Inc., as an enhancement of the 8080. In fact, the same people who designed the 8080 for Intel were responsible for designing the Z-80 at Zilog. To many people, the Z-80 represents the most significant development in the μP field over the past two years. It is faster than the 8080, with a normal clock frequency of 2.5 MHz. For example, it requires seven clock cycles (2.8 μs) to perform an ADD operation. More important, the Z-80 executes certain instructions in fewer clock cycles than the 8080, thereby gaining an even greater speed advantage.

The Z-80 has an 8-bit word size, can address up to 65,536 words of memory, and has 158 different types of instructions, including the 78 instructions of the 8080. The primary elements of the Z-80 chip are shown in Fig. 5.11. First, note that a single supply voltage, +5 V, and a single clock input, ϕ, are required. Both of these are improvements over the 8080.

There are 22 principal registers in the Z-80. As the diagram shows, the Z-80 has two sets of identical registers, each of which includes an Accumulator, a Status register, and six 8-bit General-Purpose registers. With a single instruction, the programmer can choose either set for use during a program. In addition, this μP has two 16-bit Index registers (used for indexed addressing) and a 16-bit SP.

Two special 8-bit registers are the INTERRUPT Vector (IV) and the Memory Refresh Counter (MRC). The IV register can be used during external interrupts to help determine from where in memory the μP fetches the first instruction following an interrupt. The MRC is used when dynamic memory devices are part of the μP system. These memory devices have to have their contents continually refreshed (rewritten) at some minimum rate, and the MRC keeps track of addresses in the dynamic memory as they are refreshed.

The Z-80 ALU can perform essentially the same operations as the 8080, Although at a somewhat higher speed. In addition, it can perform many operations not available in the 8080 or any other microprocessor. A principal example is the group of Z-80 instructions that can be used to test or alter the condition of individual bits of registers or memory words. Another example is an instruction that allows the contents of any number of successive memory words to be moved from one area of memory to another, or between an area of memory and a single I/O port. These and other unique instructions give the Z-80 the most powerful instruction set of any μP currently available.

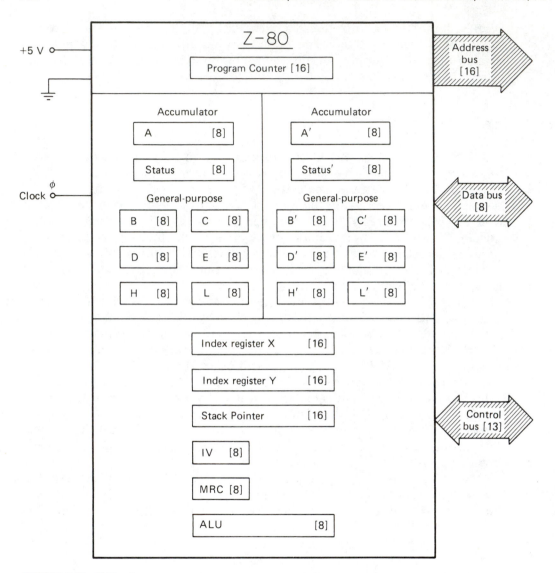

FIGURE 5.11 Z-80 microprocessor.

6800

The 6800, an NMOS microprocessor manufactured by Motorola, Inc., is at present the second most widely used μP, after the 8080A. Compared to the 8080 and Z-80, the 6800 is a model of simplicity in both its hardware and software aspects. It has an 8-bit word size, can address up to 65,536 words of memory, and has 72 types of instructions. The basic 6800 can operate with a 1-MHz clock frequency. Although this is a much lower clock frequency than the 8080A, the actual execution speed of the 6800 is not much less than the 8080A. This is because the 6800 normally requires fewer clock cycles than the 8080A to execute instructions. For example, the 6800 requires *four* clock cycles (4 µs) to execute an ADD instruction, while the 8080A requires *seven* clock cycles (3.5 µs) for the same instruction.

Figure 5.12 shows a diagram of the 6800's major elements. Note that it requires a single +5-V supply voltage and the two-phase clock inputs, ϕ_1 and ϕ_2. Also note that it contains only six principal registers: a Program Counter, two 8-bit Accumulators, a 16-bit Index register, a 16-bit Stack Pointer, and an 8-bit Status register. The two Accumulators are used independently with different instruction codes, specifying which Accumulator is to be used. The 8-bit ALU can perform the same basic operations as the 8080, including BCD arithmetic using a decimal-adjust instruction.

Motorola has developed a complete family of LSI chips used to interface the 6800 to a variety of I/O devices. This is probably the principal reason for the 6800's current popularity, since these LSI interface chips eliminate the need for a large number of MSI packages to construct a working system. Some of these interface chips are described in Chapter 7. Motorola also has faster versions of the 6800 available. The 68A00 runs at a clock frequency of 1.5 MHz and the 68B00 at a frequency of 2 MHz.

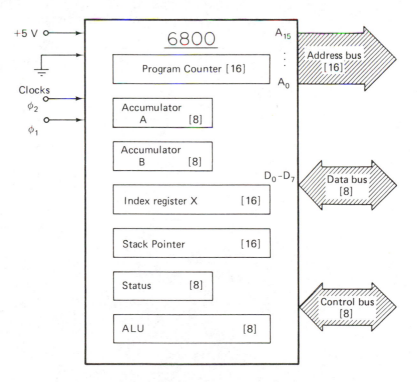

FIGURE 5.12 6800 microprocessor.

6502

The 6502 is a NMOS device manufactured by MOS Technology, Inc., as an enhancement of the 6800. It has an 8-bit word size, can address up to 65,536 memory words, and has 70 types of instructions. Like the 6800, the 6502 can use a 1-MHz clock frequency and its instruction execution speed is basically the same as the 6800. Figure 5.13, showing the principal elements of the 6502, demonstrates the simplicity of this μP.

Like the 6800 and Z-80, the 6502 chip also requires only a single power-supply voltage. A major difference between the 6502 and the other μPs is in the clock requirements. The 6502 does not require externally generated clock inputs. Instead, it generates the ϕ_1 and ϕ_2 clock signals on the chip with a frequency that is determined by an RC or crystal network connected to the clock control pins.

The 6502 contains only six principal registers: a Program Counter, an 8-bit Accumulator, two 8-bit Index registers, an 8-bit Status register, and an 8-bit Stack Pointer. The 8-bit SP is sufficient to determine the address of the stack since the 6502's stack is always located on page 01 of memory. The SP determines which location on page 01 is the next available stack location.

The 6502 ALU executes basically the same operations as the 8080 and 6800. It does, however, have an advantage in the BCD arithmetic instructions, since it does not require a decimal-adjust instruction to correct the

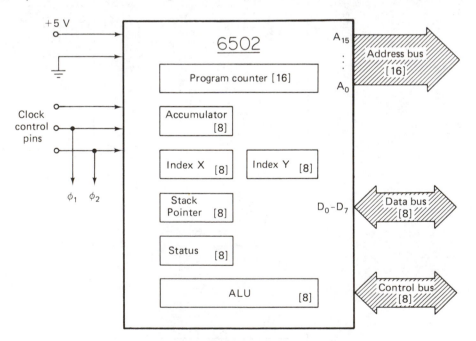

FIGURE 5.13 6502 microprocessor.

BCD results. Instead, the BCD corrections are performed automatically once the μP is instructed to operate in the BCD mode. This can be a valuable feature if the μP is to perform a large number of BCD calculations.

The manufacturers of the 6502 also make several other versions of this μP, including three higher-speed versions. The 6502A, 6502B, and 6502C devices operate at clock frequencies of 2, 3, and 4 MHz, respectively. In addition, the 6502 designers have developed several LSI interface chips to simplify the interface between the CPU and I/O devices.

5.5 16-BIT MICROPROCESSORS

Originally, microprocessors had their biggest impact in control applications where there is very limited data processing need. In the evolution of μP capabilities it was natural to enter into the field of data processing which had previously been dominated by minicomputers. Thus, the 16-bit μP has evolved in direct competition with well-established minicomputer systems. Some typical 16-bit microprocessors are the Intel 8086, Zilog Z-8000, and the Motorola 68000.

There are advantages and disadvantages to the use of a 16-bit μP. The advantage comes from the fact that with a 16-bit word size, more powerful instructions can be written which allow for a much efficient way to perform data processing tasks. Most of the present 16-bit microprocessors have instruction sets which are built around specific minicomputer instruction sets, thus allowing the user to take advantage of all the existing software available for a specific minicomputer.

The disadvantage is that being constrained to a 40-pin package necessitates *bus multiplexing*. Since there are 16 or more address lines, 16 data lines, a number of control lines, plus power-supply and clock-generation connections, more than 40 pins are needed unless bus multiplexing is used. The multiplexing of bus information increases the system complexity as far as parts count is concerned and slows down the speed of operation of the overall system. As a result of this disadvantage, most 16-bit microprocessors on the market today are not trying to compete with the 8-bit devices but are trying to get a share of the market that the minicomputers are now enjoying, since parts count is not as significant a constraint.

Texas Instruments has diverted from the standard 16-bit structure in two directions. First, it has the TMS9900, which is a 16-bit μP but in a 64-pin package. Figure 5.14 shows the architecture of this chip. This arrangement allows for a 15-bit address bus and a 16-bit data bus without the need for multiplexing. This chip has not, however, captured a large industrial market since most of industry is set up to work with 40-pin devices. It is used internally by Texas Instruments in their 990 minicomputer/microcomputer system. The other direction was a 16-bit single-chip microcomputer

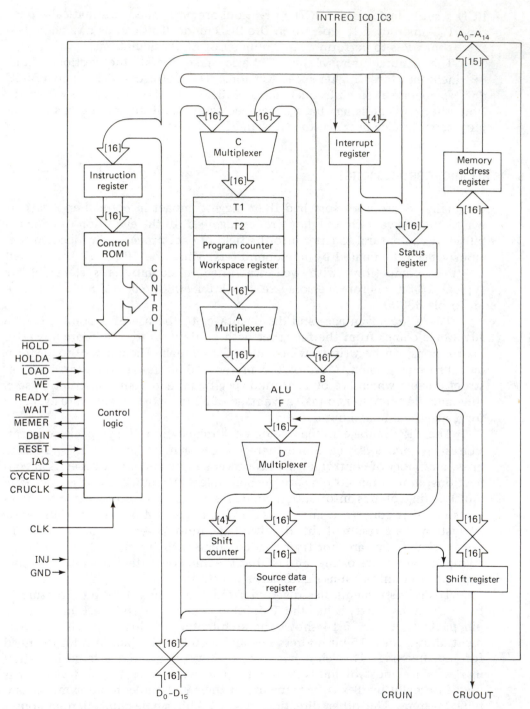

FIGURE 5.14 Architecture of the TMS 9900 16-bit microprocessor chip.

the TMS9940. Since memory is already included on this chip, a large multibit address bus is no longer necessary, and those pins can be used for input/output capability, thereby still requiring only 40 pins. The TMS9940 chip contains 2K bytes of ROM, 128 bytes of R/W memory, and 16 I/O lines.

5.6 BIT-SLICE MICROPROCESSORS

One criterion that is often looked at in a computer system selection is speed. In order to build a very fast μP one needs logic elements that have very fast switching speeds. This leads to the fact that the fastest logic families are still the bipolar devices. In particular, low-power Schottky TTL and ECL are extremely fast. Unfortunately, these devices require relatively large amounts of power dissipation and therefore cannot be implemented into a single-chip μP design. Therefore, a *bit-slice* technique of μP construction is used. The basic building block consists of a 4-bit slice which contains a 4-bit ALU, multiplexers, buses, registers, and flags. The basic bit slice can then be connected in parallel with other bit-slice devices to handle larger word lengths. For example, four 4-bit bit slices can be connected in parallel to form a complete 16-bit ALU with registers, flags, and buses, as shown in Fig. 5.15. The catch is that to perform a useful operation equivalent to a single machine language instruction the bit slice device must go through a sequence of microinstructions. These microinstructions are specified by the system designer and stored in ROM. A special device referred to as a microprogram sequencer is in control of sequencing through these microinstructions in ROM.

The bit-slice-type processors are not typically in competition with the single-chip μPs since to implement even a simple system might take a large number of chips (10 to 40); however, in applications where flexibility in design and speed are of paramount importance, the bit-slice microprocessor is found in competition with minicomputers.

5.7 SINGLE-CHIP MICROCOMPUTERS

There are a large number of industrial and consumer electronic applications that can benefit from microcomputer control and do not need vast amounts of memory capability. Furthermore, if the parts count of a complete microcomputer could be kept very low, the added features of μP control would not add appreciably to the cost of the system. This is where the single-chip microcomputer enters into the marketplace. Typically, these single-chip microcomputers consist of an 8-bit μP plus 1K bytes of ROM, 256 bytes of RAM, a number of 8-bit I/O ports, and probably some type of interval timer all on a single chip. Since the RAM and ROM are on the chip, this allows what use to be the 16 address pins to be used for I/O ports. The major dis-

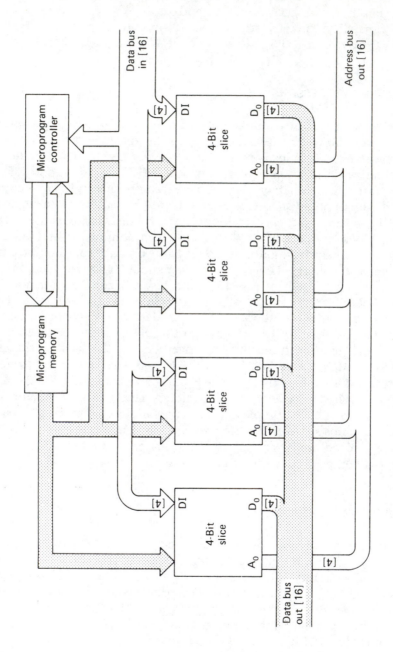

FIGURE 5.15 Simplified example of a 16-bit CPU using 4-bit bit-slice devices.

advantage of the single-chip microcomputers is that since most of the typical devices have their ROM memory mask-programmable, it is only economically feasible to use these microcomputers when quantities in the high 1000s are planned on being needed. In this case the cost per chip for such large quantities can be on the order of $1 or $2.

Intel manufactures the 8048, which is an 8-bit single-chip microcomputer that contains lK bytes of mask-programmed (unalterable) ROM and 64 bytes of RAM. There are three 8-bit ports. Two of the ports allow for individual pins to be programmed as inputs or outputs. It also has inputs that can be tested by conditional branch instructions and an 8-bit programmable timer. Intel also manufactures the 8748, which is exactly the same as the 8048 except that it has lK bytes of EPROM instead of lK bytes of mask-programmed ROM. The 8748 is used during the design and development stages. Once the control program is finalized, the 8048 is ordered in large quantities, with the control program placed in mask-programmed ROM.

Zilog manufactures the Z-8, which is an 8-bit single-chip microcomputer that contains 2K bytes of mask-programmed ROM, 124 bytes of RAM, 32 I/O lines, a UART, and two 8-bit programmable timers.

Motorola provides the MC6801, which has 2K bytes of mask-programmed ROM, 128 bytes of RAM, 31 I/O lines, a 16-bit timer, and a UART all on one chip.

These single-chip microcomputers will have a large impact on many industrial and consumer electronic applications. These devices will allow for much more sophistication in design and performance for a relatively small, and almost insignificant, increase in cost.

GLOSSARY

Bit-Slice Devices Typical CPU functions are vertically divided into separate chips. High-speed digital devices which dissipate relatively large amounts of power can be used in fabricating these chip slices. The individual chip slices can be configured to form a complete, large-word size, high-speed CPU by connecting in a parallel fashion.

Decision Block Diamond-shaped block used in a flowchart to indicate a branching instruction.

Decrement To reduce the contents of a register, being used as a counter, by one, unless otherwise specified.

Execution Speed Speed at which a μP executes instructions. It is measured by multiplying the cycle time by the number of cycles required to execute an instruction.

Extension Register Register used in conjunction with the accumulator for handling binary numbers with more than 8 bits.

Flags Single binary bits used to indicate the status of some particular μP condition: for example, Zero flag (Z) and the Carry flag (C).

Flowchart   Block diagram showing the sequence of major steps in a program such that any programmer can determine what the program is doing.

General-Purpose Register   One of a specified number of internal addressable registers in a CPU which can be used for temporary storage, such as an Index register, a Stack Pointer, an Accumulator, or any other general-purpose function.

Increment   To increase the contents of a register, being used as a counter, by one, unless otherwise specified.

Indexed Addressing   Addressing scheme in which the actual operand address called for by an instruction is the sum of the operand-address portion of the instruction plus the contents of the Index register.

Instruction Register (IR)   Internal register used to store an instruction word read from memory while instruction decoding circuitry determines which instruction is to be executed.

INT or IRQ (Interrupt Request) μP input which is used by I/O devices to interrupt the execution of the current program and cause the μP to jump to an interrupt service routine.

INTE (Interrupt Enable) μP output that indicates to external devices whether or not the μP interrupt logic is enabled or disabled. If INTE = 1, the μP will respond to an INT or IRQ input. If INT = 0, the μP will not respond to INT or IRQ signals.

LIFO   Last-in, first-out method of storage and retrieving data in a stack.

Memory Address Register (MAR)   Internal register used to hold the address of data which the CPU is reading from or writing into memory.

Nonmaskable Interrupt (NMI)   Overriding interrupt signal. If the proper signal level is present, it will always interrupt the μP, regardless of the interrupt enable status.

Program Counter (PC)   Internal register which always contains the address in memory of the next instruction which the CPU is to fetch. Many μPs divide the PC into 8-bit registers; PCH holds the 8 high-order bits, PCL holds the 8 low-order bits.

Sign Bit   MSB of a data word which can be positive (0) or negative (1).

Single-Chip μC   An individual chip contains all the functional elements necessary for a complete computer. The elements include an ALU, Control, RAM, ROM, and I/O.

Stack   Portion of RAM reserved for the temporary storage and retrieval of information, typically the contents of the μP's internal registers during an interrupt.

Stack Pointer Register   Special memory address register used only for the stack portion of RAM.

Subroutine   Sequence of instructions which perform a specific function and is available for general use by other programs.

QUESTIONS AND PROBLEMS

Section 5.1

5.1   Which of the following is *not* a function that a μP performs?
   (a)   providing timing and control signals for all elements of the μC
   (b)   transferring data to and from I/O devices

(c) performing arithmetic and logic operations called for by instructions

(d) storing programs to be executed at some later time

5.2 What are the three major functional areas of the μP chip?

5.3 Which of the following is a μP output control signal?
(a) RESET (b) IRQ (c) MREQ (d) HOLD

5.4 What μP control input causes the μP to temporarily suspend execution of the current program?

Section 5.2

5.5 The instruction register:
(a) stores flags.
(b) holds instruction addresses.
(c) is used in special address modes.
(d) stores op codes.

5.6 The Program Counter (PC):
(a) holds operand addresses.
(b) holds instruction addresses.
(c) holds data addresses.
(d) holds op codes.

5.7 The Memory Address register:
(a) holds instruction addresses.
(b) holds op-codes.
(c) holds operand addresses.
(d) holds flags.

5.8 Which register partakes in many of the operations performed by the ALU?
(a) Program Counter
(b) Instruction register
(c) Memory Address register
(d) Accumulator

5.9 Which of the following is *not* a typical use of a μP's General-Purpose register?
(a) temporary storage
(b) counters
(c) sometimes used as index registers
(d) holds address of next available location on stack

5.10 Assume that $[X] = 05_{16}$. A program contains the following instruction.

```
0400   6F   LDA,X (load accumulator indexed)
       31   lower-order address byte
       03   high-order address byte
```

From what memory address will the Accumulator be loaded?

5.11 During conditional branch instructions, the contents of this register are examined to determine the next sequence of instructions to be performed.
(a) Index register
(b) Instruction register
(c) Status register
(d) Memory Address register

5.12 The Stack:
(a) is an area of ROM used for the retrieval of information, typically tables and codes.
(b) is an area of RAM used for the temporary storage and retrieval of information, typically the μP's internal registers.

(c) is an area in RAM used for the storage of a program to be executed at some future time.

(d) an area in ROM used for controlling I/O interfacing.

5.13 Last-in, first-out describes the operation of:

(a) RAM   (b) ROM   (c) Stack   (d) ALU

5.14 Which register stores the address of the next location to be used in a special section of memory reserved for temporary storage during operations such as subroutine calls and interrupt servicing?

(a) Status register   (c) Program Counter register
(b) Memory Address register   (d) Stack Pointer register

5.15 The Stack Pointer is incremented and decremented:

(a) by the programmer in his or her main program.
(b) by the μP each time data are placed on or taken off the stack.
(c) by external logic circuits each time a READ operation is performed.
(d) by external logic circuits each time a WRITE operation is performed.

5.16 A certain microprocessor has two General-Purpose registers, X and Y, each of which is 8 bits long.

(a) Consider the flowchart in Fig. 5.4. If X were used as the General-Purpose register, what is the maximum number of times that the program can execute the instruction sequence at two?

(b) Suppose that we wanted the program to execute this instruction sequence exactly 2550 times. We could use both X and Y as counters to accomplish this task. Draw a flowchart showing exactly how this can be done.

(c) Repeat part (b) for the case where we want to execute the instruction sequence exactly 4000 times.

5.17 A table of 50 data words is stored in memory locations 1000 to 1031 (hex). Draw a flowchart for a program that will take these data words and move them to memory locations 2000 to 2031. (*Hint:* Use indexed addressing as in Fig. 5.5.)

5.18 Assume that $[SP] = 01FF_{16}$. If *three* "push" instructions are followed by *two* "pull" instructions, what will be the new $[SP]$?

Section 5.3

5.19 When the ALU performs an arithmetic or logic operation between two operands, where does the result usually end up?

5.20 Repeat Question 5.19 for single-operand operations.

5.21 Which one of the following is an ALU single-operand instruction?

(a) ADD   (b) COMPARE   (c) AND   (d) COMPLEMENT

5.22 Which one of the following is an ALU two-operand operation?

(a) INCREMENT   (c) ROTATE
(b) SHIFT   (d) COMPARE

5.23 What is the difference between a SHIFT operation and a ROTATE operation?

5.24 How does a COMPARE operation differ from the SUBTRACT operation?

5.25 What are some of the ways that the more complex arithmetic operations such as multiplication and division can be performed in μP systems?

Sections 5.4–5.7

5.26 What advantages do 16-bit μPs have over 8-bit μPs? What is one of their major disadvantages? What are they primarily designed to compete with?

5.27 What is the primary advantage of bipolar bit-slice microprocessors? Why can't they be fabricated on a single chip?

5.28 What functions are typically included on a single-chip μC? What is the principal area of application for these devices?

6

INPUT/OUTPUT MODES

In most μP and μC applications, the CPU must communicate with a variety of I/O devices. The information that passes between the CPU and these peripheral devices can be classified as either *data* or *control*. Data are typically numeric or alphanumeric information encoded in some suitable binary code, such as straight binary, BCD, or ASCII. Control information is usually one of several types: commands from the CPU, requests for service from I/O devices, control codes from the CPU, or status codes from I/O devices. In all but the simplest μP systems, the transmission of this information between the μP and I/O devices is a critical part of the system design. In this chapter we discuss the various methods of I/O transfer used in μP systems. In Chapter 7 we deal with interfacing between the CPU and I/O devices.

6.1 SOME BASIC TERMS

The discussion of I/O always involves the transmission of *data* from one device to another. Various terms are used to distinguish between the device that is sending the data and the device that is receiving the data. At various times in the subsequent sections, we will use the terms *sender, transmitter, source,* and *talker* to refer to the device sending data, and the terms *receiver, destination,* and *listener* to refer to the device receiving data.

It is important to understand that both the "sender" and "receiver" of *data* will at various times send *control* information to each other. For example, when the CPU is ready to send data to an output device, it might first send a control signal (DAV) to inform the output device that there are *data available* for it (see Fig. 6.1). The output device, upon receiving the DAV signal from the CPU, can accept the data and then send a control signal (DAC) back to the CPU to inform the CPU that it has *accepted* the data. This process of exchanging control signals during data transfer is commonly referred to as *handshaking*, a term we will use often in the discussions that follow. As we shall see, some types of I/O transfer do not use handshaking; in these cases, the data sender transmits the data to the receiver without sending a DAV signal.

6.2   SOME EXAMPLES OF I/O

Before we get into the details of interfacing, we will briefly describe two common I/O cases to give a better perspective of the types of situations that occur in μP systems.

Process/Instrument Control

In applications where a μP is used to control an instrument, a piece of equipment, or a process, the program that is to be executed is permanently stored

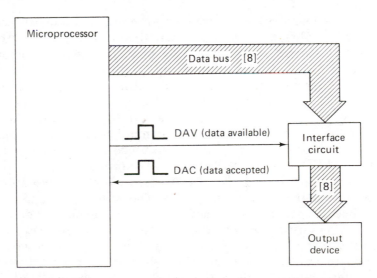

FIGURE 6.1   Handshaking between the μP and an output device.

in ROM. When the instrument or process is turned on, a signal is sent to the RESET input of the μP to begin executing instructions. For many μPs, including the 8080/8085 and Z-80, the first instruction to be executed after RESET is taken from memory location 0000_{16}. This means that the program must be stored in ROM beginning at address 0000. The 6800 and 6502 operate somewhat differently. Upon RESET, these μPs automatically read the contents of two specific address locations (FFFE and FFFF for the 6800). The two bytes obtained from these locations are sent to the program counter as the 16-bit address where the first instruction is stored. These two bytes are called the *reset vector* since they tell the μP where to get the first instruction after RESET occurs. The reset vector can specify any 16-bit address as the starting address of the program.

As the μP executes the program stored in ROM, it will be called upon to receive data inputs from devices that are monitoring some physical process variable (e.g., temperature, speed, displacement, light level, etc.). It takes these data and operates on them according to the program instructions. Based on the results of these operations, the μP sends data or control signals to the process through appropriate output devices, such as relays, digital-to-analog converters, and readouts.

In many process or instrument control applications, there is no human intervention once the operation is initiated. The μP operates automatically and continuously under the control of the program stored in ROM. The operation of the μP is changed by changing ROMs so that a different sequence of instructions is executed.

Keyboard Entry/Display

There are many situations where a μP must communicate with a human operator. An obvious example is where the μP is part of a μC that is being used as a general-purpose computing machine. This is the principal use of μCs by computer hobbyists. Another example is the μP-controlled electronic scale used in supermarkets, where the operator supplies price information to the μP, which then transmits the total cost of the purchase to the operator. Clearly, these and similar applications require an efficient and convenient means for the operator and μP to communicate. A very common technique uses a *keyboard* for an operator-controlled *input* device and hexadecimal or decimal LED displays as μP-controlled *output devices*.

In these applications, a ROM stores a *keyboard monitor* program which the μP executes upon being RESET. The keyboard and its interface circuitry will have a specific address assigned to it in the manner described in Chapter 4. The keyboard monitor program causes the μP to read the keyboard continually to look for key actuations and, when one is sensed, the μP reads the keyboard data and determines which key has been actuated. The μP then executes instructions depending on which key was actuated.

In a general-purpose μC, the operator can send various types of information from the keyboard. For example, the operator can punch in a program using a hexadecimal-encoded keyboard. As he or she keys in the hex codes for each instruction, the μP, under the control of the *monitor* program, reads the codes from the keyboard and places them in RAM. The area of RAM where the operator's program is to be stored is also keyed in by the operator. When the complete program has been placed in RAM, the operator then directs the μP to execute the program by punching in the starting address and a specific control key (e.g., RUN or GO).

When the μC finishes executing the operator's program, it can be returned to its keyboard monitoring mode by applying a RESET signal to the μP chip. This is often done with a RESET key that is part of the keyboard. The μC is then ready to accept new information from the operator.

Of course, as the μC executes the operator's program, it must transmit information and results to the operator in some manner. LED displays provide a convenient means for the μC to do this. The displays and their associated interface circuitry will have a particular address assigned to them as described in Chapter 4, and the program must contain instructions that cause the μC to write data into the displays. The displays are also often used as part of the keyboard monitor program to display the keys being actuated so that the operator can see what has been punched in.

These two examples should begin to give you an idea of the types of communication that can take place between the μC and I/O devices. As we go further in this chapter, you will learn more of the details on the interfacing required for not only these two situations but many others as well.

6.3 INPUT/OUTPUT ALTERNATIVES

There are several different ways in which I/O transfers can be initiated and controlled. For example, the transfer of data between a CPU and I/O device can be initiated either by the CPU or by the device. Once the I/O transfer

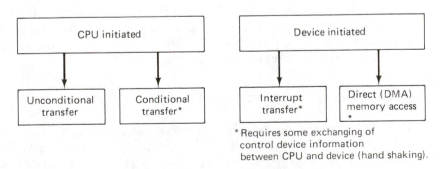

FIGURE 6.2 Basic I/O transfer alternatives.

has been initiated, it can be carried out under the control of the CPU or, in some cases, under the control of the I/O device. The basic alternatives are presented in Fig. 6.2.

When the CPU initiates an I/O transfer, it always does so under program control whereby it is called on to execute one or more instructions that transfer data between a CPU register (e.g., Accumulator) and the peripheral device. This CPU-initiated transfer can take place *unconditionally*, where the I/O device must *always* be ready for communication, or it can take place *conditionally* only when the I/O device is ready for communication. Conditional transfer always requires some form of handshaking between the CPU and the device prior to the actual transfer of data.

There are two types of device-initiated I/O transfer, both of which require an exchange of control signals between the device and the CPU. An *interrupt transfer* involves the I/O device sending a signal to the µP's INTERRUPT input (INT, IRQ, etc.) to inform the CPU that the device is ready for data transfer. The CPU, in response, will interrupt the execution of the program it is currently working on and will jump to a new program called the *interrupt service routine*, which contains instructions for transferring data to or from the interrupting device. A *direct memory access* (DMA) transfer is the other device-initiated transfer, and it is the only type of data transfer that is *not* under CPU (program) control. The data transfer takes place under the control of special interface circuits called *DMA controllers*. Direct memory access is so called because data are transferred between the I/O device and RAM directly without involving the CPU.

We will now investigate these various I/O transfer alternatives in more detail.

6.4 CPU INITIATED – UNCONDITIONAL I/O TRANSFER

This type of data transfer is used only in situations where an output device is always ready to accept data from the CPU or an input device always has data ready for the CPU. In such cases, there is no need for any exchange of control signals between the CPU and the I/O device. The CPU simply executes instructions which cause it to write data into the output device or to read data from the input device. We will look at two specific examples which illustrate how this form of transfer takes place.

CPU Transmitting Data to LED Displays

The CPU can send an 8-bit data word to be displayed on some type of readout. One possible method is shown in Fig. 6.3, where eight *light-emitting diodes* (LEDs) are used to display a single byte of data transmitted from the CPU. The output register and open-collector inverters act as the interface

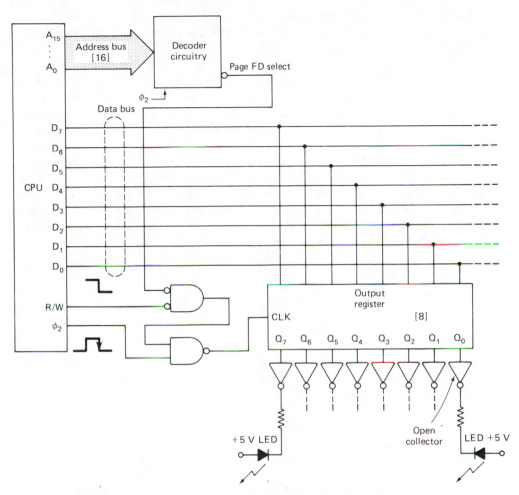

FIGURE 6.3 Eight LEDs connected as an output device for displaying a single data byte.

circuitry between the CPU data bus lines and the LEDs. The NOR* gate and NAND gate provide the logic necessary to transfer the CPU data to the LEDs at the proper time. Although not shown in the diagram, there may be need for some type of buffer circuit between each CPU data line and register input. The data lines of any MOS or CMOS microprocessor do not have enough current drive capability to drive a standard TTL load. The buffers would not be necessary if the output register is a CMOS or low-power TTL device, since these logic families require less input current.

Recall from our work in Section 4.6 that the decoder circuitry decodes

---

*From our work in Chapter 2, recall that an AND gate with inverters on its inputs is equivalent to an NOR gate.

the address bus lines to generate signals to select the various I/O devices. We have chosen the page FD select line for our LED readouts. Any address from FD00 to FDFF will produce a LOW on this select line. This LOW and the LOW from the μP's R/W line produce a HIGH at the NOR output (recall that R/W = 0 for a CPU WRITE operation). Thus, when the ϕ_2 pulse occurs, its negative-going transition will produce a positive-going transition at the NAND output. This positive-going transition transfers the byte of data from the CPU data lines to the output register, which then stores the data for the LEDs. A HIGH on a register output line causes its LED to conduct through the inverter's output transistor. The ON/OFF states of the eight LEDs, then, represent the 8 bits of data transferred from the CPU.

The CPU can be instructed to output data to the LEDs at any point during the execution of a program. For example, suppose that at a certain point in the program we want to display the contents of the Accumulator. The following three-byte instruction will accomplish this:

$$
\begin{array}{lll}
\text{byte 1} & \text{8D} \longleftarrow & \text{op code for STA} \\
\text{byte 2} & \text{00} \diagdown & \text{address of display} \\
\text{byte 3} & \text{FD} \diagup & \text{output port}
\end{array}
$$

The first byte is the op code for the Store Accumulator (STA) instruction. The code, 8D is the actual op code for a 6502 μP's STA instruction. The second and third bytes are the address where the contents of the accumulator is to be stored. In this case, the address is FD00,* which selects the LED display. Actually, any address on page FD could be used. Note that the instruction for storing the Accumulator data in the display register is no different from storing it in a RAM location. In either case, a STA instruction is used.

This same idea can be used to display the contents of any one of the μP's internal registers provided that there is an appropriate instruction in the μP's instruction set. For example, the contents of the 6502's X and Y registers can be stored using a Store X (STX) instruction and Store Y (STY) instruction, respectively. Again, these Store instructions can be used to write data into RAM or into an output device such as the LED displays.

Often, the use of single LEDs to display CPU data in binary form is not as desirable as displaying it in hexadecimal form. Special LED displays are available for this purpose. One in particular is the Hewlett-Packard 5082-7302, which is not only an LED hexadecimal display, but also contains its own 4-bit latching register and decoder/driver circuitry.

---

*For the 6502 μP, the low-order address byte comes before the high-order address byte in the instruction sequence.

Simple Input Port

As another example of CPU-initiated, unconditional transfer, we will consider a simple input port used to enter an 8-bit data word into the CPU. For purposes of illustration, we will assume that the data word is coming from a set of eight switches. These switches might be located on a μC's front panel to allow the operator to manually set the data word to be read by the CPU. They could also be switches that are part of some physical process that the μC is controlling. As part of its control program, the μC may have to examine the status of these various switches to decide what control action to take. In either case, the switch-to-μC interface would be similar to that shown in Fig. 6.4.

Tristate buffers act as the interface between the switch inputs and the CPU's data bus. These buffers are normally disabled, so their outputs are essentially disconnected from the data bus. They will be enabled (ENABLE = 1) only when the CPU performs a READ operation (R/W = 1) from any address on page FA. When enabled, the buffers will place a binary number on the data bus corresponding to the states of the switch inputs. An open switch produces a 1 and a closed switch a 0. This 8-bit number is then transferred into the CPU in the same manner as a word is read from memory.

The CPU can be instructed to read the switch data by using an instruction like the following:

byte 1   AD ⟵— op code for LDA
byte 2   00
byte 3   FA   address of switch input port

The first byte is the 6502's op code for the Load Accumulator (LDA) instruction. The second and third bytes are the address FA00, which corresponds to the switch input port. This instruction will cause the CPU to read the values of the switch inputs and load them into the Accumulator with switch S_7 loaded into the Accumulator's MSB (bit 7) and S_0 into the LSB (bit 0). For example, if switches S_7, S_6, S_2, and S_1 are closed and the others are open, the Accumulator will be loaded with the number 00111001.

Once the switch data has been entered into the Accumulator, it can be used for many different purposes. In some cases, the switch data represent a numerical value which the program will perform operations upon. Other times the switches may represent some type of code that the program has to examine to determine what instruction sequence to perform next. To illustrate, consider a typical situation where the CPU must be programmed to do the following:

1. Read the switch data.
2. Examine the status of switch S_5.

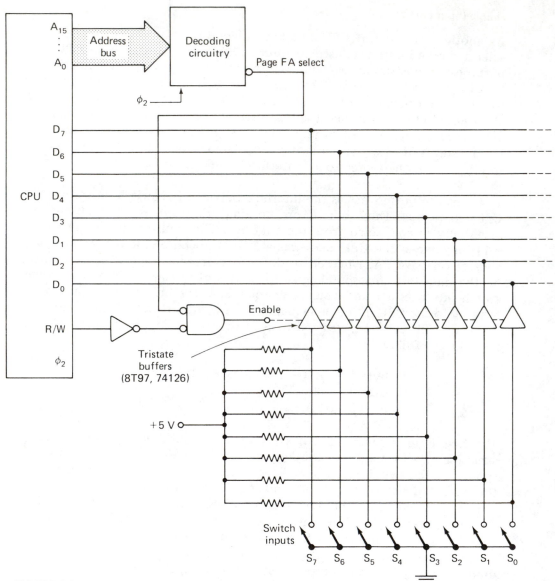

FIGURE 6.4 Use of an input port to read a single byte of switch data.

    3. If $S_5 = 0$, execute a certain sequence of instructions, which we will simply call sequence A.

    4. If $S_5 = 1$, execute a different sequence of instructions — sequence B.

The program flowchart for one means of implementing this sequence of operation is shown in Fig. 6.5. Let us follow through this flowchart for the case where the switch inputs are $S_7 S_6 S_5 S_4 S_3 S_2 S_1 S_0 = 10101001$. In block 1,

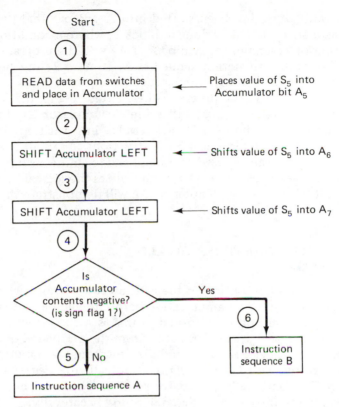

FIGURE 6.5 Flowchart for program that examines status of switch S_5 to determine which instruction sequence to follow.

these data are read into the CPU and stored in the Accumulator (i.e., LDA instruction). Thus, the Accumulator contents become

A_7	A_6	A_5	A_4	A_3	A_2	A_1	A_0
1	0	1	0	1	0	0	1

status of S_5

Note that the status of S_5 is now stored in bit A_5.

Blocks 2 and 3 each contain a SHIFT LEFT instruction so that the contents of the Accumulator are shifted two places to the left. The Accumulator contents become

A_7	A_6	A_5	A_4	A_3	A_2	A_1	A_0
1	0	1	0	0	1	0	0

status of S_5

The value of S_5 has been shifted into A_7. Recall that the CPU can interpret A_7 as a sign bit. This is done in block 4, where a conditional jump or branch instruction examines the sign bit.* If $A_7 = 0$, the program continues to block 5 to execute instruction sequence A. If $A_7 = 1$, the program branches or jumps to block 6 to execute instruction sequence B.

In summary, the program flowcharted in Fig. 6.5 loads the Accumulator with the switch data, shifts the Accumulator left the number of times needed to bring the desired switch value into the sign-bit position, and tests this sign bit to determine what instructions to execute next. There are other methods that can be used to isolate and examine a single bit of a data word. One of these is called *masking* and utilizes the logical operations (AND, OR, EX-OR) described in Chapter 5. We will demonstrate the *masking* operation in a subsequent discussion.

6.5 CPU INITIATED – CONDITIONAL (POLLED) I/O TRANSFER

In this type of I/O transfer, the CPU must determine whether the peripheral device is ready for communication before the actual data transfer takes place under program control. Normally, this is a three-step process whereby the CPU must read *status* information from the peripheral device, test this status to see if the device is ready, and then perform the data transfer when the device is ready. This type of I/O is often called *polled* I/O because the device has to be continually polled to see if it is ready. The sequence of steps is shown in the flowchart of Fig. 6.6. Study it carefully.

As the flowchart shows, the CPU keeps executing blocks 1 and 2 until the I/O device indicates that it is ready for data transfer. This loop is called a *wait loop* because the CPU operation stays in this loop while it waits for the I/O device to get ready. When the device is ready, the operation proceeds to block 3, where the CPU performs the data-transfer operation with the device. After the data transfer is completed, the CPU continues with the rest of the program.

This type of I/O transfer requires some handshaking between the CPU and the I/O device. The control signals required for this handshaking will depend on the device. We will go through a complete example using an analog-to-digital (A/D) converter as an input device. First, however, we will describe the type of A/D converter that will be used.

Tristate Output A/D Converter

For process control applications, many types of transducers are available that will change a physical quantity, such as temperature or light intensity, into a linearly proportional voltage. This voltage is an analog quantity that

*For instance, the 8080A would use a JUMP-IF-MINUS (JM) instruction and the 6502 would use a BRANCH-ON-MINUS (BMI) instruction.

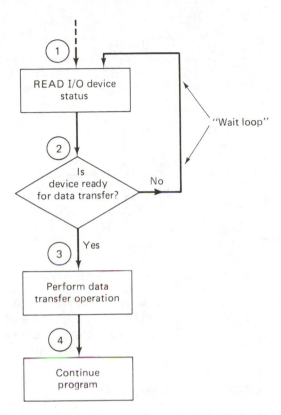

FIGURE 6.6 Flowchart showing typical sequence of steps involved in a conditional (polled) I/O data transfer.

can have any value within a given range, such as 0 V to 10 V. To interface this analog voltage to a digital controller requires that the voltage be converted to its digital representation by an A/D converter. Figure 6.7 shows one type of A/D converter, which is easily interfaced to a μP system.

This type of converter changes the analog voltage input V_A to an 8-bit digital output (D_7 through D_0) which can be either a straight binary or a BCD representation of the input. The conversion process is initiated by a pulse applied to the A/D converter's START input. The complete conversion process will take an amount of time that depends on the A/D conversion method which the particular converter uses. This time, called *conversion time*, t_c, can be as high as 100 μs for some A/D converters. During this t_c interval, as the conversion process is taking place, the A/D converter's BUSY output will go LOW. The BUSY output returns HIGH when the conversion is complete.

The digital output lines D_7 through D_0 come from tristate latches which are part of the converter. A HIGH on the ENABLE input will enable these outputs so that the digital representation of V_A is present on these lines. A LOW on the ENABLE input puts these output lines in their high-Z

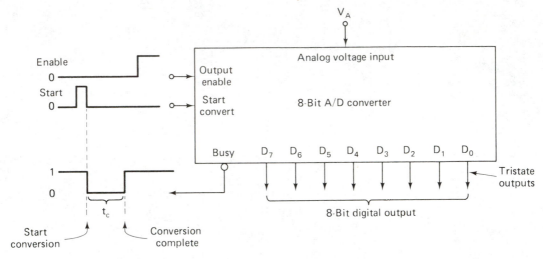

FIGURE 6.7 Typical A/D converter used in μP-based process control systems.

state. In most situations, the ENABLE input will be pulsed HIGH only after the BUSY output has indicated that the conversion is complete. If the ENABLE input is made HIGH during the t_c interval, the output lines will indicate the results of the previous A/D conversion.

Interfacing the A/D Converter to the μP

In a typical application, the input to the A/D converter is an analog voltage, V_A, generated by a process transducer and its associated circuitry. The digital output of the converter is loaded into the μP upon command. The μP then processes this digital value according to its stored program and generates appropriate control outputs to the process. The operation requires several communications between the μP and the A/D converter, as outlined below:

1. The CPU issues a START pulse to the A/D converter to tell it to convert the current value of V_A to its digital equivalent.
2. The CPU then continually reads and tests the status of the converter's BUSY output until is returns HIGH, indicating that the conversion is complete.
3. The CPU then reads the A/D digital output into one of its internal registers.

Clearly, this sequence requires *three* different control signals from the CPU to the A/D converter — one for START, one to transfer the BUSY output into the CPU to be tested, and one to transfer the A/D digital output into the CPU. One means for implementing this operation is shown in Fig. 6.8. Study it carefully before reading on.

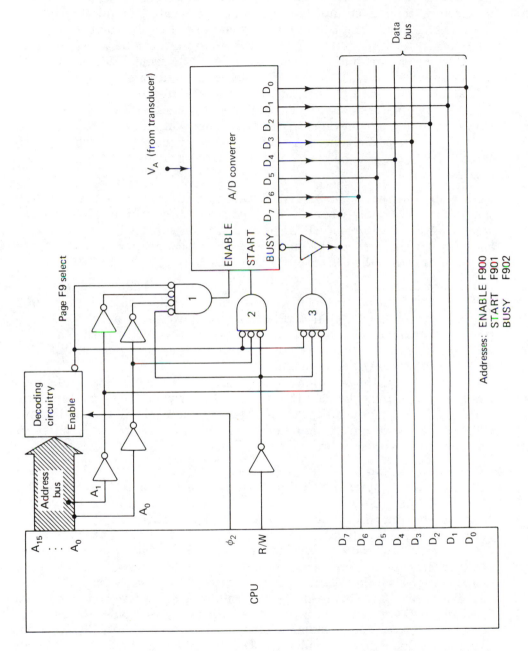

FIGURE 6.8 Interfacing an A/D converter to a μP using conditional (polled) I/O transfer.

209

The A/D outputs D_7 through D_0 are connected to the data bus so that they can be transferred into the CPU when NOR gate 1 produces a HIGH at the ENABLE input. The BUSY output is connected to the top data bus line (D_7) through a tristate buffer. Thus, the BUSY output can be transferred into the CPU when the buffer is enabled by a HIGH from NOR gate 3. The START input to the A/D converter comes from NOR gate 2, which will provide a pulse when the CPU generates the proper address code.

We have chosen to use the PAGE F9 SELECT line for the A/D converter. However, unlike our previous I/O examples, we will also need to use two of the lower-order address lines, A_0 and A_1, to allow us to select which of the three NOR gates will be activated.* Let us look at each NOR gate more closely.

NOR Gate 1   It has inputs A_0, A_1, $\overline{R/W}$, and PAGE F9 SELECT, and its output will go HIGH only when these inputs are all LOW. This condition occurs when the CPU performs a READ operation from address F900 (A_1 and A_0 are both 0). This enables the outputs of the A/D converter so that they will be transferred into the CPU over the data bus.

NOR Gate 2   It has inputs $\overline{A_0}$, $\overline{R/W}$, and PAGE F9 SELECT, and its output will go HIGH whenever the CPU performs a READ from address **F901** ($A_1 = 0$ and $A_0 = 1$). This READ operation, however, is a *dummy READ* because nothing is being placed on the data bus. It is simply used as a means for generating the F901 address code to produce a positive pulse out of NOR gate 2 to start the A/D conversion.

Incidentally, the situation where no device is placing data on the data bus is called *floating* the data bus. For most μPs, when the data bus is floating during a READ operation, an ambiguous data word will be read into the CPU's internal register. This is no problem here since we are not going to use the ambiguous word anyway.

NOR Gate 3   It has inputs $\overline{A_1}$, $\overline{R/W}$, and PAGE F9 SELECT, and its output will go HIGH whenever the CPU performs a READ from address F902. This places the BUSY output onto data bus line D_7 for transfer into the CPU. Note that the other 7 data bus lines will be floating. This again is no problem, because the CPU is only interested in the status of the BUSY output.

Now we are ready to look at how the CPU must be programmed in order to execute the transfer of data from the A/D converter. Figure 6.9 shows the program flowchart. Examine it carefully before reading on.

When the CPU gets to the point in its program where it requires data from the A/D converter, it begins by sending a START pulse (block 1). It does this by executing a dummy instruction to read address F901. An instruction to load the accumulator (LDA) from F901 would be sufficient. This will start the A/D conversion process.

*Recall from Chapter 4 that only the higher-order address lines A_8 through A_{15} are decoded to generate PAGE SELECT outputs.

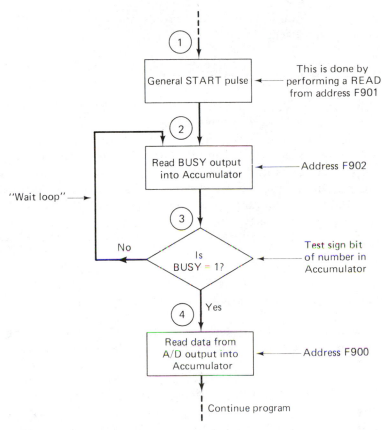

FIGURE 6.9 Flowchart showing steps taken by CPU to obtain data from A/D converter.

The CPU then proceeds to continuously read the BUSY output and test to determine if it is a 1 (blocks 2 and 3). It repeats this process as many times as necessary until the BUSY output goes high. Since the BUSY bit is connected to data bus line D_7, it will be loaded into bit 7 of the Accumulator, the sign-bit position. Thus, it can be tested using a conditional JUMP instruction such as BRANCH-IF-PLUS (BPL), which examines the Sign flag and, if it is a 0, will branch or jump back to block 2. If the Sign flag is 1 indicating BUSY = 1), the program will continue to block 4.

Here the CPU executes a LDA instruction from address F900 to transfer the A/D outputs into the Accumulator. Execution of the program then continues from that point. There may be later points in the program where the CPU must get a new value from the A/D converter and must again execute the same sequence of instructions outlined in Fig. 6.9. The programmer may choose to repeat this sequence of instructions each time it is required in the program, or may elect to just write the sequence once and have the program jump to this sequence (*subroutine*) each time it is required. This latter technique is called *subroutining*, and is a very useful programming tool that we will discuss in more detail later.

Disadvantage of Conditional I/O Transfer

This example should point out the major drawback of conditional or polled I/O transfer — the μP has to *wait* for the I/O device. In some cases, especially for slow I/O devices, the μP will waste a lot of its time reading and testing the status of the I/O device. If there is nothing else for the μP to do while the I/O device is getting ready, it does not matter. However, in many applications, the μP can be doing other tasks while it is waiting, such as processing data or communicating with other I/O devices (keep in mind that a typical μP can execute an instruction in a few microseconds). In the next section we will see how this can be accomplished using a different I/O transfer scheme.

6.6 DEVICE-INITIATED I/O TRANSFER — INTERRUPTS

This type of I/O transfer makes more efficient use of the computer's time because the μP will not have to repeatedly check to see if the device is ready for transfer. Instead, the μP is free to do other tasks, and when the I/O device is ready, it will send a signal to one of the μP's INTERRUPT inputs. This will cause the μP to suspend execution of the program it is currently working on and to perform a special *interrupt service routine*. This service routine typically contains the instructions for transferring data to or from the interrupting device. When the CPU completes execution of the interrupt service routine, it returns to the program it was executing at the time the interrupt occurred. This process is illustrated in Fig. 6.10.

Here we have a portion of the memory map for a typical situation. Memory locations 0000_{16} through $03FF_{16}$ (pages 00 through 03) contain the *main program* of instructions which the CPU must execute. An interrupt service routine (ISR) is stored in locations 0500 through 0510. During normal operation the CPU is executing the main program. Let us suppose that while it is in the process of executing the instruction at address 0250, an I/O device sends an interrupt signal to the CPU (see point 1 in Fig. 6.10). The CPU will ignore this interrupt signal until it has finished executing the instruction at 0250. When it completes that instruction, it senses the presence of the interrupt signal. The, the CPU immediately branches to address 0500 (point 2) and takes its next instruction from the interrupt service routine (ISR). It continues executing the instructions in the ISR until it reaches address 0510. This address will contain an instruction telling the CPU to return to the main program where it left off when it was interrupted. This RETURN FROM

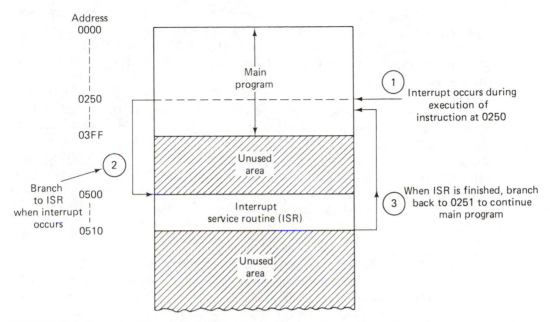

FIGURE 6.10 Example of how an interrupt causes a change in the execution of a program.

INTERRUPT (RTI) instruction will cause the CPU to return to address 0251 in the main program and to continue from there (point 3).

Interrupt Considerations

The interrupt process we have just described eliminates the need for the CPU to waste its time continually checking to see if an I/O device is ready for communication. Interrupt operation is extremely useful in applications where the CPU must interface with several I/O devices whose needs for servicing are *asynchronous* — that is, they might occur at any time and so cannot be handled through programmed unconditional I/O transfer. Although the interrupt process appears fairly straightforward, a little thought will raise several important questions about its operation. We will now consider these questions to see how μP manufacturers have dealt with them.

Return Address

1. *After executing the ISR, how does the CPU know what address in the main program it should branch back to?* This is a sensible question since an interrupt can occur at any time and there is no way of predicting what instruction the CPU will be processing when the interrupt occurs. This problem is taken care of *automatically* within the CPU by temporarily storing the

current contents of the Program Counter (PC) before branching to the ISR. Most CPUs will store the PC on the *stack* portion of memory prior to jumping to the ISR. Then, when the RETURN FROM INTERRUPT (RTI) instruction is executed at the end of the ISR, the CPU *automatically* reloads the PC from the stack.

To illustrate, for the example of Fig. 6.10, the PC is at 0250 when the interrupt occurs. As stated before, the CPU finishes executing the instruction at 0250, which includes incrementing the PC to 0251. This value, 0251, is the *return address* which the CPU stores in two successive locations on the stack (remember, the PC is 16 bits, and each memory location only stores 8 bits). Then, when the CPU executes the RTI instruction, it transfers the return address (0251) from the stack back into the PC so that the next instruction is taken from 0251 in the main program.

Disabling the Interrupt

2. *What happens when an I/O device interrupts the CPU while it is executing a portion of a program that requires continuous processing?* This might happen, for example, when the CPU is in a *timing loop* (discussed later) or when the CPU is communicating with another I/O device. In situations like these, the occurrence of an interrupt could have undesirable results. For this reason, all microprocessors have some provision for disabling the interrupt operation under program control. This is usually done by designating a single flip-flop in the μP as the Interrupt Disable flag, I, and having instructions that the programmer can use to set or reset this flag. This flag, which is also called Interrupt Mask or Interrupt Inhibit, is sometimes included as part of the μP's status register.

When an interrupt occurs, the CPU will ignore it if the Interrupt Disable flag, I, has been set to 1 by a previous program instruction. If this flag has been cleared to 0 by an earlier instruction, the CPU will respond to the interrupt in the normal manner. Thus, the programmer has the capability of disabling or enabling the interrupt operation during any or all portions of a program. This is typically done with instructions such as DISABLE INTERRUPT (DI) and ENABLE INTERRUPT (EI) which can be inserted anywhere in a program.

Types of Interrupt Inputs

3. *How many different types of interrupt inputs does a μP usually have?* Many μPs have two types of interrupt inputs—*maskable* and *nonmaskable*. A *maskable* interrupt is the type of interrupt we discussed above and whose occurrence is ignored by the CPU when the Interrupt Disable flag is set. A *nonmaskable* interrupt input operates differently since the CPU always responds to it regardless of the status of the I flag. In other words, its effect *cannot* be disabled by the programmer.

All μPs have a maskable interrupt input which goes by various symbols, such as INT, IRQ, and IREQ. We will use INT to represent this type of interrupt input. Many, but not all, μPs have a nonmaskable interrupt input which is usually given the symbol NMI. Not only does the NMI input always interrupt the μP, but it also has priority over the INT input. This means that if both INT and NMI inputs are simultaneously activated, the CPU will respond to the NMI first. A major use of the NMI input is in a power-failure shutdown routine. Here a special circuit detects whenever the system power supply voltage drops below a certain level and generates a signal to the μP's NMI input. The CPU then immediately branches to the ISR, which contains instructions for storing the contents of the CPU's internal registers and important RAM locations in a special area of memory which can operate from battery power (such as a CMOS RAM). This process only requires a few microseconds and can be completed before the power-supply voltage drops low enough to destroy the contents of these registers.

Use of the maskable interrupt, INT, often requires some handshaking between the CPU and the device that generates the INT signal. We will illustrate this for the A/D converter interface that was discussed in the previous section. Figure 6.11 shows the necessary modifications of the circuit of Fig. 6.8 for operation using the interrupt method. First, note that the BUSY output is not connected to the data bus since the CPU is not going to read the value to determine when the A/D converter has data ready. Instead, the positive-going transition of the BUSY signal will clock the JK FF, causing the CPU's $\overline{\text{INT}}$ input to go LOW when the A/D converter has a digital value ready for transmission.

If the CPU's Interrupt Disable flag, I, is LOW when $\overline{\text{INT}}$ goes LOW, the CPU will respond to the interrupt input in the manner previously outlined. If the CPU's I flag is HIGH when $\overline{\text{INT}}$ goes LOW, the CPU will ignore the interrupt input and will continue executing the instructions in its current program until an ENABLE INTERRUPT instruction clears I to 0. Then, the CPU will respond to the $\overline{\text{INT}}$ input (assuming that it is still LOW) and will go through the normal interrupt sequence.

As the CPU recognizes the interrupt and branches to the interrupt service routine (ISR), it *automatically* sets the I flag to 1. This is done to assure that the CPU will not respond to this same interrupt input again. For this example, the ISR will contain the instruction which reads the A/D output into the Accumulator. It may also contain instructions for processing these data. The last instruction in the ISR will be a RETURN FROM INTERRUPT (RTI) instruction, which returns the CPU to the program it was previously executing. In some μPs, the RTI instruction will also automatically clear I back to 0 so that subsequent interrupts can be recognized. Clearly, then, it is necessary to reset the $\overline{\text{INT}}$ input back to 1 prior to the RTI instruction or the CPU will respond to the same interrupt when it returns to the main program. This can be done by having an instruction somewhere in the ISR which sends a LOW

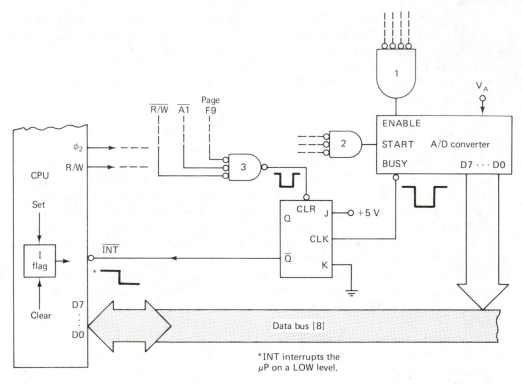

FIGURE 6.11 Interfacing the A/D converter to the μP using the maskable interrupt, $\overline{\text{INT}}$.

pulse to clear the JK FF. For our example, we are using OR* gate 3, which can be driven LOW by execution of a dummy READ instruction from address F902. Some μPs, notably the 8080A, generate an INTERRUPT ACKNOWLEDGE signal (INTA) after recognizing an interrupt. This signal can be used to reset the $\overline{\text{INT}}$ input, therefore eliminating the need for the special clearing instruction in the ISR.

Saving Register Contents

4. *What happens if the contents of one or more of the CPU's internal registers is being used by the main program when it is interrupted and the ISR changes the contents of these registers as it uses them for its own purposes?* The result will usually be disastrous because when the CPU returns to execute the main program, it will continue as if its registers' contents were the same as they were prior to the interrupt. Fortunately, this problem can be solved by storing the contents of the CPU registers somewhere before

*From our work in Chapter 2, recall that a NAND gate with inverters on its inputs is equivalent to an OR gate.

they are used in the ISR. In most μPs, this can be accomplished by using the first few instructions of the ISR to load these registers on the stack portion of memory. Then, at the end of the ISR, prior to the RTI instruction, the contents of these registers can be restored by reading them from the stack in the reverse order. We will discuss the special instructions used for storing and retrieving from the stack when we discuss programming in detail.

It might be of interest to note that the 6800 μP *automatically* takes care of saving the contents of all its registers on the stack during an interrupt without the need for special instructions. It also automatically restores the register contents upon a return from interrupt. This can be a great boon to the programmer, since it saves him/her from having to include the special stack instructions in each ISR.

Address of ISR

5. *When an interrupt occurs, how does the CPU know what address it should branch to for the ISR?* The answer to this will vary from one μP to the next and can best be determined by reading the manufacturer's literature. We will, however, describe the methods used in several of the currently popular microprocessors.

The reader may recall from our earlier discussion of the RESET operation that the 6800 and 6502 μPs obtain a 16-bit *reset vector* from two fixed locations in memory (usually ROM). This reset vector is the address where the CPU will find the first instruction of the program it is to execute. These two μPs handle the interrupt operation in the same way. When an interrupt occurs, the CPU obtains a 16-bit *interrupt vector* from two fixed locations in memory. This interrupt vector is then loaded into the program counter as the address where the CPU will go for the first instruction of the ISR.

To illustrate, Fig. 6.12 shows how the last six bytes of ROM are used to store the various address vectors for the 6502 μP. When the RESET input is activated (a LOW for the 6502), the μP automatically takes the contents of ROM locations FFFC and FFFD and loads them into the program counter. For the example in Fig. 6.12, the RESET vector is 0000, so the CPU begins executing instructions starting at that address. When the INT input is activated, the μP automatically transfers the contents of locations FFFE and FFFF into the PC. For this example, the INT vector is 0150, so the CPU begins executing the ISR at address 0150. Similarly, when an NMI occurs, the NMI vector stored in locations FFFA and FFFB will be loaded into the PC. Note that the INT and NMI vectors are different and therefore point to different interrupt service routines.

The 8080A uses a much different scheme for branching to the ISR. When a device sends an interrupt signal to the 8080A, the 8080A sends a control signal, INTA, to the device to acknowledge the interrupt. The device, when it receives INTA, must then place an 8-bit instruction code on the data

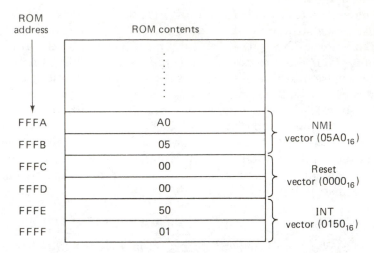

FIGURE 6.12 Memory map of reset and interrupt vectors for a 6502 μP.

bus for the CPU to read. The CPU reads this instruction and executes it the same as it would an instruction from memory. Typically, the instruction that the device places on the data bus is a RESTART (RST) instruction. The 8080A has *eight* different RST instructions, each of which causes the CPU to branch to a different address location. The interrupting device can direct the CPU to any one of these addresses for the ISR. This method of handling interrupts has the advantage that *eight* different devices can interrupt the computer, each of which can *immediately* direct the CPU to a different ISR. However, this method requires additional logic circuitry outside the μP to implement it. In applications where only one or two I/O devices are used, this extra logic can be a drawback.

The Z-80 has three different modes for handling interrupts; they are called mode 0, mode 1, and mode 2. Mode 0 is exactly the same as the method used by the 8080A. Mode 1 automatically causes the CPU to branch to address 0038 where the ISR must be located. Mode 2 utilizes the Z-80's interrupt vector (IV) register to help determine where in memory the interrupt vector is stored. The programmer chooses which interrupt mode is to be used with an INTERRUPT MODE (IM) instruction.

Interrupting an ISR

6. *Can an interrupt service routine be interrupted?* If the μP has been interrupted and is in the process of executing the ISR for the interrupting device, it cannot be interrupted by the maskable interrupt input, INT, as long as the Interrupt Disable flag, I, is 1, which is usually the case. However, if I is 0, the ISR can be interrupted by the INT input. Of course, if the μP has a nonmaskable interrupt input, NMI, it can be interrupted at any time by a signal on this input, regardless of the state of the I flag.

To illustrate the sequence of events that occurs when an ISR is interrupted, we will use the example depicted in Fig. 6.13. Here we have a 6502 μP which has separate I/O devices connected to its $\overline{\text{INT}}$ and $\overline{\text{NMI}}$ interrupt inputs (both of which are activated by a LOW signal). Also shown is the memory map which will be used for the illustration. The main program occupies address space from 0000 to 0100. The ISR for device 1 is located in addresses 0150 through 0160, and the ISR for device 2 is located in addresses 05A0 through 05B0. Locations FFFA through FFFF contain the address vectors described earlier.

Let us suppose that device 1 sends a LOW signal to INT while the μP is executing the instruction at 0036 in the main program. When the μP finishes executing this instruction, it recognizes the interrupt (assume that I = 0) and will fetch the INT vector from locations FFFE and FFFF. This address vector, 0150, is placed in the Program Counter after the previous contents of the PC (which were 0037) have been stored on the stack. The μP then begins executing the ISR for device 1 at 0150.

Now let us further suppose that device 2 sends a LOW signal to NMI while the μP is executing the instruction at 0154. Regardless of the status of I, the μP will recognize this interrupt as soon as it finishes this instruction and will fetch the NMI vector from locations FFFA and FFFB. This address

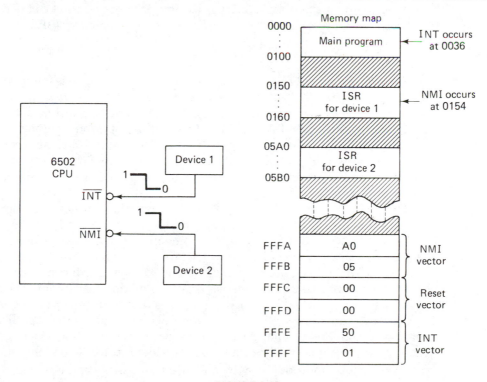

FIGURE 6.13

vector, 05A0, is placed in the PC after the previous PC contents (0155) have been stored on the stack. (At this point, the addresses 0155 and 0037 are stored on the top of the stack, in that order.) The μP now begins to execute the ISR for device 2 at 05A0.

The last instruction of this ISR is a RETURN FROM INTERRUPT (RTI), which tells the CPU to branch back to where it was when the NMI occurred. To accomplish this, the CPU reads the top two bytes from the stack and places them in the PC. This will set [PC] = 0155 so that the CPU can now continue executing the ISR for device 1. The last instruction of this ISR is also a RTI which tells the CPU to branch back to where it was when the INT occurred. The CPU again removes the top two bytes from the stack and loads them into PC so that [PC] = 0037. (Remember that when the CPU previously read 0155 from the stack, the Stack Pointer would have been incremented twice, once per byte, so that the top two locations on the stack would then hold 0037.)

With [PC] = 0037, the CPU returns to the main program and continues executing instructions from that point. This example not only illustrates the interrupt process, but also shows the usefulness of the stack in assuring that everything returns to normal after each ISR has been executed. As explained earlier, although it was not mentioned in this example, the stack could also have been used to store the contents of one or more of the CPU registers if those registers were to have their contents altered during the ISR.

Multiple Interrupts

7. *If a μP has only one or two interrupt input pins, how can it service a greater number of I/O devices?* There are several different ways in which μPs handle multiple interrupts from many I/O devices. Some μPs, such as National Semiconductor's PACE, have four interrupt input pins and so can easily handle four different interrupting devices. Most μPs, however, have only one or two interrupt inputs and so must use different methods to handle multiple interrupts. Most of the methods which are used have the basic arrangement shown in Fig. 6.14.

Here we see how several I/O devices can share a common interrupt input line to the μP. The interface circuitry for each device generates an INTERRUPT REQUEST (IRQ) output connected to the μP INT input. These outputs have to be open-collector or tristate types which are normally in the high-Z state. A LOW from any one of the IRQ outputs will drive the INT pin LOW to interrupt the μP. In this way, any number of different I/O devices can interrupt the μP. When the μP recognizes that an interrupt has occurred, it must then somehow determine *which* device has generated the interrupt signal so it will know what ISR to execute to service that device. This is where the various methods for handling multiple interrupts differ greatly.

The various methods can be classified as either *vectored interrupts* or

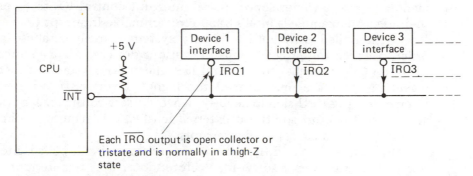

Each $\overline{IRQ}$ output is open collector or tristate and is normally in a high-Z state

FIGURE 6.14 Any number of I/O devices can be connected to a common interrupt line if each device generates an open-collector or tristate interrupt request signal ($\overline{IRQ}$).

polled interrupts. Vectored interrupts are faster but require more external hardware. Typically, the CPU responds to an interrupt by sending out an INTERRUPT ACKNOWLEDGE signal (INTA) to all the devices connected to the interrupt line. Only the device that generated the IRQ signal will respond to INTA, and it does so by supplying the CPU with the address of its ISR in some manner. For example, with the 8080A, the device places a RESTART instruction on the data bus, as explained earlier. Thus, the CPU is directed immediately to the interrupting device's ISR with very little delay.

Polled interrupt methods are slower but generally require less external hardware. When an interrupt occurs, the CPU goes to a general ISR where it executes a sequence of programmed instructions to determine the source of the interrupt. This is commonly done by having the CPU poll the status of each device, one at a time (as was done in our earlier example of conditional I/O transfer from an A/D converter) until it finds the device that is ready for I/O transfer. Depending on which device this turns out to be, the program will cause the CPU to branch to the proper service routine for that device. Clearly, this method will be slower than the vectored interrupts, but it is easier to implement and is usually the method used when the number of interrupting devices is small or when speed is not a prime consideration.

Whether vectored or polled interrupts are used, there has to be some provision for handling *simultaneous* interrupts from two or more devices. Usually, a *priority* system is set up where each device is assigned a different priority. When two devices interrupt the CPU at the same time, the CPU will service the higher-priority device first and then the lower-priority device. With vectored interrupts, this priority scheme is often accomplished by using a process called *daisy chaining*. In this process, the CPU sends the INTA signal to the highest-priority device first. If this device is not the interrupting device, it passes the INTA signal on to the next-highest priority device, and so on down the line until INTA reaches an interrupting device. This adds even more logic to that required for vectored interrupts. In fact, some μP manufacturers have developed special interrupt control ICs to be used with their μPs. An example is Intel's 8259 Programmable Interrupt Controller.

With polled interrupts, a priority system is easily established by the order in which the program polls the various devices. When an interrupt occurs, the CPU branches to a general ISR and polls the status of each device, beginning with the one assigned the highest priority. If two devices had interrupted the CPU simultaneously, it would service the higher-priority device first. Thus, no additional external hardware is required to implement a priority system using polled interrupts.

In summary, the difference between vectored and polled interrupts is one of hardware versus software. Vectored interrupts require more external hardware, are generally faster, and require less software. Polled interrupts use less hardware, are slower, and require more software to carry out the polling process.

Summary of Complete Interrupt Sequence

The steps that the μP follows while servicing a *maskable* interrupt are summarized in Fig. 6.15. Each of these steps is performed automatically by the μP and does not require special instructions from the program. Of course, the programmer has to write the ISR and make sure that it is at the correct address location specified by the interrupt vector.

Note that the μP checks the interrupt input each time it completes the execution of an instruction in the main program to see if it is being activated by an interrupting device. Also note that the stack is used to save both the *Return Address* (PC) and the *Status register*. The reason for saving the Status register will become clear during our detailed discussion of programming.

The μP follows these same steps for the nonmaskable interrupt (NMI) except that the Interrupt Disable flag is not checked since the NMI cannot be disabled.

6.7 DEVICE-INITIATED I/O TRANSFER – DIRECT MEMORY ACCESS

Up to now we have considered only the transfer of data between the CPU and I/O devices. There are many times, however, when data transfer must take place between memory and external devices. An *input* device may have information that has to be placed in RAM. An example of this would be the use of tape-cassette or "floppy-disk" storage units to store programs or data. At the appropriate time, a program or a block of data may have to be transferred from these storage devices into the μC's RAM for eventual processing by the CPU. Alternatively, an *output* device may require information that is

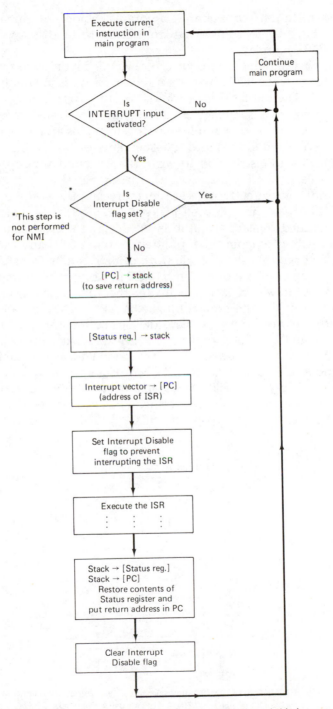

FIGURE 6.15 Steps that the μP follows to service a maskable interrupt.

stored in RAM. For example, a complete block of alphanumeric characters might have to be transferred from RAM to be displayed on a cathode-ray-tube (CRT) display.

For situations where an I/O device is involved in transferring blocks of data to or from RAM, there are two basic ways in which the transfer can be handled. The most obvious way is to use *programmed* transfer whereby the CPU executes a sequence of instructions for transferring the data between RAM and I/O. For example, the CPU executes an instruction to read a word from RAM and load it into the Accumulator (e.g., a LDA instruction). Then it executes an instruction to write the Accumulator contents into an output device (e.g., a STA instruction). Clearly, in this method, the information does not pass directly between memory and the peripheral device because it must first pass through the CPU (see Fig. 6.16). The same idea holds true for programmed transfer from an input device to RAM. The information transfer actually goes from the input device to the CPU and then to RAM.

For typical μPs, a single word of data can be transferred between memory and a peripheral device in 5 to 10 μs using programmed transfer. A lot of this time, however, is taken up by the CPU fetching instructions and the need to transfer the data through the CPU. If the data could be transferred *directly* between the peripheral device and memory, the transfer of one data word would typically require only 1 μs. This is called *direct memory access* (DMA) and is the alternative to programmed transfer. DMA offers a substantial increase in data transfer rate (words per second) over programmed transfer, especially when relatively large blocks of data are to be transferred.

DMA involves the direct transfer of data between memory and a peripheral device without involving the CPU. This means that the interface cir-

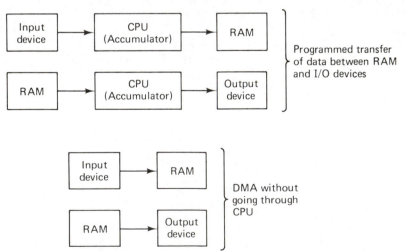

FIGURE 6.16 DMA allows faster, direct transfer of large amounts of data between I/O devices and RAM without using the CPU.

cuitry for this device must be capable of accessing memory for READ and WRITE operations in much the same way as the CPU does. A DMA interface circuit must be able to do the following:

1. Respond to a DMA request from the peripheral device by generating a control signal to the μP to place the μP in a HOLD state. [In this state, the μP suspends its operations and relinquishes its control of the system buses by placing its address, data, and memory control (R/W) lines in a high-Z state, effectively disconnecting them from the μC buses.]

2. Once the μP acknowledges that it is in a HOLD state (by sending an appropriate signal back to the DMA interface circuit), the DMA interface circuit takes control of the address and control buses. It places the addresses of the RAM locations being accessed by the peripheral device onto the address bus, and it generates the control signals necessary for completing the data transfer between RAM and the peripheral.

3. The DMA interface circuit keeps track of the locations of RAM being accessed and when the data transfer is complete, it removes the μP from its HOLD state. The μP then regains control of the system bus and can continue executing its program.

From this description, it is clear that a DMA interface circuit will be relatively complex, since it duplicates many of the same functions normally carried out by the μP. Many μP manufacturers have developed LSI chips called *DMA controllers* that are designed to be used with their μPs. These DMA controllers can be used to control the direct transfer of data between memory and several (usually 4 to 8) I/O devices. One example is Intel's 8257 DMA controller, which can handle DMA for four I/O devices when used with the 8080A μP. The 8257 contains all the logic necessary for performing the operations outlined above.

Cycle-stealing DMA

In the DMA technique just described, the DMA interface circuit disables the CPU and tkes control of the address and control buses for the period of time required to perform the transfer of a complete block of data. There is a second approach to DMA that does not disable the CPU for long periods of time. Instead, the DMA operations are performed only during those portions of time that the CPU is not using the system buses. For instance, the CPU does not use the buses during the portion of the instruction cycle after it has fetched the instruction op code. During that time, the CPU is decoding the op code and generating internal control signals. When DMA is performed only at those times, it is called *cycle-stealing* DMA. The advantage of cycle stealing is that the CPU continues to execute the program without having its operations suspended; in fact, the CPU does not even know that DMA transfer is taking place. The disadvantage is that the data-transfer rate will be limited to one word per CPU instruction cycle.

GLOSSARY

A/D Converter Analog-to-digital converter. Used to convert analog signals into a digital representation (straight binary, BCD) of the analog value.

Conditional CPU-Initiated Transfer (Polled) CPU-initiated transfer of information only when I/O device is ready for communication. This process usually involves "handshaking."

Control Commands from CPU, requests for service from I/O devices, or status codes from I/O devices.

Cycle-stealing DMA Transfer of data between RAM memory and I/O device directly without involving the μP. This transfer takes place only when the μP is not using the system buses: for example, when the μP is performing an internal register-to-internal register transfer.

Daisy Chaining Technique used in a multiple interrupt system whereby the highest-priority device receives the INTERRUPT ACKNOWLEDGED signal first. If this device is not the interrupting device, it passes the INTA signal onto the next-highest-priority device.

Data Typically, numeric or alphanumeric information encoded in a suitable binary code.

Direct Memory Access (DMA) Device-initiated transfer of information in which data are transferred between the I/O device and RAM memory directly under the control of special interface circuits called direct memory access controllers.

Floating Data Bus A READ command is generated but no device places data on the data bus. This technique is used in some μP systems to generate signals necessary for starting or terminating operation of devices.

Handshaking Exchange of control signals during a data transfer between the μP and I/O device.

Interrupt Service Routine Special program in memory containing instructions for transferring data to or from an interrupting I/O device.

Interrupt Transfer I/O device initiates transfer of information by sending a signal to the μP's interrupt input.

Interrupt Vector Address of interrupt service routine to be executed when μP is interrupted. This address is usually stored in ROM and is fetched by the μP during its response to the interrupt.

Maskable Interrupt Type of interrupt procedure which allows the interrupt request to be ignored if the Interrupt Disable flag is set.

Masking Method of examining or changing a single bit of a data word, utilizing the logical operations of AND, OR, and EX-OR.

Nonmaskable Interrupt   Type of interrupt procedure which forces the CPU to respond to the interrupt request, regardless of the status of the Interrupt Disable flag.

Reset Vector   Address location of first instruction to be executed after the actuation of the μP's RESET input. This address is usually stored in ROM and is fetched by the μP as it responds to the reset signal.

Unconditional CPU-Initiated Transfer   CPU initiates transfer of information to I/O device. The I/O device must always be ready for communication. This process does not usually involve "handshaking."

QUESTIONS AND PROBLEMS

Sections 6.1–6.5

6.1 When interfacing an input/output device to a μP, the term "handshaking" refers to:
  (a)   the conversion of the μP parallel data to a serial format for the I/O device.
  (b)   the exchange of control signals between the μP and I/O device.
  (c)   circuitry to ensure that the voltage levels of the I/O device are compatible with the μP.
  (d)   the I/O device has control of the buses when the μP is not using them.

6.2 Direct memory access refers to:
  (a)   the ability of the μP to read or write information in any location of memory.
  (b)   the ability of the μP to read information from any location in memory in the same amount of time as any other location.
  (c)   under the control of special interface circuits an I/O device can transfer information directly to or from memory without the control of the μP.
  (d)   a special memory chip designed to speed up the transfer of information between the μP and memory by having a shorter access time.

6.3 Unconditional CPU-initiated I/O transfer does *not* involve:
  (a)   the μP executing instructions that cause it to write data into an output device.
  (b)   the μP executing instructions that cause it to read data from an input device.
  (c)   the μP performing read or write operations as if the I/O device were simply a location in memory.
  (d)   handshaking between the CPU and the I/O device.

6.4 When Conditional (polled) CPU-initiated I/O transfer is used, data are transferred when:
  (a)   the μP has data to send to the output device.
  (b)   the input device has data to send to the μP.
  (c)   the μP has read and tested status information from the I/O device to determine if the device is ready for transfer.
  (d)   whenever a read or write to the I/O device is encountered in a program.

6.5 One of the major disadvantages of using conditional (polled) CPU-initiated I/O transfer is:
  (a)   additional hardware is required in interfacing the I/O device to the μP.
  (b)   the μP might waste a lot of time reading and testing the status of the I/O device.

(c)   the μP will waste a lot of time since it will have to jump to an interrupt service routine before I/O transfer can take place.

(d)   the I/O device must always be ready to send or receive data upon μP request.

6.6   Suppose that the circuits of Figs. 6.3 and 6.4 are combined in the same μC. Can the same page address be used for both the input and output ports? Explain.

6.7   Assume that the circuits of Figs. 6.3 and 6.4 are combined as stated in Problem 6.6. Draw a flowchart showing the steps the CPU must be programmed to execute to do the following:

(a)   Read the switch data.

(b)   If *any* of switches S_4 through S_7 are closed, the CPU will send 15_{10} to the output register.

(c)   If S_4 through S_7 are all open but S_3 is closed, the CPU sends 240_{10} to the output register.

(d)   If S_3 through S_7 are all open, the CPU sends all 0s to the output register.

(e)   After each transfer of data to the output register, the CPU continues on to a new instruction sequence.

6.8   Refer to Figs. 6.8 and 6.9. What would happen if the CPU was erroneously programmed to read the BUSY bit from address F903 instead of F902?

6.9   In Fig. 6.8 the ϕ_2 signal is used to enable the decoder circuitry only when ϕ_2 is HIGH. What might happen if this were not done?

Sections 6.6 and 6.7

6.10   Which of the following tells the μP where the ISR is located?
(a)   reset vector   (b)   INT input   (c)   interrupt vector   (d)   PC

6.11   Describe the function of the Interrupt Disable flag? Is it possible for the programmer to instruct the μP to ignore *all* types of interrupts?

6.12   After executing the ISR, how does the μP know what address to return to in the main program?

6.13   Explain the differences between the INT and NMI inputs.

6.14   During the execution of an interrupt service routine, which one of the following is *not* true?
(a)   The μP can be interrupted by a nonmaskable interrupt.
(b)   The μP cannot be interrupted by a maskable interrupt if the Interrupt-Disable flag is a logic 1.
(c)   The μP can be interrupted by a maskable interrupt if the Interrupt-Disable flag is a logic 0.
(d)   The μP cannot be interrupted during the execution of an interrupt service routine.

6.15   Refer to Fig. 6.11. Why is the FF used to drive the $\overline{\text{INT}}$ input instead of simply using the BUSY output through an inverter?

6.16   What is the function of OR gate 3 in Fig. 6.11? When is it activated?

6.17   In many μPs the NMI input is *edge-sensitive*; that is, it only interrupts the μP when a HIGH-to-LOW transition occurs. Show how using the NMI input in Fig. 6.11 can eliminate the FF and OR gate.

6.18 Describe the major differences between the polled and vectored methods of handling multiple interrupting devices.

6.19 Arrange the following list of events in the order in which they occur as the μP services an interrupting device.
   (a)   The return address is placed on the stack.
   (b)   The μP is directed to the ISR by the interrupt vector.
   (c)   The μP returns to the main program.
   (d)   The ISR is executed.
   (e)   The μP checks the Interrupt Disable flag.
   (f)   The return address is put back into the PC.

6.20 Cycle-stealing DMA involves:
   (a)   an interface circuit taking over the address, control, and data buses while a block of data is transferred from an input device to memory.
   (b)   an interface circuit waits for the μP to finish executing the program it is working on and then takes over the address, data, and control buses.
   (c)   while the μP is executing a program an interface circuit takes over control of the address, data, and control buses when not in use by the μP.
   (d)   data are transferred between the I/O device and memory during every other clock cycle.

6.21 Compare DMA data transfer and programmed data transfer as to:
   (a)   speed
   (b)   circuit complexity

6.22 Describe the sequence of steps that must take place when a peripheral device transfers data directly to the μP main memory (RAM) using DMA.

7

INPUT/OUTPUT
INTERFACING

In Chapter 6 we studied the different methods by which the μP communicates with I/O devices. In this chapter we deal with the principal considerations involved in constructing the interface between the μP and various types of I/O devices. The examples that are presented, although not exhaustive, are representative of the techniques and devices in use today.

7.1 PRACTICAL INTERFACE CONSIDERATIONS

The I/O section of a computer is the interface between the computer and the outside world. Very often the computer and the external devices operate in very different ways. The computer is a digital electronic device which operates at a specific clock frequency and uses specific voltage levels to represent 0s and 1s. The interface circuits for I/O devices must convert data output from the computer into a form which the external devices can understand, and must convert data input from external devices into a form which the computer can understand. This conversion can sometimes be a relatively complex task.

The design of interface circuitry requires the consideration of several characteristics of the signals being transmitted between the computer and I/O devices. We will discuss some of these characteristics now to see how they affect the I/O interface circuitry.

Logic Levels

External devices which are digital in nature generally use two different voltage levels to represent the two logic levels. These voltage levels, however, may be different than those used by the computer. Most μCs use TTL logic nominal voltages of 0 V and +5 V to represent logic 0 and logic 1, respectively. Some I/O devices, such as certain types of computer terminals, use much different voltage levels (e.g., –12 V for a 0 and +12 V for a 1). There are even some devices, such as the standard teletypewriter (TTY), which use *current* levels rather than voltage levels. The interface circuitry used for such devices must be able to convert or *translate* from one set of logic levels to another. An example of this conversion process is shown in Fig. 7.1.

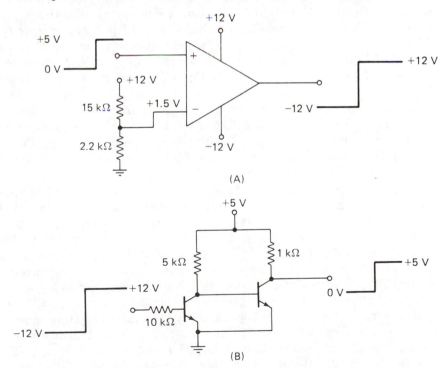

FIGURE 7.1 Circuits used to translate logic levels between two different systems.

The circuit in Fig. 7.1A uses an operational amplifier comparator to translate TTL logic levels, 0 V and +5 V, into –12 V and +12 V, respectively. The TTL levels are connected to the op amp's noninverting input and compared to a +1.5-V reference level which is connected to the inverting terminal. The reason a +1.5-V reference level is used is to allow for variations in the TTL levels which can range from 0 V to +0.8 V for a logic 0 and 2.0 V to 5.0 V for a logic 1. The circuit in Fig. 7.1B converts the –12-V and +12-V logic levels back to TTL levels using cascaded transistor inverters.

Signal Drive Capabilities (Loading)

As stated several times before, whenever we connect an output signal line to any loads, we must be concerned with the output's drive capabilities. We cannot interconnect two devices without first assuring that the output device can maintain its output voltage in the proper range while satisfying the load's requirements. Most of the large-scale integration (LSI) chips used in a μC belong to either the NMOS or CMOS logic families. This includes the μP, RAM and ROM chips, and special interface and UARTs (to be discussed shortly). These NMOS and CMOS devices have no trouble driving NMOS or CMOS loads because these loads require very little input current (typically 10^{-11} A). This is not true, however, when it comes to driving TTL loads.

TTL has been, over the past several years, the leading series of logic families, since it includes a wider variety of devices than any other logic family (although CMOS is gaining ground). In a μC, TTL devices are often used in the address decoding circuitry and in much of the I/O interface circuitry. The three most widely used TTL families are the 74LSxx (low-power Schottky), 74xx (standard TTL), and 74Sxx (high-speed Schottky). For example, a dual JK flip-flop chip in these three families would be designated 74LS76, 7476, and 74S76, respectively.

The 74LSxx requires the least amount of input current of these three families. Typically, an MOS output can drive four 74LSxx inputs. By contrast, it can drive only one 74xx input and no 74Sxx inputs. For this reason, 74LSxx devices are often used for much of a μC's external logic. If an MOS output has to drive more than four loads or, if 74LSxx devices are not available, some type of buffer circuits must be used between the output and the loads. TTL inverting and noninverting buffers can provide a good interface between MOS outputs and TTL or other higher-power loads. These buffers can increase the current-driving capability by a factor of 10 or more.

In summary, when configuring a μC system, particular attention must be paid to the drive capabilities of the μP and other MOS devices. The manufacturer's data sheets generally supply this information.

Driving Heavy Loads

Standard TTL buffer circuits such as the 7406 and 7407 hex* buffers can be used to drive loads requiring up to 30 V and 40 mA. Figure 7.2A shows how eight 7406 *inverting* buffers can be used to interface a μC output port (e.g.,

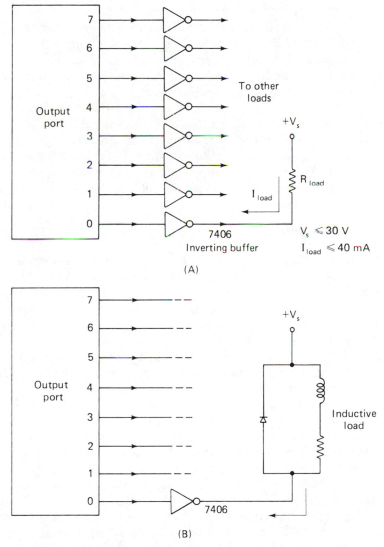

FIGURE 7.2 Using buffers to drive heavy loads.

*"Hex" indicates six buffers on one chip.

an 8-bit output register) to these loads. The 7406 has open-collector transistor outputs which can withstand up to 30 V in the OFF state and can *sink* (conduct) up to 40 mA of current in the ON state. Since the 7406 is an inverting buffer, a logic 0 input will turn OFF its output transistor, thereby cutting off current to the load. A logic 1 input turns ON the output transistor, providing a path to ground for the load current. The opposite logic is available using the 7407 noninverting buffer.

When used to control current to an inductive load (e.g., motor, relay, or solenoid), these buffers have to be protected against the "inductive kick" that occurs when the current through the load is switched off. A diode placed across the load provides this protection by offering a path for the inductive current to decay slowly (Fig. 7.2B).

For higher-current loads, there are buffers available which can handle more current. One example is the Texas Instrument 75462 dual NAND buffer chip with open collector outputs that can switch up to 300 mA of load current. For load currents greater than a few hundred milliamps, it is necessary to use a single-power transistor, or a Darlington power transistor to provide both current amplification and high-current-handling capability.

Driving AC Loads

When the μC outputs are to be used to control power to an ac load operating from the 60-Hz power line, it is necessary to *isolate* the load circuit from the logic circuit output that is controlling it. In other words, an output logic level from the μC must control a high-voltage, high-power device without actual electrical connections between the two devices. This is done so that the 60-Hz line voltage and its associated noise signals are not coupled back into the logic, where they could cause serious malfunctions.

The necessary isolation can be provided with either an electromagnetic relay or a solid-state relay. Small electromagnetic relays called *reed relays* are available in dual-in-line packages (DIPs) just like digital ICs. Some reed relays can be energized with 5 V and a few mA and can be easily driven from a buffer such as in Fig. 7.3. Here the relay is the inductive load, which becomes energized when the input to the 7406 is a high logic level. The relay controls the set of contacts that switches ac power to the load.

A solid-state relay can also supply the necessary isolation for ac loads. Many solid-state relays use the phenomenon of *optoisolation*, where light energy is used to switch power to the load. Called *optoisolators*, these devices contain an LED and a light-sensitive element, such as a photocell, photodiode, phototransistor, or light-activated SCR (LASCR), encapsulated in one package. Figure 7.4 shows several of the more common optoisolators, which are used to isolate a logic signal from a heavy load. In each case, current flows through the LED when the logic input is HIGH, causing light energy

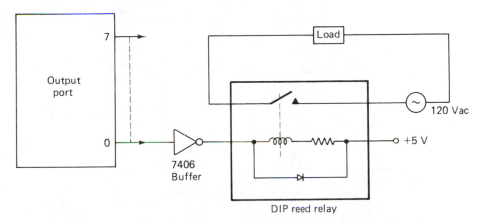

FIGURE 7.3   Reed relay used as interface between output logic level and ac load.

from the LED to switch power to the load. In Fig. 7.4A, a photodiode acts as the photodetector to supply current to a Darlington transistor pair. In 7.4B, the LASCR is both the photodetector and switching device. It can be used to switch ac power to the load, but it will conduct for only half of the line voltage cycle. Full-cycle ac can be applied to the load with the optoisolator in Fig. 7.4C, which employs a TRIAC. The cadmium sulfide (CDS) photoresistive cell becomes a low resistance when the LED conducts, allowing current to flow to the gate of the TRIAC during both half-cycles of the line voltage, thereby turning on the TRIAC.

Signal Format

The μC handles *digital* data in a parallel format where all 8 bits of an 8-bit word are transmitted simultaneously. Many external devices do not adhere to this digital, parallel format. One large class of devices uses *analog* rather than digital signals. These devices require the use of D/A and A/D converters as interface circuits in order to communicate with the μC. This is particularly true when μPs are used in process control applications or as part of process-measurement instrumentation.

Another signal format incompatibility occurs when the external device transmits and/or receives digital data in a *serial* format, that is, 1 bit at a time. Teletypewriters and tape-cassette units are examples of devices that use a serial data format. When a μC must communicate with a serial device, there are two basic methods for handling the incompatibility. In the first method, the μC communicates with the serial device over a *single* line of the data bus. The data are transmitted from the μC to the device (and vice versa) over this data line in serial fashion.

This method is essentially a *software* approach because a large number

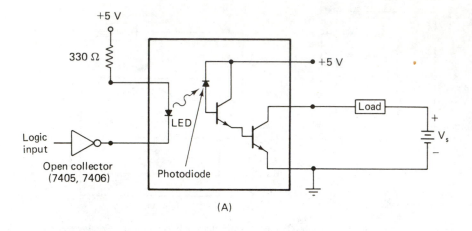

(A)

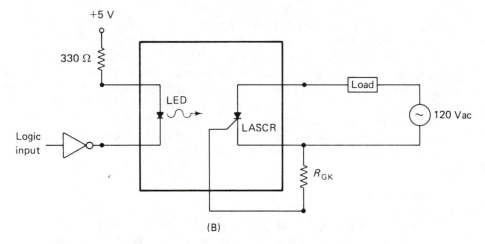

(B)

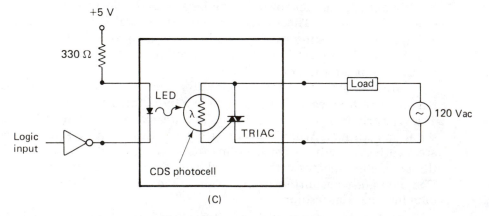

(C)

FIGURE 7.4 Three types of optoisolators.

of programmed instructions are required for the μC to transmit or receive serial data with the proper timing. Although this method requires a minimum of external hardware, it does have the disadvantage of requiring a serial/parallel conversion program. Furthermore, with this technique, the μC's time is taken up during the complete transmission of a serial data word. With slow devices, such as a teletypewriter, the time required to transmit a single serial data word can be as long as 0.1 s. In some applications, this use of μC time would be prohibitive and it becomes necessary to use a *hardware* approach to perform serial-to-parallel and parallel-to-serial conversions. This approach is important enough to warrant a detailed discussion in the next section.

7.2 ASYNCHRONOUS SERIAL DATA TRANSMISSION

When a computer (or, in fact, any device) has to communicate with a serial I/O device, one common means for doing so is called *asynchronous serial data transmission*. It is *asynchronous* because the transmitting device can send data to the receiving device at *any* time without being synchronized to the receiver. Figure 7.5 is a block diagram of such a data-transmission system. This system performs these two basic operations:

1. Takes an 8-bit parallel data word from the μP data bus and converts it to a serial data word to be sent to the serial device.
2. Takes a serial data signal from the serial device and converts it to an 8-bit parallel data word which is transferred to the μP via the data bus.

Clearly, the main function of the interface circuitry is to convert parallel data to serial data, and vice versa. Before we discuss how this can be done, we will first look at the serial data signal format.

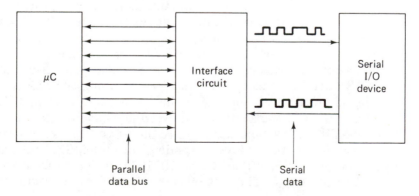

FIGURE 7.5 μC interfaced to a serial device.

Serial Data Signals

A serial data signal is broken up into time intervals called *bit times* (see Fig. 7.6). During each bit time (T_B), the value of the signal can be either 0 or 1, and the signal can only change levels at the start of each bit time.

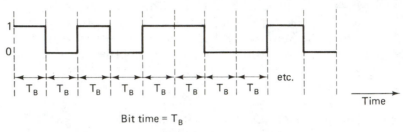

Bit time = T_B

FIGURE 7.6

When asynchronous serial data are transmitted between two devices such as a μP and a teletypewriter, a standard format is used to transmit a single data word. This format (Fig. 7.7A) consists of three (or optionally, four) parts:

1. A START bit, which is always a 0.
2. Five to 8 data bits, representing the actual information being transmitted.
3. An optional *parity* bit for error-detection capability. If the parity bit is included, either odd or even parity can be used.
4. One, $1\frac{1}{2}$,* or 2 STOP bits, which are always 1s. Most frequently, there will be 2 STOP bits.

For a given system, the number of data bits, the parity-bit option, and the number of STOP bits are fixed by the design. Figure 7.7B shows an example of a serial data word that uses 7 data bits, an *even*-parity bit, and 2 STOP bits. This is the format used by most teletypewriters, where the 7 data bits are the ASCII code for the alphanumeric character being transmitted.

The complete serial data word in Fig. 7.7B begins with a START bit of 0. The signal line is assumed to be transmitting a constant HIGH level prior to the START bit. This is called *marking* or *idling*. Whenever a data word is not being transmitted, the signal line will always be *marking*. Thus, the beginning of each transmitted data word is characterized by a 1 to 0 transition when the START bit occurs. Here the START bit is followed by 7 bits of data, beginning with the LSB and ending with the MSB. Thus, the actual data being transmitted here are read as 1001011, which happens to be the ASCII code for the letter K. The data bits are followed by an *even*-parity bit; in this

*One-and-a-half STOP bits would be represented as a 1 level, which lasts for $1\frac{1}{2}$ bit times (i.e., 1.5 T_B).

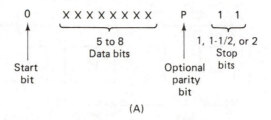

(A)

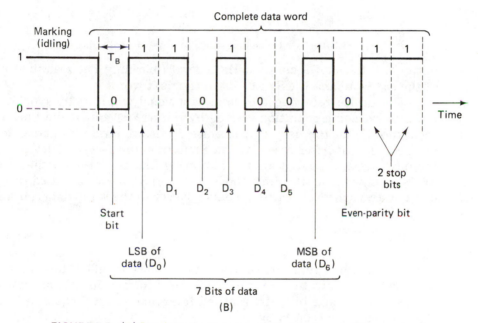

(B)

FIGURE 7.7 (A) Standard asynchronous serial data format; (B) example of a serial data word using 7 data bits, an even-parity bit, and 2 STOP bits. The data represented here are 1001011, which is the ASCII code for the letter K.

case it is a 0, since the 7 bits of data contain an even number of 1s. The parity bit is followed by 2 STOP bits, which are always 1s.

Asynchronous serial data transmission is often used to transmit several consecutive words from one device to another. Figure 7.8 shows the serial signal for transmitting two consecutive words. The first word is the same as that in Fig. 7.7B. After the 2 STOP bits of the first word, the START bit of the second word occurs followed by 7 data bits, a parity bit, and 2 STOP bits. The data bits of the second word are read as 1011001, which is the ASCII code for Y. When serial data words are transmitted one right after the other, the START bit of each new word immediately follows the last STOP bit of the preceding word. This represents the maximum rate of data transmission. When serial data words are not transmitted at the maximum rate, the trans-

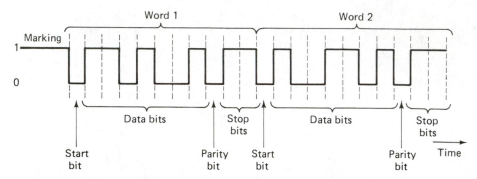

FIGURE 7.8 Transmitted serial signal for two consecutive words.

mitter will transmit a constant HIGH level (marking) between the STOP bits of the last word and the START bit of the next word.

The device receiving the serial data signal will initially synchronize to the negative-going transition created by the START bit of the first word. It then knows that the next 10 transmitted bits are data plus parity, followed by 2 STOP bits. After receiving the STOP bits, the receiving device waits for the next negative-going transition, knowing that it represents the START bit of the next word. In this way, the START and STOP bits are used to synchronize and resynchronize the serial data receiver to the serial data transmitter.

Baud Rate

The rate at which serial transmission takes place is called the *baud rate*. It is essentially equal to the number of bits of information that are transmitted per second. Since 1 bit is transmitted for a time interval equal to 1 bit time, T_B, the baud rate is given by

$$\text{baud rate} = \frac{1}{\text{bit time}} = \frac{1}{T_B} \text{ (bits/s)}$$

For example, in a teletypewriter (TTY) system, T_B is 9.09 ms. This gives a baud rate of 110 bits/s. In a tape-cassette system, baud rates of 300 to 1200 bits/s are very common. For proper interpretation of received data, it is necessary that the receiver of the serial data be operating at the same baud rate as the transmitter.

7.3 PARALLEL/SERIAL INTERFACE – THE UART

Now that we are familiar with the format used in asynchronous serial data transmission, let us return to the situation of Fig. 7.5, where we found that an interface circuit is needed to convert between parallel data and serial data.

Because of the extensive use of asynchronous serial transmission, several semiconductor manufacturers have developed a single-chip LSI device called a UART, or *universal asynchronous receiver transmitter*. The UART is used to implement the serial/parallel conversions required when a μP communicates with a serial I/O device (Fig. 7.9). Although there are slight differences among various manufacturers, all UARTs have the basic elements shown: (1) a *serial* Receiver (Rx), which takes a serial input and converts it to a parallel format that is stored in the Receiver Data Register (RxDR) for eventual transmission to the μP; (2) a *serial* Transmitter (Tx), which takes a parallel data word from the Transmitter Data Register (TxDR) and converts it to a serial format for transmission; (3) a bidirectional Data Bus Buffer, which passes *parallel* data from the μP to the TxDR or from RxDR to the μP over the system data bus; and (4) externally applied clock inputs, RxCLK, and TxCLK.

When the μP wants to transmit a data word to a serial output device, it sends the data word to the UART's Transmitter Data Register (TxDR). Con-

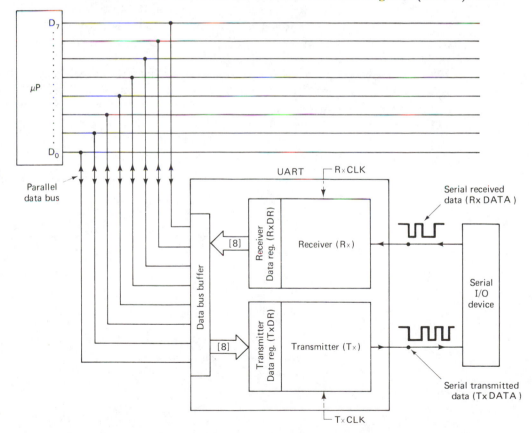

FIGURE 7.9 Basic structure for a UART.

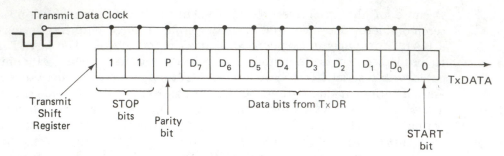

FIGURE 7.10

trol logic in the Tx section takes this data word and adds a START bit, a parity bit (if used), and the desired number of STOP bits to it. The complete data word is then placed in a register called the Transmit Shift register (Fig. 7.10). The contents of this register are shifted right at a rate determined by the Transmit Data Clock. This produces a serial data word (TxDATA) which is transmitted to the output device. The Transmit Data Clock* must have a frequency equal to the desired baud rate. For example, for TTY data transmission this clock would be 110 pulses/s, producing a baud rate of 110 at the TxDATA output.

When a serial input device wants to send data to the μP, it transmits a serial data word to the UART's Receiver section through the RxDATA input. When control logic in the Rx section senses a HIGH-to-LOW transition on the RxDATA line, it interprets this as the START bit. It then shifts the remainder of the serial data word into the Receiver Shift register (Fig. 7.11) at a rate determined by the Receiver Data Clock.* When the complete serial data

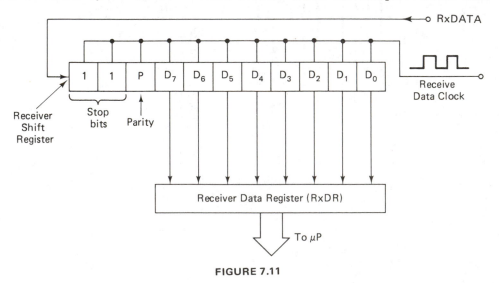

FIGURE 7.11

*As we shall see, these clock frequencies are derived from TxCLK and RxCLK, respectively.

word is in the Shift register, the data portion (D_7 through D_0) is parallel-transferred to the RxDR. The μP will eventually read the contents of the RxDR over the system data bus just like a memory location.

Clearly, for proper operation of the asynchronous serial data system of Fig. 7.9 there must be agreement between the UART and serial I/O device as to the format of the serial data; that is, number of data bits, parity bit (odd, even, or none), and number of STOP bits. This information is usually programmed into the UART by the μP. The UART has an internal Control Register which the μP can write into just like a memory location. The μP's program will contain instructions that cause the μP to send an 8-bit code to the Control register over the system data bus. This code will tell the UART the characteristics of the serial data. More will be said on this when we describe the 6850 UART in detail.

Syncing the Receiver Section to the Serial Data

As noted earlier, the Receiver initially synchronizes itself on the negative-going transition produced by the START bit. This tells the Receiver that the data bits, parity bits, and STOP bits will follow. In order to facilitate its synchronization to the serial data, a UART uses an external clock which is a much higher frequency than the baud rate, usually by a factor of 16. For example, if a baud rate of 110 is to be used, the externally applied receiver clock, RxCLK, must have a frequency of $16 \times 110 = 1760$ Hz. This is the actual clock frequency applied to the UART's RxCLK input pin. Since the frequency of RxCLK is 16 times the baud rate, one period of RxCLK is equal to 1/16 of 1 bit time, that is, $T_B/16$.

After it senses the first negative-going transition, the Receiver waits for eight periods of RxCLK and then samples the serial input (Fig. 7.12) to see if it is still LOW. This ensures the Receiver that this is a START bit and not a glitch on the serial data line. Note that this sample is taken at approximately* the middle of the START bit interval, since eight RxCLK pulses will occur in about $\frac{1}{2}$ of 1 bit time. After sampling the START bit, the Receiver samples the serial data at intervals of 16 RxCLK periods (approximately 1 bit time) providing samples which are centered quite close to the middle of each bit time. Each of these samples is then shifted into the Receiver Shift register on the rising edge of the Receive Data Clock, which is derived by putting RxCLK through a divide-by-16 counter (MOD-16). Note that this makes the frequency of the Receive Data Clock equal to the baud rate.

Once the complete serial data word has been shifted into the Receiver Shift register, circuitry in the UART automatically checks to see that the required number of STOP bits are 1s. If any of the STOP bits are 0, a *Framing Error* flag is set. This flag is part of the UART's internal Status register, which

---

*It is approximate because RxCLK is a clock signal generated independent of the clock signal used by the device that is sending the serial data.

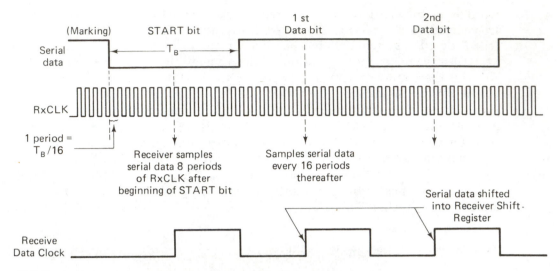

FIGURE 7.12 Receiver samples serial data using RxCLK, which has a frequency that is 16 times the baud rate.

the μP can read just like a memory location. As part of its routine for reading a received word from the UART, the μP can read the UART's Status register; if it sees that a framing error has occurred, it can take appropriate action.

The UART circuitry also checks the parity of the data portion of the received word if a parity bit has been included in the format. For example, if even parity is being used, the UART circuitry determines if the received data (including parity bit) contains an even number of 1s. If it does not, a *Parity Error* flag is set. This flag is also part of the Status register, which the μP checks as part of its routine. If the μP sees that a parity error has occurred, it can then take appropriate action.

As shown in Fig. 7.11, the data bits are transferred in parallel to the RxDR, which holds the data for the μP. Once the transfer into RxDR has taken place, the Receiver begins looking for the next serial data word from the serial input device and shifts it into the Receiver Shift register. This second word will not be transferred into the RxDR, however, until the μP reads the previous word stored there. Thus, it is possible that a third serial data word could be shifted into the Receiver Shift register before the second word was transferred to the RxDR, thereby effectively losing the second word. When this occurs, the UART will set an *Overrun Error* flag in its Status register, which tells the μP, upon reading the Status register, that it has missed a data word. It should be realized that overrun errors can be easily avoided by ensuring that the μP reads the data from the RxDR within the time it takes for a new serial data word to be completely shifted into the Receiver. This time, of course, will depend on the baud rate being used.

7.4 MOTOROLA 6850 UART

We now have enough background to look closely at a specific IC UART, the MC6850, which Motorola calls an Asynchronous Communications Interface Adapter (ACIA). A thorough examination of this particular chip will illustrate the concepts and operations involved in using other UARTs and other types of interface chips. Figure 7.13 shows a block diagram of the MC6850.

In the block diagram there are six major functions, which are shown blocked off:

1. CHIP SELECT and READ/WRITE control.
2. Data bus buffers.
3. Transmit Data register (TxDR) and Transmit Shift register (TSR).
4. Receive Data register (RxDR) and Receive Shift register (RSR).
5. Status register.
6. Control register.

The TxDR and TSR, RxDR and RSR, and the data bus buffer were explained previously, so we will concentrate on the other functions in some detail.

Chip Select and Read/Write Control Function

The μP can be operating with many input/output devices. The three CHIP SELECT inputs (CS0, CS1, $\overline{CS2}$) are input lines used to address a particular UART so that the μP can communicate with the serial I/O device which the UART is interfacing. The UART is selected when CS0 and CS1 are HIGH and $\overline{CS2}$ is LOW. Once the UART is selected, the μP can perform one of four operations:

1. *Read the Status Register.* Information concerning the status of the UART's TxDR, RxDR, and error logic is stored in the Status register. The μP obtains this information when a read Status register operation is performed.
2. *Read the RxDR.* When the UART has received a serial word from an input device, the μP can acquire these data by performing a read RxDR operation.
3. *Write to the Control Register.* The UART's Control register is an 8-bit write-only register whose contents determine such things as clock-frequency divider ratio, word size, number of stop bits, and parity. These characteristics are controlled by the μP, which writes an 8-bit control word into the Control register.

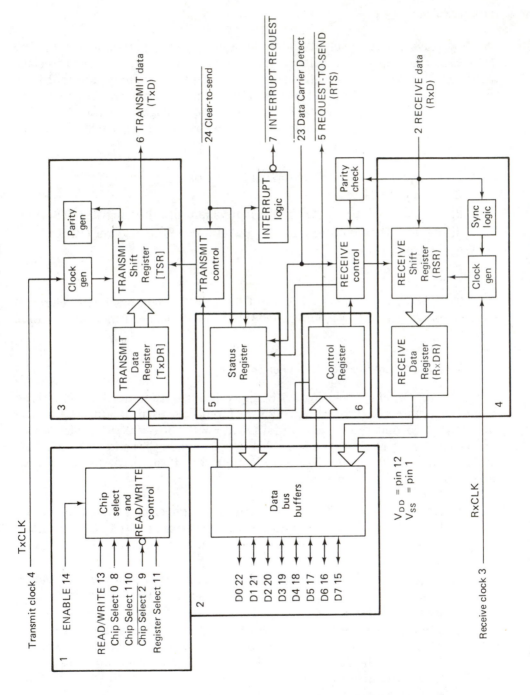

FIGURE 7.13 Six functional blocks of the MC6850 UART.

246

4. *Write to the TxDR*. When the μP wants to send a data word to the output device, it does so by performing a write data into TxDR operation. The UART then transmits the data serially to the device.

These four operations involve the μP reading or writing the contents of the RxDR, TxDR, Status, or Control registers. The actual operation being performed at any time is determined by the levels on the CHIP SELECT, REGISTER SELECT (RS), R/W, and ENABLE inputs according to the following table:

Operation	CS0	CS1	$\overline{CS2}$	RS	R/W	Enable
Read Status register	1	1	0	0	1	1
Write Control register	1	1	0	0	0	1
Read RxDR	1	1	0	1	1	1
Write TxDR	1	1	0	1	0	1

For all four operations the UART chip must be selected (CS0 = CS1 = 1, $\overline{CS2}$ = 0). These inputs are normally derived from address decoding circuitry. In addition, the ENABLE line must be HIGH. This input is usually connected to the ϕ_2 clock signal so that all data transfers occur when ϕ_2 is high. Recall that this is the time when the data are stable on the data bus.

The R/W input must be driven HIGH for either of the read operations and the RS input selects which register (Status or RxDR) will be read. Similarly, R/W has to be LOW for either write operation, and RS selects either the TxDR or the Control register to be written into.

The Status Register

The 6850's Status register is an 8-bit read-only register from which the μP can read information concerning the status of the UART. The functions of the different bits are as follows:

Status Register

SR7	SR6	SR5	SR4	SR3	SR2	SR1	SR0
Interrupt Request (IRQ)	Parity Error (PE)	Receiver Overrun (OVRN)	Framing Error	$\overline{\text{Clear-to-Send}}$	$\overline{\text{Data Carrier Detect}}$	Transmit Data Register Empty (TDRE)	Receive Data Register Full (RDRF)

Modem Status spans SR3 and SR2.

Receive Data Register Full (RDRF)   This bit is automatically set high when the Receive Shift register transfers its contents to the RxDR. This bit is cleared after the μP reads the contents of the RxDR, indicating that the contents of RxDR are no longer current.

Transmit Data Register Empty (TDRE)   This bit is set high when the TxDR contents have been transferred to the Transmit Shift register. A low indicates that the TSR is still full and the μP should not transfer another word to the UART at this time for transmission to the output device.

Data Carrier Detect ($\overline{DCD}$) and Clear-to-Send ($\overline{CTS}$)   Special status bits used in conjunction with modem* transmission of data. We will not consider these at this time.

Framing Error (FE), Receiver Overrun (OVRN), and Parity Error (PE)   These bits have been discussed in the previous general discussion of UARTs.

Interrupt Request (IRQ)   This bit always indicates the status of the UART's $\overline{IRQ}$ output line. Anytime the $\overline{IRQ}$ output is LOW, the IRQ bit of the Status register will be HIGH, and vice versa. (This is useful when a number of devices are connected to the μP's interrupt input. When interrupted, the μP can read the UART's Status register to see if the IRQ bit is 1. This will indicate that the UART's $\overline{IRQ}$ output line is 0 and the UART is the device generating the interrupt signal to the μP.) The IRQ bit is cleared whenever the μP performs a read RxDR or a write TxDR operation.

The Control Register

The function of the 8 bits of this register are given below. The μP will write the appropriate word into this register to define the characteristics of the serial data transmission.

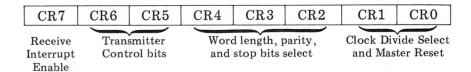

CR7	CR6	CR5	CR4	CR3	CR2	CR1	CR0
Receive Interrupt Enable	Transmitter Control bits		Word length, parity, and stop bits select			Clock Divide Select and Master Reset	

Clock Divide Select Bits (CR1, CR0)   Recall from Figs. 7.11 and 7.12 that there is a specific ratio between RxCLK, the clock signal applied to the UART's RxCLK input, and the Receive Data Clock, which is used to shift the received data into the UART. This ratio can be selected as either 1, 16, or 64 using the CR1, CR0 bits of the Control register, as follows:

---

*A *modem* is a device used to access a computer from a remote location over telephone lines. It converts digital information to be transmitted into a series of audio tones. It also converts received audio tones into their corresponding digital codes. A modem is used on both ends of a communication link.

CR1	CR0	Clock Divide Ratio
0	0	÷1
0	1	÷16
1	0	÷64
1	1	Master Reset for UART

It is important to realize that the Receive Data Clock = RxCLK/clock divide ratio, and this has to equal the baud rate of the serial data. For example, if the baud rate is to be 110 and a clock divide ratio of 16 is to be used, the frequency of RxCLK must be $110 \times 16 = 1760$ Hz. This is the frequency that has to be applied to the UART's RxCLK input. The same holds true for the TxCLK input.

Word Select Bits (CR4, CR3, CR2) These bits control word-length parity and the number of stop bits. The following table shows how these functions are determined.

CR4	CR3	CR2	Data Bits	Function Parity	Stop Bits
0	0	0	7	Even	2
0	0	1	7	Odd	2
0	1	0	7	Even	1
0	1	1	7	Odd	1
1	0	0	8	None	2
1	0	1	8	None	1
1	1	0	8	Even	1
1	1	1	8	Odd	1

Transmitter Control Bits (CR6, CR5) The most significant states for our purposes are shown below. $\overline{\text{RTS}}$ is a UART output signal that can be used for any purpose.

CR6	CR5	Function
0	0	$\overline{\text{RTS}}$ = 0; Transmit Interrupt Disabled
0	1	$\overline{\text{RTS}}$ = 0; Transmit Interrupt Enabled
1	0	$\overline{\text{RTS}}$ = 1; Transmit Interrupt Disabled

It can be set or cleared by the μP via the UART's Control register. When the TRANSMIT INTERRUPT is enabled, the UART's $\overline{\text{IRQ}}$ output line will go LOW whenever the TDRE status bit goes HIGH, indicating that the TxDR is empty

and is ready for a word from the μP. This $\overline{\text{IRQ}}$ output can be used to interrupt the μP whenever TDRE = 1.

Receive Interrupt Enable Bit (CR7) A HIGH on this bit enables the RE-
CEIVE INTERRUPT so that the UART's $\overline{\text{IRQ}}$ line will go LOW whenever the
RDRF status bit goes HIGH, indicating that the UART has a data word for
the μP. The $\overline{\text{IRQ}}$ output can be used to interrupt the μP whenever RDRF = 1.

    If both TRANSMIT INTERRUPT and RECEIVE INTERRUPT are enabled
(CR6 = 0, CR5 = 1, CR7 = 1) and $\overline{\text{IRQ}}$ is connected to the μP's INTERRUPT
line, the μP will read the Status register as part of its interrupt service routine
to determine whether TDRE = 1 or RDRF = 1 caused the interrupt. If nei-
ther interrupt is enabled or if $\overline{\text{IRQ}}$ is not connected to the μP, the UART
cannot interrupt the μP. The μP would then communicate with the UART
using the conditional (polled) I/O technique.

Interfacing the 6850 to a μP

Figure 7.14 shows the circuit diagram for interfacing the 6850 UART to a μP
for communication with a serial I/O device such as a teletypewriter (TTY).
The circuit is set for both interrupt operation and conditional transfer. If
interrupt operation is not going to be used, the $\overline{\text{IRQ}}$ connection can be eliminated or the μP can disable the UART interrupts via bits CR7, CR6, and
CR5 of the Control register.

    With the address decoding circuitry shown, the UART is assigned ad-
dresses on page BF. Any address on page BF will produce a LOW on the $\overline{\text{CS2}}$
input, thereby selecting the UART chip, since CS0 and CS1 are kept permanently HIGH. Note that the RS input is connected to the A_0 address line.
Thus, by using addresses BF00 and BF01, the μP can select the UART and
control the RS input.

    A 1760-Hz clock signal is externally generated and applied to both the
TxCLK and RxCLK inputs. This signal might be obtained from a crystal
oscillator and frequency divider. If we assume that a UART clock divide ratio
of 16 is being used, this 1760-Hz clock input will produce a data-transmission
rate of 110 bits/s. This is the baud rate used by standard TTYs. In actual
practice, a frequency of 1760 Hz ± 5 percent will be sufficient to guarantee
reliable data transmission.

    There are *four* basic operations which the μP can perform on the
UART: writing into the Control register, reading the Status register, writing
into the TxDR, and reading the RxDR. These operations involve the μP either writing a word into, or reading a word from, one of the UART registers.
The three-byte instructions for each of these operations is illustrated using
6502 op codes and using the Accumulator as the μP source or destination
register.

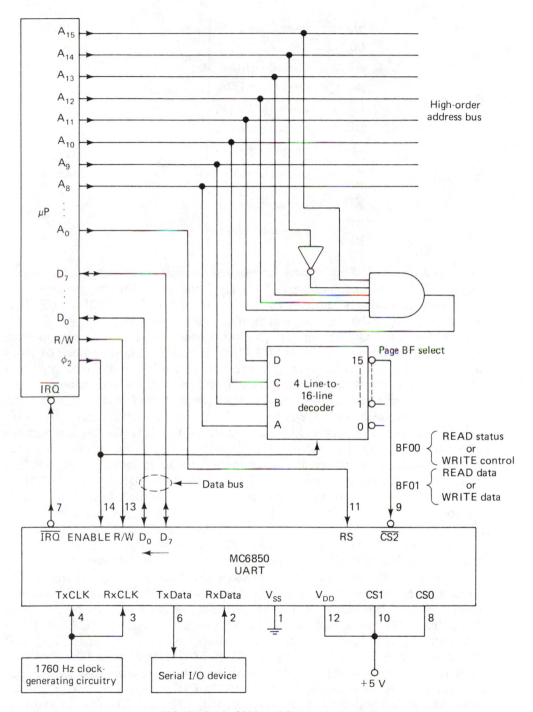

FIGURE 7.14 6850 UART interfaced to a μP.

8D ←—— op code for STA   } write into
00 >—— address of UART
BF   Control register   } Control register

AD ←—— op code for LDA   } read Status
00 >—— address of UART
BF   Status register   } register

8D ←—— op code for STA
01 >—— address of TxDR   } write into TxDR
BF >

AD ←—— op code for LDA
01 >—— address of RxDR   } read RxDR
BF >

Note that address BF00 is used for both the Control register and the Status register. This is no problem because the R/W line determines which one is being accessed. Similarly, address BF01 is used for both the TxDR and RxDR, with the R/W line determining which of the two is selected.

These four instructions are used whenever the μP communicates with the serial I/O device via the UART. Let us examine the sequence of steps which the μP must perform when it wants to transmit a single data word or a block of data to a serial output device. Refer to the flowchart shown in Fig. 7.15. Before any communication can take place, the μP has to *initialize* the UART by sending a control word to its Control register. This serves to set up the UART for the proper baud rate, number of data bits, parity, and number of STOP bits. After this is done, the μP will execute some intermediate program of instructions. When it has some data ready to transmit, the μP first reads the Status register and checks bit SR1 to see if TDRE = 1. With TDRE = 0, the UART is not ready for data and the μP loops back to read the Status register again. If TDRE = 1, the UART is ready for the next data word. The μP then proceeds to write a data word into the TxDR to be eventually transmitted serially to the output device. This same sequence of operations is repeated until the μP has written all its data into the output device.

Next, let us take a look at the steps involved in the μP *receiving* data from a serial input device. For efficient use of the μP's time, interrupt operation would be preferable. If interrupt operation is to be used for receiving data, the UART has to have its RECEIVE INTERRUPT enabled (CR7 = 1) during the initialization process. Thereafter, whenever the UART has a data word ready (RDRF = 1), its $\overline{IRQ}$ output will go LOW, interrupting the μP. Figure 7.16 is the flowchart for a typical interrupt service routine (ISR) which the μP will execute in response to the UART's $\overline{IRQ}$ signal. Essentially, the μP reads the Status register and checks bits SR6, SR5, and SR4 for any error in-

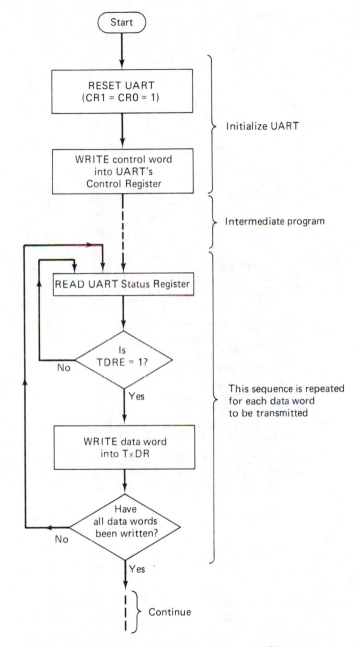

FIGURE 7.15 Flowchart of μP operations for transmission to a serial output device.

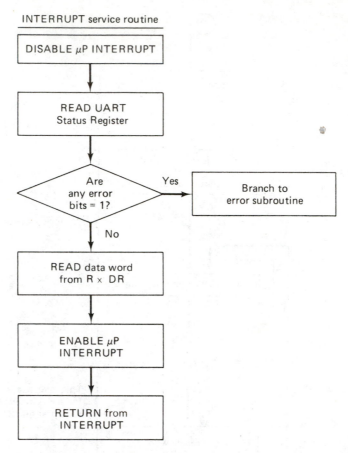

INTERRUPT service routine

FIGURE 7.16 Flowchart of μP ISR executed in response to an interrupt signal from UART; it is assumed that the UART has been previously initialized with the Receiver Interrupt *enabled* and the Transmit Interrupt *disabled*.

dication. If an error is indicated, the μP branches to an error subroutine to take appropriate action. Otherwise, it reads the data from the RxDR into the Accumulator. It then returns to the program it was executing prior to being interrupted. When the UART has a new data word ready, this process is repeated.

It should be pointed out here that interrupt operation is not necessary if the μP has nothing else to do while it is waiting for data from the UART. On the other hand, interrupt operation is preferable if the μP has other functions it can perform while waiting for data. This is especially significant when the data are coming from the input device at a very slow rate. A prime example is a μP that is waiting for data being punched in from a TTY keyboard.

When one microprocessor system communicates with another microprocessor system over long distances, or when it communicates with peripheral devices such as teletypes, printers, or CRT terminals, data are often transmitted serially. Serial transmission requires only two wires to carry all the necessary data, address, and control information, but it does so one bit at a time, and so is much slower than parallel transmission. Serial data can be transmitted using voltage levels, current levels, or audio tones (for transmission over telephone lines). We will briefly describe the serial transmission standards that are in common use today.

Current Loops

Teletypes often send and receive serial data using the presence or absence of current to represent 0s and 1s. The nominal values are:

no current ("space"):   logical "0"
nominal 20 mA ("mark"):   logical "1"

The terms *space* and *mark* are often used to indicate the absence and presence of current in teletype communication links. Some teletypes use 60 mA as the nominal current level.

Figure 7.17 shows a typical situation where a teletype is communicating with a device that uses TTL data levels. The teletype sends data to the device's receiver data input, RxDATA, and receives data from the devices's transmit data output, TxDATA. The RxDATA and TxDATA lines might be part of a UART which is interfacing the teletype to a microcomputer. Or they might be two pins of an input/output interface chip used for the same purpose.

The TxDATA signal is a TTL-level signal (e.g., 0 V and +5 V) which controls Q2 so that a 1 at TxDATA produces 20 milliamperes (mA) of current through the printer solenoid in the teletype, while a 0 produces no current through the solenoid. If TxDATA is an ASCII-coded serial signal, the pattern of current and no current through the solenoid sets up internal electromagnets to print the desired character.

The teletype sends data to the microcomputer interface by opening and closing an internal switch. When it is not transmitting, the teletype's switch is normally closed so that Q1 is ON and +5 V is applied to the RxDATA input. This is the idling or marking condition. The teletype begins its transmission by opening the switch that turns OFF Q1 and applies 0 V to RxDATA. This is the START bit, which begins the serial transmission. The teletype then opens and closes the switch according to the ASCII code of the keyboard character it is transmitting.

The arrangement of Figure 7.17 is called the *full duplex* mode of data transmission. In this mode, data can be transmitted in both directions, *and* they can be transmitted in both directions simultaneously. In the *half-duplex* mode, data can be transmitted in only one direction at a time.

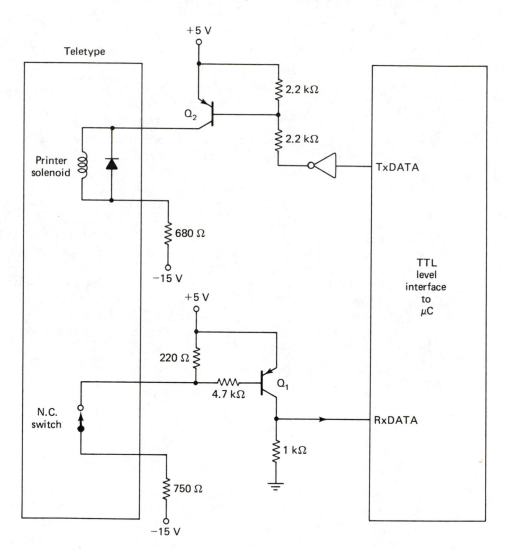

FIGURE 7.17   20-mA current-loop teletype interfaced to a microcomputer.

EIA Standards

The Electronics Industry Association (EIA) has adopted a serial data communication standard called the RS-232-C standard. This standard specifies signal voltage levels and handshake signals. The RS-232-C voltage levels are defined as follows:

$$\text{logic 1 (mark)} \quad \text{voltage more negative than } -3 \text{ V}$$
$$\text{logic 0 (space)} \quad \text{voltage more positive than } +3 \text{ V}$$

Typically, a RS-232-C system uses –12 V and +12 V for 1 and 0, respectively. Note that this convention uses the more positive voltage as logic 0 and the more negative voltage as logic 1.

Since the RS-232-C voltage levels are not compatible with the voltage levels used by the standard IC families and microcomputer components, it is usually necessary to use some type of interface circuit to convert RS-232-C to TTL levels, and vice versa. Figure 7.18 shows how this can be done using two ICs designed especially for this purpose. The Motorola MC 1488 converts TTL to ± 12 V RS-232-C, and the MC1489 converts RS-232-C to TTL.

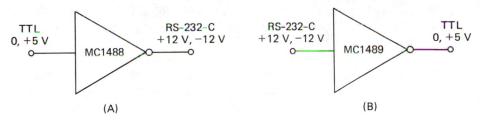

FIGURE 7.18 ICs used to convert between TTL and RS-232-C levels.

The RS-232-C standard for serial data transmission is typically used for baud rates up to 20K bits/s using signal line lengths up to 50 ft. For higher transmission rates over longer distances, the EIA has adopted two improved standards, RS-422 and RS-423. These standards require lower-impedance line drivers to drive the long transmission lines, and they use *differential* (two-line) transmitted signals and differential receivers to reduce the effects of common-mode noise.

Serial Data Formats

Earlier in our discussion of serial data transmission and UARTs, we used the *asynchronous* format for serial data. Recall that this format utilized a START bit, and one or more STOP bits to separate each word or character being transmitted. This was necessary so that the receiver could synchronize itself to the data without the need for transmitting a clock signal along with the data. Asynchronous transmission, then, requires at least 2 extra bits per character other than the actual data bits.

A *synchronous* serial transmission format can be used in which these extra START and STOP bits are not attached to each data word. Instead, the data words are transmitted continuously one after the other. The synchronization between transmitter and receiver is obtained by transmitting a special synchronizing word between every 100 data words. The receiver has to have the circuitry to detect this synchronizing word and use it to sync itself to transmitted data. This method, called *synchronous serial communication*, requires fewer extra bits than asynchronous communication, but more complex receiver circuitry. Special chips called universal synchronous receiver-transmitters (USRTs) are available for this purpose.

Modems

Computer systems often use the standard telephone lines to send digital data between a remote terminal (e.g., teletype keyboard or video keyboard terminal) and the computer. The bandwidth of these telephone lines, however, is only about 3 kHz, so that they will drastically distort normal digital pulses probably beyond recognition. For this reason, digital data are transmitted over these phone lines using *sine waves* instead of pulses.

Called *frequency shift keying* (FSK), this method represents a logic 0 as a burst of sine waves at one frequency, and a logic 1 as a burst of sine waves at another frequency. Special circuits are needed to convert logic levels to the appropriate sine waves for transmission (called *modulation*), and to convert the received sine waves into logic levels (*demodulation*). A circuit that can perform both these functions (modulation and demodulation) is called a *modem*.

Figure 7.19 illustrates a typical situation where a CPU is communicating with a remote terminal (teletype) over a single phone line. When the CPU

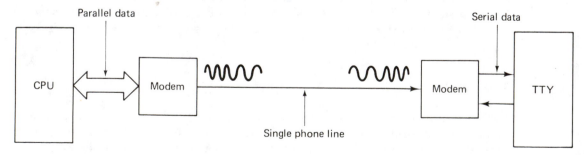

FIGURE 7.19 Modems used for serial data transmission over phone lines.

transmits data to the terminal, the CPU's logic levels are converted to a FSK waveform by its modem and transmitted over the phone lines. The terminal's modem receives the FSK waveform and converts it to a serial logic waveform (e.g., RS-232-C or 20-mA loop) for the teletype. The opposite operations occur when the terminal is sending information to the CPU.

When a modem is transmitting, it is called the *originate* modem; when it is receiving, it is called the *answer* modem. An originate modem sends the following sine-wave frequencies:

mark (logic 1)   1270 Hz
space (logic 0)   1070 Hz

The answer modem, after accepting these signals and converting them to logic levels, communicates back to the originate modem using the following frequencies:

mark (logic 1)   2225 Hz
space (logic 0)   2025 Hz

Using two different sets of frequencies allows for *simultaneous* two-way communication over the same wire. Again, this is called a *full-duplex* mode of communication.

7.6 PROGRAMMABLE INPUT/OUTPUT (PIO) INTERFACE CHIPS

In an earlier section we took an in-depth look at a fairly sophisticated and complex peripheral support device. We will now investigate some other programmable input–output support chips. Because of limited space these devices will not be described in as much detail as the UART, but the basic structure and functions of some common I/O support chips will be presented. Integrated-circuit manufacturers are making great advances concerning the number of capabilities per chip that can be offered to the user. Needless to say, this is an area that is changing very rapidly, and it is our intention here to expose the reader to a few of the common devices in use today.

The MCS6520 PIA — Peripheral Interface Adapter

This device, manufactured by MOS Technology, Inc., is referred to as a Peripheral Interface Adapter (PIA). The terms "PIA" and "PIO" are synonomous; no standard terminology for these devices has been agreed upon by the industry. The purpose of this device is to provide communication capabilities between the μP and peripheral devices such as displays, keyboards, and printers. Figure 7.20 shows a simplified block diagram of the MCS6520. From this diagram we can see that the device communicates with the μP over an 8-bit bidirectional data bus which is simply connected to the μP's data bus. Two completely independent 8-bit bidirectional ports are available to be connected to various peripheral devices. In this very basic arrangement the μP can send information to port A or port B by simply performing a WRITE operation to the specific port address. The μP can also receive information from peripheral devices by way of port A or port B by performing a READ operation from the specific port address of the PIA.

A more in-depth look at the MCS6520 is necessary to get a full grasp of the power and flexibility that this chip provides μC system designers. Figure 7.21 is a more detailed block diagram of the MCS6520. The chip can be thought of as two completely independent 8-bit I/O ports. Ports A and B contain *Data Direction registers* (DDRA, DDRB) which allow the programmer to specify independently each pin of both ports as either an input or an output pin. Putting a "0" in a Data Direction register bit causes the corresponding pin on the port to act as an input. Placing a "1" in a particular bit position of the DDR causes the corresponding pin on the port to act as an output.

The *Control registers* (CRA, CRB) allow the programmer to choose certain interrupt and peripheral control capabilities. Also, the Control register provides certain status information concerning interrupt activity.

The *Output registers* (ORA, ORB) hold data that are to be sent to output devices until such devices are ready to accept it. Inputs CA1, CA2, CB1,

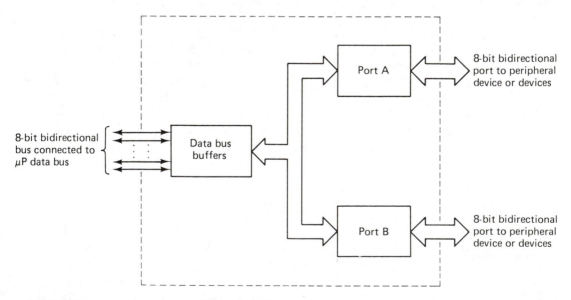

FIGURE 7.20 Simplified function of the MCS 6520.

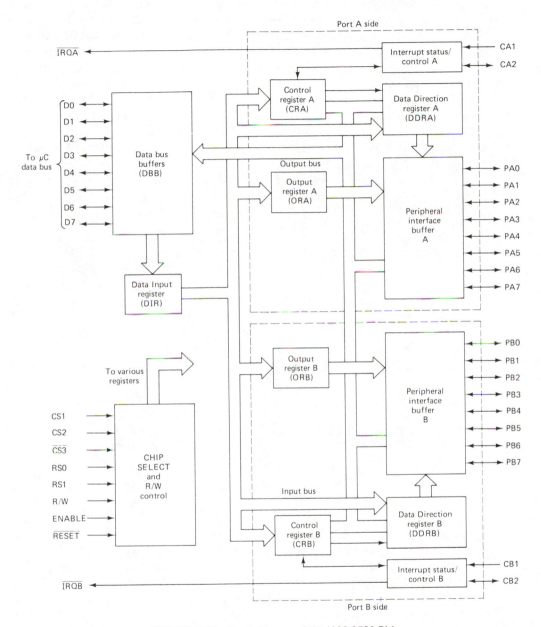

FIGURE 7.21 Block diagram of the MCS 6520 PIA.

and CB2 can be used as status inputs for conditional I/O transfer, or for interrupt interfacing capabilities. Under software control CA2 and CB2 can be programmed, via the Control register, to act as peripheral control *outputs* that can be used in various handshaking schemes. We will describe these functions in more detail later.

In dealing with this chip the μP must be able to communicate with six different registers. In Figure 7.21 you will notice that the CHIP SELECT and R/W control section has only two register select inputs, RS0, RS1. This seems to indicate that the μP can only communicate with four registers. However, one bit in each Control register is used to distinguish between addressing of the Data Direction register and the Output register. This allows the choice then of communicating with one of *six* different registers, two Data Direction registers, two Control registers, and two Output registers. The REGISTER SELECT and CHIP SELECT inputs operate similar to those of the 6850 UART.

Using the 6520 for Unconditional Transfer   The 6520 can easily be used to implement the I/O formats discussed in Chapter 6. The format for μP-initiated unconditional transfer is implemented by connecting the data bus buffers of the 6520 to the μP data bus while port A, port B, or both are connected to I/O devices. To set up port A as an *output* port, for example, the μP must write all 1s into the Data Direction register A (DDRA). The port A pins are thereby set up to act as outputs, and whenever the μP needs to send data to the output device connected to port A, it simply performs a WRITE operation to Output register A (ORA). The main advantage of this type of interface chip is its programability. If at some future point in time port A needs to be made an input port, the μP simply writes all 0s into Data Direction register A. Then whenever the μP performs a READ operation of port A, whatever logic levels are present on PA_0 through PA_7 will be placed onto the data bus to be latched into the μP. These same ideas pertain to the port B portion of the chip.

Using the 6520 for Conditional Transfer   Microprocessor-initiated conditional transfer of data can easily be implemented using the 6520. Each Control register has two read-only bits or flags reserved for status information. These flags are activated by inputs CA1, CA2 or CB1, CB2, respectively. The device can be programmed via the Control register to respond to either positive- or negative-going transitions on these inputs. Thus, the appropriate transitions on the CA or CB inputs will set corresponding status flags in the Control register, and for conditional transfer the μP would read the contents of the Control register and test these status bits before any transfer of information takes place. These status flags are cleared whenever the μP performs a READ operation for the corresponding port or when a RESET is generated.

EXAMPLE 7.1   Figure 7.22 shows how the 6520 PIA would be used in a typical application. Here port B is used as an output port driving a D/A converter (DAC), while port A is an input port being driven by an A/D converter (ADC). Describe the steps involved in the two types of I/O transfer.

Solution:

(a) *Output:* The transfer of data from the CPU to the DAC is *unconditional* transfer. Pins PB_0 through PB_7 are programmed as *output* pins by having the CPU WRITE all 1s into DDRB; this is usually done at the beginning of the program. Then, when the CPU wishes to send an 8-bit data word to the DAC, it simply does a WRITE operation to ORB. The addresses used for DDRB, ORB, and the other PIA registers are determined by the address decoder logic just as they were for the UART.

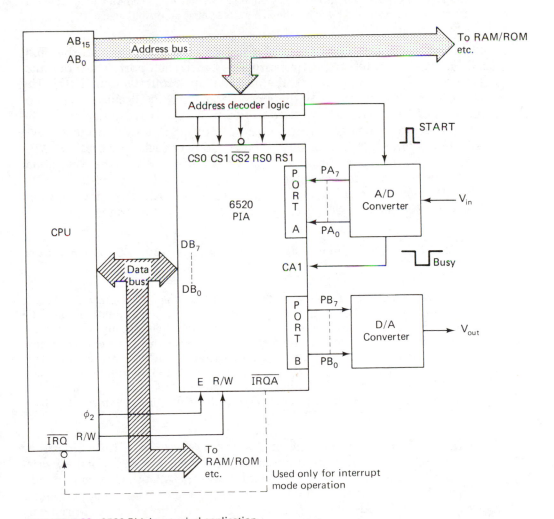

FIGURE 7.22 6520 PIA in a typical application.

(b) *Input:* The transfer of data from the ADC to the CPU is *conditional* transfer based on the status of the BUSY signal. Recall that BUSY makes a positive-going transition when the A/D conversion is complete. Pins PA_0 through PA_7 are programmed as *input* pins by having the CPU *write* all 0s into DDRA. The CPU must also send the appropriate control word to Control register A (CRA) for making input CA1 respond to positive-going transitions. Thus, when BUSY goes from LOW to HIGH, it will set the flag in CRA that is activated by CA1. The CPU can determine the status of this flag by reading the contents of CRA. If this flag is HIGH, the CPU then knows that the ADC has valid data, and it can perform a READ operation on port A to get the data.

Note that a START pulse is required for the ADC and it can be generated from the address decoder circuitry as was done in Chapter 6. The START pulse could alternatively be provided by using the PIA's CA2 pin as an output signal.

6520 Interrupt Mode For I/O transfer using the interrupt mode, the 6520 has an active-LOW interrupt output associated with each port. These outputs, $\overline{IRQA}$ and $\overline{IRQB}$, can be tied to the μP interrupt request input ($\overline{IRQ}$). The operation of these interrupt outputs can be enabled or disabled under program control by writing appropriate words to the Control register. When the interrupt feature is utilized, an INTERRUPT output is activated (goes LOW) whenever the *Interrupt* flag in the associated Control register is set.

The Interrupt flag is the same flag used as a status flag in the conditional transfer mode, and is activated (set HIGH) by appropriate transitions on the CA or CB inputs. Thus, the CA or CB inputs act as INTERRUPT inputs which can be driven by an I/O device. The following example illustrates.

EXAMPLE 7.2 Describe how the ADC in Fig. 7.22 can interrupt the CPU for data transfer.

Solution: For interrupt operation several things must be done. First, since the ADC is using port A, the $\overline{IRQA}$ output is connected to the CPU $\overline{IRQ}$ input. Second, the CPU must write a control word in CRA to enable $\overline{IRQA}$ and specify that a positive transition on CA1 will set the Interrupt flag. Thus, when the ADC completes a conversion, the BUSY signal produces a positive transition at CA1 which sets the Interrupt flag in CRA. This in turn causes $\overline{IRQA}$ to go LOW to interrupt the CPU. When the CPU responds to this interrupt, it will read the ADC data from port A. This READ operation will automatically clear the Interrupt flag and drive $\overline{IRQA}$ back high.

6520 Handshaking Features One of the unique features of this chip is that CA2 and CB2 can be made to function as outputs instead of inputs. By writing an appropriate word into the Control register, CA2 and CB2 can operate as outputs in three different modes for handshaking purposes and peripheral control. The first mode allows CA2 or CB2 outputs to be set or cleared corresponding to the logic level written into a bit position of the Control Register.

The second mode used in handshaking arrangements works such that when an input device interrupts the CPU using input CA1, output CA2 is made to go HIGH. When the μP READS port A to get the new data, output CA2 is made to go LOW, signaling the peripheral device that data have been accepted and new data can be sent. For port B operation, the CB2 output is cleared when the μP performs a WRITE operation to port B. When the out-out device accepts this information, it sends a signal back, activating input CB1, which can then interrupt the μP by use of $\overline{\text{IRQB}}$, signaling the μP that the output device has accepted this new information. Because of this second mode, port A is more easily interfaced when used in conjunction with an input device and port B for an output device.

The third mode, referred to as a pulsed mode, causes output CA2 to generate a pulse each time the μP READS the contents of port A, and output CB2 to generate pulse whenever the μP WRITES to port B.

As can be seen, this device is fairly sophisticated and allows great freedom to the system designer. The main advantage of this chip over hand-wired logic is its programability. Under software control its basic operation can easily be changed even while the system is in full operation.

The 8255 PPI — Programmable Peripheral Interface

The 8255, manufactured by Intel, is referred to as a Programmable Peripheral Interface (PPI). Figure 7.23 shows the block diagram of the PPI. The device has three ports (A, B, C) for a total of 24 I/O pins, which can be programmed in two groups of 12 (port C being broken down to two 4-bit groups) and used in three modes of operation. In Mode 0 port A (8 bits), the upper-half of port C (4 bits), port B (8 bits), and the lower-half of port C (4 bits) can be programmed as independent blocks allowing for 16 variations of input/output configurations. In Mode 1 of each group of 12 I/O pins can be programmed to have 8 input or output lines (port A, port B). Three of the remaining 4 pins of port C are used for "handshaking" and interrupt control signals. In Mode 2 port A is used as an 8-bit bidirectional bus port while 5 bits of port C are used for "handshaking." Port B cannot be used in this fashion.

The MCS6530 — Peripheral Interface/Memory Device

The MCS6530, manufactured by MOS Technology, Inc., is an example of how advances in technology have brought forth I/O interface devices with greatly expanded functional capabilities. As shown in the block diagram (Fig. 7.24), this device contains a 1K $\times$ 8 ROM memory, 64 $\times$ 8 RAM memory,

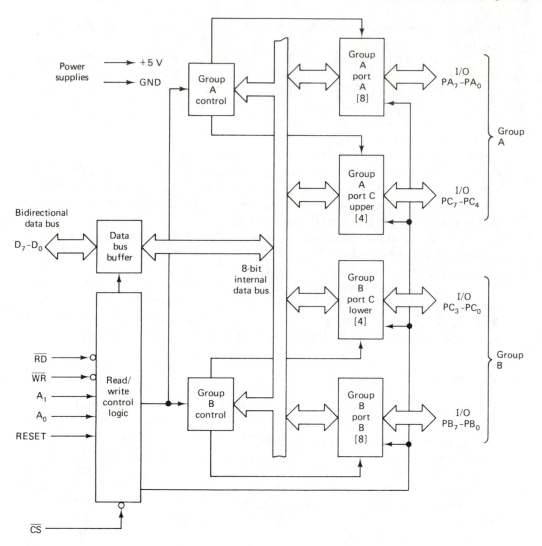

FIGURE 7.23   INTEL's 8255 PPI block diagram.

two 8-bit bidirectional ports, a Programmable Interval Timer capable of timing from 1 to 256 units of 1024 clock periods, and a Programmable Interval
Timer Interrupt output, which can be used to interrupt the μP after the programmed number of clock cycles have been counted. All of this is software
programmable, leading to a very flexible and powerful capability for a single-
chip interface device.

In summary, as the technology evolves, interface chips will be designed
and manufactured with more and more functional capabilities per chip. This
can only improve the sophistication and ease of interfacing, so that the role

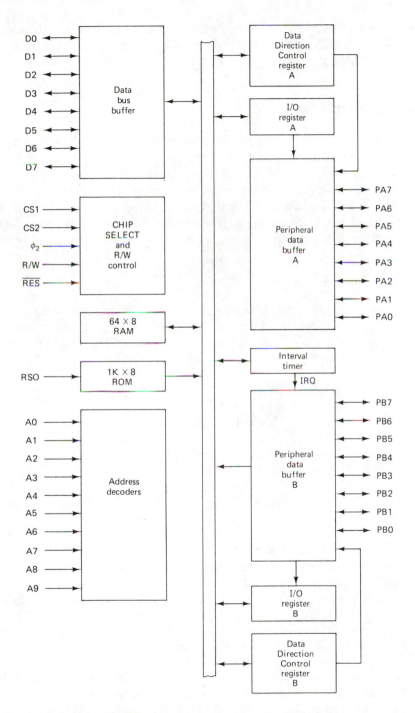

FIGURE 7.24 Block diagram of the MCS 6530.

267

of μP's in our lives will expand even more significantly than at present. For a more detailed discussion of the operation of these devices, the manufacturers' literature should be consulted.

7.7 PARALLEL BUS STANDARDS

We know that a microprocessor-based system uses data, control and address buses for communication between the microprocessor and its associated devices. When one microprocessor system is to communicate with another microprocessor system or some complex peripheral device, it is desirable to have a standard format for the buses. Unfortunately, there is no single bus standard which has been universally accepted by the various segments of the industry. We will discuss some of the most widely used bus standards.

The S-100 Bus

In 1976, MITS, Inc., introduced the S-100 bus as part of their Altair microcomputer, which is based on the 8080 microprocessor, and it became the "hobby computer" bus standard. It consists of 100 lines or wires allocated as follows:

      8 data-input lines   } connected to microprocessor data bus
      8 data-output lines }
   16 address lines — from microprocessor address bus
   48 control-signal lines — to and from the microprocessor
    6 power-supply and ground lines
   14 unused lines — for future expansion

Note that separate data-in and data-out lines are used as required by some systems. Also note the large number of control lines. There are many more than would ever be needed by a given system. Several of these control lines were originally required because of some 8080 limitations that have been overcome by its successors. The abundance of control lines makes the S-100 bus suitable for microprocessors other than the 8080.

A microcomputer which uses the S-100 format generally consists of a large chassis that contains the power supply, the CPU PC board with the microprocessor and its support chips, and several slots where other PC boards can be added. These added PC boards may be static or dynamic RAM boards, ROM boards, floppy-disk controller boards, interrupt controller boards, or some other type of interface board. Each PC board, including the CPU board, plugs into a double-sided 100-pin connector whose 100 pins are connected in common with the pins on all the other connectors. In this way, each PC board and its devices are connected to the various buses simply by plugging the board into a slot. Since all the connectors are identically wired, boards can be interchanged or moved from one slot to another without any problem.

There have been over 500 different types of S-100 boards developed by numerous manufacturers. These boards are primarily intended for use in hobby computer systems similar to the Altair 8080-based microcomputer. It is possible to purchase boards from several different manufacturers, plug them into slots on the main chassis, and have everything work satisfactorily as long as each board is S-100-compatible.

The S-100 bus standard, despite its wide use, has not been without problems. The original developers of the 100-pin layout were lax in their consideration of such problems as "cross-talk" between the clock lines and other control lines on adjacent connector pins, and potential shorting between adjacent power-supply pins.

Altair-680B System Bus

Also developed by MITS, Inc., the 680B bus format is based on systems using microprocessors such as the 6800 or 6502. It is a well-thought-out format compared to the S-100; it has none of the pin layout problems and it uses substantially fewer pins to accomplish the same results. The bus allocations are:

> 8 bidirectional data lines (combine data-in and data-out)
> 16 address lines
> 11 control lines, including R/W, ϕ_2, NMI, RESET, $\overline{\text{IRQ}}$

IEEE-488 Bus (HPIB)

Hewlett-Packard, Inc., developed an interface bus to connect instruments such as digital voltmeters, signal generators, and frequency counters. Known as the Hewlett-Packard interface bus (HPIB), it was later accepted by the IEEE as a standard bus called the IEEE-488.* The main function of the IEEE-488 bus is to allow a computer to be connected with several test instruments to form a computer-controlled test system.

This bus format consists of eight bidirectional data lines and eight control lines. It does not include any dedicated address lines. Address information is carried by the data lines at certain times. In fact, the data lines will at various times carry data, commands, or addresses. The control lines determine the function of the data bus.

*It is also known as the general-purpose interface bus (GPIB).

Figure 7.25 shows the diagram for a typical microprocessor-controlled measurement system, where the various devices are connected via the IEEE-488 bus. Note that all the devices are connected in parallel to the 16 different bus lines. The various devices can perform one or more of the following functions:

Talker   can transfer data to other devices via the data bus

Listener   can receive data from other devices via the data bus

Controller   manages the operation of the bus system primarily by sending addresses and commands over the data bus and control signals over the control lines

In Fig. 7.25, device A is the microprocessor and it can perform all three functions: TALK, LISTEN, and CONTROL. Device B can TALK and LISTEN. It could be a programmable instrument suh as a digital multimeter

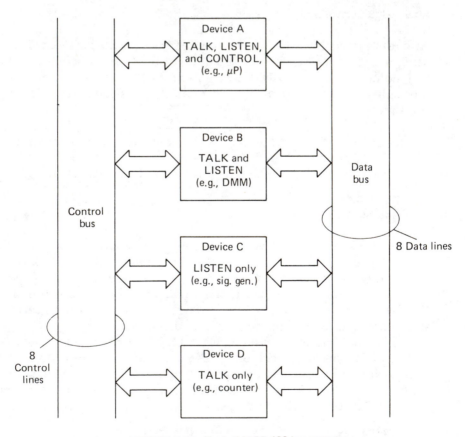

FIGURE 7.25 Typical IEEE-488 bus system.

which would LISTEN to receive a command code (from the microprocessor) telling it what measurement to perform, and would TALK to send its measurement (to the μP or a printer, for example).

Device C is only able to LISTEN. It might be a device such as a programmable signal generator which receives a command code from the microprocessor telling it the parameters of the signal it is to produce. Device D is only able to TALK. It could be a device such as a counter which sends its reading over the data bus to other devices (e.g., the microprocessor, a printer, etc.).

Only one Talker is allowed to put data on the data bus at a given time, but more than one Listener can receive the data. The Controller sends a TALK address out over the data lines while activating the appropriate control line. The device whose address this is will be the only Talker that is activated, while all other Talkers are disabled. A similar procedure selects the one or more Listeners which will receive data from the Talker. The Talker will subsequently send data to the Listeners *asynchronously*. That is, the data are not transmitted in synchronism with any particular clock signal; instead, they are transmitted when the Talker decides it has data available and the Listeners decide that they are ready to accept the data. This requires the use of several *handshake* signals between the Talker and Listener. These are transmitted over several of the control lines.

Clearly, the proper operation of this system is fairly complex. It has not been our intention to go into all of its details but rather to show the reader how a microprocessor can be interfaced to an instrumentation setup, where it can control the measurement, logging, and processing of data. The use of this standard bus format makes the task easier, especially if the instrumentation being used is designed to be interfaced to the IEEE-488 standard bus. At present over 300 instruments from more than 80 different manufacturers meet this requirement.

7.8 KEYBOARD INPUT DEVICES

A microprocessor is a complex LSI device that is one of the marvels of semiconductor technology. Even so, this device is rendered useless unless it has a program of instructions to execute. When used in dedicated applications such as process controllers, equipment and appliance controllers, and traffic controllers, the μP executes fixed programs that are stored in ROM. Any operation change to be made in such applications simply requires replacing the ROM with a different ROM. On the other hand, there are numerous situations where the μP must not only execute many different programs, but these programs must be continually modified. For these applications, the programs have to be stored in RAM. This is particularly true of general-purpose and hobbyist μCs, where the user is continually developing, testing, and running different programs. The same holds true for the development systems that engineers use to develop programs for μP-based equipment. All the extensive testing, modifying, and debugging of these programs is done using RAM. Then the final programs are put into ROM as part of the finished product.

When RAM is to be used for program storage, there has to be some means for easily entering programs and data into memory. One of the more common techniques used in low-cost microcomputers and μP development systems utilizes a *hexadecimal keyboard*. This keyboard contains 16 digit keys, one for each hex digit 0 through F, and several control keys. A typical hex keyboard format is shown in Fig. 7.26. In addition to the hex digit keys, this keyboard has four control keys, which determine the keyboard function being performed. For example, to read the contents of memory location 80AB, the user punches the hex keys 8-0-A-B, in that order, and then punches the EXAMINE key. This will cause the μP to read address location 80AB and display its contents, usually on LED readouts. A new word can then be stored in this address location by punching in the two hex digits and then punching the STORE key. Punching in a four-digit hex address and then punching the GO key causes the μP to go to that address to begin executing instructions. The RESET key is used to activate the μP's RESET input and to reset other conditions in the system.

There are a wide variety of methods used to interface a keyboard such as this to a μP. We will not attempt to show them all here. Instead, we will

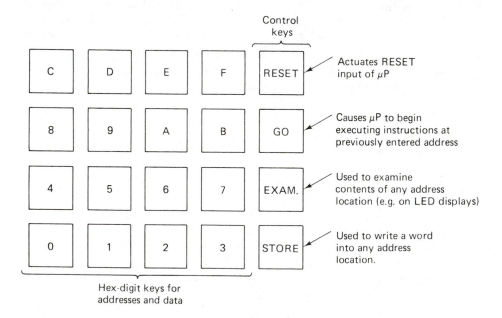

FIGURE 7.26 Typical hex keyboard format.

examine one of the more popular approaches, referred to as *software keyboard scanning*. This technique requires a *keyboard monitor program*, stored in ROM, which controls all the keyboard operations. The basic operation proceeds as follows:

1. Depressing the RESET key resets the μP and causes it to begin executing the keyboard monitor program stored in ROM. This means that the monitor program must be located at the address where the μP takes its first instruction after being reset. In the 6502 μP, this is determined by a reset vector.

2. As the μP executes the monitor program, it continually scans the keyboard outputs until it senses that a key has been depressed, and then determines which of the keys it is.

3. If the monitor program determines that it is one of the hex-digit keys, the 4-bit code for that particular key if fetched from a KEY-CODE table stored in ROM. For example, if the "A" key has been depressed, the code 1010 will be fetched from the KEY-CODE table. This code will then usually be sent to an LED readout for display and also to a RAM location for temporary storage until it is needed.

4. If the monitor program determines that one of the control keys has been depressed, the program performs the corresponding operation. For example, if the EXAM key is actuated, the monitor program fetches the word stored in the address location specified by the preceding *four* key actuations and sends it to LED readouts for display.

5. The monitor program continues to scan the keyboard looking for key actuations until the GO key is depressed. Upon sensing that the GO key has been actuated, the monitor program executes an unconditional jump to the address location specified by the preceding *four* key actuations. The codes for these key actuations were previously stored in RAM (step 3). This will cause the μP to stop executing the monitor program and begin executing the program stored at the punched-in address. Since the monitor program is no longer being executed, the keyboard relinquishes control over to the μP (i.e., all subsequent key actuations are ignored). The keyboard will regain control when the user punches the RESET key (step 1).

Interface Circuitry for Keyboard Scanning

Implementation of this keyboard scanning technique requires some means for allowing the μP to read the status of each key under the control of the monitor program. For this purpose the keyboard is treated as an input device and is assigned a specific address which the μP uses to communicate with it. Figure 7.27 shows one possible scheme for interfacing the keyboard of Fig. 7.26 to a μP.

In this arrangement, each keyswitch, when actuated, will connect one horizontal conductor to one vertical conductor. For example, depressing the "C" key will connect the output of inverter 4 to the input of tristate buffer 3; similarly, depressing the "GO" key will connect the output of inverter 0 to the input of buffer 2. With none of the keys depressed, the outputs of inverters 0 through 4 will be disconnected from all the inputs of buffers 0 through 3. In this condition, the pull-up resistors will keep the buffer inputs at a logic HIGH level. The BUFFER outputs are connected to the lower four lines (D_3 through D_0) of the system data bus and will be enabled by a HIGH level from the AND-gate output.

The keyboard is assigned addresses on page F8. Specifically, each column of keys is assigned a different address on page F8 according to the following table:

Column	Assigned Hex Address
4	F810
3	F808
2	F804
1	F802
0	F801

The μP can read the status of the keys in any column by using the appropriate address. For example, as part of the monitor program, the μP can read the status of the keys in column 3 by executing the instruction Load Accumulator (LDA) from Address F808. During this instruction, the higher-order address lines will produce a LOW at the decoder's PAGE F8 SELECT output. This LOW is inverted and applied to the AND gate along with the R/W line, which will be HIGH since the μP is performing a read operation. This produces a HIGH at the AND output enabling the BUFFERS and connecting their outputs to the data bus for transfer into the μP Accumulator.

The low-order address lines will have the hex code 08, which is the binary code 00001000, so the address line A_3 is HIGH. This produces a LOW at the inverter 3 output. Inverters 0, 1, 2, and 4 will have HIGH outputs, since address lines A_0, A_1, A_2, and A_4 are all LOW. This means that if any key in column 3 is down at the time the μP is executing the LDA F808 instruction, a LOW will be applied to the corresponding BUFFER input and then transferred to the Accumulator over the data bus. For example, if key "9" is down, the LOW from inverter 3 will be connected to the input of buffer 2 (point x). All other BUFFER inputs will be HIGH. Thus, the levels 1011 will be applied to the data bus and will enter the four lower-order

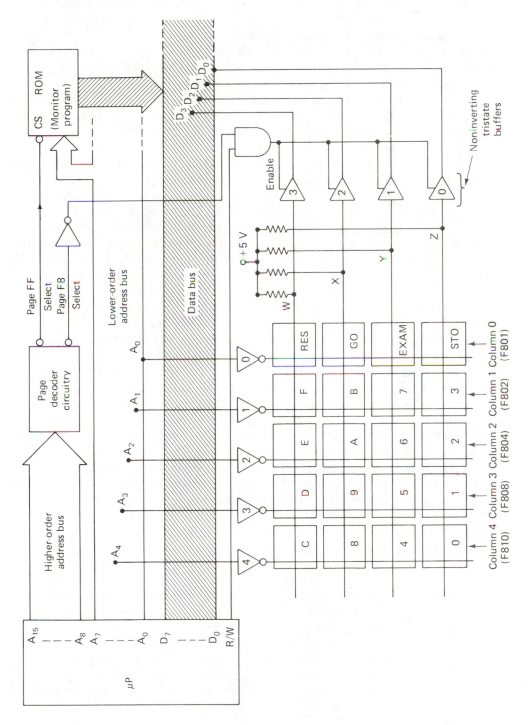

FIGURE 7.27 Hex keyboard interface for software scanning technique.

bits of the Accumulator. Similarly, if key "5" is down, the levels 1101 will be transmitted to the Accumulator. If none of the keys in column 3 is down at this time, the levels 1111 will be transmitted to the Accumulator.*

After completing the LDA F808 instruction, the monitor program will examine the contents of the Accumulator to see if any of the four lower-order bits is a 0. This tells it that a key from column 3 has been actuated, and the location of the 0 tells it which key. If none of the bits are 0, this indicates that none of the keys in column 3 are down.

Likewise, the μP can execute a LDA F810 instruction to read the status of the keys in column 4, a LDA F804 to read the keys in column 2, a LDA F802 for column 1, and a LDA F800 for column 0. The keyboard monitor program continually sequences through these instructions, reading the various keyboard columns one at a time until it reads a 0 into the Accumulator. The program keeps track of which column is being read and which bit of the Accumulator is zero to determine which key is depressed. For example, if the monitor program reads a 0 into bit 2 of the Accumulator (i.e., ACC = 11111011) while it is executing a LDA F810 (column 4), it knows that key "8" is down. Once it determines the key, the monitor program will execute a sequence of instructions, depending on which key it was.

Developing a keyboard monitor program is a fairly complex task and should not be undertaken by an inexperienced programmer. Fortunately, such programs are usually available from μP and μC manufacturers and are often presented in computer magazines. Of course, the actual monitor programs will vary depending on the μP and the type of keyboard being used. Some of the practical considerations that the monitor program must deal with include keyswitch bounce, multiple reading of the same key, and actuation of a second key before the first key is released.

Keyswitch bounce occurs when a key is first depressed and rarely lasts for more than 10 ms. When this bounce occurs it can appear to the μP that the same key has been actuated several times instead of just once. The monitor program can eliminate this problem by not servicing the keyboard more often than, say, every 20 ms. In other words, after sensing a key actuation, the monitor program will *delay* for about 20 ms before scanning the keyboard for a new key actuation. This delay is obtained by having the μP go through a *timing loop* in the monitor program. A timing loop is a sequence of dummy instructions that the μP repeats for a specified number of times which are usually counted in one of its index or general-purpose registers. Timing loops are discussed more fully in Chapter 8.

A typical monitor program can completely scan and service a typical hex keyboard in less than 1 ms. This means that the same key depression might be erroneously detected many times before the key is released. To avoid this, the monitor program must check to see that the actuated key has

---

*If any key in the other columns is down, it will not produce a LOW at the BUFFER inputs because its INVERTER output is HIGH.

been released before it scans the keyboard for new key actuations. A some-what related problem occurs when the user depresses a second key before the first key is released. Again, the monitor program solves this problem by checking for the release of the first key before it scans the keyboard for new key actuations. This is called a *two-key rollover* technique, and it allows the user to punch in a fast succession of key inputs without error.

Other Techniques

We have shown one scheme for utilizing a hex keyboard for inputting information to a μC. This software scanning method requires a somewhat complex monitor program (software) but uses a minimum of hardware. A completely opposite approach requires more complex circuitry but a less complex monitor program. This hardware approach uses a keyboard encoder circuit that converts each key actuation into a parallel binary code that is transferred to the μP over the data bus (Fig. 7.28). The circuitry also includes a KEY ACTUATION output, which indicates when any key is down. The μP monitor program does not need to scan the entire keyboard. Instead, it merely keeps polling the KEY ACTUATION output and, when a key actuation is indicated, it reads the encoder outputs into the Accumulator. Alternatively, an *interrupt* mode of operation can be used. For this mode, the KEY ACTUATION output is connected to one of the μP's interrupt inputs so that when any key is depressed, the μP ceases execution of its current program and branches to the interrupt service routine where it executes instructions for reading the encoder outputs into the Accumulator.

This software vs. hardware trade-off is something that μP users are continually confronted with. Generally speaking, performing a function in hard-

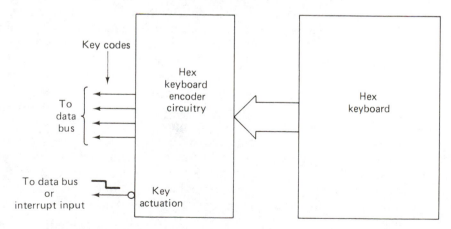

FIGURE 7.28 Hardware encoder for hex keyboard converts a key actuation into a 4-bit code to be sent to μP over data bus.

ware is usually faster than performing it in software; this is because the μP can perform only one operation at a time while external hardware can do several operations simultaneously. Doing it with software, however, is usually cheaper, is easier to modify, requires less assembly time and troubleshooting, and is more reliable, since fewer parts are used. A designer has to weight the advantages of both approaches carefully to see which one is best for his particular application.

ASCII Keyboard Interface

A hex keyboard is used to communicate with a computer using only the 16 hex digits 0 through F. The next higher level of communication uses the familiar English alphabet, numerals, punctuation marks, and other commonly used symbols (e.g., %, $, #, etc.). The universal binary code used for this type of communication is the 7-bit ASCII code (Chapter 1). With 7 bits, there are $2^7 = 128$ possible codes, representing 94 different characters and 34 different machine commands (e.g., carriage return, backspace, etc.). With 128 ASCII characters it would appear that an ASCII keyboard requires 128 key switches. Fortunately, an ASCII keyboard uses a shift key just like in a typewriter, to allow each key to have two functions. Thus, only 64 keys are needed.

ASCII keyboards are laid out similar to a conventional typewriter keyboard for easy two-hand operation. Each key is a switch which, when depressed, connects two points together in the same manner as shown for the hex keyboard. ASCII keyboards normally operate into a keyboard encoder circuit which generates the 7-bit ASCII code bit pattern for the key being depressed. This bit pattern is transferred to the μP over the data bus. Again, a KEY ACTUATION output allows either polled operation or interrupt operation to be used. ASCII keyboard encoders are more complex than hex keyboard encoders because of the greater number of keys and codes.* Some of the more sophisticated keyboard encoder chips (such as National Semiconductor's MM5740AF) also contain special *debouncing* and *two-key rollover* features.

ASCII keyboards can also be interfaced to a μP using a software scanning technique such as that illustrated in the last section for the hex keyboard. This method is used, for example, in the TRS-80, Radio Shack's popular business and hobbyist microcomputer.

Figure 7.29 illustrates another method of interfacing an ASCII keyboard to a μP for software scanning. It uses a PIA chip to provide the row-scanning function (port B) and the column-scanning function (port A). The μP keyboard monitor program scans a keyboard row by sending a word to

---

*An ASCII keyboard encoder chip often contains a ROM which stores the ASCII codes of the various keyboard characters and functions.

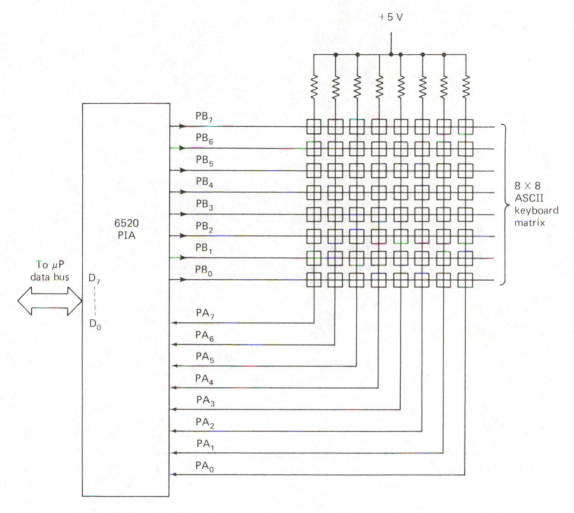

FIGURE 7.29   ASCII keyboard interfaced to a μP through a 6520 PIA.

port B with only a single 0 in that row position, and then reads port A. If a key in that row is down, the word read from port A will have a 0 in a position corresponding to the column of the actuated key.

7.9   TELETYPEWRITERS

A teletypewriter (TTY) is a computer I/O device that uses an ASCII keyboard for transmitting information to a computer and also has a printing unit for printing out information sent by the computer. Figure 7.30 is a picture of the most popular TTY in use today, the ASR 33 manufactured by

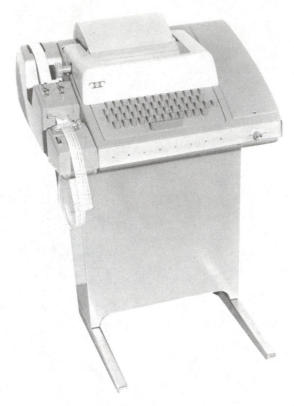

FIGURE 7.30   Model ASR 33 teletypewriter from Teletype Corporation.

Teletype Corporation. This model was first introduced in 1962 and over a
half million are presently being used. Although several companies manufacture teletypewriters, the popularity of the ASR 33 has made the word *teletype* a standard term in the computer field. In fact, people commonly use
the term "teletype" to refer to any teletypewriter unit.

The TTY is popular because it provides both an input device and output device in the same unit. Although the keyboard and printer are located
in the same mainframe, it should be noted that they are independent devices
which are not interconnected. They can be connected, if desired, so that the
printer prints out the characters as the keys are depressed, just like a typewriter. There is a switch at the bottom of the keyboard which, when placed
in the LOCAL position, causes the TTY to operate in this manner.

However, if this switch is in the LINE position, the TTY is connected
to the microcomputer, which takes sole control of the printer. When the μC
transmits the ASCII code for a character to the TTY, the printer will print
out that character. In this mode the keyboard does not control the printer.
Instead, when a key is pressed, the TTY transmits the ASCII code for that
key to the μC, which will read it into one of the μP registers. If the program

the μP is executing takes this key code and transmits it back to the TTY to be printed, the TTY appears to respond just like a typewriter would. This process is called *echoing*. If the program does not send the code back to the TTY printer, no printout occurs for that key depression.

As stated earlier, data transmission to and from the TTY is done in a serial format at a baud rate of 110. Each serial word consists of 11 bit times of 9.09-ms duration; this includes a START bit, 7 data bits (the ASCII code), an *even*-parity bit, and 2 stop bits. Thus, each serial word requires 11×9.09 ms ≈ 100 ms, so a TTY can transmit or receive characters at a maximum rate of 10 characters/s. It was also mentioned earlier that a TTY often sends and receives information as a series of current pulses, a logic 1 being represented by a flow of 20 mA of current and logic 0 by no flow of current. This *current* operation requires special interfacing circuitry to convert between the 0-V and +5-V TTL logic levels of a UART and the 20-mA current levels required by the TTY.

Many TTY units also have a paper-tape punch and paper-tape reader. Paper tape is a storage medium consisting of 1-inch-wide paper in rolls of several hundred feet in length. A paper-tape punch can punch holes into this tape conforming to a binary code such as ASCII. A paper-tape reader is a device used to detect the holes that have been punched in the tape and to generate logic levels corresponding to the bit pattern. The TTY considers the paper-tape punch and the printer to be the same physical unit; that is, when the paper-tape punch is turned on, anything which the printer prints out will also be punched on paper tape. This means that paper tape can be used to store programs that the TTY user punches into the keyboard.

These programs can then be stored and reused without the need for the user to enter them from the keyboard again; instead, the paper tape is fed through the tape reader, which then sends the codes to the μC. The rate at which information is punched into or read from the paper tape will be the standard TTY rate of 110 baud or 10 characters/s. Paper-tape punches and readers are available as separate equipment, not tied to a TTY. They come in various operating speeds, the faster units being more costly. Currently, paper-tape punches are available that can punch up to 200 characters/s at an average cost of $2000. Paper-tape readers that can read up to 1000 characters/s are commonplace at an average cost of about $800.

7.10 MAGNETIC-TAPE STORAGE

Undoubtedly, the most popular *bulk* storage device used by microcomputer owners is magnetic tape. By bulk storage we mean the storage of large quantities of information (programs, data, etc.) that are not in constant use by the computer, but must be available when the computer requires them. Magnetic-tape units can utilize the same magnetic tape used in audio-tape recorders, or, for higher-speed recording, a higher-quality tape designed for digital storage. By far the most popular units used by μC owners are the familiar audio-tape cassettes and cassette recorders. These devices record digital information on tape in exactly the same manner as they record audio; one particular audio frequency (tone) is used to represent a logic 0, and a different tone is used to represent a logic 1.

Cassette storage enjoys widespread use for several reasons, including its relatively low cost, convenience, and ease of handling. It also enjoys a speed advantage over TTY-connected paper-tape units. A suitable cassette recorder can be purchased for as little as $25. Of course, more expensive units are available which can perform at higher data-transfer rates and with better reliability.

The magnetic tape itself is very inexpensive. A typical cassette costing about $2.50 can store more than 100,000 bytes of information, while $2.50 worth of paper tape can store only about 10,000 bytes. Magnetic tapes are much easier to handle and store compared to unwieldy paper tape. In addition, magnetic tapes can be erased and used over and over again.

Magnetic-tape units interfaced to microcomputers operate at data-transmission rates that range from 300 to 3000 bauds. For these units, data are recorded serially along the length of the tape and read from the tape serially. Faster units are available which use parallel digital recording across the width of the tape; however, these units are generally priced out of the range of the μC user.

Recording Format

One of the most popular formats for recording data on cassette tapes is called the Kansas City Standard, which uses the following to represent logic levels:

> logic "0"   *four* cycles of a 1200-Hz tone
> logic "1"   *eight* cycles of a 2400-Hz tone

Figure 7.31 illustrates how a sequence of binary levels is recorded on tape using this format.

A special interface circuit between the μC and recorder converts the binary levels from the computer into the appropriate audio tones to be recorded on the tape. Another part of the interface circuit is used for the reverse process, where the audio tones are played back (not into a speaker) and converted into logic levels to be fed into the computer. A significant part of this interface is a UART which is used to convert between the computer's parallel data and the tape's serial format.

A typical cassette can hold over 100,000 bytes—a large amount of data

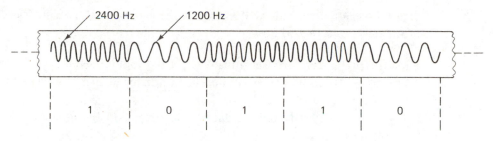

FIGURE 7.31 Using two audio frequencies recorded on magnetic tape to represent 1s and 0s.

or instructions. This is a lot more than a μC can use at any one time. For this reason, the information stored on the tape is divided into blocks called *records*. Each record stores a related group of bytes that could be a block of data or a program that the μC will require at various times. When more than one record is stored on a cassette tape, there has to be a gap separating individual records. This is illustrated in Fig. 7.32A, where the shaded regions represent records consisting of strings of 0s and 1s recorded as audio tones, and the clear areas are the *interrecord gaps*, where no audio tone is recorded. These gaps are required because the starting and stopping of the tape between records takes a certain amount of time.

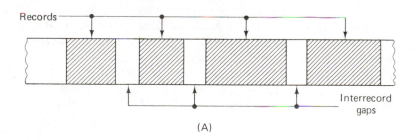

(A)

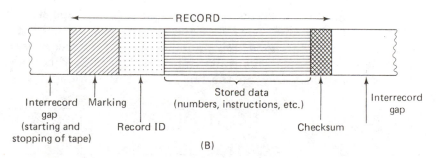

(B)

FIGURE 7.32 (A) Cassette tape divided into records; (B) format of a typical record.

The individual records will each have the format shown in Fig. 7.32B. The four parts of a record are:

MARKING: a standard amount of recorded logic 1 levels.

RECORD ID: an identification code and other information used to identify this particular record.

STORED DATA: the actual data or information being stored for eventual use by the μC.

CHECKSUM: a calculated numerical value used in error detecting.

The ID portion typically consists of two bytes that serve as an identifying code for the record to distinguish it from other records. It may also contain information regarding the number of bytes contained in the record so that the μC, when reading the record, will know when it has reached the end of the recorded data.

The CHECKSUM is a value that is calculated as data are being recorded on the tape. As the computer sends a block of data from its memory (RAM) to be stored on tape, it treats each byte as a number and keeps a running sum (ignoring overflows) in its Accumulator. At the end of the record, this final total (CHECKSUM) is recorded on the tape immediately following the recorded data. Later, when the computer is reading this record from the tape, it keeps a running sum of the data bytes as it reads them. At the end of the record the μC compares the final total to the value of CHECKSUM, which it also reads from the tape. If the two values do not agree, an error has occurred either in recording or reading the data. The same record can be then reread, and hopefully there will be no CHECKSUM error the second time. If there is, the data on the tape probably contain one or more errors that occurred during recording.

Redundant Recording

Errors could be the result of a scratched or worn tape surface or simply a bad spot on the tape. A well-designed μC system will help to combat these errors by using *redundant recording*, whereby each record is recorded twice on the cassette tape. This is illustrated in Fig. 7.33, where each record is recorded twice in a row on the tape. With this system, if the μC detects a

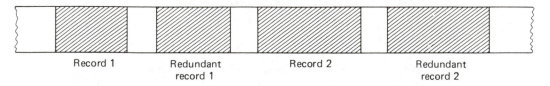

Record 1   Redundant   Record 2   Redundant
                   record 1   record 2

FIGURE 7.33 Using redundant records reduces the effect of errors.

CHECKSUM error when reading record 1, it will proceed to read redundant record 1, with a good chance that this record is error-free. Of course, if no CHECKSUM error occurs in record 1, the μC will skip over redundant record 1. This technique is useful in reducing the effects of tape recording errors, but it uses twice as much tape to record the same information.

Interfacing the Cassette Recorder to the μP

Figure 7.34 shows a typical arrangement for interfacing a cassette recorder to a μP. As noted earlier, a major component of the system is a UART,

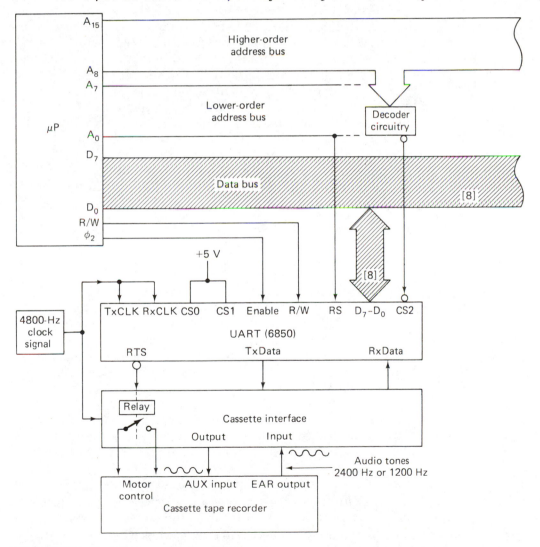

FIGURE 7.34 Typical cassette interface arrangement.

which is needed to convert the parallel data bytes from the μP to the serial format required by the tape recorder. The UART also adds 1 START bit and 2 STOP bits to each data byte before transmitting it to the recorder. A parity bit is normally not used, since CHECKSUM is used for error detection. The TxCLK and RxCLK inputs are shown driven from a 4800-Hz clock signal. If the UART uses a clock divide ratio of 16, this gives a baud rate of 4800/16 = 300, which is normally the lowest baud rate used in cassette recording. Each bit time is thus equal to 1/300 = 3.33 ms. This is exactly the amount of time required to record eight cycles of a 2400-Hz tone or four cycles of a 1200-Hz tone.

The UART is connected to the recorder through the *cassette interface*, which performs three basic functions. First, it contains the circuitry used to transform the UART's serial output (TxData) from TTL logic levels to audio tones. This circuitry utilizes the 4800-Hz clock to obtain the 2400-Hz and 1200-Hz frequencies. These audio signals are fed to the recorder's auxiliary (AUX) input for recording on the tape. The second function of the cassette interface is to take the audio signals from the tape (earphone output) during playback and transform them back into serial logic levels for the UART's RxDATA input. The cassette interface is also used to turn the tape recorder motor on and off. It does this through a relay that is controlled by the UART's $\overline{\text{RTS}}$ output. Recall that the μP can set this output level to a 0 or 1 through the UART's Control register (bits CR5 and CR6). Thus, by writing the appropriate code into the Control register, the μP can turn the recorder on or off.

Software

The entire process of writing information onto and reading information from the cassette tape is done under program control. There has to be a *tape I/O control program* somewhere in the μC memory, usually ROM, which the μC can execute whenever the tape is to be accessed. Very often this program utilizes a keyboard to allow the μC user to enter the commands and parameters required for a data transfer. The tape I/O program, when it is being executed, waits for keyboard actuation to give it information including:

Beginning Address (BA): the location in μC memory (RAM) of the first word of data to be placed on tape; or, during a tape-read operation, it is the address in RAM where the first data word read from the tape is to be placed.

Ending Address (EA): the location in μC memory of the last word of data to be written on tape; or, during a tape-read operation, it is the RAM address where the last word read from the tape is to be placed.

Identifier (ID): a four-digit (hex) code used to identify the record being recorded or read.

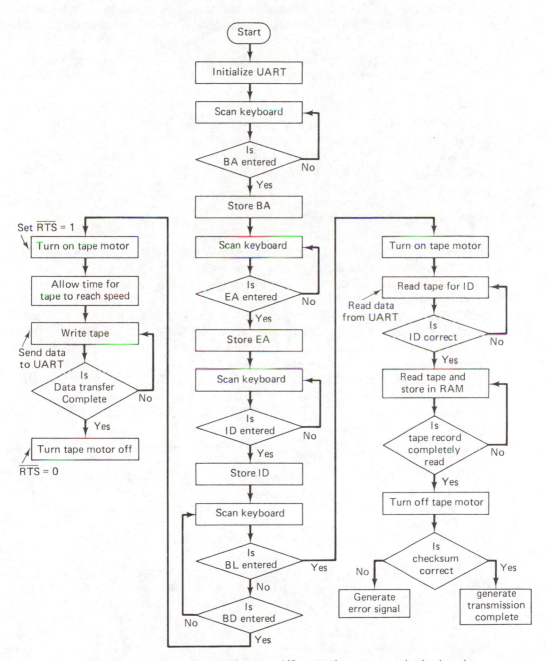

FIGURE 7.35 Flow diagram for tape I/O control program under keyboard control.

Begin Dump (BD): a command to the tape I/O program telling the μC to *write* data from RAM onto the tape using addresses specified by BA and EA.

Begin Load (BL): a command telling the μC to *read* data from the tape record specified by ID and place in RAM locations specified by BA and EA.

A simplified flowchart of a typical tape I/O control program is shown in Fig. 7.35. It is not meant to show all the details involved in such a program; rather, it shows the various major steps performed in the process of accessing the tape under keyboard control.

7.11   FLOPPY DISKS (or DISKETTES)

Magnetic tape offers higher performance at a lower cost than paper tape for the bulk storage of data and programs. Magnetic tape, however, does possess a major drawback, in that information on the tape must be accessed sequentially. For example, this means that if the cassette tape is positioned at record 1 and it is desired to read data from record 15, it is necessary to wind through the intervening records before record 15 is reached. Even if fast-forward operation is used, the time required to locate the desired record may be anywhere from several seconds to several minutes. For some applications or for some μC users, this long access time would be prohibitive. Another disadvantage of cassette-tape storage is that most cassette recorders cannot be completely controlled by the μC. For instance, the μC cannot switch the recorder to the rewind or fast-forward modes.

A bulk storage device that overcomes these disadvantages, at an increase in cost, is the *floppy disk*. A floppy disk (also called a *diskette*) is a flexible disk which looks like a 45-rpm phonograph record without grooves. The surface of the disk is coated with a magnetic material that is used to store digital information in the form of magnetized spots. Because floppy disks are flexible and bend easily, they are enclosed in a protective cardboard envelope. This keeps them rigid as they are spun around by the disk drive unit in much the same way as phonograph records.

Figure 7.36 shows the standard floppy disk, which has a diameter slightly less than 8 inches. The protective envelope has cutouts for the drive spindle, the READ/RECORD head, and an index position hole. The access slot allows the READ/RECORD head to make contact with the surface of the disk as it spins inside the envelope. The index hole allows a photoelectric sensor to be used to determine a reference point for all the tracks on the disk.

Floppy disks are normally rotated at a speed of 360 rpm, which corresponds to one rotation in about 167 ms. As the disk rotates, the READ/

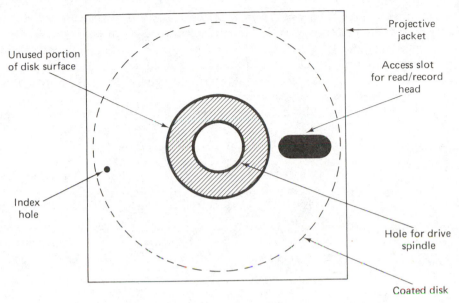

FIGURE 7.36 Floppy disk.

RECORD head makes contact with it through the access slot so that it can write or sense magnetic pulses on the disk surface. The standard 8-inch disk surface is divided into 77 concentric tracks numbered 0 to 76 (see Fig. 7.37A) with track number 0 being the outside track. These tracks are normally spaced about 0.02 inch apart, with track 0 having a total length of about 25 inches and track 77 a total length of 15 inches. This means that

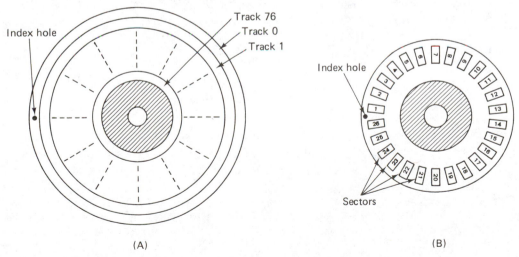

FIGURE 7.37 (A) Disk is divided into 77 concentric tracks; (B) each tract is divided into 26 equal sectors.

the longer outside tracks have space for more information than the shorter inside tracks. For convenience in accessing a given point on the disk, the disk is divided into 26 equal-sized *sectors* (see Fig. 7.37B) in which information can be stored. This means that the same amount of storage space is used on each track irrespective of the length of the track; thus, more space is wasted (not used) on the longer tracks.

The index hole is placed between the last sector (26) and the first sector (1). Using a light source/photodetector combination, the disk-drive controller will know when the disk is in its reference position, with sector 1 next to the index hole. Special identification information is recorded at the start of each sector to allow the disk controller to keep track of which sector is under the READ/WRITE head. This arrangement using a single index hole is referred to as *soft sectoring*. Some floppy disks use a *hard sectoring* format where, in addition to the index hole, there are sector holes at the start of each sector. This eliminates the need for identification information recorded at the start of each sector.

Disk Capacity

When discussing disk capacity, it must be clear whether you are talking about *formatted* or *unformatted* capacity. A substantial amount of disk space is allotted for functions such as sector and record identification, error checking, and interrecord gaps. Thus, the capacity available for data storage (*formatted* capacity) is less than the total available capacity (*unformatted* capacity).

To illustrate, disks that use the popular IBM 3740 format have a formatted capacity of 128 bytes/sector. Thus, the total formatted capacity of one disk surface will be

$$128 \, \frac{\text{bytes}}{\text{sector}} \times 26 \, \frac{\text{sectors}}{\text{track}} \times 77 \, \frac{\text{tracks}}{\text{disk}} \approx 256{,}000 \, \frac{\text{bytes}}{\text{disk}}$$

The unformatted capacity of this same disk would be around 382,000 bytes.

Some disk systems use *dual-density* storage, which crams 256 bytes into each sector. Another means for increasing disk capacity uses double-sided disks and disk drives. A double-sided disk has a magnetic oxide coating on both sides and uses a separate READ/WRITE head for each side of the disk.

A smaller floppy disk called a *mini-floppy* is also in common use. It has a diameter of slightly more than 5 inches and a typical formatted capacity of 90,000 bytes/disk, although more densely packed mini-floppies are available.

Access Time

Data are recorded or read from the disk surface 1 bit at a time at a nominal rate of 1 bit every 4 μs or 1 byte every 32 μs. This rate, however, occurs after the READ/RECORD head has been positioned on the desired sector of the desired track. It takes approximately 6 ms for the head-positioning mechanism to move the head from one track to the next and 16 ms more to lower the head onto the track. With 77 tracks, it will take about 1/2s in the worst case for the head to move from its present track to the track that is to be accessed for reading or writing. Once the head is on the desired track, it has to find the desired sector on that track. Since the disk makes one revolution in 167 ms, it will take 167 ms to find the right sector in the worst case. Thus, even in the worst case it takes a little over 0.6 s to find the desired record on the disk. On the average, this access time will be more like 0.3 s. This is much faster than the time required to randomly access a record on even the fastest magnetic-tape system.

Cost

A complete floppy-disk system includes the disk, the disk drive, the controller, and a computer interface. The disk drive includes the 360-rpm motor which spins the disk, the READ/WRITE head positioner, and the photosensor that detects the index and sector holes. The controller includes all of the electronics that accepts commands from the computer and translates them into control signals for the disk drive. The interface circuitry between the computer and the controller can be as complex as a complete PC board, or as simple as a single floppy-disk controller chip. The total cost for a typical system that handles two floppy disks is around $2000.

Software

The software that controls the disk drive is called the *disk operating system* (DOS). The DOS is usually a fairly complex program that is provided by the computer manufacturer.

Hard Disks

Another type of disk system which has been adopted by microcomputer users differs from the floppy disk. It uses a hard aluminum disk that cannot be removed, and is referred to as a Winchester disk drive. The Winchester drive uses a flying head that floats on a cushion of air and does not rub against the disk surface. This eliminates disk surface wear. Winchester drives have faster access times and higher capacities than floppies. A typical for-matted capacity is 10 million bytes/disk.

7.12 TVT or VIDEO DISPLAY

A TVT or TV typewriter is a low-cost way of displaying large quantities of alphanumeric information on an ordinary television set. It is an I/O device suitable for use with a µC system that allows easy and fast transfer of infor-mation from µP to operator and operator to µP.

Video Display Introduction

Before we can get into the details of how to display information on a TV monitor, we need to have some idea of the basics of video display. Let us assume that we have a certain amount of memory reserved for display pur-poses. This memory space will store the information that we wish to display on the TV monitor. Each memory address will store one ASCII-coded char-acter and the format chosen for display will determine the actual memory requirements. Typical formats are 16 lines of 32 characters, 16 lines of 64 characters, and 16 lines of 80 characters. If we choose the simplest format of 16 lines of 32 characters, we will need a minimum of $16 \times 32 = 512$ memory spaces to store a complete screen of information. Figure 7.38 shows

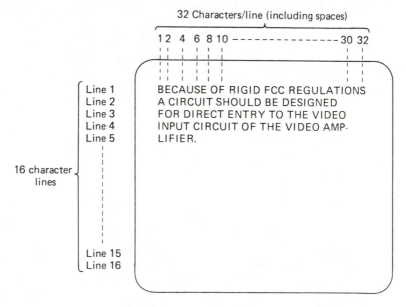

FIGURE 7.38 Partial TV display.

a partial display. One horizontal line consists of a maximum of 32 characters, including spaces. A complete display would consist of a maximum of 16 such horizontal character lines.

The display consists of digital information being sequentially read from memory and converted to the appropriate video signals to be fed into the TV. Of course, certain timing and control signals will also need to be generated. To understand how binary information stored in memory can be converted to video information, we need to discuss some basic television operation. This topic will be presented in a somewhat simplified manner so as not to detract from the more pertinent concepts.

Television Operation Introduction

We will only look at the simplest television display to be used solely for displaying alphanumeric information. The actual display (see Fig. 7.39) is made up of an electron beam being horizontally swept across the picture tube from left to right in about 53.5 μs, starting at the upper left-hand corner of the screen. The beam is then blanked and returned (retraced) back to the left side of the screen in about 10 μs. During this retrace the beam is gradually deflected downward by a small amount.* This sequence is repeated until the electron beam traverses the entire screen, ending up in the lower right-hand corner of the screen. This complete scan of the TV screen is referred to as a *frame* or *vertical sweep*. *Vertical retrace* occurs when the electron beam is blanked and returned to the upper left-hand corner of the screen. One complete vertical sweep and retrace requires 16.67 ms (a rate of 60 Hz). Since vertical retrace takes about 1.25 ms, we are left with 15.42 ms for one vertical sweep time. Since each horizontal line takes 63.5 μs, this

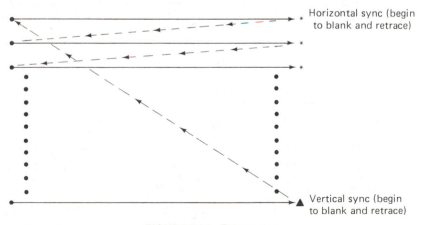

FIGURE 7.39 TV scanning.

*In actual practice, the beam is continuously being deflected downward as it moves horizontally.

gives a total of 15.42 ms/63.5 μs = 242 possible lines per frame. As shown in Fig. 7.39, to synchronize operation of the system we need to generate one horizontal sync pulse at the end of each horizontal line and one vertical sync pulse at the end of each frame (242 lines).

The next question we must deal with is: How can we get ASCII-coded data stored in memory to be displayed as alphanumeric characters on the TV screen? The answer to this comes in the form of an integrated circuit known as a *character generator*.

Character Generation   The data stored in each memory location correspond to a particular ASCII code. We must be able to convert this information into a form that can be used by the video section. This is accomplished by converting each ASCII code into a *dot-matrix* pattern. Typical patterns consist of a 5 $\times$ 7 matrix or a 7 $\times$ 9 matrix.

Figure 7.40A shows a 5 $\times$ 7 dot-matrix pattern for the letter E. Each solid dot can be represented by a logic 1 and each blank dot by a logic 0, as shown in Fig. 7.40B. With this format the dot-matrix equivalent of an ASCII character can be transmitted as seven serial bit patterns, one for each row of dots.

Figure 7.41 shows the 2513 character-generator integrated circuit which transmits these bit patterns. It has two sets of inputs. One set consists of the ASCII code bits which select the particular character. The 2513 generates only the uppercase characters so that only 6 ASCII code bits are needed. The second set of inputs are row select inputs that select which row of each character's dot matrix will be present at the five output pins. For example, $R_2 R_1 R_0 = 001$ selects row 1, 010 selects row 2, and so on up to row 7. For row inputs $R_2 R_1 R_0 = 000$, no row is selected and the five outputs will all be 0. This can be used to provide vertical spacing between characters in a complete system.

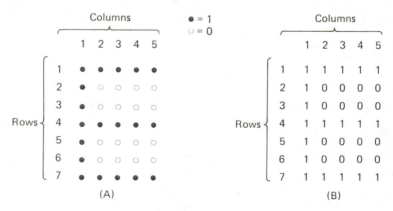

FIGURE 7.40   (A) Dot-matrix representation of the letter E; (B) logic-level representation of the letter E.

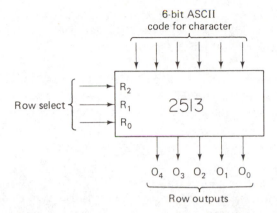

FIGURE 7.41   Model 2513 character-generator integrated circuit.

In order to output the complete dot matrix of a character, we must sequence through all seven rows. Each row pattern appears at the character-generator outputs. These outputs are in a parallel format, and to be able to display this information on a television system, it must be converted to a serial signal. As a row of information is made available at the output of the 2513, it is transferred to a Shift register and shifted out serially. As the electron beam is sweeping horizontally across the TV screen, the 1s and 0s contained in the row of information being shifted out are used to turn the electron beam on and off. In this fashion the TV would have to complete seven horizontal scans to display the full character. Figure 7.42 shows the arrangement of the 2513 and the use of a Shift register to shift out the row information serially.

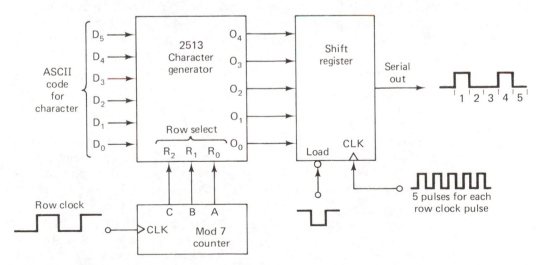

FIGURE 7.42   Parallel-to-serial conversion of row information.

Complete Display System A block diagram for the complete system operation is given in Fig. 7.43. The overall system can be broken down into several segments, described below.

1. *Memory:* a total of 512 RAM memory spaces. Each memory location stores the ASCII code for one character. We can visualize this memory space arranged at 16 lines of 32 characters per line.

2. *Character Counter (CC):* a mod-32 counter used to select one character out of the 32 possible per character line using address lines A_4 through A_0.

3. *Character Line Counter (CLC):* a mod-16 counter used to select one character line out of the 16 possible using address lines A_8 through A_5. The combined function of the preceding two counters is to determine what character position on the TV screen is being written onto at a given point in time. As the CLC is sequenced, it selects which character line of 16 is written on the screen. As the CC is sequenced, it selects which character of the 32 in a given character line is written onto the screen.

4. *ROW Select Counter (RSC):* a mod-10 counter used to select a particular row of the selected character. Count 0 selects row 0 of the character matrix; this puts 0s at outputs O_4 through O_0 of the character generator. These 0s produce a black level (blank) on the screen and provide a row of spacing above the character. Counts 8 and 9 generate a signal that is fed to the video combiner and used to produce two more rows of blanking. Therefore, between character lines we have a total of three blank lines for spacing.

5. *Shift Register:* a 7-bit register used to convert the 5-bit parallel output of the character generator to a 7-bit serial output. The two LSBs of the Shift register are always loaded as lows and used to provide two blanking spaces for horizontal character spacing.

6. *Dot Counter:* a mod-7 counter used to keep track of which dot of a character matrix row is being shifted out. It is also used to increment the character counter and generate a load pulse for the Shift register.

7. *O.S. Delay:* a one shot used to provide a delay so that when the dot counter is reset and a new memory address selected, enough time is provided for the new data out of memory and the outputs of the character generator to become stable before loading the Shift register.

8. *Timing and Control:* circuitry that might consist of such things as crystal-controlled oscillators, counters, gates, phase-locked loops, or special function-integrated circuits used to generate the master clock signal, horizontal sync, vertical sync, and blanking signals.

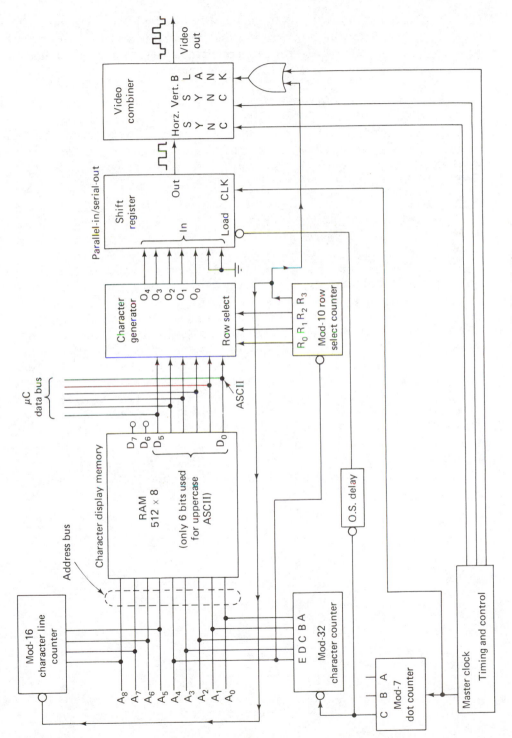

FIGURE 7.43 Complete display system.

9. *Video Combiner:* discrete circuitry used to combine the data information from the Shift register and the timing and control information into one signal with proper voltage levels. This signal is then fed to the TV monitor and provides the display.

A more detailed description of this complete system is beyond the intended scope of this book. The interested reader can find a great deal more information on TVT systems in the following two publications by Don Lancaster: *TV Typewriter Cookbook* and *The Cheap Video Cookbook*. Both are published by Howard W. Sams, Inc., and both are written for relative novices to the computer field.

Final Words on Video Display

You might now ask how the information contained in RAM initially gets there. With proper interfacing and control, the address bus and data bus can be tied into the μC system such that the μP can read from or write into the display memory like any other memory location in the system. A keyboard can be interfaced to the μP such that information can be entered into the μP and then echoed (transferred) to the display memory. This allows for great flexibility in software control of the system.

To enter data into the system, we need to know where the character we want to enter will be placed on the display. This is taken care of by adding another feature to our basic display, called a *cursor*. The cursor is usually a blinking box, underline, or overline that shows the user where a new character will be placed on the display. Figure 7.44 shows the cursor on the screen, indicating that the next piece of information to be entered will be next to the H in the second line.

Generally, the keyboard will allow one to change the position of the

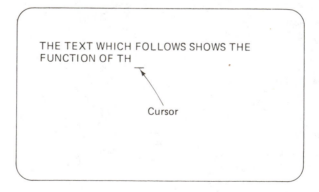

THE TEXT WHICH FOLLOWS SHOWS THE
FUNCTION OF TH

Cursor

FIGURE 7.44 Adding a cursor to the display.

cursor by moving it to the right or left (backspace) one space at a time and one line up or down at a time. With these four controls we can easily locate the cursor anywhere on the display and insert new information.

GLOSSARY

Baud Rate Number of bits of information transmitted serially per second:

$$\text{baud rate} = \frac{1}{\text{bit time}}$$

Bit Time Period of time allotted to 1 data bit in serial transmission system.

Character Generator Specialized IC that will accept an ASCII-coded word for input and produce a dot-matrix pattern of that character.

Checksum Value that is the arithmetic sum of all the bytes in a record and recorded on the tape immediately following the recorded data. Later, when the computer is reading this record from the tape, it keeps a running sum of the data bytes as they are read. The μP then compares this final value to the CHECKSUM, which it also reads off the tape; if they are equal, it is assumed that the record was loaded without error.

Cursor Special symbol used in a TVT system to indicate the position where the next character will be placed on the screen.

Echoing Process whereby when a teletype key is depressed, a program will cause the μP to read the key code into an internal register and immediately transmit the same key code back to the printer.

Floppy Disk Flexible-disk bulk storage device which looks like a 45-rpm phonograph record. The surface of the disk is coated with a magnetic material that is used to store digital information in the form of magnetized spots.

Full Duplex Data in a serial transmission scheme can be transmitted in both directions simultaneously.

GPIB General-purpose interface bus (*see* IEEE-488 Bus).

Half Duplex Data in a serial transmission scheme can be transmitted or received but not simultaneously.

HPIB Hewlett-Packard interface bus (*see* IEEE-488 Bus).

IEEE-488 Bus (HPIB, GPIB) Parallel bus designed by Hewlett-Packard and accepted by the IEEE as a standard. Utilized in the interconnection of a computer to several test instruments.

Interrecord Gaps Spacing between records on tape or disk where no information is recorded. This allows for a certain amount of time for the starting and stopping of the tape drive (typically 0.5 s).

Kansas City Standard Audio cassette recording format standard which uses four cycles of a 1200-Hz tone for a logic 0 and eight cycles of a 2400-Hz tone for a logic 1.

Marking Whenever there is no serial data word being transmitted in an asynchronous serial transmission system, the signal line is kept at a logic HIGH (1) level.

Modem Device used to transmit or receive digital information using standard telephone lines. Frequency-shift keying is used in this scheme and the device is used to modulate and demodulate the signals.

Monitor Program Program stored in ROM utilized to scan a keyboard upon application of a RESET signal.

Optoisolator Solid-state device that can be used to electrically isolate the load from the source. Light energy is used to turn power on and off to a load.

PARITY Bit Extra bit attached to a code group to make the number of 1s conform to a predetermined form (odd or even). This is used in error-detection schemes in transmission of data.

Record Related group of bytes that could be a block of data or a program stored on magnetic tape or disk. On disk, it is often called a "file."

Reed Relay Miniature electromagnetic relay used to switch ac loads under control of the μP.

RS-232-C Electronics Industry Association (EIA) standard for serial transmission voltage levels utilizing –12 V and +12 V for logic 1 and 0, respectively.

S-100 Bus Parallel "hobby computer" bus standard consisting of 100 lines used for data I/O, address, control, power supply, and future expansion connections.

Software Keyboard Scanning Upon RESET of the μP the keyboard monitor program, stored in ROM, continually scans the keyboard outputs until it senses that a key has been depressed. It then determines which key was depressed and takes appropriate action.

START Bit Logic Low for a period of 1 bit time used in asynchronous serial data transmission to indicate the initiation of data transmission.

STOP Bit Logic HIGH for a period of 1 to 2 bit times used in asynchronous serial data transmission to indicate termination of a data word.

TVT (TV Typewriter) Relatively inexpensive I/O device consisting of a teletype keyboard for input and a TV monitor (or television) for output.

Two-Key Rollover Technique whereby the keyboard monitor program incorporates checking to see that the first key depressed is released before scanning the keyboard for new key actuations.

Unconditional CPU-Initiated Transfer CPU initiates transfer of information to I/O device. The I/O device must always be ready for communication. This process does not usually involve "handshaking."

Winchester Disk Drive Hard disk used in μC systems.

QUESTIONS AND PROBLEMS

Section 7.1

7.1 Design the necessary circuitry for translating TTL logic levels (0, +5 V) to RS-232C levels which are +12 V and –12 V for logic 0 and 1, respectively.

7.2 Design the circuitry for translating from RS-232C to TTL.

7.3 Why should relays or optoisolators be used when an output port drives an ac load?

Section 7.2

7.4 Which of the following are not part of the standard asynchronous serial data format?
  (a) a START bit (0)
  (b) 5 to 8 data bits
  (c) a STATUS bit
  (d) one or more STOP bits (1s)
  (e) an optional parity bit

7.5 Using the standard asynchronous serial format with 7 data bits, odd parity, and 2 stop bits, draw the complete waveform for the transmission of the message "HELP."

7.6 If the transmission in Problem 7.5 is taking place at a baud rate of 1200 bits/s, how long will it take for the complete message to be transmitted?

Section 7.3

7.7 Which of the following are not part of a UART?
  (a) a serial receiver   (e) Receive and Transmit Shift registers
  (b) a serial transmitter   (f) a Memory Address register
  (c) an internal baud-rate generator   (g) a Parity Checker
  (d) a bidirectional data bus buffer

7.8 Describe the steps that take place when a μP transmits a data word to a serial output device through a UART.

7.9 Describe the steps that take place when a μP receives a data word from a serial input device through a UART.

7.10 How does the UART Receiver section sync itself to the incoming serial data?

Section 7.4

7.11 Name the *four* 6850 UART registers that the μP can communicate with.

7.12 Which one of the following is *not* one of the four basic operations a μP can perform on a UART?
  (a) read the Control register
  (b) read the Status register
  (c) write to the Transmit Data register
  (d) read from the Receiver Data register

7.13 Information that determines the serial transmission characteristics between a UART and an I/O device is in the UART's:
  (a) Status register   (c) Transmit Data register
  (b) Receiver Data register   (d) Control register

7.14 If a μP and UART are set up for μP-initiated conditional transfer, the μP can determine if the UART has data for it by:
  (a) reading and testing the Status register
  (b) reading and testing the Receiver Data register
  (c) reading and testing the Control register
  (d) reading and testing the Transmit Data register

7.15 What control word must the μP send to the 6850 Control register if the following operation is desired?
(a) a baud rate of 110 bits/s using an external clock frequency of 7040 pulses/s
(b) 8 data bits
(c) even parity
(d) 1 STOP bit
(e) RTS = 0 and TRANSMIT INTERRUPT DISABLED
(f) RECEIVER INTERRUPT DISABLED

7.16 Refer to Fig. 7.14. Assume that the microprocessor has previously written the word "5A" into the UART Control register. Draw the serial waveform that is generated at the TxData output if the microprocessor then writes the word "C9" into the UART Transmit Data register (TxDR). Show the exact timing.

7.17 Refer to the flowchart of Fig. 7.15. Why is it necessary to read the Status register contents before writing a new word into the TxDR for transmission? What would happen if this were not done? Remember, the microprocessor executes instructions in several microseconds.

7.18 Change the circuit of Fig. 7.14 so that address 3001 is used for Status and Control, and address 3000 is used for Data.

Section 7.5

7.19 What common I/O device often uses the presence and absence of current to represent logic levels?

7.20 Using the serial transmission format described in Problem 7.15, draw the waveform for the transmission of the character "A" using RS-232C voltage levels.

7.21 What is the main advantage of synchronous serial communication over asynchronous serial communication? What is the disadvantage?

7.22 Why is FSK used instead of pulses when transmitting digital data over telephone lines?

7.23 Describe the functions performed by a modem.

Section 7.6

7.24 What is the function of the Data Direction registers in the 6520 PIA?

7.25 The 6520 does not contain any specific Status registers. Where, then, is status information stored for examination by the μP?

7.26 Draw a flowchart showing the steps performed by the CPU in Fig. 7.22 if the CPU is doing the following.
(a) reading a value V_{in} from the process
(b) performing calculations on V_{in}.
(c) sending a value V_{out} to the process.
(d) repeating (a) through (c).
Include all CPU/PIA communication steps in the flowchart.

Section 7.7

7.27 What is the "hobby computer" bus standard?

7.28 What is the measurement/instrumentation bus standard?

7.29 In the IEEE-488 bus format there are no dedicated address lines. Over what lines is address information conveyed? What is the only type of device that can supply address information?

Section 7.8

7.30 Which one of the following is *not* an advantage of interfacing a μP to a keyboard using a software keyboard scanning technique as opposed to a hardware keyboard encoder?
(a) cheaper   (c) faster
(b) more reliable   (d) easier to modify

7.31 When interfacing a hexadecimal keyboard to a μP using the software keyboard scanning technique:
(a) a keyboard monitor program must be stored in RAM memory.
(b) a keyboard monitor program must be stored on audio tape so that it can be loaded when needed.
(c) a keyboard monitor program must be stored in ROM memory.
(d) a keyboard monitor program must be entered each time power is applied.

7.32 Refer to Fig. 7.27. Assume that the μP is executing a LDA F802 operation while the "6" key is being depressed. What will be in the four lower-order bits of the Accumulator as a result of this operation? Repeat for the "8" key.

7.33 How does a keyboard monitor program handle the problem of keyswitch bounce? How does it handle the possibility of a new key being depressed before the old key is released?

7.34 What is the purpose of the resistors connected to W, X, Y, and Z in Fig. 7.27?

7.35 Is it really necessary to connect R/W to the AND gate in Fig. 7.27? What could happen if this connection were eliminated?

7.36 How does an ASCII keyboard differ from a hex keyboard?

Section 7.9

7.37 If a TTY is operated in the LOCAL mode, what controls the characters that are printed out on paper?

7.38 What controls the TTY printer in the LINE mode?

7.39 Describe the process of *echoing*.

7.40 What is the advantage of using a TTY that has a paper-tape unit?

Section 7.10

7.41 What are some of the advantages of magnetic-tape storage?

7.42 Which one of the following is *not* part of a standard format for an individual record recorded on an audio tape cassette?
(a) MARKING   (b) RECORD ID   (c) CHECKSUM   (d) OVERRUN

7.43 Which one of the following is used to determine if a program recorded on audio tape has been properly read into the μP?
(a) SYNC bit   (b) parity bit   (c) CHECKSUM   (d) START bit

7.44 When recording data on an audio cassette using the "Kansas City" format, a digital logic 0 consists of:
(a) 8 cycles of a 4800-Hz signal.
(b) 4 cycles of a 2400-Hz signal.
(c) 8 cycles of a 2400-Hz signal.
(d) 4 cycles of a 1200-Hz signal.

7.45 Refer to Fig. 7.34 and assume that the tape recording scheme being used is:

logic 0   4 cycles of a 2-kHz tone
logic 1   2 cycles of a 1-kHz tone

What clock frequency should be applied to the UART?

7.46 What are some types of circuitry that would be used to transform the UART logic levels to audio tones in Fig. 7.34? Note that it is not usually necessary for the 2400-Hz and 1200-Hz signals to be pure.

7.47 Repeat Question 7.46 for the reverse process of converting the tape output to logic levels.

Section 7.11

7.48 What disadvantages of cassette-tape storage are overcome by floppy disks?

7.49 Explain the difference between soft sectoring and hard sectoring.

7.50 Why is a disk's formatted capacity always less than its unformatted capacity?

7.51 How does the access time of floppy-disk storage compare to magnet tape? How does it compare to semiconductor RAMs?

7.52 For each of the statements below, indicate whether it refers to floppy-disk drives or Winchester disk drives.
(a) The disks are flexible.
(b) The READ/WRITE head does not make physical contact with the disk surface.
(c) The disks are not removable or interchangeable, but rather, one disk stays on the drive spindle at all times.
(d) A typical formatted capacity is 10^7 bytes/surface.

Section 7.12

7.53 Refer to Fig. 7.42. Assume that the ASCII code for uppercase "E" is applied to the 2513 and the row select inputs are 010. The Load and CLK inputs to the shift register are shown in Fig. 7.45. Draw the serial output waveform.

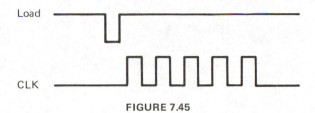

FIGURE 7.45

7.54 In the display system of Fig. 7.43, why are the two LSBs of the shift register loaded with 0s?

7.55 In the video display system of Fig. 7.43, which block contains information about all of the character positions on the CRT? Which block holds the actual pattern of dark and bright spots which are to be displayed on the CRT?

7.56 Why is the row select counter in Fig. 7.43 a MOD-10 counter when there are only seven rows in each character dot pattern?

PART 3

MICROCOMPUTER SOFTWARE

8

MICROCOMPUTER PROGRAMMING

Now that we have become familiar with many of the hardware aspects of microcomputers and microprocessors, we will concentrate on the concepts and techniques used to program these versatile devices so that they can perform all the marvelous tasks they are capable of performing. To discuss the programming of microprocessors, we must discuss the types of instructions they can perform. Rather than trying to include all the instructions currently used by the wide variety of available microprocessors, we have chosen, instead, to concentrate on the instruction set of one microprocessor (the 6502). We feel that once the terminology, ideas, and techniques of programming are learned, it is relatively easy to understand and use the instruction sets of any microprocessor.

We hasten to caution the reader, however, against expecting too much from this chapter. No amount of reading will teach one how to program. The only way to learn how to program is to sit down, write programs, and run them on a computer. Most programmers will tell you that they learn something new with each program they write. Hopefully, after mastering the following material, you will be able to go to a computer, pick up its programming manual, and begin your real education.

8.1 PROGRAMMING LANGUAGES

In our discussion of the various computer languages in Chapter 3, we saw that there are essentially three levels of language. These are machine language, assembly (symbolic) language, and high-level languages such as BASIC and FORTRAN. The machine and assembly languages are unique to a given microprocessor, while a high-level language, except for minor variations, is independent of the microprocessor.

This chapter is devoted to programming a microprocessor using machine language and some elements of assembly language. This will serve to tie together many of the hardware concepts presented in the previous chapters. The background acquired in those chapters will make the job of learning machine and assembly language programming relatively easy. Once one has mastered these types of programming, it is a rather simple task to learn how to program in higher-level languages.

8.2 MICROPROCESSOR INSTRUCTION SETS

An *instruction set* is the group of instructions that a particular microprocessor is designed to execute. Each manufacturer designs a different instruction set into his microprocessor according to the intended applications of the device. There are, however, many types of instructions that are common to all microprocessors, so learning one microprocessor set will provide a meaningful introduction to the capabilities of microprocessors in general.

Instructions can be grouped together in several categories or classifications to emphasize specific features of the instruction set. We will describe some of the common classifications below, keeping in mind that some instructions will fit well into more than one category, while some specialized instructions defy classification.

Data Manipulation Instructions

Instructions in this category are those which change *data* in any way. This includes arithmetic and logic instructions, shift and rotate instructions, and decrement/increment instructions. These operations are the heart of most programs, since they do the actual processing of data.

Data-Transfer Instructions

These are instructions that involve the movement of a binary word from one location to another. The transfer of data can be from one microprocessor register to another, between memory and a register, or between a microprocessor register and an I/O device. Instructions that transfer information between the microprocessor and the stack are also in this category.

Program Control Instructions

These instructions are used to alter the normal sequence that a program follows by loading a new address into the Program Counter (PC). This includes unconditional jump instructions, which always place a new value in PC, and conditional jump or branch instructions, which place a new value in PC only if a specified condition is met. Other instructions in this category include those which allow a program to jump to and from subroutines.

Machine Status Control Instructions

These instructions control the operation of the microprocessor itself. Included in this group are instructions that halt the microprocessor, clear specific flags, set specific flags, and cause the microprocessor to perform no operation (no-ops).

Memory Reference Instructions

This group includes all instructions that specify a memory address where a word is to be stored or from which a word is to be read. Memory reference instructions will include many instructions that also fall into the data-manipulation and data-transfer classifications.

6502 REGISTER

Before we examine the 6502's instruction set, let us review its register structure, since these registers play an important part in most of the instructions. Figure 8.1 shows only those registers that are of concern to the programmer.

Recall that the 6502 uses an 8-bit data bus and a 16-bit address bus so that it can access up to 65,536 different addresses. Thus, the program counter (PC) is a 16-bit register. It is shown as two 8-bit registers, PCH and PCL, which hold the 8 high-order bits and 8 low-order bits, respectively.

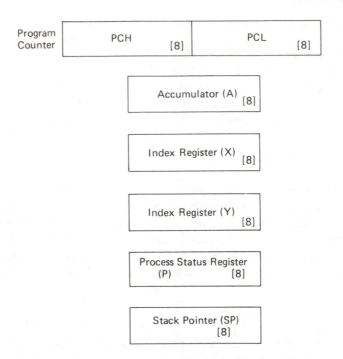

FIGURE 8.1 These 6502 registers are those involved in machine and assembly language programming.

The 6502 has a single 8-bit Accumulator (A) and two 8-bit Index registers, X and Y. The Accumulator takes part in most of the data-manipulation instructions. X and Y can be used as counters in repetitive loops, as temporary data storage, and are used in several indexed addressing modes. These register applications were discussed in Chapter 5, but we will review them and elaborate on them as we go along.

The Stack Pointer register (SP) is only 8 bits long because the stack in a 6502 system is always located on memory page 01. The contents of SP give the location on page 01 where the stack is located. For example, if $[SP] = 01100111_2 = 67_{16}$, the next available location on the stack is in address location 0167. Since the stack will always be on page 01, it should be clear that memory page 01 has to be RAM. As we shall see later, the stack and stack pointer can give a programmer headaches if he is not careful how he uses them in the program.

The 6502 has an 8-bit Processor Status register (P), which stores the various microprocessor flags. Actually, only seven flags are used (see Fig. 8.2), and bit 5 of this register has no meaning. The meaning of each of these flags will be described.

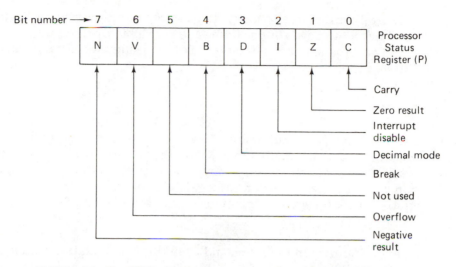

FIGURE 8.2 The 6502's flags are stored in the 8-bit Processor Status register.

Carry Flag

The Carry flag (C) reflects the carry status of arithmetic operations such as addition and subtraction. For example, if the microprocessor is performing an addition instruction where it adds two 8-bit data words, the value of the carry out of the MSB position becomes the value of the Carry flag. This is illustrated below for two cases.

$$
\begin{array}{ll}
10101000 & \longleftarrow \text{ original contents of A} \\
+01010110 & \longleftarrow \text{ operand (from memory)} \\
\hline
11111110 & \longleftarrow \text{ result to be stored in A}
\end{array}
$$

— no carry

Here no carry occurs when the MSBs are added. The microprocessor thus causes the C flag in the Status register to be cleared to 0.

$$
\begin{array}{ll}
10101000 & \longleftarrow \text{ A} \\
+01100110 & \longleftarrow \text{ operand}
\end{array}
$$

carry $\longrightarrow$ 1 00001110 ⌐ to be stored in A

Here a carry of 1 occurs; this causes the microprocessor to set the C flag to 1.

The C flag bit also takes part in the various shift and rotate instructions, which will be described shortly. Recall from our discussion in Chapter 5 that the C flag acts as a *ninth* bit during shift or rotate operations.

The programmer can set or clear C using two separate instructions, SEC and CLC.

Zero Flag

The Zero flag (Z) is automatically set to 1 whenever the results of any data-transfer or data-manipulation operation is an 8-bit word of 00000000. Z is automatically cleared to 0 for any other result. This means that any instruction that processes data or causes data to be moved from one location to another will affect the Z flag. Here are three examples of operations that will cause Z to be set to 1.

1. Subtraction of an operand from the Accumulator, producing a result of 00000000_2.
2. Loading Accumulator with a byte from memory that is equal to 00000000.
3. Decrementing the contents of the X register such that [X] = 00000000.

Interrupt Disable Flag

The Interrupt Disable flag (I) was described during our discussion of interrupts in Chapter 6. Its purpose is to disable the effects of the 6502's INTERRUPT REQUEST pin (IRQ). When I = 1, the effect of $\overline{IRQ}$ is disabled; when I = 0, the $\overline{IRQ}$ input can be used to interrupt the microprocessor. The value of I does not affect the operation of the 6502's NONMASKABLE INTERRUPT pin ($\overline{NMI}$).

The I flag can be cleared or set by the programmer using the SEI and CLI instructions to be discussed shortly. It is also cleared or set automatically by the microprocessor at various times. For example, before branching to an INTERRUPT SERVICE ROUTINE (ISR) in response to an interrupt, the microprocessor sets I = 1. This prevents another interrupt signal on $\overline{IRQ}$ from interrupting the execution of the ISR, but it does not disable the effect of the $\overline{NMI}$ input.

Decimal Mode Flag

The arithmetic circuitry of the 6502 can perform addition and subtraction either in the straight binary system or in the BCD system. The Decimal Mode flag (D) controls which mode will be used. If D = 0, the microprocessor will perform all add and subtract operations in binary; if D = 1, the microprocessor will perform all add and subtract operations in BCD. Below are examples of the addition of two bytes of data for the two values of D.

$$
\begin{array}{ll}
\begin{array}{r}
01101000(104) \\
+\ 00010010(\ 18) \\
\hline
01111010(122)
\end{array}
&
\begin{array}{l}
\text{D = 0, addition is} \\
\text{done in binary}
\end{array}
\end{array}
$$

$$
\begin{array}{ll}
\begin{array}{r}
01101000(68) \\
+\ 00010010(12) \\
\hline
10000000(80)
\end{array}
&
\begin{array}{l}
\text{D = 1, addition is} \\
\text{done in BCD (including correction)}
\end{array}
\end{array}
$$

The programmer decides which arithmetic mode is to be used for a particular program or portion of a program by setting or clearing D with the appropriate instructions. Once D is given a particular value, all arithmetic operations will be performed in the corresponding mode until the program changes the value of D.

Break Flag

The Break flag (B) is used by the microprocessor to indicate that a BREAK instruction, BRK, has been executed. This instruction is a "software interrupt," which will be discussed later. There are no instructions for setting or clearing this flag.

Overflow Flag

The Overflow flag (V) is used to indicate *overflow* whenever *signed* numbers are being added or subtracted. Recall that for signed numbers, the MSB (bit 7) is used as a sign bit with 0 = positive and 1 = negative. This leaves only 7 bits to represent the magnitude of a number, giving a range from -127_{10} to $+127_{10}$ that can be represented in 8 bits. The overflow flag is automatically set high whenever an arithmetic operation produces a result outside this range. An example of an overflow situation is the following:

sign bits

$$
\begin{array}{r}
\boxed{0}\ 1100000 \quad (+96_{10}) \\
+\ \boxed{0}\ 1000001 \quad (+65_{10}) \\
\hline
\boxed{1}\ 0100001
\end{array}
$$

result is a *negative* number — thus, V = 1

Here the addition of two positive numbers produces a result that has a 1 in the sign bit. This would erroneously be interpreted as a negative number. The error is due to overflow and the microprocessor automatically sets V = 1. An overflow condition occurs whenever two numbers with the same sign produce a result with the opposite sign.

The V flag should not be confused with the C flag. V is used *only* when signed arithmetic operations are performed and indicates an overflow of the 7-bit word capacity. C is used for unsigned operations and indicates an overflow of the 8-bit word capacity. Of course, C is also involved in shift and rotate instructions while V is not.

The V flag can be cleared by the programmer using a CLV instruction, but there is no instruction for setting V. Interestingly, there is a 6502 input pin called *Set Overflow* (S.O.), which can be used to set V from an external signal. This allows V to be used as a sense flag for sensing the status of some external device. The program can test the V flag to determine if the device has been sent a signal to the S.O. input.

Negative Flag

As already discussed, the microprocessor can perform arithmetic operations on signed numbers. The Negative flag (N) is used to indicate the sign of the result of any data-manipulation or data-transfer operation. In fact, N is *always* equal to bit-7 (the sign bit) of the result. It should be clear that the N flag is the same as the Sign flag we discussed in Chapter 5.

It is important to realize that N will be equal to bit 7 of the result even when the program is not using signed numbers. The microprocessor has no way of knowing whether the data represent unsigned numbers, signed numbers, or non-numerical information for that matter (the programmer has to keep track of those things). This means that the N flag can be tested at any time to determine the value of bit 7 after any data manipulation or data movement operation. This will be put to good use later.

Summary of Flags

The P register holds a series of seven status flags which indicate specific conditions in the microprocessor or in the program being executed. Each of these flags conveys certain information to the programmer at various points in time. By using a series of conditional branch instructions which are part of the 6502 instructions set, the program can test the values of some of these flags to determine what sequence of instructions to follow next. This represents a powerful programming tool and is the basis for all the decision-making capabilities of any computer.

8.4 6502 INSTRUCTION SET
AND ADDRESS MODES

Table 8.1 is an alphabetical listing of the different instructions used by the 6502. Although there are 55 instructions in this list, the 6502 actually uses 145 different op codes* to specify 145 different instructions. This is due to the various *addressing modes* that can be used for those instructions that access a memory location. An addressing mode refers to the way in which the operand address portion of an instruction is determined. The 6502 has 13 possible address modes, although no single instruction will utilize all of them. For example, the STA instruction can use any of seven different address modes. This means that seven different op codes are required to distinguish between these various modes so that the microprocessor knows which one the programmer is using and can respond accordingly.

Many of the available address modes use the X or Y index registers to produce various *indexed addressing* capabilities. These will be described later. For now we will concentrate on some of the nonindexed address modes.

Absolute Addressing

This is the address mode we have used in all the examples and discussions up to now. *Absolute addressing* (also called *direct addressing* in some microprocessors) always uses a three-byte instruction sequence, the first byte being the op code and the next two bytes specifying the 16-bit operand address. Following is the instruction sequence for storing the contents of the Accumulator in address location 3A06 (all values are in hex code):

$$8D \longleftarrow \text{op code for STA (ABS)}$$
$$06 \longleftarrow \text{low-order operand address, ADL}$$
$$3A \longleftarrow \text{high-order operand address, ADH}$$

Note that the mnemonic we will use for this instruction is STA (ABS), to denote that absolute addressing is being used. Also note that the first address byte listed is the low-order address, ADL, followed by the high-order address byte, ADH. (Some microprocessors, like the 6800, use the *opposite* order, with ADH followed by ADL.)

Here is another example:

$$AE \longleftarrow \text{op code for LDX (ABS)}$$
$$25 \longleftarrow \text{ADL}$$
$$01 \longleftarrow \text{ADH}$$

*These 6502 op codes are listed in the Appendix.

TABLE 8.1   Alphabetical Listing of 6502 Instruction Set

ADC	ADD Memory to Accumulator with CARRY	**LDA**	LOAD Accumulator with Memory
AND	"AND" Memory with Accumulator	**LDX**	LOAD Index X with Memory
ASL	SHIFT LEFT One Bit (Memory or Accumulator)	**LDY**	LOAD Index Y with Memory
		LSR	SHIFT RIGHT One Bit (Memory or Accumulator)
BCC	BRANCH on CARRY CLEAR	**NOP**	No Operation
BCS	BRANCH on CARRY SET		
BEQ	BRANCH on RESULT EQUAL to ZERO	**ORA**	"OR" Memory with Accumulator
BIT	TEST Bits in Memory with Accumulator	**PHA**	PUSH Accumulator on Stack
BMI	BRANCH on RESULT MINUS	**PHP**	PUSH Processor Status on Stack
BNE	BRANCH on RESULT NOT EQUAL to ZERO	**PLA**	PULL Accumulator from Stack
		PLP	PULL Processor Status from Stack
BPL	BRANCH on RESULT PLUS	**ROL**	ROTATE One Bit Left (Memory or Accumulator)
BRK	Force BREAK		
BVC	BRANCH on OVERFLOW CLEAR	**ROR**	ROTATE One Bit Right (Memory or Accumulator
BVS	BRANCH on Overflow Set		
		RTI	RETURN FROM INTERRUPT
CLC	CLEAR CARRY Flag	**RTS**	RETURN FROM SUBROUTINE
CLD	CLEAR Decimal Mode Flag		
CLI	CLEAR INTERRUPT DISABLE Flag	**SBC**	SUBTRACT Memory from Accumulator with Borrow
CLV	CLEAR OVERFLOW Flag	**SEC**	SET CARRY Flag
CMP	COMPARE Memory and Accumulator	**SED**	SET Decimal Mode Flag
CPX	COMPARE Memory and Index X	**SEI**	SET INTERRUPT DISABLE Flag
CPY	COMPARE Memory and Index Y	**STA**	STORE Accumulator in Memory
		STX	STORE Index X in Memory
DEC	DECREMENT Memory by One	**STY**	STORE Index Y in Memory
DEX	DECREMENT Index X by One		
DEY	DECREMENT Index Y by One	**TAX**	TRANSFER Accumulator to Index X
		TAY	TRANSFER Accumulator to Index Y
EOR	"EXCLUSIVE-OR" Memory with Accumulator		
INC	INCREMENT Memory Contents by One	**TSX**	TRANSFER Stack Pointer to Index X
INX	INCREMENT Index X by One	**TXA**	TRANSFER Index X to Accumulator
INY	INCREMENT Index Y by One		
		TXS	TRANSFER Index X to Stack Pointer
JMP	JUMP to New Location		
JSR	JUMP to Subroutine (Saving Return Address)	**TYA**	TRANSFER Index Y to Accumulator

This instruction will load the contents of memory location 0125 into the X register. Instructions that use the absolute addressing mode require *four* clock cycles to execute; one to fetch the op code, one to fetch ADL, one to fetch ADH, and one to fetch or store the data.

Immediate Addressing

The immediate addressing mode is used only for instructions that transfer data from memory into one of the microprocessor registers or into the arithmetic unit for processing. The immediate mode does not specify a numerical address for the operand. Instead, it always means that the operand is stored in the address location *immediately* following the location of the op code. That is, a two-byte instruction sequence is used, with the op code followed by the actual value of the operand. This is illustrated below:

$$A2 \longleftarrow \text{op code for LDX (IMM)}$$
$$37 \longleftarrow \text{operand (data) to be loaded into X}$$

The first byte, A2, is the op code which specifies that the X register is to be loaded with the operand (data) stored in the second byte. When the microprocessor control section detects this op code, it knows that it must fetch the value from the next sequential memory location and load this value into X. For the example above, the X register will be loaded with the value 37_{16} = 00110111_2. Note that the op code for LDX (IMM) is A2 and the op code for LDX (ABS), which we used earlier, is AE. Both operations are LDX instructions but use different modes for obtaining the data, and therefore require different op codes.

The immediate mode is used whenever the value of the operand is a constant that is known at the time the program is being written. Since it does not require fetching the operand from a specified address, instructions using this mode are executed faster than those using absolute addressing. We will now look at a short programming example which utilizes both absolute and immediate addressing. All values are *hexadecimal*.

Memory Address	Label	Instruction Code	Mnemonic	Comments
0100	START	A9	LDA (IMM)	Set [A] = 20
0101		20		
0102		8D	STA (ABS)	Set [COUNTER] = 20
0103		00		
0104		02		
.		.		
.		.		
.		.		
0200	COUNTER	??		

This example and all subsequent examples use a five-column format. The first column lists the addresses in memory where each byte of the program is stored. The second column, called Label, is used to give labels or names to certain of these address locations. For example, location 0100 is given the label START, and location 0200 is given the label COUNTER. For our purposes here, these labels are just a convenient way to refer to certain steps in the program or certain data-storage locations. In assembly language, these labels are actually part of the assembly language program and are used in place of actual numerical addresses.

The third column lists the hex codes stored in each address location. This, of course, is the only information which the computer receives. It is the actual machine language program. The fourth column gives the mnemonics corresponding to each instruction op code.

The fifth column includes explanatory comments which are helpful in following and understanding the program. These comments are not only a help to one who is reading someone else's program, but they also allow the programmer to keep track of what his program is doing as he is writing it.

This particular program example is used to place a specific number, 20, into a memory location (0200) labeled COUNTER. This operation requires two steps, loading 20 into A, and then storing [A] into COUNTER. Recall that [A] stands for "the contents of register A." We will use this format for all registers and also for memory locations. For example, [COUNTER] = 20 means that the contents of memory location 0200 is equal to 20_{16} = 00100000_2.

The two-byte instruction sequence beginning at address 0100 loads the data word stored at address 0101 into A. The three-byte sequence beginning at 0102 then stores the contents of A into memory location 0200. At that point, both [A] and [COUNTER] are equal to 20.

Zero-Page Addressing

Zero-page addressing uses a two-byte instruction sequence where the second byte specifies the low-order address byte; the high-order address byte is assumed to be 00. In other words, the operand address is always on page 00, and the exact location on page 00 is specified by the second byte of the instruction. An example is as follows:

$$85 \longleftarrow \text{op code for STA (ZP)}$$
$$7E \longleftarrow \text{low-order address (high-order address = 00)}$$

This instruction will store the contents of the Accumulator in address location 007E. Here is another example:

A4 ←— op code for LDY (ZP)
62 ←— low-order address, ADL

This instruction will read memory location 0062 and load its contents into the Y register.

The zero-page address mode is more efficient than the absolute mode because it uses two bytes and requires only three clock cycles to execute; one for the op code, one to fetch ADL, and one to fetch or store the data. In order to take advantage of zero-page addressing, the programmer should organize his program so that the most frequently accessed memory locations are on page 00. This can result in a significant savings in the number of bytes of memory needed to store the program, and a shortening of the program execution time.

Implied Addressing

Implied addressing is really not an addressing mode, since no memory address is specified. Implied addressing refers to those single-byte instructions that do not require an operand address. Instructions of this type contain only a single-byte op code. Examples include instructions for clearing and setting various microprocessor flags, incrementing and decrementing the X and Y registers, and transferring the contents of one microprocessor register to another.

Study the example program below and note the various address modes that are used. Especially note that the TXA and DEX instructions use implied addressing since they require no operand address. What data will be stored in memory location 0069 as a result of the STX (ZP) instruction?

Memory Address	Label	Instruction Code	Mnemonic	Comments
0000	BEGIN	A2	LDX (IMM)	Set [X] = OF
0001		0F		
0002		8A	TXA	Transfer [X] ⟶ [A]
0003		CA	DEX	Decrement [X]
0004		86	STX (ZP)	Set [XVALUE] = [X]
0005		69		
.		.		
.		.		
.		.		
0069	XVALUE	??		

The answer is OE.

Accumulator Addressing

The 6502 has three shift instructions which can be used to shift the contents of a memory word or the contents of the Accumulator. When used to shift a *memory* word, these instructions require an operand address. However, an operand address is not required if the *Accumulator* is the operand. For these instructions the appropriate op code is all that is needed to tell the microprocessor that the operand is in the Accumulator. This is illustrated as follows:

this instruction causes contents of memory location C037 to be shifted left 1 bit

$\begin{cases} \text{0E} \longleftarrow \text{op code for ASL (ABS)} \\ \text{37} \longleftarrow \text{ADL} \\ \text{C0} \longleftarrow \text{ADH} \end{cases}$

this instruction causes contents of Accumulator to be shifted left 1 bit; no operand address is required

OA $\longleftarrow$ op code for ASL (ACC)

Other Address Modes

We have described only five of the 6502's available address modes. These five, together with *relative addressing*, which will be described under conditional branching instructions, can now be used to help us demonstrate the various 6502 instructions. The other address modes will be discussed after we become more familiar with the instruction set.

8.5 MACHINE STATUS CONTROL INSTRUCTIONS

The machine status control group consists primarily of instructions for controlling certain flags in the Processor Status register (P). All of these are single-byte instructions requiring no operand (implied addressing).

CLC — CLEAR CARRY Flag
    This instruction clears the C Flag.

SEC — SET CARRY Flag
    This instruction sets the C flag.

CLD — CLEAR Decimal Flag
    This instruction clears the D flag to enable all arithmetic operations to be performed in binary.

SED — SET Decimal Flag

This sets the D flag to enable all arithmetic operations to be performed in BCD.

CLI — CLEAR INTERRUPT DISABLE Flag

This clears the I flag to allow the microprocessor to respond to external interrupts.

SEI — SET INTERRUPT DISABLE Flag

This sets the I flag and prevents the microprocessor from responding to interrupt requests (except for nonmaskable interrupt).

CLV — CLEAR OVERFLOW Flag

This clears the V flag.

NOP — No Operation

This instruction is actually a noninstruction. It tells the microprocessor to go through the motions of an execution cycle without performing any operation. There are two uses for NOP instructions: they can be inserted at various points in a program where the programmer feels he may later have to add instructions, or they can be inserted between other instructions to achieve a time delay. With regard to this latter application, each NOP takes two µP clock cycles to execute. The following example shows NOPs used in this manner.

Memory Address	Label	Instruction Code	Mnemonic	Comments
0300	CONVERT	AD	LDA (ABS)	Send START signal to A/D converter using "dummy" READ operation
0301		01		
0302		F9		
0303		EA	NOP	Time delay
0304		EA	NOP	
0305	READ	AD	LDA (ABS)	Read A/D output data
0306		00		
0307		F9		
.		.		
.		.		
.		.		

This short program sequence sends a START signal to a fast A/D converter using a "dummy" READ operation (refer to our discussion of Fig. 6.8), and then reads the A/D data outputs into the Accumulator. The addresses assigned to the A/D converter's START input and data outputs are F901 and F900, respectively. Two NOP instructions are inserted between these steps to allow for the A/D converter's conversion time. These two NOPs use up *four* clock cycles, which translates into 4.0 μs if a 1-MHz clock frequency is used. It is assumed that the A/D conversion time will be less than 4.0 μs.

Using NOPs for time delay becomes impractical for delays of greater than a few microseconds, because each NOP produces only 2 μs of delay. Later we will see how *timing loops* can be used to achieve relatively long delays with just a handful of instructions.

8.6 ARITHMETIC INSTRUCTIONS

The class of data manipulation instructions for the 6502 can be subdivided into five groups: *arithmetic* instructions, *logical* instructions, *shift* instructions, *decrement/increment* instructions, and *compare* instructions. In this section we describe the 6502's various arithmetic instructions. We stated earlier that most microprocessors are only able to execute a few simple arithmetic operations (i.e., addition and subtraction). Any other mathematical operations have to be derived from these basic operations combined with other instructions. Most microprocessors do not have the capability to multiply or divide. These operations can be provided by developing sequences of instructions that effectively produce the desired multiplication (or division) results. These instruction sequences are called *subroutines* and are actually short programs used over and over.

Addition

The 6502 has one basic addition instruction, ADC, which can be used with eight different address modes. The ADC instruction adds the value of the operand and the Carry flag to the contents of the Accumulator and stores the result in the Accumulator. The symbolic representation of this operation is

$$[A] + [M] + C \longrightarrow [A]$$

where [M] stands for the contents of the memory location where the operand is stored. The addition will be performed in binary or BCD, depending on the current state of the D flag.

Let us do two examples of binary addition. In the first example, we assume that the C flag is 0 prior to the addition, and in the second example, we assume that C = 1.

EXAMPLE 8.1

$$
\begin{array}{lr}
\text{operand (from memory)} & 00111010 \\
\text{+Accumulator (A)} & +00100101 \\
\text{+Carry (C)} & +\underline{\qquad 0} \\
\text{result (ends up in A)} & 01011111
\end{array}
$$

└─ no carry; therefore, C = 0

EXAMPLE 8.2

$$
\begin{array}{lr}
\text{operand} & 00101001 \\
+ & \\
\text{A} & +10001110 \\
+ & \\
\text{C} & +\underline{\qquad 1} \\
\text{result (A)} & 10111000
\end{array}
$$

└─ no carry; therefore, C = 0

The reader might be wondering why the C bit is added to the two data words. The reason has to do with *multibyte* addition, which is used to add numbers that are longer than one byte. This operation will be described later. For the addition of two 8-bit numbers, however, we do not usually want the C flag to affect the result. Thus, we must ensure that C = 0 prior to the add instruction by using a CLC (CLEAR CARRY Flag) instruction prior to each add operation.

Signed Number Addition The ADC operation is executed the same way for signed numbers. The only difference is in how the program interprets the sign-bit position. For example, the results of Example 8.1 would be interpreted as a positive number equal to $+95_{10}$. The results of Example 8.2 would be interpreted as a negative number equal to -72_{10} (recall that negative numbers are in 2's-complement form).

Affected Flags The results of the ADC instruction execution will affect the Carry (C), Negative (N), Zero (Z), and Overflow (V) flags. The results of each of the preceding examples show no carry from the MSB position, so the C flag would be cleared to 0 at the end of the operation. Both examples produce a nonzero result, so the Z flag would be 0 in both cases. In Example 8.1, the N flag would be 0 since bit 7 of the result is 0; for Example 8.2, the N flag would be set to 1. In both examples no overflow occurs, so V = 0.

Decimal Addition The programmer can select BCD arithmetic operation by setting the D flag using a SED instruction. All subsequent add and subtract operations will treat each data byte as two BCD digits. The result will be in correct BCD form without any need for corrections.

EXAMPLE 8.3 The following program sequence performs the addition of decimal numbers 32 and 49 using BCD addition.

Memory Address	Label	Hex Instruction Code	Mnemonic	Comments
1000	BEGIN	18	CLC	Clear C flag
1001		F8	SED	Set for BCD mode
1002		A9	LDA (IMM)	
1003		32		
1004		6D	ADC (ABS)	Add DATAX
1005		4F		
1006		10		
1007		8D	STA (ABS)	Store result in 1050
1008		50		
1009		10		
.		.		
.		.		
.		.		
104F	DATAX	49		Location of operand
1050	RESULT	??		Location of result

The program begins by clearing the C flag and setting the D flag. The first BCD number (32) is loaded into the Accumulator using immediate addressing. (Note that the hex code for a BCD coded number is the same as the BCD code.) The ADC (ABS) instruction is then used to fetch the second BCD number (49) from address 104F and add it to the Accumulator. The result (81) is then stored in address location 1050. Of course, this result still remains in the Accumulator.

EXAMPLE 8.4 The program sequence below is used to add two *signed* numbers, referred to as Data 1 and Data 2. Follow the instructions through to address 0050 and determine the following: (a) the contents of location 0101; and (b) the status of the C, N, Z, and V flags.

Memory Address	Label	Instruction Code	Mnemonic	Comments
0047	START	18	CLC	
0048		D8	CLD	Use binary mode
0049		A5	LDA (ZP)	Load Data 1
004A		7A		
004B		6D	ADC (ABS)	Add Data 2

Memory Address	Label	Hex Instruction Code	Mnemonic	Comments
004C		00		
004D		01		
004E		8D	STA (ABS)	Store result
004F		01		
0050		01		
.		.		
.		.		
.		.		
007A	DATA 1	B8		Data 1 = -72_{10}
.	.	.		
.	.	.		
0100	DATA 2	C0		Data 2 = -64_{10}
0101	RESULT	??		

Solution:
  (a) The words DATA 1 and DATA 2 are added to produce RESULT, which is stored in location 0101.

$$\text{DATA } 1 = B8_{16} = 10111000_2 = -72_{10}$$
$$\text{DATA } 2 = C0_{16} = 11000000_2 = -64_{10}$$

$$+$$
$$1\ \underbrace{01111000}$$

to C flag ←┘   └ ends up in Accumulator

The binary addition of DATA 1 and DATA 2 produces an 8-bit sum, 01111000, and a carry of 1. This 8-bit sum ends up in the Accumulator, and is stored in location 0101 by the STA instruction.

  (b) As the result above shows, C = 1. Since the 8-bit sum is neither *zero* or *negative*, both the N and Z flags will be 0. However, the fact that two *negative* numbers produced a *positive* indicates that arithmetic overflow has occurred. Thus, V = 1.

Subtraction

The SBC instruction subtracts the value of the operand and the *borrow* from the contents of the Accumulator and stores the result in the Accumulator. The *borrow* is defined as the Carry flag inverted ($\overline{C}$). The symbolic representation for this operation is

$$[A] - [M] - \overline{C} \longrightarrow [A]$$

borrow

The subtraction is performed in binary or BCD, depending on the current state of the D flag.

The borrow, $\overline{C}$, is used in multibyte subtraction, which will be considered later. For our purposes here, we will want $\overline{C} = 0$, so that it will not affect our results. This can be taken care of by setting $C = 1$ with a SEC instruction prior to each subtract operation.

The binary subtraction is performed using the 2's-complement method whereby the 2's-complement of the operand is *added* to the Accumulator. This is illustrated as follows:

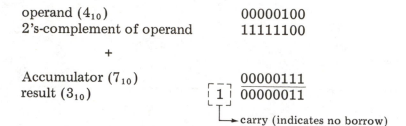

```
operand (4₁₀)                          00000100
2's-complement of operand              11111100

            +

Accumulator (7₁₀)               ┌──┐   00000111
result (3₁₀)                    │ 1│   00000011
                                └──┘
                                 └──→ carry (indicates no borrow)
```

Here the operand, 4_{10}, was subtracted from the Accumulator, 7_{10}. The operand was 2's-complemented and then added to the Accumulator. The result is a 9-bit number, with the ninth bit being the Carry flag. The other 8 bits end up in the Accumulator. The Carry bit indicates the borrow condition. $C = 1$ ($\overline{C} = 0$) indicates no borrow (operand < Accumulator) and $C = 0$ ($\overline{C} = 1$) indicates a borrow (operand > Accumulator).

Signed-Number Subtraction   The SBC instruction is executed in exactly the same way for signed numbers. For instance, the operand in the example above would be $+4_{10}$, and its 2's-complement would represent -4_{10}. The Accumulator holds $+7_{10}$ and the result is $+3_{10}$.

Affected Flags   The results of a SBC operation will affect the C, N, Z, and V flags in the same way as the ADC instruction.

Decimal Subtraction   When the D flag is set to 1, all subtractions will be performed in the BCD system, treating each data byte as two BCD digits and producing a corrected BCD result.

EXAMPLE 8.5   The program sequence below performs the subtraction of decimal 49 from decimal 76 using BCD subtraction. The operand 49 is stored in memory location 004F.

Memory Address	Label	Code	Mnemonic	Comments
2000	START	F8	SED	Set for BCD mode
		38	SEC	Set C flag
		A9	LDA (IMM)	
		76		
		E5	SBC (ZP)	
		4F		
		85	STA (ZP)	Store result in 0050
		50		

This program loads 76 into the Accumulator using immediate addressing. It then performs BCD subtraction of the operand (49) fetched from location 004F using zero-page addressing. The result (37) is then stored in 0050 using zero-page addressing.

8.7 LOGICAL INSTRUCTIONS

This group of instructions takes the contents of the Accumulator and an operand from memory, performs a bit-by-bit logic operation on them, and stores the results in the Accumulator. There are three such logic instructions available on the 6502.

AND performs the logical AND operation
ORA performs the logical OR operation
EOR performs the logical EX-OR operation

These three operations are illustrated below for the same Accumulator and operand values:

```
 7  6  5  4  3  2  1  0
┌──┬──┬──┬──┬──┬──┬──┬──┐
│1 │0 │1 │0 │1 │0 │1 │0 │  Accumulator (A)
├──┼──┼──┼──┼──┼──┼──┼──┤
│1 │1 │0 │1 │0 │0 │1 │1 │  Operand
├──┼──┼──┼──┼──┼──┼──┼──┤
│1 │0 │0 │0 │0 │0 │1 │0 │  AND result ┐
├──┼──┼──┼──┼──┼──┼──┼──┤            │
│1 │1 │1 │1 │1 │0 │1 │1 │  ORA result ├ stored in A
├──┼──┼──┼──┼──┼──┼──┼──┤            │
│0 │1 │1 │1 │1 │0 │0 │1 │  EOR result ┘
└──┴──┴──┴──┴──┴──┴──┴──┘
```

It is important to realize that these logic operations work on each bit position separately and independently from the others. For example, bit 7 of the

Accumulator is ANDed with bit 7 of the operand to produce bit 7 of the result; likewise, bit 6 of A is ANDed with bit 6 of the operand to produce bit 6 of the result, and so on for the other bits.

Affected Flags These logical instructions will affect only the Z and N flags. If the result is 00000000, the Z flag will be set; otherwise, it will be cleared. If the result has a 1 in bit 7, the N flag will be set; otherwise, the N flag will be cleared.

AND Operation-Selective Clearing

The most common use of the AND instruction is to selectively *clear* specific bits of a data word while not affecting the other bits. This can be done by ANDing the data word with another word, called a *mask*, which the programmer chooses to select which bits he wants to clear. This is illustrated as follows:

D_7	D_6	D_5	D_4	D_3	D_2	D_1	D_0	Data word

0	1	1	1	1	0	1	1	Mask for clearing bits 2 and 7

0	D_6	D_5	D_4	D_3	0	D_1	D_0	Result of ANDing

Here the bits of the data word, D_7 through D_0, can be any pattern of 1s and 0s. The mask word has 1s in each bit position except bits 7 and 2. The result of ANDing the data word with the mask word shows that bits 7 and 2 are 0 while the other bits are the same as the data word. This is because of the properties of the AND operation—anything ANDed with 0 is 0, and anything ANDed with 1 is unchanged.

Thus, the overall effect of the operation is to clear bits 2 and 7 of the data word without affecting the other bits. Clearly, any of the data bits can be cleared by putting a 0 in the appropriate position of the mask word. This process is often referred to as *AND masking*.

This masking technique is also often used to isolate the value of a single bit of a data word. The data word might be a status word read from an input device (e.g., a UART) and a particular bit of the status word could be used to tell the microprocessor what sequence of instructions to follow. This is illustrated as follows:

D_7	D_6	D_5	D_4	D_3	D_2	D_1	D_0	Status word from input device

0	0	0	1	0	0	0	0	Mask for isolating D_4

0	0	0	D_4	0	0	0	0	Result of ANDing

The mask has a 1 only in the bit 4 position, so the result of the AND operation has 0s in all bit positions except bit 4, which will equal D_4. If D_4 is 0, the result will be all 0s, so the Z flag is set to 1. If D_4 is 1, the Z flag will be cleared to 0. Thus, by testing the Z flag, the program can determine the D_4 status and alter its instruction sequence accordingly. This testing is done using conditional branch instructions, which we will be discussing shortly.

ORA Operation-Selective Setting

The ORA instruction can be used to selectively *set* specific bits of a data word while not affecting the other bits. This is done by using a mask word which has 1s only in those bit positions that are to be set. This is illustrated as follows:

D_7	D_6	D_5	D_4	D_3	D_2	D_1	D_0	Data word
0	1	1	1	0	0	0	0	Mask for setting bits 4, 5, 6
D_7	1	1	1	D_3	D_2	D_1	D_0	Result of ORing

Here the mask word has 1s in bit positions 4, 5, and 6. The result of ORing the mask with the data word produces a word with 1s in these positions regardless of the values of D_6, D_5, and D_4. The other data word bits are unaffected. This is due to the properties of the OR operation—anything ORed with 1 is 1, and anything ORed with 0 is unchanged. This process of selective bit setting is called *OR masking*.

Masking Application — BCD-to-ASCII Conversion

A useful application of AND and OR masking occurs when BCD-coded data are to be transmitted from the computer's memory to a teletypewriter. The BCD data have to be converted to ASCII code before they can be output to the TTY. For example, suppose that the BCD code for decimal 64 is stored in a particular memory location as a single byte.

$$\underset{6}{\underbrace{\overset{MSD}{0110}}} \quad \underset{4}{\underbrace{\overset{LSD}{0100}}} \qquad \text{BCD data word}$$

This two-digit decimal number has to be transmitted to the TTY one digit at a time using the proper ASCII code for each digit.

```
00110110     ASCII code for 6
00110100     ASCII code for 4
```

Note that the ASCII code for any decimal digit has *0011* in the four MSB positions followed by the digit's BCD code.

The MSD of our decimal number has to be transmitted to the TTY first. This can be done using the following steps:

1. Load the Accumulator with the BCD data word:

$$[A] = 01100100$$

2. Shift the Accumulator contents *four* places to the right with 0s shifted in from the left. This can be done using four successive LSR instructions, and leaves the Accumulator with

$$[A] = 00000110$$

   The BCD code for 6 is now in the proper position for the ASCII code.

3. OR the Accumulator with the mask word 00110000. This leaves the Accumulator with

$$[A] = 00110110$$

   which is the complete ASCII code for 6. This word can now be transmitted to the TTY.

Now we have to transmit the LSD of our decimal number to the TTY using the following steps:

1. Load the Accumulator with the BCD data word.

$$[A] = 01100100$$

2. AND the Accumulator with the mask word 00001111 to clear the four MSBs. This produces

$$[A] = 00000100$$

3. OR the Accumulator with the mask word 00110000. This produces

$$[A] = 00110100$$

   which is the complete ASCII code for 4. This word can now be transmitted to the TTY.

The sequence of 6502 instructions for this complete process of changing a BCD data word into two ASCII codes is given below. It is assumed that the BCD data word is stored in location 009A. It is also assumed that a UART is used as an interface between the microcomputer and TTY and that the UART's Transmit Data register (TxDR) has an address of BF01,* as in Fig. 7.14.

Memory Address	Label	Instruction Code	Mnemonic	Comments
0100	START	A5	LDA (ZP)	Put BCD data word in A
0101		9A		Zero-page address of data
0102		4A	LSR (ACC)	Shift Accumulator four places to right
0103		4A	LSR (ACC)	
0104		4A	LSR (ACC)	
0105		4A	LSR (ACC)	
0106		09	ORA (IMM)	OR Accumulator with 00110000 to complete ASCII code
0107		30		
0108		8D	STA (ABS)	Transmit MSD to TTY via UART
0109		01		Address of UART TxDR
010A		BF		
010B		A5	LDA (ZP)	Put BCD data word in A
010C		9A		
010D		29	AND (IMM)	AND Accumulator with 00001111 to clear bits 4–7
010E		0F		
010F		09	ORA (IMM)	OR Accumulator with 00110000 to get ASCII code
0110		30		
0111		8D	STA (ABS)	Transmit LSD to TTY via UART
0112		01	.	.
0113		BF	.	.

Note that the shift-right instructions (LSR) use Accumulator addressing and do not require an operand address. Each LSR, when executed, shifts the Accumulator contents 1 bit to the right and puts a 0 into bit 7. It should be clear that this program will work for any BCD data word, since the shifting and masking operations do not depend on the contents of the data word.

*For clarity, we will not include the instructions for testing the UART status prior to transmitting data, and we will assume that the UART has been initialized.

EOR — Selective Inversion

The EOR instruction is often used to selectively *invert* specific bits of a data word while not affecting the other bits. This is illustrated as follows:

D_7	D_6	D_5	D_4	D_3	D_2	D_1	D_0

Data word

0	0	1	0	0	0	0	0

EOR mask for inverting D_5

D_7	D_6	$\overline{D_5}$	D_4	D_3	D_2	D_1	D_0

Result of EOR operation

The result shows that D_5 has been inverted, as the result of the 1 in the mask word, while the other bits of the data word are unchanged. This is a result of the following EX-OR truth table:

Data Bit (D)	Mask Bit (M)	Result = D ⊕ M
0	0	0
1	0	1
0	1	1
1	1	0

Whenever the mask bit is a 1, the result is the inverse of the data bit; whenever the mask bit is a 0, the result is the same as the data bit.

One common application of the EOR operation occurs when the microcomputer reads a data word from an input device that places *inverted* data on the microcomputer data bus. This could be taken care of by the addition of tristate inverters between the device outputs and the data bus. A less costly solution is to read the data into the microcomputer and then use an EOR instruction to invert the complete data word. This is easily accomplished using the following instruction sequence:

Instruction Code		
AD	LDA (ABS)	Load data from input device
00		⎫
F7		⎬ Address of input device
49	EOR (IMM)	Invert Accumulator contents
FF		

The mask word FF (hex) = 11111111_2 is used to invert each bit of the Accumulator.

8.8 SHIFT AND ROTATE INSTRUCTIONS

The 6502 has three instructions for shifting the contents of the Accumulator or a memory location. We have already used one of these, LSR, in a previous example. The three instructions are described below. The operand in each case can be in the Accumulator or in any memory location (see the Appendix for address modes).

ASL – Shift Left One Bit

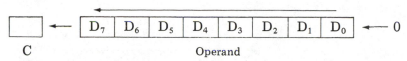

The operand is shifted left with D_7 shifting into the C flag and a 0 shifting into D_0. This is illustrated below:

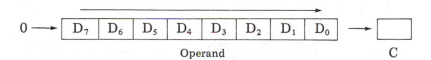

LSR – Shift Right One Bit

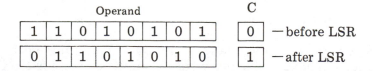

The operand is shifted right with D_0 shifting into the C flag and a 0 shifting into D_7. This is illustrated as follows:

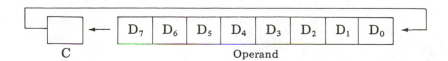

ROL – Rotate Left One Bit

The operand is shifted left with D_7 shifting into C and C shifting into D_0. This becomes essentially a 9-bit circulating shift register. An example is as follows:

```
C                        Operand
┌───┐   ┌───┬───┬───┬───┬───┬───┬───┬───┐
│ 0 │   │ 0 │ 1 │ 1 │ 0 │ 1 │ 0 │ 1 │ 1 │ — before ROL
└───┘   └───┴───┴───┴───┴───┴───┴───┴───┘
┌───┐   ┌───┬───┬───┬───┬───┬───┬───┬───┐
│ 0 │   │ 1 │ 1 │ 0 │ 1 │ 0 │ 1 │ 1 │ 0 │ — after ROL
└───┘   └───┴───┴───┴───┴───┴───┴───┴───┘
```

ROR – Rotate Right One Bit

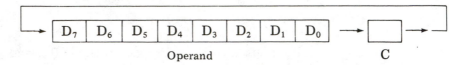

The operand is shifted right with D_0 shifted into C and C shifted into D_7. An example is shown below.

```
            Operand                   C
┌───┬───┬───┬───┬───┬───┬───┬───┐   ┌───┐
│ 0 │ 1 │ 1 │ 0 │ 1 │ 0 │ 1 │ 1 │   │ 0 │ — before ROR
└───┴───┴───┴───┴───┴───┴───┴───┘   └───┘
┌───┬───┬───┬───┬───┬───┬───┬───┐   ┌───┐
│ 0 │ 0 │ 1 │ 1 │ 0 │ 1 │ 0 │ 1 │   │ 1 │ — after ROR
└───┴───┴───┴───┴───┴───┴───┴───┘   └───┘
```

Affected Flags

Each of these shift instructions can affect the C, N, and Z flags. The C flag is obviously affected, since it is involved in the shifting. The N flag will take on the value of bit 7 of the operand *after* the shift operation. For the LSR operation, N will always become 0. The Z flag will be set if the operand becomes 00000000 *after* the shift; otherwise, Z will be cleared.

Address Modes

As stated earlier, the operand for each of these shift operations can be the Accumulator or a memory word. When the operand is a memory word, the complete shift operation can take up to *seven* clock cycles, depending on the address mode used.* This is one of the longest execution times of any of the 6502 instructions, and is due to the fact that the microprocessor has to

---

*The absolute address mode requires six cycles and the zero-page mode requires five cycles. The indexed address mode requires seven cycles.

read the operand from memory, send it to the ALU to be shifted, and then write it back into memory.

We have already seen one application of a shift operation in the BCD-to-ASCII conversion example of the preceding section. There are many more uses that occur in a wide variety of situations. Some of these will be demonstrated in subsequent examples as we continue through the 6502 instruction set and programming techniques.

8.9 DECREMENT/INCREMENT INSTRUCTIONS

This group of instructions can be used to add 1 or subtract 1 from the current contents of the X register, Y register, or a memory location. Let us look first at the instructions that affect X and Y.

INX — INCREMENT X by 1; symbolically $[X] + 1 \longrightarrow [X]$.
INY — INCREMENT Y by 1; symbolically $[Y] + 1 \longrightarrow [Y]$.
DEX — DECREMENT X by 1; symbolically $[X] - 1 \longrightarrow [X]$.
DEY — DECREMENT Y by 1; symbolically $[Y] - 1 \longrightarrow [Y]$.

These instructions affect only the N and Z flags. If the result of the operation has a 1 in bit 7, the N flag is set; otherwise, it is cleared. If the result is exactly zero, the Z flag is set; otherwise, it is cleared. The C and V flags *are not affected* by these instructions. For example, if the value of X is 11111111, the value after an INX operation becomes 00000000 and the value of C remains at the value it had prior to INX.

INC — INCREMENT the operand from memory by 1; $[M] + 1 \longrightarrow [M]$.
DEC — DECREMENT the operand from memory by 1; $[M] - 1 \longrightarrow [M]$.

These operate in exactly the same way and affect the same flags as the corresponding X and Y operations, except that the operations are performed on the contents of a memory location. As such, these instructions require an operand address (see the Appendix for address modes).

The major uses of DECREMENT/INCREMENT instructions occur when a register or a memory location is being used as a *counter*. Counters are often used for keeping track of the number of times a specific sequence of operations is performed, as illustrated in Chapter 5. They are also used for keeping track of addresses in indexed addressing operations. We shall present examples of these applications after conditional branch instructions are introduced. For now, we will just show some of the different methods for setting up a register or memory location as a counter.

Code	Mnemonic	
A2 20	LDX (IMM) ⎱ ⎰	This sets up the X register as a down counter with initial count = 20
. . . CA	. . . DEX	
A0 00	LDY (IMM) ⎱ ⎰	This sets up the Y register as an up counter with initial count = 00.
. . . C8	. . . INY	
A9 FF 85 20	LDA (IMM) ⎱ ⎰ STA (ZP) ⎰	This sets up the memory location 0020 as a down counter with initial count = FF
. . . C6 20	. . . DEC (ZP)	

In all cases, the register or memory location is loaded with an initial value. This value gets decremented or incremented at various points in the program and is periodically tested to see if it has reached a prescribed limit. Note that a greater number of instruction bytes are required to set up and decrement (or increment) a memory location. This, coupled with the fact that the DEC and INC instructions have very long execution times, leads to the conclusion that memory locations should be used as counters only when X and Y are being used for other purposes.

8.10 COMPARE INSTRUCTIONS

This group of instructions performs the subtraction operation but does not store the result anywhere. These instructions are designed only to affect certain flags for testing with conditional branch instructions.

CMP — Compare Memory with Accumulator

The CMP instruction subtracts [M], the contents of the specified memory location, from [A], the contents of the Accumulator. The result of the subtraction is *not* placed in the Accumulator, however, but is used to set or clear the C and Z flags.*

	C	Z
[A] less than [M] :	Cleared	Cleared
[A] equal to [M] :	Set	Set
[A] greater than [M] :	Set	Cleared

The purpose of the CMP instruction is to allow the program to compare the contents of the Accumulator with a data word from memory or an input device without changing the value stored in the Accumulator. An example of where this is extremely useful is when the microprocessor is reading data from an input device such as an A/D converter. The input data, depending on their value, can cause the program to branch to one of several different sequences of instructions. It is fairly simple to use the CMP instruction followed by the appropriate flag-testing instructions to determine where the program should branch to. We will illustrate this technique after we introduce the conditional branching instructions.

EXAMPLE 8.6 Assume that the Accumulator is loaded with the data word 01101101 and that the contents of memory address 0120 is 01001001. For each of the following, determine the values of the C and Z flags after the execution of the CMP instruction. All values are hex.

Case	Code	Mnemonic	Comments
I	CD 20 01	CMP (ABS)	Compare [A] with [0120]
II	C9 6F	CMP (IMM)	Compare [A] with 6F
III	C9 6D	CMP (IMM)	Compare [A] with 6D

Solution:

Case I. Since [A] is greater than [0120], the C flag is set to 1 and Z is 0.

Case II. Here [A] is compared to the data word 6F = 01101111_2 using immediate addressing. Since [A] is equal to 6D, which is less than 6F, the C flag will be 0 and the Z flag will be 0.

---

*The CMP instruction also affects the N flag, but the resultant value of the N flag can be either 0 or 1 for cases where [A] ≠ [M] depending on the signs of [A] and [M]. Thus, N is not useful for determining whether [A] > [M] or [A] < [M].

Case III. Here [A] is compared to the data word 6D using immediate addressing. Since they are equal, the C flag will be 1 and the Z flag will be 1.

Register Compare Instructions

There are two other compare instructions which use the X and Y registers. They operate in the same way as the CMP instruction except that the X register (or Y register) is used in place of the Accumulator.

CPX — COMPARE Memory with X register.

CPY — COMPARE Memory with Y register.

Execution of these instructions affects the C and Z flags in the same manner as the CMP instruction.

8.11 THE BIT-TEST INSTRUCTION

The bit-test instruction (BIT) is a very useful 6502 instruction. It can be used in testing bits of a data word from memory or an input device without loading the data word into one of the 6502 internal registers. When the BIT instruction is used to operate on a data word, two distinct operations take place.

1. The data word is ANDed with the contents of the accumulator, but the result is *not* placed in A. If the result is 00000000, the Z flag is set to 1; otherwise, Z = 0.
2. The result of the AND operation does not affect the N and V flags. Instead, the N flag takes on the value of bit 7 (MSB) of the data word, and V takes on the value of bit 6 of the data word.

The following example illustrates. Assume that [A] = 00100000 and that an input device with address F800 has the data word $D_7 D_6 D_5 D_4 D_3 D_2 D_1 D_0$ = 11011000. The BIT instruction is as follows:

2C	BIT (ABS)	Bit-test data from
00		input device
F8		

The ANDing of [A] and the data word produces 00000000, so that Z = 1. This tells the computer that bit D_5 of the data word was 0. [A] remains at 00100000. The N flag takes on the value of D_7; thus, N = 1. The V flag takes on the value of D_6; thus, V = 1. The program can now use conditional branch instructions to examine Z, N, and V to decide what to do next.

8.12 DATA-TRANSFER INSTRUCTIONS

Data-transfer instructions can be subdivided into three groups: transfers between memory and microprocessor registers, transfers between microprocessor registers, and transfers to and from the stack portion of memory.

Memory/Register Transfers

The LDA, LDX, and LDY instructions will read a word from memory* and load it into the A, X, and Y registers, respectively. The memory location can be specified using one of several address modes, including absolute, zero-page, and immediate addressing. The word transferred into a register will affect the N and Z flags in the normal manner.

The STA, STX, and STY instructions will store the contents of the A, X, and Y registers, respectively, into a specified memory location.* The contents of the register involved will not change as a result of the transfer. No flags will be affected by these instructions.

Register-to-Register Transfers

These six instructions transfer data between the microprocessor's internal registers. They are single-byte instructions which use implied addressing because no operand address is required.

$$\text{TAX} - \text{Transfer contents of Accumulator to X register: } [A] \longrightarrow [X].$$
$$\text{TAY} - \text{Transfer contents of Accumulator to Y register: } [A] \longrightarrow [Y].$$
$$\text{TXA} - \text{Transfer contents of X register to Accumulator: } [X] \longrightarrow [A].$$
$$\text{TYA} - \text{Transfer contents of Y register to Accumulator: } [Y] \longrightarrow [A].$$
$$\text{TSX} - \text{Transfer contents of Stack Pointer to X: } [SP] \longrightarrow [X].$$
$$\text{TXS} - \text{Transfer contents of X to Stack Pointer: } [X] \longrightarrow [SP].$$

In all these transfer instructions, the contents of the *source* register is transferred to the *destination* register without affecting the contents of the source register. For all but the TXS instruction, the N and Z flags will be affected by the data word being transferred.

The TXS instruction is normally used by the programmer to initialize the Stack Pointer register (SP) at the beginning of the program. Recall that the SP always points to the next available stack location on page 01. Normally, the programmer sets [SP] equal to FF so that the stack is located at 01FF. This is done using the following sequence:

A2	LDX (IMM)	Set [X] = FF
FF		
9A	TXS	Set [SP] = FF

*Or I/O device.

Stack Transfers

These four instructions are used to transfer the contents of the Accumulator and Processor Status Register (P) to and from the stack.

PHA—Push Accumulator onto Stack This instruction transfers the contents of the Accumulator to the next available location on the stack, as indicated by the SP Register, and decrements SP to point to the next location on the stack. To illustrate, let us assume that [SP] = FF so that the SP is pointing to address 01FF. Consider the following instruction sequence.

A9	LDA (IMM)	Set [A] = 25
25		
48	PHA	Store A on stack
A9	LDA (IMM)	Set [A] = B7
B7		
48	PHA	Push A on stack

The Accumulator is loaded with the value 25. This value is then pushed onto the stack at location 01FF, and the SP is decremented to FE. The Accumulator is then loaded with the value B7. This value is pushed onto the stack at location 01FE (since [SP] = FE), and SP is then decremented to FD.

PHP—Push Processor Status onto Stack This instruction transfers the contents of the Processor Status register (P) onto the stack and decrements the SP register. This instruction is used to save the status of the microprocessor flags when an interrupt occurs so that the program can continue properly after returning from the interrupt service routine.

PLA—Pull Accumulator from Stack This instruction *increments* the SP register and then loads the Accumulator from the stack location indicated by SP. Incrementing SP causes it to point to the last stack location that was written into. To illustrate, let us assume that [SP] = FF and consider the following sequence:

A9	LDA (IMM)	Set [A] = 32
32		
48	PHA	Push A onto stack
.	.	.
.	.	.
.	.	.
68	PLA	Pull A from stack

The Accumulator is loaded with 32, which is then pushed onto the stack at location 01FF. The SP is decremented to FE at the conclusion of the PHA instruction. Some time later a PLA instruction is executed which increments the SP back to FF and then transfers the contents of memory location 01FF back into the Accumulator.

PLP — Pull Processor Status from Stack This *increments* SP and then loads the Status register from the stack location indicated by SP. This instruction is used to restore the status flags to their preinterrupt values prior to returning from an interrupt service routine.

These "push" and "pull" instructions are often referred to as *save* and *restore* instructions, respectively. This is because they are used to save the contents of microprocessor registers whenever a break in the normal program sequence occurs, and to restore their contents upon returning to the normal program sequence. A prime example occurs during the processing of an interrupt request from an external device.

Saving Microprocessor Registers during Interrupts

When an interrupt occurs, the microprocessor stops executing the current program and branches to the interrupt service routine (ISR). During this process, the microprocessor *automatically* stores the contents of the Program Counter (PC) on the stack with the high-order byte (PCH) stored first and the low-order byte (PCL) stored on top of it. This is illustrated in Fig. 8.3, where a portion of the stack is shown. If we assume that [SP] = FF prior to

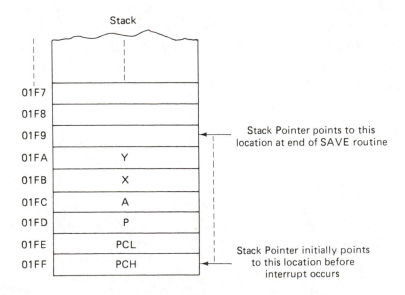

FIGURE 8.3 Saving the contents of μP registers on the stack during an interrupt.

the occurrence of the interrupt, PCH will be placed in stack location 01FF and PCL in location 01FE. The SP is then pointing to 01FD as the next available stack location.

Once the microprocessor branches to the ISR, the programmer may wish to save the contents of various microprocessor registers. This can be done by using the following instruction sequence at the beginning of the ISR. It is called a SAVE routine.

SAVE routine

08	PHP	Save [P]
48	PHA	Save [A]
8A	TXA	
48	PHA	Save [X]
98	TYA	
48	PHA	Save [Y]

.   .
.   .
.   .

(continue ISR)

Since the SP is at 01FD after PCH and PCL have been placed on the stack, this routine will first store P* at location 01FD and then A at location 01FC. The TXA, PHA combination then stores X at location 01FB. Similarly, the TYA, PHA combination stores Y at 01FA. At this point, the stack holds the contents of all the microprocessor registers and the SP is pointing to address 01F9 at the top of the stack (see Fig. 8.3).

At the end of the ISR, the contents of the microprocessor registers have to be restored before returning to the main program. This is done using the following instruction sequence, called a RESTORE routine.

RESTORE routine

68	PLA	
A8	TAY	Restore [Y]
68	PLA	
AA	TAX	Restore [X]
68	PLA	Restore [A]
28	PLP	Restore [P]
40	RTI	Return to main program

Notice that the RESTORE routine takes the registers off the stack in the opposite order that they were put on the stack. This is because the SP is at 01F9 and the first "pull" instruction will increment SP to 01FA, where Y

---

*Actually, the 6502 µP also *automatically* saves P when an interrupt occurs. However, many µPs do not, so it is included here in the SAVE and RESTORE routines for illustrative purposes.

is stored. The second "pull" instruction increments SP to 01FB, where X is stored; and so on. After the final PLP instruction restores the status register, the SP will be at 01FD. The return-from-interrupt (RTI) will *automatically* pull PCL and PCH from the stack and restore them to the program counter so that the microprocessor will continue execution of the program that was interrupted. At this point SP is back to 01FF, where it was prior to the interrupt.

It should be pointed out that it is not always necessary to save the contents of all the microprocessor registers during an interrupt service routine. It is only necessary to save those which are used during the ISR. In some cases this involves only saving the Accumulator, the processor status register, and the PC (which is saved automatically). This, of course, reduces the number of instructions required in the SAVE and RESTORE routines.

Programmer Concerns with the Stack

Although these "push" and "pull" instructions involve transferring data to and from memory, they require no operand address since the memory address is supplied by the SP. Thus, the programmer is not concerned with addressing when he uses these stack transfer instructions. However, the programmer must be concerned with two aspects of the stack:

1. When power is first applied to the microprocessor, the SP value will be random. One of the first things the programmer must do is to load a value into SP using the TXS instruction as shown earlier. Usually, this value is FF. The programmer must also decide what portion of page 01 is to be allocated for the stack. For example, he may allocate addresses 01A0 through 01FF for the stack and 0100 through 019F as program memory.

2. The SP is decremented each time a word is pushed onto the stack. This occurs whenever an interrupt or a JUMP TO SUBROUTINE (JSR) occurs, and whenever a PHA or PHP instruction is executed. The SP is incremented during a RETURN FROM INTERRUPT (RTI) and RETURN FROM SUBROUTINE (RTS), and whenever a PLA or PLP is executed. The programmer has to make certain that the SP does not get decremented too many times in succession before being incremented, or the SP might drift into the program area of page 01. This could prove to be disastrous, since portions of the program could be destroyed. This could be a problem when *nested subroutines* are used and the programmer has not allocated enough space for the stack. Most often it happens due to a programming error that somehow pushes data onto the stack more often than it pulls data off the stack.

8.13 UNCONDITIONAL JUMP (JMP)

We will begin our discussion of program control instructions with the simple unconditional jump instruction, JMP, which is used to change the program sequence. It is illustrated as follows:

Memory Address	Code	Mnemonic	Comments
0500	4C	JMP (ABS)	Jump to location 0520
0501	20		New PCL byte
0502	05		New PCH byte
.	.		.
.	.		.
.	.		
0520	Op code		New instruction

The JMP instruction sequence located at addresses 0500 through 0502 will cause the microprocessor to load the program counter with 0520 so that the next instruction will be taken from memory location 0520 rather than 0503. Thus, the address portion of the JMP instruction determines the new location from which the program execution will proceed.

This operation is called an *unconditional* jump since it always produces a change of program sequence. It does not perform any tests of status flags to determine whether or not to jump. This JMP instruction is used whenever it is necessary to change the program sequence no matter what conditions have occurred. The 6502 JMP instruction can use the absolute address mode (used above), or the indirect address mode which will be explained later.

8.14 CONDITIONAL BRANCH INSTRUCTIONS

This group of instructions is used to produce a change in the program sequence based on the status of the microprocessor flags. Each of the conditional branch instructions operates as follows:

1. The microprocessor interprets the op code.
2. Then it tests or checks the specified flag to see if it has the specified value (e.g., test for C = 1).
3. If the test is passed, the PC is set to a new value, which specifies the location the program will branch to.
4. If the test fails, the PC is incremented and the program continues its normal sequence.

Figure 8.4 illustrates how a conditional branch instruction could be used. In

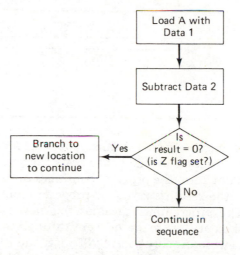

FIGURE 8.4 Typical use of conditional branching.

this example, it should be clear that a result of zero from the subtract operation will cause the program to branch to a new location; otherwise, the program will continue in its normal sequence.

Relative Addressing

All the 6502's conditional branch instructions use a two-byte format. The first byte is the op code, which specifies the flag being tested and the value it is being tested for. The second byte is an *offset*, which is *added* to the current contents of the PC, if the test passes, to obtain the new program address. This is called *relative addressing*.

The 6502 μP treats the offset byte as a *signed* binary number using 2's-complement representation for negative values. Thus, the offset can range from -127_{10} to $+127_{10}$. This means that the contents of the PC can be increased by up to 127_{10} for *forward* branching, or decreased by up to -127_{10} for *backward* branching. The machine-language programmer determines the offset value required to achieve branching to the new location when the flag test passes.

To illustrate, below is an example (continued on page 348) using the BEQ instruction which causes branching on a result equal to zero (Z = 1).

Address	Code	Mnemonic	Comments
0260	AD	LDA (ABS)	Load data from input device
0261	00		
0262	F8		
0263	F0	BEQ (REL)	If zero, branch ahead to 0280

Address	Code	Mnemonic	Comments
0264	1B ←———————————————		Offset
0265	AA	TAX	If not, transfer A to X
.	.	.	.
.	.	.	.
.	.	.	.

This program sequence begins by loading a data word into the Accumulator. The instruction at 0263 then tests for a result of zero (Z flag = 1). If the result is not zero, the program continues on to 0265 for the next instruction. But, if the result is zero, the program branches to 0280 for its next instruction. The programmer specifies this new address with an offset byte, 1B. Let us look at the process he went through to obtain this value.

The PC will normally go to 0265 after the BEQ instruction. For branching to the new address, the PC must become 0280. The value of the necessary offset can be obtained by subtracting these two values:

$$\begin{array}{rl} \text{new PC value} & 0280 \\ \text{current PC value} & -0265 \\ \hline & 1B \longleftarrow \text{ offset (hex)} \end{array}$$

This subtraction can be performed in hexadecimal, decimal or binary. The binary value of the offset is $00011011 = 27_{10}$. This is within the required range of -127_{10} to $+127_{10}$.

In this final example, the program branched *forward*, necessitating a *positive* offset. Here is an example where the branching will be *backward*, requiring a *negative* offset:

Address	Code	Mnemonic	Comments
0260	AD	LDA (ABS)	Load data
0261	00		
0262	F8		
0263	F0	BEQ (REL)	If zero, branch back to 0240
0264	DB ←———————————————		Offset
0265	AA	TAX	If not, transfer A to X
.	.	.	.
.	.	.	.
.	.	.	.

Here the BEQ instruction causes the program to branch backward to location 0240 if the result is zero. The PC will normally go to 0265. The difference is

$$
\begin{array}{ll}
\text{current PC value} & 0265 \\
\text{new PC value} & -0240 \\
\hline
& 25 \text{ (hex)} = 00100101_2 = 37_{10}
\end{array}
$$

which is within the specified range. However, the offset must be a *negative* binary number so that it reduces PC to 0240 when it is added. The required negative offset is obtained by 2's-complementing the difference obtained above.

$$
\begin{array}{lll}
\text{difference} & 00100101_2 & = +37_{10} \\
\text{2's-complement} & \underbrace{11011011}_{\text{offset}} & = -37_{10}
\end{array}
$$

This negative offset can be written as DB (hex) and is the byte shown in the above program immediately following the op code for BEQ.

Page-crossing

The new PC value and the current PC value can be on different pages of memory. For instance, branching can occur forward from a location on page 02 to a location on page 03, or backward to a location on page 01. The only stipulation is that the size of the offset be between -127_{10} and $+127_{10}$.

The steps followed in the preceding examples for determining the offset byte are the same for all conditional branch instructions and are summarized as follows:

1. For a branch forward, subtract the current value of the PC from the desired new value. The current value will always be the address of the instruction byte following the offset byte (0265 in our examples) since the PC is incremented after fetching the offset byte. The result of this subtraction will be the required positive offset. Note that the maximum positive offset is $127_{10} = 7F_{16}$.

2. For a branch backward, subtract the desired new PC value from the current PC value. The result is the number of locations to be branched, and should be less than $127_{10} = 7F_{16}$. The binary equivalent of this value is then 2's-complemented and represents the required negative offset.

Branching Out of Range

The conditional branch instructions are limited to branching forward 127 bytes or backward 127 bytes from the next instruction. This limitation of relative addressing might appear to be a severe disadvantage. In most programs, however, the branching is usually within this range, and the few exceptions can be handled using a special trick, as we shall see. The major advantage of relative addressing is the fact that it only requires one byte after the op code. Since most programs contain many conditional branch instructions, this can produce a significant savings in program bytes.

To handle cases where branching must occur outside the range of the relative addressing mode, we can employ an unconditional jump. This is illustrated in the example below, which is the same as the previous two examples except that it is desired to branch to address 03F0 when a zero result occurs. Note that a BNE (branch when result is *not* equal to zero) is used instead of BEQ. Study the example carefully.

Address	Code	Mnemonic	Comments
0260	AD	LDA (ABS)	Load data
0261	00		
0262	F8		
0263	D0	BNE (REL)	If *not* zero, branch ahead to 0268
0264	03		
0265	4C	JMP (ABS)	If zero, jump to 03F0
0266	F0		
0267	03		
0268	AA	TAX	Come here if result not zero
.	.	.	.
.	.	.	.
.	.	.	.

The BNE instruction tests for a result *not* equal to zero, and if this condition is met, it causes the program to branch to 0268. (Note that the offset byte is 03.) If the result is equal to zero, the BNE instruction does not cause any branching but goes on to the next instruction at 0265. The JMP instruction at 0265, however, produces an unconditional jump to 03F0. The overall result, then, is that the program branches ahead to 03F0 for a result of zero, or it continues on to 0268 for a nonzero result. This technique should be used whenever a conditional branch must be made forward or backward by more than 127 bytes.

Various Conditional Branch Instructions

Following is the list of the eight 6502 instructions that fall into this category.

Mnemonic	Causes Branching When:
BEQ	Result equals zero (Z = 1)
BNE	Result not equal to zero (Z = 0)

Branch

Mnemonic	Causes Branching When:
BCS	Carry flag set (C = 1)
BCC	Carry flag cleared (C = 0)
BMI	Result is minus (N = 1)
BPL	Result is plus (N = 0)
BVS	Overflow flag is set (V = 1)
BVC	Overflow flag is cleared (V = 0)

Each of these instructions tests one specific microprocessor flag condition. If the condition is met, branching occurs; if not, the program continues to the next instruction sequence.

We will now look at some typical programming applications of conditional branch instructions. In each example, the reader should verify the value of the offset.

EXAMPLE 8.7   Write a sequence of instructions beginning at 0200 which will cause a branch to address 024A whenever the least significant bit (LSB) of an input port equals 1.

Solution:

Address	Code	Mnemonic	Comments
0200	AD	LDA (ABS)	Load Accumulator from input device
0201	00		
0202	F7		
0203	4A	LSR (ACC)	Shift LSB of A into C
0204	B0	BCS (REL)	Branch to 024A if C = 1
0205	44		Offset = +68 (decimal)
0206			Otherwise, continue
.	.	.	.
.	.	.	.
.	.	.	.

The LSR instruction shifts the LSB of the Accumulator into the C flag. The BCS then tests for C = 1 and produces a branch to location 024A if this condition is met. (Note that the offset byte = 44.) If C = 0, then the program continues in sequence to 0206.

EXAMPLE 8.8   Repeat Example 8.7 using the most significant bit (MSB) of the input port.

Solution:

Address	Code	Mnemonic	Comments
0200	AD	LDA (ABS)	Load Accumulator
0201	00		
0202	F7		
0203	30	BMI (REL)	If [A] is negative, branch to 024A
0204	45		Offset = +69 (decimal)
0205	.		Otherwise, continue
.	.	.	.
.	.	.	.
.	.	.	.

Here it is not necessary to perform a shift operation. Instead, the N flag is tested (using the BMI instruction) because its value will equal the value of the MSB of the data word.

EXAMPLE 8.9   Write a sequence of instructions starting at 0400 which will do the following: (A) load A with a data word from an input device; (B) branch to address 044A if the LSB is a 0; and (C) branch to 03F0 if the LSB is 1 and bit 4 is a 0.

Solution: This sequence requires two tests and two decisions and is flowcharted in Fig. 8.5. The LSB is tested first to see if it is a 0. If it is not, bit 4 is then tested to see if it is a 0. The instruction sequence is given below.

Address	Code	Mnemonic	Comments
0400	AD	LDA (ABS)	Load A with input data
0401	00		
0402	F7		
0403	4A	LSR (ACC)	Shift LSB of A into C
0404	90	BCC (REL)	If C = 0, branch to 044A
0405	44		Offset = +68 (decimal)
0406	29	AND (IMM)	If C = 1, isolate bit-3
0407	04		
0408	F0	BEQ (REL)	If result is zero, branch to 03F0
0409	E6	.	Offset = –26 (decimal)
040A	.	.	Otherwise, continue
.	.	.	.
.	.	.	.
.	.	.	.

The LSR instruction shifts the LSB into the C flag and the BCC instruction tests for C = 0. If C = 1, the program sequences to 0406. Here an AND-masking operation is performed to isolate bit 3 of the Accumulator, which was the original bit 4 prior to the LSR operation. The subsequent BEQ instruction determines if this bit is 0 and branches to 03F0 if it is. This branch is an example of page-crossing.

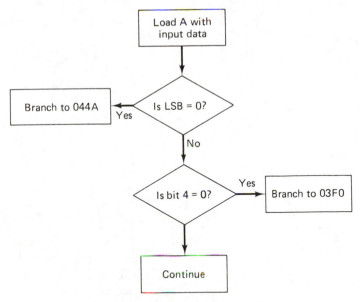

FIGURE 8.5 Flowchart for Example 8.9.

EXAMPLE 8.10 A microprocessor is being used in a control application where it receives coded commands from a switch-register input port. Write a sequence of instructions starting at C070 which does the following: (A) load register X with the command code from the input port; (B) branch to C0A6 if the command code is 3C; (C) branch to C0C3 if the command code is 78; (D) otherwise, branch to C0F9.

Solution: A flowchart for this sequence is shown in Fig. 8.6. Here we are performing tests on a complete byte of data rather than on one of its bits. This type of testing is best done using Compare instructions. The instruction sequence is shown below.

Address	Code	Mnemonic	Comments
C070	AE	LDX (ABS)	Load X from input port
C071	00		
C072	F7		
C073	E0	CPX (IMM)	Compare [X] with 3C
C074	3C		
C075	F0	BEQ (REL)	If [X] = 3C, branch to C0A6
C076	2F		
C077	E0	CPX (IMM)	If not, compare [X] with 78
C078	78		
C079	F0	BEQ (REL)	If [X] = 78, branch to C0C3
C07A	48		
C07B	4C	JMP (ABS)	If not, jump to C0F9
C07C	F9		
C07D	C0		

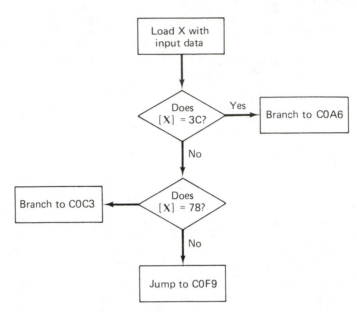

FIGURE 8.6 Flowchart for Example 8.10.

The first CPX instruction compares [X] with the value 3C. If they are equal, the Z flag will be set and the subsequent BEQ instruction will cause the program to branch to C0A6. Otherwise, the program proceeds to C077, where it compares [X] to the value 78. If [X] = 78, the subsequent BEQ produces a branch to C0C3. If [X] ≠ 78, the program continues to C07B where an unconditional jump instruction sends the program to C0F9.

Determining the Branched-to Location

When analyzing someone else's program, it is often necessary to determine the new location a program is branching to. This can be done by reversing the steps followed for determining the offset value. The method is illustrated below for forward and backward branching.

1. *Positive offset.* When the hexadecimal offset has a MSD of 7 or less, its binary equivalent has a MSB of 0, indicating a positive offset. For this case the new PC value is determined by adding the offset to the current PC value. To illustrate, if the current PC value is 02A2 and the offset is 38_{16}, the new PC is found as

$$
\begin{array}{ll}
\text{current PC} & 02A2 \\
+ & 38 \\
\hline
\text{new PC} \longrightarrow & 02DA
\end{array}
$$

If the offset is changed from 38 to 78, we have

$$
\begin{array}{ll}
\text{current PC} & \text{02A2} \\
\text{offset} & +\ \underline{\quad 78} \\
\text{new PC} \longrightarrow & \text{031A}
\end{array}
$$

2. *Negative offset.* When the MSD of the hex offset is 8 or more, the MSB of the binary offset is 1, which indicates a negative offset. First, convert the binary offset to a positive value by 2's-complementing. Then subtract this value from the current PC to obtain the new PC value. To illustrate, assume that the current PC is 0237 and the offset is 95_{16}.

$$
\text{Offset} = 95_{16} = 10010101_2
$$
$$
\text{2's-complement of } 10010101 = 01101011 = 6B_{16}
$$

$$
\begin{array}{ll}
\text{current PC} & \text{0237} \\
\text{offset} & -\ \underline{\quad 6B} \\
\text{new PC} \longrightarrow & \text{01CC}
\end{array}
$$

The reader should try the foregoing method on some of the earlier examples to see that it works.

8.15 SUBROUTINES

Very often a program will require that a certain function be performed at various times during the program. For example, a program might be outputing ASCII-coded data to a TTY at several points during the program. As another example, a program could require the multiplication of two numbers many times during the program's execution. The sequences of instructions needed to perform these functions can be repeated in the program each time they are needed. This would be acceptable when the sequences are relatively short and the number of repetitions is not too great. Often, this is not the case, so the programmer treats the sequences as *subroutines*.

A subroutine is a sequence of instructions which performs a specific function and which the program can branch to any time. A subroutine only has to be written once and stored in a specific area of memory. Then, whenever the main program requires the function, it can branch to the address of the subroutine, execute the subroutine, and return to the main program. This should be recognized as being very similar to the action that takes place during an interrupt when the program branches to the interrupt service routine.

Figure 8.7 is a flowchart that illustrates how a subroutine may be used

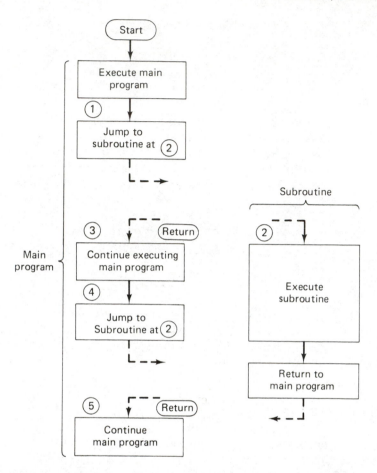

FIGURE 8.7 A subroutine can be used at any point during the execution of a program; the operation returns to the main program at the end of the subroutine.

in a program. Here we see that the main program jumps to the subroutine at two different times (point 1 and point 4). In each case, after the subroutine is executed, operation returns to the main program to continue execution (point 3 and point 5 respectively). This same sequence can occur many times during the execution of the main program. Clearly, this will generally be more efficient in the use of memory space than the alternative approach of repeating the subroutine instruction sequence each time it is needed in the main program.

A jump to a subroutine is often referred to as a *subroutine call* and the program can be said to "call the subroutine." For example, in Fig. 8.7 the main program calls the subroutine at two different times. We will use the terms "call" and "jump to subroutine" interchangeably.

Subroutine Instructions — JSR and RTS

The JSR and RTS instructions control the branching to and return from a subroutine. The jump-to-subroutine instruction, JSR, is a three-byte instruction that contains the absolute address of the subroutine. It operates similar to the JMP instruction, in that it replaces the contents of the PC with the subroutine address. This is illustrated as follows:

Address	Code	Mnemonic	Comments
C100	20	JSR (ABS)	Jump to subroutine at CA25
C101	25		Low-order address of subroutine
C102	CA		High-order address of subroutine

This instruction sequence causes the microprocessor to begin executing the subroutine that starts at CA25. At the end of the subroutine, there has to be a return-from-subroutine instruction, RTS, which transfers the operation back to the main program. The RTS instruction is a single-byte instruction with an op code of 60. For the example above, the RTS instruction will send the program counter back to C103 to continue execution of the main program.

The reader should notice a similarity between the RTS instruction and the RTI instruction (Chapter 6) used for returning from interrupt service routines. They both cause a return to the main program. As we described for RTI, the return address for RTS is stored on the stack when the subroutine call occurs. The contents of the program counter at the end of the JSR instruction sequence (C102 for the example above) is automatically pushed onto the stack. Later, when RTS is executed, this value (C102) is automatically pulled off the stack and placed into the PC. The PC is then incremented (C103) to bring it to the proper point for continuation of the main program.

Saving Microprocessor Registers during Subroutine Calls

It may be necessary to store the contents of registers on the stack during the execution of a subroutine if the subroutine uses a register whose contents is crucial to the main program. This can be done using the steps described in Section 8.12 for branching to an interrupt service routine. The SAVE routine can be placed at the start of the subroutine, and the RESTORE routine at the end of the subroutine prior to the RTS instruction. Alternatively, the SAVE routine can be placed in the main program just before the JSR instruction, and the RESTORE routine just after the JSR. This is illustrated below for saving the A and X registers.

Address	Code	Mnemonic	Comments
0200	48	PHA	Save [A]
0201	8A	TXA	
0202	48	PHA	Save [X]
0203	20	JSR (ABS)	Call subroutine at 1F36
0204	36		
0205	1F		
0206	68	PLA	
0207	AA	TAX	Restore [X]
0208	68	PLA	Restore [A]
0209	.	.	
.	.	.	
.	.	.	
.			

The A and X registers are pushed on the stack just prior to the subroutine call. When the subroutine returns control to the main program, the RESTORE routine will be executed to pull X and A off the stack. This method is sometimes preferred over placing the SAVE and RESTORE routines in the subroutine because there may not be a need to save registers during every subroutine call.

We can get a better idea of how the stack is used in subroutine calls by following through the sequence of operations for the example above. Let us assume that [SP] = FF prior to the subroutine call.

1. *Save A* — store [A] on stack at 01FF. Decrement [SP] to FE.
2. *Save X* — store [X] on stack at 01FE and decrement [SP] to FD.
3. *Execute JSR*
   (a) *Save return address* — store [PC] on stack at 01FD and 01FC (PCL = 05 stored at 01FD and PCH = 02 stored at 01FC). [SP] is now equal to FB.
   (b) *Load PC with subroutine address* — [PC] now equals 1F36.
4. *Execute subroutine* beginning at 1F36.
5. *Execute RTS at end of subroutine.*
   (a) *Restore return address* — increment [SP] to FC and load 02 into PCH; increment [SP] to FD and load 05 into PCL. [PC] now = 0205.
   (b) *Increment PC* — [PC] is now 0206 and operation returns to main program.
6. *Restore X* — increment [SP] to FE and load value at 01FE into A, then transfer to X. [X] has now been restored to its original value.

7. *Restore A* — increment [SP] to FF and load value at 01FF into A. [A] has now been restored, and execution of the main program can continue.

Nested Subroutines

The use of the stack in saving the return address and register contents during a subroutine call can be extended to more complex situations. In particular, it is possible to perfom *nested* subroutine calls whereby the main program

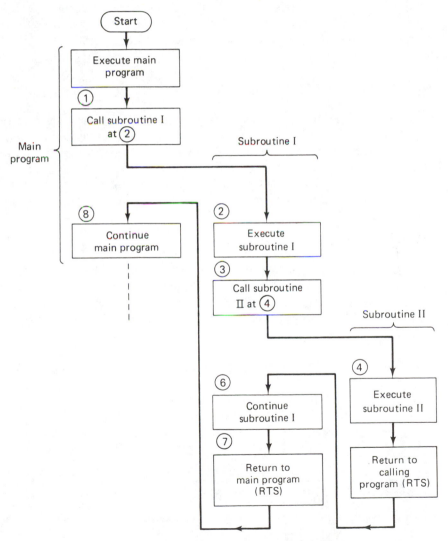

FIGURE 8.8 Flowchart showing how subroutines can be "nested" — one subroutine calling another.

calls a subroutine and that subroutine, during its execution, calls another subroutine, and so on. A flow diagram depicting this situation is shown in Fig. 8.8.

Here we see the main program performing a call to subroutine I (point 1), which in turn performs a call to subroutine II (point 3). At the completion of subroutine II, operation returns to subroutine I (point 6). When subroutine I is complete, operation returns to the main program (point 8). The return addresses in each case are automatically saved on the stack during the JSR instruction execution and restored to the PC during the RTS instruction. Each subroutine's RTS instruction will cause a branch back to the program that called the subroutine, because the calling program's return address will have been the last thing placed on the stack.

8.16 INDEXED ADDRESSING MODES

In Chapter 5 we saw how a microprocessor's Index registers could be used for special addressing techniques referred to as *indexed addressing*. With indexed addressing, the effective operand address is determined by a combination of the address portion of the instruction and the contents of an Index register. The 6502 has several indexed addressing modes which use the X or Y register as Index registers.

Absolute Indexed Addressing

The absolute indexed addressing mode uses a two-byte absolute address to which the contents of an index register is added. The *effective* address, which is the actual data address, is the sum of the 16-bit absolute address and the 8-bit index register. For example, if the X register is being used, we have

$$\text{effective address} = \text{absolute address} + [X]$$

In this addition process, the [X] is treated as a positive 8-bit number which can range from 00 to FF (hex) or 0 to 255 (decimal).

The following instruction sequence illustrates how this address mode works:

Address	Code	Mnemonic	Comments
0100	A2	LDX (IMM)	Set [X] = 25
0101	25		
0102	9D	STA (ABS,X)	Store [A] in 0160 + [X]

Address	Code	Mnemonic	Comments
0103	60		ADL
0104	01		ADH
.	.	.	.
.	.	.	.
.	.	.	.

The STA instruction at 0102 uses absolute indexed addressing with the X register, as indicated by the (ABS,X) notation. The absolute address portion of this instruction is 0160. The value of X has to be added to this to find the address in memory where [A] is to be stored. That is:

$$\text{effective address} = \overset{\text{Absolute}}{0160} \quad + \overset{\text{X}}{25}$$
$$= \quad 0185$$

Thus, the [A] will be stored at location 0185.

This same operation can take place using the Y register as the Index register. For example, the instruction mnemonic LDA (ABS,Y) will load the Accumulator from the memory location whose address is given by the sum of the absolute address and the Y register.

Zero-Page Indexed Addressing

The zero-page indexed addressing mode is exactly like the zero-page address mode except that the effective address (on page 00) is obtained by adding the contents of the Index register to the single-byte zero-page address:

Address	Code	Mnemonic	Comments
0100	A2	LDX (IMM)	Set [X] = 42
0101	42		
0102	35	AND (ZP,X)	AND [A] with data in 0020 + [X]
0103	20		ADL (ADH = 00)
.	.	.	.
.	.	.	.
.	.	.	.

The AND instruction at 0102 uses zero-page indexed addressing with the X register, as indicated by the (ZP,X) notation. The effective address of the data to be used by this instruction can be obtained as follows:

$$\text{effective zero-page address} = \overbrace{20}^{\text{Zero-page}} + \overbrace{42}^{X}$$

$$= 62$$

Thus, the data word at address 0062 is ANDed with the Accumulator. Note that instructions which use this address mode are two-byte instructions, since the high-order address byte is always 00.

Now that we have introduced indexed addressing, let us look at some of the many programming applications where indexed addressing is extremely helpful.

Movement of Data Blocks

One operation that occurs quite often is the movement of blocks of data from one area of memory to another. To illustrate, let us pose a typical problem with the help of Fig. 8.9A. Here we see a group of six data bytes stored in memory locations 0270 through 0275. Call this block 1. We want to transfer these bytes into memory locations 03A3 through 03A8, which we will call block 2. This operation could be programmed in a straightforward manner by simply repeating the following sequence *six* times (once per data byte):

```
AD    LDA (ABS)      Load Data 0
70              ⎫
02              ⎬   Address in block 1
8D    STA (ABS)      Store Data 0
A3              ⎫
03              ⎬   Address in block 2
 .        .      (Repeat with different block 1
 .        .         and block 2 addresses)
 .        .
```

This would require 18 bytes of program codes. Clearly, this method would become prohibitive as the *size* of the data blocks increased.

A more efficient method using indexed addressing is flowcharted in Fig. 8.9B. The X register is used as the index register for addressing and also as a loop counter to keep track of the number of bytes of data being moved. Note that [X] is initially set equal to 05 and is decremented following the transfer of each byte from block 1 to block 2. After the *sixth* byte transfer, [X] will be decremented from 00 to FF (remember that X is being used as a down counter) and, since $FF_{16} = 11111111_2$, the N flag will be 1. Thus, the program will stop looping and no further transfers will take place.

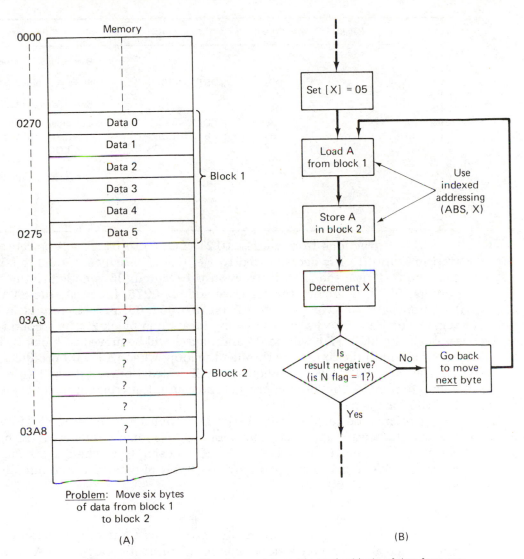

FIGURE 8.9 Indexed addressing can be used in moving blocks of data from one area of memory to another.

The sequence of instruction codes for this process follows. Study it carefully before proceeding.

Address	Label	Code	Mnemonic	Comments
0125		A2	LDX (IMM)	Set [X] = 05
0126		05		
0127	LOOP	BD	LDA (ABS,X)	Load A from block 1

Address	Label	Code	Mnemonic	Comments
0128		70		Base address in block 1
0129		02		
012A		9D	STA (ABS,X)	Store A in block 2
012B		A3		
012C		03		Base address in block 2
012D		CA	DEX	Decrement counter
012E		10	BPL (REL)	If [X] is positive, return to LOOP
012F		F7		
0130				Otherwise, continue
.		.	.	.
.		.	.	.
.		.	.	.

The instructions from address 0127 (LOOP) to 012E will be repeated six times until [X] is decremented to FF. [X] is initially set equal to 05, so that the first time the LDA instruction is executed, 05 is added to the base address, 0270, to obtain the effective address 0275. Likewise, the STA instruction uses the effective address 03A3 + 05 = 03A8. This results in the transfer of Data 5 to its corresponding location in block 2. The second time through the loop, [X] will be 04 and data 4 will be moved to block 2. This continues until the sixth time through the loop, when [X] = 00 produces the transfer of data 0. The subsequent DEX instruction results in [X] = FF, which terminates the looping process and causes the program to continue on to 0130 for the next instruction.

This method requires only 11 program bytes as compared to 18 using the straightforward approach. Furthermore, this same sequence of 11 bytes can be used to move up to 256 bytes of data simply by changing the initial contents of X. For example, to move 64 bytes of data, X would initially be loaded with 3F (hex) = 63_{10}.

Tables

The use of memory *tables* can significantly speed up microcomputer operations, such as code conversions, complex arithmetic calculations, message generation, and control output generation. Tables are simply lists of related data that are stored in sequential memory locations. The data in these tables usually are constant for a given application and are typically stored in ROM or loaded into RAM from a tape or disk storage unit.

The principal advantage of a table is that it eliminates the need to perform any calculations in order to produce an answer. An answer is obtained simply by finding the correct address in the table and reading the contents of that location. Proper use of a table requires setting up the data in the table and establishing a means for accessing any entry in the table. We will look at a typical application that lends itself to the use of tables.

Figure 8.10A shows part of a microprocessor-based process control sys-

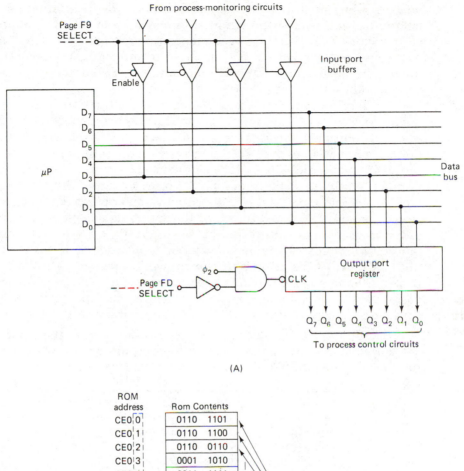

(A)

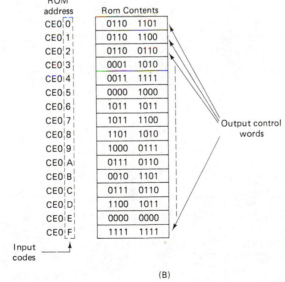

(B)

FIGURE 8.10 (A) Partial diagram of a μP-based process control system; (B) a table of output control words stored in ROM.

365

tem. A 4-bit input port is used to transfer process information into the microprocessor. This information is obtained from process-monitoring circuits such as limit switches, over-temperature sensors, level detectors, and so on, whose outputs have been converted to proper logic levels. The tristate input port buffers are enabled when any page F9 address is placed on the system address bus (not shown).

An 8-bit output port register is used to latch control outputs from the microprocessor and transmit them to various process control circuits such as solenoid-controlled valves, relays, and triacs. Data are latched into the output register when any page FD address is placed on the address bus.

The microprocessor periodically reads data from the input port to determine the status of the process-monitoring circuits. With four inputs there are 16 possible input status codes, so the microprocessor must determine which code is present and then load the appropriate control outputs into the output register. The most efficient way to do this is to store the various output control words in a table and use the input code to access the table. Figure 8.10B shows the 16 output control words stored in a ROM table at address CE00 through CEOF. The least significant hex digit of each address corresponds to the input code. For example, an input code of $1001_2 = 9$ (hex) corresponds to address CE09 and an output control word of 10000111.

The following instruction sequence is used to read the input port, find the correct table entry, and transmit the output control word. It uses an input port address of F900 and an output port address of FD00.

Address	Label	Code	Mnemonic	Comments
0226	CONTROL	AD	LDA (ABS)	Read input port
0227		00		
0228		F9		
0229		29	AND (IMM)	Clear four MSBs
022A		0F		
022B		A8	TAY	Transfer input code to Y
022C		B9	LDA (ABS,Y)	Fetch output control word
022D		00		
022E		CE		Base address of output table
022F		8D	STA (ABS)	Write control word into
0230		00		output port
0231		FD		

Let us follow through this sequence step by step assuming that the input data are 1011_2.

Step 1. The accumulator is loaded from the input port and its contents becomes

$$[A] = X\ X\ X\ X\ 1\ 0\ 1\ 1$$

The four MSBs will be ambiguous (indicated by an "X"), since the input port only drives the four lower-order data bus lines.

Step 2. The AND instruction is used to clear the four MSBs of the Accumulator without affecting the other bits. This results in

$$[A] = 0 \ 0 \ 0 \ 0 \ \underbrace{1 \ 0 \ 1 \ 1}_{\text{input code}}$$

Step 3. $[A] \longrightarrow [Y]$, so now $[Y] = 00001011 = 0B$ (hex).

Step 4. The LDA (ABS,Y) instruction now enters the control word table at address CE00 + 0B = CE0B and loads A with 00101101.

Step 5. This control word is written into the output register.

8.17 INDIRECT ADDRESSING

In this addressing mode, the address portion of the instruction is *not* the operand address; instead, it is the address in memory where the operand address can be found. In other words, it is the *address of the operand address.* To illustrate, consider the following instruction sequence:

0100	64*	LDA (IND)*	Load Accumulator (indirect)
0101	20		} Pointer address
0102	D1		
.	.		.
.	.		.
.	.		.
Pointer { D120	3A		ADL } Operand address
locations { D121	02		ADH

The LDA (IND) instruction is a three-byte instruction with the second and third bytes representing an address, D120. This address is called a *pointer*, since it points to the location where the operand address is stored. In executing this instruction, the microprocessor uses the pointer address to fetch the *operand* address (023A), which is stored at D120 and D121. Note that the pointer address location holds the ADL and the following location holds the ADH of the operand address. Once the microprocessor has fetched

---

*This op code and mnemonic are fictitious since the 6502 does not have this particular instruction. It is used here merely for illustrative purposes.

the operand address, it then fetches the data from that address and loads it into the Accumulator.

Clearly, indirect addressing is more time-consuming than the other address modes because it requires *six* memory accesses — one to fetch the op code, two to fetch the pointer address, two more to fetch the operand address, and one to fetch the operand. For this reason, indirect addressing is used only when necessary. There are certain types of programming problems where it is necessary to have an operand address that is a variable or computed value which will be different under different conditions. For these problems, indirect addressing is useful because each time a new operand address is computed, it can be stored in the pointer address locations (D120, D121 in our example) which have to be RAM locations. The instruction which is accessing the variable operand address will often be stored in ROM. This is why the absolute address mode cannot be used since the operand address could not be varied.

The 6502 has only one instruction that uses the indirect addressing mode just described. The unconditional jump, JMP, can use indirect addressing as well as absolute addressing. For example, if we replace the LDA (IND) instruction in the previous illustration with JMP (IND), the program will execute an unconditional jump to location 023A.

The 6502 does have two other address modes which combine indirect addressing with indexed addressing. We will not describe these here, but refer the reader to the 6502 Programming Manual for a detailed discussion of all the indirect addressing modes.

8.18 TIMING LOOPS

There are many situations which require that a time delay be inserted into a program. One common case is when the execution rate of the program has to be slowed down to match the speed of a slower I/O device. We saw an example of this earlier when we discussed the NOP instruction (Section 8.5). Another common application of "software" time delays is when the program is used to send control signals with specific time durations to peripheral devices.

There are two basic ways to produce a time delay between two points in a program. The first way simply uses a straight sequence of dummy instructions which performs no useful function. This is what we did earlier with the NOP instructions. As we stated, then, this method is limited to short delays because the number of program bytes *required* is proportional to the size of the required delay. The second approach uses a sequence of dummy instructions which is repeated as many times as are needed to produce the required delay. The sequence is put into a loop and a register keeps track of the number of times the loop is executed. Loops used for this purpose are called *timing loops*.

Regardless of which method is used to produce a time delay, the amount of delay will depend on the execution times of the various instructions, which in turn depend on the microprocessor clock frequency. Each instruction takes a certain number of clock cycles to execute. For the 6502 this number can range anywhere from two to seven cycles. The table of 6502 instruction codes in Appendix A also lists the number of clock cycles, N, for each instruction. For example, a LDA instruction using absolute addressing takes *four* cycles to execute, while a LDA instruction using immediate addressing requires *three* cycles.

Software One-Shot

Let us consider using a software delay to generate a single pulse at an output port. We will use the output register of Fig. 8.10 and the pulse will appear at the Q_0 output. The process requires three steps: (1) write a 1 in bit 0 of the output register; (2) go through a time delay; and (3) write a 0 in bit 0 of the output register.

The complete instruction sequence is given below. The number of clock cycles for each instruction is shown in brackets after the op code.

Address	Label	Code	Mnemonic	Comments
0320	OSHOT	A9 [2]	LDA (IMM)	[A] = FF
0321		FF		
0322		8D [4]	STA (ABS)	Set Q_0 = 1
0323		00		
0324		FD		
0325	DELAY	EA [2]	NOP	
0326		48 [3]	PHA	} For delay purposes only
0327		68 [4]	PLA	
0328		A9 [2]	LDA (IMM)	[A] = FE (bit 0 = 0)
0329		FE		
032A		8D [4]	STA (ABS)	Clear Q_0 = 0
032B		00		
032C		FD		

We will assume that Q_0 = 0 initially. Thus, Q_0 will be set to 1 when the STA (ABS) instruction at 0322 is executed. This occurs at the end of the last clock cycle of that instruction (falling edge of ϕ_2). Instructions 0325 through 0327 are dummy instructions used for delay, and the instructions at 0328 and 032A are used to clear Q_0 to back to 0. Q_0 will be cleared to 0 at the end of the last clock cycle of the STA (ABS) instruction at 032A. The total time that Q_0 is high, then, will be the time required to execute instructions 0325 through 032A, or a total of 15 clock cycles. For a 1-MHz clock frequency, this becomes a 15-μs pulse duration (see Fig. 8.11).

The pulse duration can be varied by increasing or decreasing the amount of delay. For the sequence above, the minimum pulse duration would be six clock cycles, which is obtained by removing the NOP, PHA, and PLA instructions. The LDA (IMM) and STA (ABS) instructions have to be kept, hence the six-cycle delay. The maximum pulse duration is theoretically unlimited since we can add as many dummy instructions as we like.* Practically, however, this is limited by the amount of memory space available. For instance, to obtain a 1-ms pulse duration using straight sequences of dummy instructions for the delay would take up about 300 memory locations.

To achieve delays of more than 20 or 30 cycles, then, it is better to use a timing loop. This is illustrated below for the software one-shot program, where we have inserted a counting loop in the delay path using the Y register as a loop counter. Study the sequence carefully.

Addresses	Label	Code	Mnemonic	Comments
0320	OSHOT	A9	LDA (IMM)	[A] = FF
0321		FF		
0322		8D	STA (ABS)	Set $Q_0 = 1$
0323		00		
0324		FD		
0325	DELAY	A0 [2]	LDY (IMM)	Initialize loop counter (Y = 5) for number of passes through loop
0326		05		
0327	LOOP	EA [2]	NOP	
0328		88 [2]	DEY	Decrement counter
0329		D0 [3]	BNE (REL)	If [Y] $\neq$ 0, branch back to LOOP
032A		FC		
032B		A9 [2]	LDA (IMM)	If [Y] = 0, load [A] = FE
032C		FE		
032D		8D [4]	STA (ABS)	Clear $Q_0 = 0$
032E		00		
032F		FD		

Here the total delay is the time required to execute the sequence from 0325 through 032D. This includes the instructions at 0327, 0328, and 0329,

*Remember to balance each PHA with a PLA, or the Stack Pointer may get into portions of page 01 that are reserved for nonstack uses.

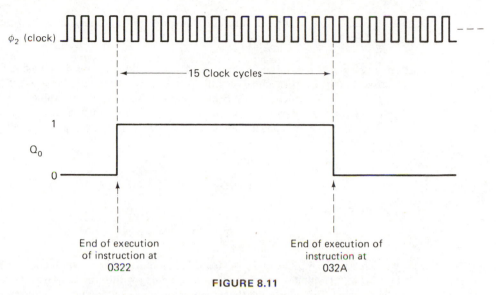

FIGURE 8.11

which form the timing loop and which will be executed *five* times before the counter (Y) is decremented to zero. The total delay is calculated as follows:

$$\text{total delay} = T_L \times N_L + T_E$$

where T_L is the total of the execution times of the *loop* instructions. N_L is the number of times the program passes through the loop, and T_E is the total of the execution times of the instructions *external* to the loop. For our example, $T_L = 2 + 2 + 3 = 7$ cycles, $N_L = 5$, and $T_E = 2 + 2 + 4 = 8$ cycles. This gives a total delay of 43 cycles or 43 μs for a 1-MHz clock.

EXAMPLE 8.11 How would you modify this program to produce a pulse at Q_0 with a duration of 1 ms?

Solution: The easiest way to do it is to determine how many times the program has to execute the loop instructions to produce a total delay if 1 ms = 1000 μs.

$$1000\ \mu s = 7 \times N_L + 8\ \mu s$$

so that

$$N_L = 141.7 \approx 142$$

Thus, if we change the initial value of the loop counter from 05 to 8E (hex equivalent of decimal 142), the program will execute the loop 142 times for a total delay of approximately 1 ms. This can be accomplished by changing the code at address 0326 from 05 to 8E.

EXAMPLE 8.12 How would you modify this program to produce an output pulse duration of approximately 10 ms?

Solution: Using the method of Example 8.11, we would come up with a value for N_L of approximately 1420 (decimal) = 58C (hex). This value is too large to load into the loop counter, Y, which is only 8 bits long and has a maximum value of FF (hex) = 255 (decimal). Since we cannot go through the loop enough times for the delay we need, perhaps we can consider increasing T_L, the delay within the loop. We have

$$\text{total delay} = T_L \times N_L + T_E$$

$$10{,}000 \ \mu s = T_L \times N_L + 8 \ \mu s$$

Therefore,

$$T_L \times N_L = 9992 \ \mu s$$

We can use $N_L = 222$ and $T_L = 45 \ \mu s$. This requires that the loop counter be initialized to 222 (decimal) = DE (hex) and the delay within the loop be increased to 45 clock cycles. This additional delay can be obtained by adding more dummy instructions within the loop. One possibility is shown below, where we have expanded the loop to include instructions from 0327 through 0335 to replace the instructions from 0327 through 0329.

Address	Label	Code	Mnemonic	
0327	LOOP	48	PHA	
•		68	PLA	
•		48	PHA	
•		68	PLA	
•		48	PHA	
•		68	PLA	
•		48	PHA	
•		68	PLA	Loop delay,
032F		48	PHA	$T_L = 45$ cycles
0330		68	PLA	
0331		E6	INC(ZP)[a]	
0332		00		
0333		88	DEY	
0334		D0	BNE	
0335		F1		

[a]INC(ZP) is being used as a dummy instruction for a five-cycle delay. It is assumed that location 0000 is not being used for other purposes.

The number of bytes in the loop has been increased from 4 to 15 to provide the necessary 45 cycles of delay. Once again, a more efficient way to achieve this 45 cycle delay would be to use a loop. In other words, we could use a timing loop within a timing loop. This is easily done by setting up the X register as a second loop counter and inserting another loop in place of all the dummy instructions.

Time-Delay Subroutines

When time delays are to be used often in a programming application, it is good programming practice to set up time-delay subroutines which can be called at any time. Using the techniques described earlier, it is a relatively easy matter to write a subroutine for a specific time delay. The subroutine can then be called by the main program whenever the specific value of delay is needed. To illustrate, let us assume that we have a 10-ms time-delay subroutine stored in ROM at locations C800 through C820. This subroutine requires 10 ms to execute and includes instructions for saving and restoring microprocessor registers that are used in the subroutine. With this subroutine available, we can now rewrite the one-shot program as follows:

Address	Label	Code	Mnemonic	Comments
0320	OSHOT	A9	LDA (IMM)	[A] = FF
0321		FF		
0322		8D	STA (ABS)	Set Q_0 = 1
0323		00		
0324		FD		
0325	DELAY	20 [6]	JSR (ABS)	Jump to 10-ms delay subroutine
0326		00		
0327		C8		
0328		A9 [2]	LDA (IMM)	Load [A] = FE
0329		FE		
032A		8D [4]	STA (ABS)	Clear Q_0 = 0
032B		00		
032C		FD		

This program will actually produce an output pulse duration of 10.012 ms, because the execution times of the instructions at 0325, 0328, and 032A have to be added to the 10-ms execution time of the subroutine.

Delay times which are multiples of the 10 ms can be obtained by putting the JSR instruction in a loop and setting up a loop counter for the required number of times you want the subroutine executed. For example, the program above can be modified to produce a 50-ms output pulse by replacing the JSR instruction with the following sequence, which causes the 10-ms delay to be repeated *five* times.

Address	Label	Code	Mnemonic	Comments
0325	DELAY	A2	LDX (IMM)	Initialize counter
0326		05		
•	LOOP	20	JSR	Execute 10-ms delay
•		00		
•		C8		
•		CA	DEX	Decrement counter
•		D0	BNE (REL)	If not zero, branch back to
•				LOOP for another 10-ms
032C		FA		delay

Applications for Time Delays

As we have seen, software time delays are valuable in generating software-controlled output pulses. An application related to this uses the microprocessor to control the sequencing of external events under program control. A

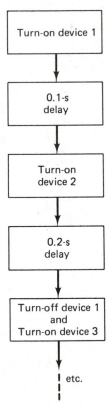

FIGURE 8.12 A μP can be programmed to act as a sequencer with timing loops used to produce the delays between events.

portion of a typical flowchart for such an application is shown in Figure 8.12. The delays shown between successive events are obtained using time-delay subroutines.

Another common use of time delays is in keyboard monitoring programs where keyswitch bounce has to be dealt with. When the monitor program detects a key actuation, it will go through a short delay (usually about 20 ms) before it reads the keyboard data into the microprocessor. This allows enough time for the depressed keyswitch to stabilize.

Time delays are also useful when the microprocessor has to communicate with slow I/O devices. For example, when the microprocessor wants to record information on a tape-cassette unit, it first generates a signal to start the tape motor (usually through a control relay). Then, the microprocessor goes through a delay of about 0.5s to allow the motor to reach full speed before starting the tape recording process.

8.19 MULTIBYTE ARITHMETIC OPERATIONS

Like most microprocessors, the 6502 arithmetic unit operates on 8-bit numbers. This means that the maximum value of the numbers is limited to 255 (decimal) when binary representation is being used or 99 (decimal) when BCD representation is used.

If the microprocessor is to perform arithmetic operations on numbers greater than these, it will be necessary to represent these numbers as a series of bytes. For example, two serial bytes can represent numbers up to 65,535 in binary or up to 9999 in BCD. Numbers represented in more than one byte are called multibyte numbers.

Multibyte Addition

In order to add two multibyte numbers, the individual bytes are operated on separately with the carry from one byte position added to the next byte position. Let us consider the addition of two 16-bit numbers, which we will represent as follows:

	High-Order Byte	*Low-Order Byte*
First number	H 1	L 1
Second number	H 2	L 2

Each of these bytes will be stored in memory. To add these numbers, the microprocessor has to be programmed to perform the following steps:

1. Clear Carry flag (C = 0).
2. Add lower-order bytes L1 and L2 and C (ADC instruction).
3. Store the result, L3, in memory. The C flag will be set if the result exceeds 11111111_2.
4. Add high-order bytes H1 and H2 and C (the carry out of the addition of the low-order bytes).
5. Store the result, H3, in memory. The H3 and L3 bytes represent the 16-bit result. The C flag will be set if the sum exceeds 16 bits.

This process is illustrated below for two binary numbers.

first number: 01000000 ¦ 00100000   (16,416)
second number: 00100000 ¦ 11100100   (8,420)

Add low-order bytes with carry = 0:

$$
\begin{array}{rl}
00100000 & \text{L1} \\
11100100 & \text{L2} \\
\underline{\hspace{1em}0} & \text{C} \\
C = [1]\ 00000100 & \text{L3}
\end{array}
$$

Add high-order bytes with carry from the previous addition:

$$
\begin{array}{rl}
01000000 & \text{H1} \\
00100000 & \text{H2} \\
\underline{\hspace{1em}1} & \text{C} \\
C = [0]\ 01100001 & \text{H3}
\end{array}
$$

The final result is H3, L3 = 0110000100000100 = 24,836.

This process can be easily extended to numbers more than two bytes long by repeating the same steps for each byte position.

Multibyte Subtraction

A similar procedure can be followed for the subtraction of multibyte numbers. The procedure for the subtraction of two 16-bit numbers is outlined below:

1. Set the Carry flag (C = 1).
2. Subtract L2 from L1 with a borrow (SBC instruction). Remember, borrow = $\overline{C}$.

3. Store result, L3, in memory. C flag will be 0 if a borrow occurred from subtraction of lower-order bytes (L2 > L1).
4. Subtract H2 and H1 with a borrow.
5. Store the result, H3, in memory. The H3 and L3 bytes represent the 16-bit result.

It should be pointed out that the procedures outlined above for multi-byte addition and subtraction can also be used for signed numbers and BCD-coded numbers. Of course, if BCD arithmetic is to be performed, the microprocessor has to be set for the decimal mode with a SED instruction.

8.20 6502 ADDRESS VECTORS

In Chapter 6 we discussed the way in which the 6502 branched to particular address locations during a reset or interrupt operation. The address vectors for these branches have to be stored in locations FFFA through FFFF — in the order shown here:

Address	
FFFA — ADL	
FFFB — ADH	NMI vector
FFFC — ADL	
FFFD — ADH	RES vector
FFFE — ADL	
FFFF — ADH	IRQ vector

The microprocessor user has to decide what areas of memory to use for the interrupt service routines (ISR) and the reset routine, and then he must store the starting addresses of these routines in the locations above. Typically, page FF will be in ROM and these address vectors will be permanently stored.

Interrupt Operation

The 6502 has two interrupt pins, $\overline{\text{IRQ}}$ and $\overline{\text{NMI}}$. $\overline{\text{IRQ}}$, the *maskable* interrupt input, is active-LOW and its effect on the microprocessor is disabled as long as the interrupt disable flag, I, is set to 1. $\overline{\text{NMI}}$ responds to negative-going transitions and always interrupts the microprocessor regardless of the state of the I flag. Each of these interrupt inputs, when active, will cause the microprocessor to suspend operations and branch to an ISR at the locations specified by their particular address vector. At the end of each ISR, a RE-TURN FROM INTERRUPT instruction, RTI, sends microprocessor operation back to where it was when the interrupt occurred.

The Break Instruction, BRK

In addition to its external interrupt capabilities, the 6502 has the capability of undergoing an interrupt sequence under program control using the BRK instruction. The BRK instruction is a single-byte instruction (op code = 00) which causes the microprocessor to respond as if the IRQ input were activated. The program branches to the location specified by the IRQ vector and executes the ISR.

The most typical use of the BRK instruction is in the process of program debugging. A BRK can be inserted at any point in a program to force the microprocessor to branch to the ISR. The ISR can be programmed to store all the microprocessor registers in known memory locations which the user can examine from the computer console. The user can then instruct the computer to continue executing the program until the next BRK instruction is encountered.

Reset Operation

The 6502 has a RESET input, $\overline{RES}$, which responds to a negative-going pulse. When the reset pulse is applied, the microprocessor branches to the address location given by the RES vector and begins executing instructions there. These first instructions are normally used to initialize such things as the stack pointer contents and the I and D flags. Operation is then usually transferred to a keyboard monitor program to await commands from the user.

8.21 WRITING A PROGRAM

Now that we have examined the instruction set of a typical microprocessor and have seen some of the common programming techniques, the obvious question becomes: How does one develop and write a program for a particular application? The process of successfully using a computer to solve a problem requires that the programmer execute a series of equally important steps. We will briefly describe these steps and then we will illustrate them in detail by going through a complete application.

1. *Define the problem.* The programmer has to decide exactly what needs to be done. It is helpful to write down a description of what the problem is and what the program is to accomplish.

2. *Break the overall process down into small steps* showing the progression of events that lead to the final objective. This step helps one to see the logic the program must follow and helps to determine the possibility of using subroutines.

3. *Draw a flowchart showing the logical steps the program* must follow, including all jumps and branches. It helps to put labels on those blocks in the flowchart which can be entered from more than one direction.

4. *Write a symbolic (assembly) program* using mnemonics for instructions, labels for all addresses, and comments to explain the purpose of each instruction. Do not enter op codes or address codes yet. The symbolic program can then be evaluated for correctness of logic and modified if necessary. The reasons for not entering op codes or address codes at this point are several. First, the area of memory where the program is to be placed has not yet been determined yet, so some addresses would not be known. Second, the programmer may add or delete instructions after evaluating the symbolic program. This could result in having to change many address codes. In addition, address modes for certain instructions may not be determined yet, so the op codes cannot be entered.

5. *Write the machine language program.* The process of converting the symbolic (assembly) program into a machine language program with all the address and op codes is called *assembly.* If the programmer does it himself by looking up the codes for the various instructions, assigning addresses, and so on, it is called *hand assembly.*

6. *Checkout and debugging.* The need for this step is significantly diminished if the previous steps have been carefully followed. However, seldom is it possible to develop a machine language program of any reasonable complexity and have it work perfectly the first time. Checkout and debugging of a program consist of observing the operation of the program under controlled test conditions. One commonly used technique involves "stepping" the computer through each instruction one at a time. This is called *single stepping*, and in this mode the computer will execute an instruction and then stop to allow the operator to examine the status of various microprocessor registers and memory locations. Many monitor programs used with hex or ASCII keyboards provide this valuable single-step capability. Another technique is the use of program "breaks" which the programmer can insert at various points in the program to cause the computer to temporarily stop program execution so that registers and memory can be examined. For 6502 systems, the BRK instruction serves this purpose.

Example of Complete Process

The example we have chosen is practical enough to provide a meaningful exercise, yet simple enough to provide a clear illustration of the programming process.

Define the Problem The problem is to write a program for using a microprocessor system as an IC tester. Figure 8.13 shows the I/O hardware needed to simultaneously test two quad NAND-gate chips. The microprocessor is to be

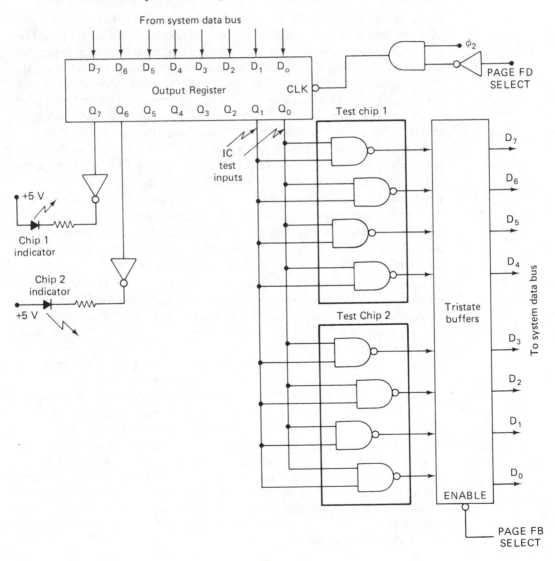

FIGURE 8.13 Diagram of IC tester.

programmed to generate the various logic conditions for the NAND inputs, monitor the NAND outputs, and activate the appropriate indicator if a chip is found to be faulty.

The Q_1 and Q_0 outputs of the output port register serve as the test inputs for the two NAND chips. A complete test sequence would require cycling through the four different combinations of these inputs. For our purposes, however, only the 00 and 11 conditions will be used, to keep the program at a reasonable length. The Q_7 and Q_6 outputs driving the LED indicators are to be pulsed on for a 10-ms duration each time the program determines that a chip is faulty. It is assumed that an operator will be continually replacing the test chips and discarding the faulty ones.

Tristate buffers are used as an input port through which the microprocessor can read the various NAND outputs. After the microprocessor reads these outputs, it checks to see if they are all at the proper level for the applied input conditions, and turns on the appropriate indicator if they are not.

Break into Small Steps We can now write down the steps that the program must follow to produce the operation described above.

1. Turn off all indicators.
2. Generate $Q_1 = Q_0 = 0$ and apply it to test chips.
3. Read chip outputs.
4. If they are all correct, go to step 6.
5. If not, determine which chip is faulty and activate corresponding indicator for 10 ms.
6. Generate $Q_1 = Q_0 = 1$ and apply it to chips.
7. Read chip outputs.
8. If they are all correct, go to step 10.
9. If not, determine which chip is faulty and activate corresponding indicator for 10 ms.
10. Jump back to step 2 and repeat test sequence.

If we examine these steps carefully, we see that the most complex programming task involves determining if any incorrect outputs have occurred and then pulsing the appropriate indicator. This operation takes place *twice* during a complete test sequence (steps 4 and 5 and 8 and 9). Rather than write this portion of the program twice, we will write it once and use it as a subroutine. We will call it the FAULT subroutine, since it is used to determine if either of the chips is faulty.

Draw a Flowchart The flowchart showing the steps above is presented in Fig. 8.14, with the main program sequence on the left and the FAULT subroutine on the right. Read through the flowchart carefully and try to follow the logic for one complete test sequence before reading the next paragraph.

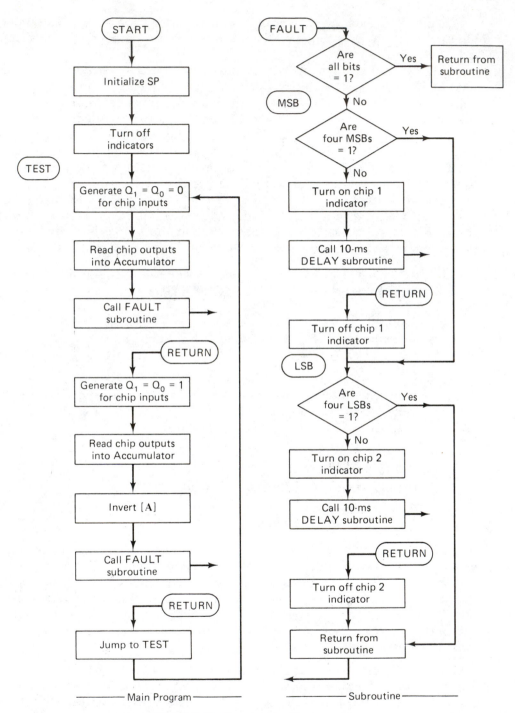

FIGURE 8.14 Flowchart for IC tester program.

You should have noticed the following important points as you progressed through the flowchart:

1. The first operation in the main program is used to initialize the Stack Pointer. This is a good practice to follow.

2. The main program calls the FAULT subroutine after each loading of the chip outputs into the Accumulator. Note that for the second test condition ($Q_1 = Q_0 = 1$), the [A] is inverted before jumping to the FAULT subroutine. This is because the subroutine is designed to check for all 1s as the correct result.

3. If the FAULT subroutine determines that the [A] is *not* all 1s, it then checks the four MSBs to see if chip 1 has produced a faulty output. Then it checks the four LSBs to see if chip 2 has produced a faulty output.

4. The FAULT subroutine utilizes a time-delay subroutine to produce the 10-ms pulses for the indicators. This is an example of nested subroutines. The flowchart for the DELAY subroutine is not shown and we will not bother to include it as part of the complete program. We will just assume that such a subroutine is available.

5. The main program branches back to repeat the test sequence over and over. Thus, when a chip is faulty, its indicator will be continuously pulsing. The fact that the program runs continuously allows the operator to keep inserting different chips into the test sockets without having to restart the program each time.

Write a Symbolic Program   With the flowchart completed, we are almost ready to write the actual sequence of instructions. Before we can do that, however, we have to determine the details of how the FAULT subroutine will test the contents of the Accumulator for a faulty output. There are several ways to do this and the method we have chosen to use may not be the most efficient, but it works.

First, we can test for all 1s in the Accumulator by using a Compare instruction (CMP) and comparing [A] with 11111111_2 = FF. Recall that the CMP instruction does not affect the contents of the Accumulator but only affects the status flags. If [A] = FF, the Z flag will be set. This means the outputs are correct and no indicators are to be activated. If [A] $\neq$ FF, Z will be cleared. Then we must proceed to find out which half of A does not have all 1s.

We can check for all 1s in the four MSBs (chip 1 outputs) by using a compare instruction to compare [A] with 11110000 = F0. If the four MSBs are *not* all 1, the CMP instruction will clear the C flag since [A] < [M]; otherwise, it will set the C flag.

We can check for all 1s in the four LSBs (chip 2 outputs) by first clearing the four MSBs and then comparing [A] with 0F. If the four LSBs are all 1, the Z flag will be set; otherwise, it will be cleared.

With these ideas in mind, we can now write the symbolic program shown in Table 8.2. Before reading through it, note that in a symbolic program each line contains one complete instruction, including the operand or operand address. For example, the first line (START) has the instruction LDX #$ FF. The # sign indicates that FF is the *actual data* to be loaded into X and is not an address.* Now look at the fourth line, which is STX OUT-PORT. This instruction says to store [X] in address OUTPORT. Here the label OUTPORT represents the address of the output port register in Fig. 8.13. In the symbolic program we use labels for addresses. The actual numerical values will be added later. This is also true for each conditional branch instruction, where we write the symbolic address that the program will branch to; the actual numerical offset will be added later.

We have not included the time-delay subroutine in this symbolic listing. We will assume that it is already available and resides in memory locations CE00 through CE20. The label DELAY will represent the starting address of this subroutine.

Write the Machine Language Program If the computer you are using has an assembler program stored in its memory and an ASCII keyboard for input, the symbolic program can be entered into the computer as is. However, if your system can only accept machine language inputs (i.e., hex keyboard input), it is necessary to convert the symbolic program into machine language by hand. This process involves two steps: (1) looking up the hex op code for each instruction mnemonic and (2) assigning a numerical value to each address label.

The first step simply involves referring to the microprocessor op-code table and finding the one-byte code for each instruction. The table for the 6502 is in Appendix A.

The second step is a bit more involved. First, we will assign an address to the first instruction of the main program. Let us use START = 0200. Since this first instruction requires loading X with a specific value, we must use immediate addressing which requires two bytes. This automatically makes the address TEST = 0203. The address assigned to OUTPORT and INPORT are FD00 and FB00, respectively, as indicated by the circuit of Fig. 8.13. The FAULT subroutine will be assigned a starting address of 0300, and as mentioned earlier, the DELAY subroutine starts at address CE00.

The three remaining address labels, MSB, LSB, and RETURN, will have their numerical values automatically determined once we set FAULT = 0300. Actually, these addresses are not *directly* referenced by any instructions in the program. Instead, they are referenced by conditional branch instructions.

---

*$ is used if the data are in hex; % is used if the data are in binary; no prefix is used if the data are in decimal.

TABLE 8.2   Symbolic Program for IC Tester

Address Label	Instruction/Operand		Comments
START	LDX	#$FF	Initialize stack pointer
	TXS		
TEST	LDX	#$00	Turn off indicators and make $Q_1 = Q_0 = 0$
	STX	OUTPORT	
	LDA	INPORT	Load chip outputs into A
	JSR	FAULT	Call FAULT subroutine
	LDX	#$03	Apply $Q_1 = Q_0 = 1$ to chips
	STX	OUTPORT	
	LDA	INPORT	Load chip outputs into A
	EOR	#$FF	Invert [A]
	JSR	FAULT	Call FAULT subroutine
	JMP	TEST	Unconditional jump to TEST
.	.	.	.
.	.	.	.
.	.	.	.
FAULT	CMP	#$FF	Are all bits = 1?
	BNE	MSB	If not, branch to MSB to check MSBs; if they are, return from subroutine
	RTS		
MSB	CMP	#$FO	Are four MSBs = 1?
	BCS	LSB	If they are, branch to LSB to check LSBs
	LDX	#$80	If not, turn on chip 1 indicator
	STX	OUTPORT	
	JSR	DELAY	Call 10-ms delay subroutine
	LDX	#$00	Turn off chip 1 indicator
	STX	OUTPORT	
LSB	AND	#$0F	Clear four MSBs
	CMP	#$0F	Are four LSBs = 1?
	BEQ	RETURN	If yes, branch to RETURN
	LDX	#$40	If no, turn on chip 2 indicator
	STX	OUTPORT	
	JSR	DELAY	10-ms delay
	LDX	#$00	Turn off chip 2 indicator
	STX	OUTPORT	
RETURN	RTS		Return to main program

The offsets for these conditional branch instructions have to be calculated for the machine language program using the method outlined earlier.

The reader should now try writing the machine language program for the symbolic program of Table 8.2. Hopefully, when finished, the result will match the machine language program of Table 8.3. If it does not, go over it carefully to find where you went wrong.

The machine language listing in Table 8.3 is in the exact form that it would be entered into the computer from a keyboard and is the end product

TABLE 8.3 Machine Language Listing for IC Tester Program

	Main Program			FAULT Subroutine	
	Address	Code		Address	Code
(START)	0200	A2	(FAULT)	0300	C9
	0201	FF		0301	FF
	0202	9A		0302	D0
(TEST)	0203	A2		0303	01
	0204	00		0304	60
	0205	8E	(MSB)	0305	C9
	0206	00		0306	F0
	0207	FD		0307	B0
	0208	AD		0308	0D
	0209	00		0309	A2
	020A	FB		030A	80
	020B	20		030B	8E
	020C	00		030C	00
	020D	03		030D	FD
	020E	A2		030E	20
	020F	03		030F	00
	0210	8E		0310	CE
	0211	00		0311	A2
	0212	FD		0312	00
	0213	AD		0313	8E
	0214	00		0314	00
	0215	FB		0315	FD
	0216	49	(LSB)	0316	29
	0217	FF		0317	0F
	0218	20		0318	C9
	0219	00		0319	0F
	021A	03		031A	F0
	021B	4C		031B	0D
	021C	03		031C	A2
	021D	02		031D	40
				031E	8E
				031F	00
				0320	FD
				0321	20
				0322	00
				0323	CE
				0324	A2
				0325	00
				0326	8E
				0327	00
				0328	FD
			(RETURN)	0329	60

of the machine language programming process. In practice, a programmer would include mnemonics and comments along with this listing to make it easier to follow and to help in the debugging process.

8.22 FINAL COMMENTS

With these last few words, our introduction to microcomputer programming will come to an end. For the reader, however, the venture into the marvelous world of computers should be just beginning. As we stated in the introduction to this chapter, the best way to learn how to program and apply microprocessors is to get hands-on experience. Only then will you experience the thrill of seeing your hardware and software finally working together after countless testing, debugging, modifying, and troubleshooting efforts. Hopefully, we have prepared you well for this step. Your fun has just begun. Enjoy.

GLOSSARY

Absolute (Direct) Addressing   Three-byte instruction sequence with the first byte being the op code and the next two bytes specifying the 16-bit address.

Absolute Indexed Addressing   Effective address is found by adding the contents of an index register to the 16-bit absolute address.

Assembler   Computer program that converts an assembly language program into an executable object (machine language) program.

Assembly Language (Symbolic Language)   Operator-oriented language that uses alphabetic abbreviations (mnemonics) for each type of instruction, rather than binary or hex machine language, because they are more easily remembered.

Data-Manipulation Instructions   Instructions that change data in any way: for example, arithmetic and logic instructions.

Data-Transfer Instructions   Instructions that involve the movement of a binary word from one location to another.

Effective Address   *Actual* data address when indexed addressing is used. The actual data address is generally found by adding the address portion of the instruction and the contents of an index (X or Y) register.

High-Level Language   Computer language that uses symbol and command statements an operator can easily read. Typically, each instruction statement contains many steps, corresponding to many machine language instructions. Examples of high-level languages are BASIC, FORTRAN, and COBOL.

Immediate Addressing   Two-byte instruction sequence used only for instructions that transfer data from memory into one of the μP registers or into the arithmetic unit for processing. The operand is always stored in the address location immediately following the location of the op code.

Implied Addressing Refers to single-byte instructions that do not require an operand address.

Indirect Addressing Addressing mode in which the address portion of the instruction "points" to the address of the operand address.

Instruction Set Group of instructions that a particular μP is designed to execute.

Machine Language Binary equivalent of a computer's instruction set.

Machine Status Control Instructions Instructions that control the operation of the μP itself: for example, halt, clear specific flags, and no-ops.

Memory Reference Instructions Instructions that specify a memory address where a word is to be stored or from which a word is to be read.

Nested Subroutine Programming technique whereby the main program calls a subroutine and that subroutine, during its execution, calls another subroutine, and so on.

Program Sequence of instructions that causes the computer to perform some useful function.

Program Control Instructions Instructions that alter the normal sequence which a program follows by loading a new address into the Program Counter (PC).

Relative Addressing Type of addressing used in conditional branch instructions which specifies the new program address by adding an offset byte to the contents of the Program Counter (PC).

Subroutine Program segment that performs a specific function and to which the main program can branch at any time.

Timing Loop Sequence of dummy instructions, which performs no useful function but which is repeated as many time as are needed to produce a specified delay.

Zero-Page Addressing Two-byte instruction sequence in which the second byte specifies the lower-order address byte; the higher-order address byte is assumed to be 00_{16}.

Zero-Page Indexed Addressing Effective address on page zero is found by adding the contents of an 8-bit index (X or Y) register to the single-byte, zero-page address specified by the instruction.

QUESTIONS AND PROBLEMS

Sections 8.1–8.5

8.1 Draw a diagram showing the important 6502 registers and indicating the size of each.

8.2 Identify the 6502 flag being described in each statement.
   (a) Can be used to prevent μP from being interrupted.
   (b) Is affected by both arithmetic and shift operations.
   (c) Indicates the sign of the result.
   (d) Indicates if result is zero.
   (e) Controls arithmetic mode.
   (f) Indicates overflow in signed arithmetic operations.

8.3 Which flags can be *cleared* by specific program instructions? Which ones can be *set*?

8.4 Following are three different instructions for loading data into the Accumulator. For each, indicate where the data come from.

A9	LDA (IMM)	A5	LDA (ZP)	AD	LDA (ABS)
4E		4E		4E	
				25	

8.5 Which of the following instructions use *implied* addressing, where no operand address is required?

TYA   LDX   DEY   STA   CLC

8.6 What are two uses for the NOP instruction?

Sections 8.6 and 8.7

8.7 Modify Example 8.3 by changing the CLC instruction to SEC and the SED instruction to CLD. Then determine the result stored in RESULT.

8.8 Modify Example 8.4 by changing the ADC (ABS) instruction to SBC (ABS) and the CLC instruction to SEC. Determine the contents of location 0101 and the values of the C, N, Z, and V flags after the program has been executed.

8.9 Repeat Problem 8.8 with Data 2 = B8.

8.10 Where does the result of an arithmetic instruction always end up?

8.11 Three values are stored in memory locations 0050, 0051, and 0052. Write a program to add these three values and store their sum in 0253. (*Hint:* Choose the best address mode; you cannot assume [A] = 00 before starting.)

8.12 Assume that the value 10110110_2 is stored in memory location 0050. Determine the contents of the Accumulator after the execution of the following instruction sequence. Also determine the N and Z flags.

A5	LDA (ZP)
50	
25	AND (IMM)
7A	

8.13 Repeat Problem 8.12 when $[0050] = 85_{16}$.

8.14 Replace AND (IMM) by ORA (IMM) and repeat Problem 8.12.

8.15 Replace AND (IMM) by EOR (IMM) and repeat Problem 8.12.

8.16 Write an instruction sequence that will take a word from memory location 0200, *clear* bits 6 and 7 of the word, and restore it in memory.

8.17 Repeat Problem 8.16 except that bits 6 and 7 are to be *set*.

8.18 Which logic operation can be used to invert a data word?

Sections 8.8 and 8.9

8.19 Determine the contents of the accumulator and the values of the N, Z, and C flags after the following sequence is executed.

$$
\begin{array}{ll}
18 & \text{CLC} \\
\text{A9} & \text{LDA (IMM)} \\
\text{8B} & \\
\text{0A} & \text{ASL (ACC)}
\end{array}
$$

8.20 Change ASL to LSR and repeat Problem 8.19.

8.21 Change ASL to ROR and repeat Problem 8.19.

8.22 Change ASL to ROL and repeat Problem 8.19.

8.23 Write an instruction sequence, using shift or rotate instructions, which takes a word stored in memory location 0070 and interchanges the four MSBs with the four LSBs.

8.24 In Section 8.7 we saw an example of how a byte containing two BCD digits could be converted to two ASCII code words for transmission. Now, consider the opposite problem. Assume that two ASCII-coded decimal digits (e.g., 00110111-ASCII for "7" and 00111001-ASCII for "9") are stored in memory locations 0020 and 0021, respectively, with 0020 holding the MSD. Write an instruction sequence that produce the two-digit BCD code (e.g., 01111001-BCD for 79) and store it in memory location 0022. (*Hint:* Outline your procedure or draw a flowchart first.)

8.25 Determine the contents of X, Y, and memory location 0320 after the following instruction sequence has been executed. Also determine N and Z.

$$
\begin{array}{ll}
\text{A2} & \text{LDX (IMM)} \\
01 & \\
\text{8E} & \text{STX (ABS)} \\
20 & \\
03 & \\
\text{E8} & \text{INX} \\
\text{CE} & \text{DEC (ABS)} \\
20 & \\
03 & \\
\text{AC} & \text{LDY (ABS)} \\
20 & \\
03 & \\
88 & \text{DEY}
\end{array}
$$

Sections 8.10–8.12

8.26 Explain how the CMP instruction differs from the SBC instruction.

8.27 Assume that $[00A5] = 32_{16}$ and determine the C and Z flags after the execution of the following instruction sequence. Also determine [A] at the completion of the sequence.

```
A9    LDA (IMM)
57
C5    CMP (ZP)
A5
```

8.28　Assume that $[A] = [X] = [Y] = 00_{16}$ and $[0325] = 2A_{16}$ prior to the following instruction sequence.

```
AD    LDA (ABS)
25
03
AA    TAX
E0    CPX (IMM)
29
CA    DEX
8A    TXA
A8    TAY
C0    CPY (IMM)
29
```

Go through the instructions one at a time and indicate the contents of A, X, Y, and the values of the C, Z, and N flags as each instruction is executed. Assume that C = 0 initially.

8.29　Assume that $[A] = 04_{16}$ and $[C300] = 36_{16}$. What are the values of the Z, N, and V flags after the following instruction is executed?

```
2C    BIT (ABS)
00
C3
```

8.30　For the following SAVE routine, determine the exact addresses where the Status register A, X, and Y are stored.

```
A2    LDX (IMM)
FA
9A    TXS
08    PHP
48    PHA
98    TYA
48    PHA
8A    TXA
48    PHA
```

8.31　What is the advantage of using stack "push" instructions to store register contents rather than using store instructions? What concerns must the programmer take care of if the stack is to be used?

Sections 8.13–8.14

8.32 Explain the differences between the unconditional jump (JMP) and the conditional branch instructions.

8.33 For each pair of PC values given below, calculate the offset required for branching from the current PC to the new PC. Express the offset in hex, and indicate if it is within the allowable range.

	Current PC	New PC
(a)	073A	0782
(b)	073A	071C
(c)	073A	06D2
(d)	2062	20F1
(e)	F035	EFF7

8.34 Write an instruction sequence, starting at address 0280, which loads data into A from input port address F800 and then tests bit 2 of the data. If bit 2 = 0, the program must branch to 0250; otherwise, it must branch to 0400. Do this problem *two* different ways, first using shift operations, then using bit masking. Decide which method is most efficient for this problem.

8.35 Refer to the flowchart of Fig. 7.16 for the UART receiver interrupt service routine. Write the instruction sequence using 0300 as the ISR starting address and 0350 as the address of the error subroutine.

8.36 Consider the following instruction sequence:

0200	E0	CMP (IMM)
0201	35	
0202	90	BCC
0203	3C	
0204	F0	BEQ
0205	D0	
0206	4C	JMP
0207	90	
0208	02	

Determine where the program branches to for each of the following initial values of [A]: (a) 37, (b) 29, and (c) 35.

8.37 For the following instruction sequence, [A] is initially 25_{16}.

0300	A2	LDX (IMM)
0301	FA	
0302	0A	ASL (ACC)
0303	E8	INX
0304	30	BMI (REL)
0305	FC	
0306	4A	LSR (ACC)

Determine [A] after the LSR instruction is executed.

Section 8.15

8.38 What is the difference between an unconditional jump, JMP, and a jump to subroutine, JSR?

8.39 When an RTS instruction is executed, how does the μP know where to return to in the main program?

8.40 What is the advantage of using subroutines?

8.41 What are *nested* subroutines?

Sections 8.16 and 8.17

8.42 For each of the following instruction sequences, determine the effective address being accessed by the second instruction.

	(a)			(b)	
A2	LDX (IMM)		A0	LDY (IMM)	
B3			15		
75	ADC (ZP,X)		15	STX (ABS,Y)	
25			35		
			02		

8.43 In the example of Fig. 8.9, we moved six bytes of data from one area of memory to another. Write a sequence of instructions that will move a block of 100 bytes which are stored in locations 0005 through 0068 to a new area of memory, C450 through C4B3.

8.44 What hardware and software changes would have to be made for the configuration of Fig. 8.10 if *six* inputs are used?

8.45 Refer to the UART interface circuit of Fig. 7.14. The following program is used to transmit an ASCII-coded message to the output device using the basic scheme shown in the flowchart of Fig. 7.15.

0300	A9	LDA (IMM)	Reset UART
0301	03		
0302	8D	STA (ABS)	
0303	00		
0304	BF		
0305	A9	LDA (IMM)	Initialize UART
0306	19		
0307	8D	STA (ABS)	
0308	00		
0309	BF		
030A	A2	LDX (IMM)	Initialize word counter
030B	15		
030C	AD	LDA (ABS)	Load UART status
030D	00		

030E	BF		
030F	29	AND (IMM)	Mask TDRE
0310	02		
0311	F0	BEQ (REL)	Reload status if TDRE = 0
0312	F9		
0313	BD	LDA (ABS,X)	Load A with next ASCII code word
0314	60		
0315	C0		
0316	8D	STA (ABS)	Send it to UART TxDR
0317	01		
0318	BF		
0319	CA	DEX	Decrement word counter
031A	D0	BNE (REL)	If $\neq 0$, get next ASCII code word
031B	F0		If $= 0$, message is finished; continue
031C			with program
031D			

Study the program carefully and answer parts (a) through (c).

(a) What baud rate is being used?

(b) How many data bits, stop bits, and types of parity bit are being transmitted per word (character)?

(c) How many ASCII-coded data words does the message contain? Where must these ASCII codes be stored?

(d) List the required codes and their memory locations for the message "PROCESS UNDER CONTROL."

8.46 When is the indirect address mode useful?

Section 8.18

8.47 Assume a 1-MHz clock and determine the total time required to execute the instruction sequence of Problem 8.37.

8.48 Modify the one-shot program for an output pulse duration of approximately 0.25 ms.·

8.49 Modify the one-shot program for a pulse duration of 50 ms.

8.50 (a) Write an instruction sequence that takes approximately 50 μs to execute (assume a 1-MHz clock). The last instruction in the sequence should be an RTS (return from subroutine), since this sequence is going to be used as a time-delay subroutine.

(b) Use this time-delay subroutine and develop a program that will do the following:

(1) Set all the bits at an output register (address C900) to 1 for approximately 1 ms.

(2) Clear all the bits at this output port to 0 for approximately 1 ms.

(3) Repeat steps (1) and (2) continuously.

(c) Sketch the waveforms present at the output register.

8.51 Modify Problem 8.50 so that only the LSB of the output register gets alternately set and cleared every 1 ms without affecting the other bits.

8.52 Modify the program of Problem 8.50 such that the binary contents of the output register are *incremented* every 1 ms. Sketch the output register waveforms.

Section 8.19

8.53 A 16-bit number is stored in address locations 0040 and 0041 with the high-order byte in location 0040. Likewise, a second 16-bit value is stored in locations 0050 and 0051. Write an instruction sequence for adding these two 16-bit numbers and storing the result in locations 0060 and 0061.

Section 8.21

8.54 List the six major steps in the process of developing a program.

8.55 How would you modify the IC tester hardware and software to test quad NOR gate chips?

8.56 The IC tester program developed in the text did not test the gates for the 01 and 10 input conditions. In practice, this condition would have to be tested since the 00 and 11 input conditions could not detect a gate with shorted inputs. Modify the flowchart and the program to include these conditions.

APPENDIX

6502 INSTRUCTION SET AND OP CODES*

The table below gives the various 6502 instruction mnemonics and op codes. Note that many of the instructions use more than one address mode and have a different op code for each one. Each instruction op code is accompanied by two other numbers, N and #. The value for N gives the number of clock cycles required to execute that particular instruction; the value of # gives the number of program bytes required for the instruction. For example, the LDA instruction using zero-page addressing has an op code of A5, requires *three* clock cycles to execute, and uses *two* program bytes.

Mnemonic Instructions	Op Code	N	#	Mnemonic Instructions	Op Code	N	#
ADC (IMM.)	69	2	2	ADC (IND,X)	61	6	2
ADC (ABS.)	6D	4	3	ADC (IND),Y	71	5	2
ADC (Z.P.)	65	3	2	ADC (Z,P,X)	75	4	2

*This information is presented through the courtesy of MOS Technology, Inc.

Mnemonic Instructions	Op Code	N	#	Mnemonic Instructions	Op Code	N	#
ADC (ABS,X)	7D	4	3	DEY (IMPL.)	88	2	1
ADC (ABS,Y)	79	4	3	EOR (IMM.)	49	2	2
AND (IMM.)	29	2	2	EOR (ABS.)	4D	4	3
AND (ABS.)	2D	4	3	EOR (Z.P.)	45	3	2
AND (Z.P.)	25	3	2	EOR (IND,X)	41	6	2
AND (IND,X)	21	6	2	EOR (IND),Y	51	5	2
AND (IND),Y	31	5	2	EOR (Z.P.,X)	55	4	2
AND (Z.P.,X)	35	4	2	EOR (ABS,X)	5D	4	3
AND (ABS,X)	3D	4	3	EOR (ABS,Y)	59	4	3
AND (ABS,Y)	39	4	3	INC (ABS.)	EE	6	3
ASL (ABS.)	0E	6	3	INC (Z.P.)	E6	5	2
ASL (Z.P.)	06	5	2	INC (Z.P.,X)	F6	6	2
ASL (ACCUM.)	0A	2	1	INC (ABS,X)	FE	7	3
ASL (Z.P.,X)	16	6	2	INX (IMPL.)	E8	2	1
ASL (ABS,X)	1E	7	3	INY (IMPL.)	C8	2	1
BCC (REL.)	90	2[a]	2	JMP (ABS.)	4C	3	3
BCS (REL.)	B0	2[a]	2	JMP (IND.)	6C	5	3
BEQ (REL.)	F0	2[a]	2	JSR (ABS.)	20	6	3
BIT (ABS.)	2C	4	3	LDA (IMM.)	A9	2	2
BIT (Z.P.)	24	3	2	LDA (ABS.)	AD	4	3
BMI (REL.)	30	2[a]	2	LDA (Z.P.)	A5	3	2
BNE (REL.)	D0	2[a]	2	LDA (IND,X)	A1	6	2
BPL (REL.)	10	2[a]	2	LDA (IND),Y	B1	5	2
BRK (IMPL.)	00	7	1	LDA (Z.P.,X)	B5	4	2
BVC (REL.)	50	2[a]	2	LDA (ABS,X)	BD	4	3
BVS (REL.)	70	2[a]	2	LDA (ABS,Y)	B9	4	3
CLC (IMPL.)	18	2	1	LDX (IMM.)	A2	2	2
CLD (IMPL.)	D8	2	1	LDX (ABS.)	AE	4	3
CLI (IMPL.)	58	2	1	LDX (Z.P.)	A6	3	2
CLV (IMPL.)	B8	2	1	LDX (ABS,Y)	BE	4	3
CMP (IMM.)	C9	2	2	LDX (Z.P.,Y)	B6	4	2
CMP (ABS.)	CD	4	3	LDY (IMM.)	A0	2	2
CMP (Z.P.)	C5	3	2	LDY (ABS.)	AC	4	3
CMP (IND,X)	C1	6	2	LDY (Z.P.)	A4	3	2
CMP (IND),Y	D1	5	2	LDY (Z.P.,X)	B4	4	2
CMP (Z.P.,X)	D5	4	2	LDY (ABS,X)	BC	4	3
CMP (ABS,X)	DD	4	3	LSR (ABS.)	4E	6	3
CMP (ABS,Y)	D9	4	3	LSR (Z.P.)	46	5	2
CPX (IMM.)	E0	2	2	LSR (ACCUM.)	4A	2	1
CPX (ABS.)	EC	4	3	LSR(Z.P.,X)	56	6	2
CPX (Z.P.)	E4	3	2	LSR (ABS,X)	5E	7	3
CPY (IMM.)	C0	2	2	NOP (IMPL.)	EA	2	1
CPY (ABS.)	CC	4	3	ORA (IMM.)	09	2	2
CPY (Z.P.)	C4	3	2	ORA (ABS.)	0D	4	3
DEC (ABS.)	CE	6	3	ORA (Z.P.)	05	3	2
DEC (Z.P.)	C6	5	2	ORA (IND,X)	01	6	2
DEC (Z.P.,X)	D6	6	2	ORA (IND),Y	11	5	2
DEC (ABS,X)	DE	7	3	ORA (Z.P.,X)	15	4	2
DEX (IMPL.)	CA	2	1	ORA (ABS,X)	1D	4	3

Mnemonic Instructions	Op Code	N	#	Mnemonic Instructions	Op Code	N	#
ORA (ABS,Y)	19	4	3	SBC (ABS,Y)	F9	4	3
PHA (IMPL.)	48	3	1	SEC (IMPL.)	38	2	1
PHP (IMPL.)	08	3	1	SED (IMPL.)	F8	2	1
PLA (IMPL.)	68	4	1	SEI (IMPL.)	78	2	1
PLP (IMPL.)	28	4	1	STA (ABS.)	8D	4	3
ROL (ABS.)	2E	6	3	STA (Z.P.)	85	3	2
ROL (Z.P.)	26	5	2	STA (IND,X)	81	6	2
ROL (ACCUM.)	2A	2	1	STA (IND),Y	91	6	2
ROL (Z.P.,X)	36	6	2	STA (Z.P.,X)	95	4	2
ROL (ABS,X)	3E	7	3	STA (ABS,X)	9D	5	3
ROR (ABS.)	6E	6	3	STA (ABS,Y)	99	5	3
ROR (Z.P.)	66	5	2	STX (ABS.)	8E	4	3
ROR (ACCUM.)	6A	2	1	STX (Z.P.)	86	3	2
ROR (Z.P.,X)	76	6	2	STX (Z.P.,Y)	96	4	2
ROR (ABS,X)	7E	7	3	STY (ABS.)	8C	4	3
RTI (IMPL.)	40	6	1	STY (Z.P.)	84	3	2
RTS (IMPL.)	60	6	1	STY (Z.P.,X)	94	4	2
SBC (IMM.)	E9	2	2	TAX (IMPL.)	AA	2	1
SBC (ABS.)	ED	4	3	TAY (IMPL.)	A8	2	1
SBC (Z.P.)	E5	3	2	TSX (IMPL.)	BA	2	1
SBC (IND,X)	E1	6	2	TXA (IMPL.)	8A	2	1
SBC (IND),Y	F1	5	2	TXS (IMPL.)	9A	2	1
SBC (Z.P.,X)	F5	4	2	TYA (IMPL.)	98	2	1
SBC (ABS,X)	FD	4	3				

[a]Add 1 to "N" if branching occurs to same page. Add 2 to "N" if branching occurs to a different page.

(IMM.) — IMMEDIATE ADDRESSING: The operand is contained in the second byte of the instruction.

(ABS.) — ABSOLUTE ADDRESSING: The second byte of the instruction contains the 8 low-order bits of the effective address. The third byte contains the 8 high-order bits of the effective address.

(Z.P.) — ZERO-PAGE ADDRESSING: The second byte contains the 8 low-order bits of the effective address (EA). The 8 high-order bits are zero.

(ACCUM.) — ACCUMULATOR: One-byte instruction operating on the Accumulator.

(Z.P.,X)/(Z.P.,Y) — ZERO-PAGE INDEXED ADDRESSING: The second byte of the instruction is added to the index (carry is dropped) to form the low-order byte of the EA. The high-order byte of the EA is zero.

(ABS,X)/ABS,Y) — ABSOLUTE INDEXED ADDRESSING: The effective address is formed by adding the index to the second and third bytes of the instruction.

(IND,X) — INDEXED INDIRECT ADDRESSING: The second byte of the instruction is added to the X index, discarding the carry. The result points to a location on page-zero which contains the 8 low-order bits of the EA. The next byte contains the 8 high-order bits.

(IND),Y — INDIRECT INDEXED ADDRESSING: The second byte of the instruction points to a location in page zero. The contents of this memory location is added to the Y index, the result being the low-order 8 bits of the EA. The carry from this operation is added to the contents of the next page-zero location, the result being the 8 high-order bits of the EA.

INDEX